.NET

SECURITY AND
CRYPTOGRAPHY

.NET
SECURITY AND
CRYPTOGRAPHY

PETER THORSTEINSON
G. GNANA ARUN GANESH

PRENTICE
HALL
PTR

Prentice Hall PTR, Upper Saddle River, NJ 07458
www.phptr.com

Library of Congress Cataloging-in-Publication Data

Thorsteinson, Peter.
    .NET security and cryptography / Peter Thorsteinson and Arun Ganesh.
      p. cm.
    Includes bibliographical references and index.
    ISBN 0-131-00851-X (alk. paper)
    1. Computer security.   2. Cryptography.   3. Microsoft .NET.   I. Ganesh, Arun.   II. Title.

    QA76.9.A25T48 2003
    005.8—dc21
                                                     2003051438

Editorial/Production Supervision: Jacquelyn Doucette
Acquisitions Editor: Karen Gettman
Marketing Manager: Curt Johnson
Manufacturing Buyer: Carol Melville
Cover Design: Anthony Gemallaro
Cover Design Direction: Jerry Votta
Interior Series Design: Gail Cocker-Bogusz

© 2004 Pearson Education, Inc.
Publishing as Prentice Hall Professional Technical Reference
Upper Saddle River, NJ 07458

PRENTICE
HALL
PTR

Prentice Hall books are widely used by corporations and government agencies for training, marketing, and resale.

The publisher offers discounts on this book when ordered in bulk quantities. For more information, contact Corporate Sales Department, phone: 800-382-3419; fax: 201-236-7141; email: corpsales@prenhall.com. Or write Corporate Sales Department, Prentice Hall PTR, One Lake Street, Upper Saddle River, NJ 07458.

Product and company names mentioned herein are the trademarks or registered trademarks of their respective owners.

Printed in the United States of America

10 9 8 7 6 5 4 3 2 1

ISBN 0-131-00851-X

Pearson Education LTD.
Pearson Education Australia PTY, Limited
Pearson Education Singapore, Pte. Ltd.
Pearson Education North Asia Ltd.
Pearson Education Canada, Ltd.
Pearson Educación de Mexico, S.A. de C.V.
Pearson Education—Japan
Pearson Education Malaysia, Pte. Ltd.

CONTENTS

PREFACE

Over the last several years, security and cryptography technologies have been continually increasing in importance to Windows users and software developers. Additionally, in some respects the security and cryptographic capabilities of 32-bit Windows has reached parity with larger mini and mainframe computing platforms, where security has always been a major priority. Now, with the advent of .NET, these security capabilities have become much easier to implement than ever before. Of course, a significant investment in effort is still required in understanding the concepts and acquiring the skills necessary to leverage the many security features provided by .NET. Indeed, that is exactly what this book is all about. Although much of the same functionality was provided in the form of an arcane Win32 C Windows library, the advent of .NET has made security and cryptography programming much simpler and much more powerful than ever before. The .NET Security Framework provides a powerful set of security and cryptographic classes that are relatively easy to use, and this framework is explored throughout this book.

This book is intended to provide a practical and comprehensive coverage on implementing both cryptography and security functionality on the .NET platform. It is an effective tutorial, providing a large number of clear and focused code examples.

Organization

The book is organized into 10 chapters and five appendixes. Chapter 1 introduces cryptography and security on the .NET platform and provides a non-technical overview of the topics that are described in greater detail in subsequent chapters. This first chapter also provides the reasoning behind the layout of the book and how the two main topics of cryptography and security interrelate. The purpose of this chapter is not to provide significant depth or code examples, but rather to convey conceptual understanding and to provide an overview of cryptography and security technologies on the .NET platform. Chapter 2 provides a solid theoretical background to promote a deeper insight into all subsequent chapters. The point is made that all security is based on cryptography, and, to understand cryptography in a meaningful way, it is necessary to first understand several basic theoretical cryptographic concepts. Chapters 3, 4, 5, and 6 provide detailed hands-on .NET programming examples, using symmetric algorithms, asymmetric algorithms, digital signatures, and XML cryptography, respectively. Chapters 7 and 8 cover .NET programming with user-based security and code access security, respectively. Chapter 9 introduces ASP.NET security programming, and Chapter 10 introduces .NET Web Services security programming.

Each aspect of .NET cryptography and security is dealt with in the proper context and sequence, where they are most relevant and most easily understood. Appendixes describe a few additional topics, such as security attacks and additional cryptography-related mathematical topics.

This book is intended to be a practical tutorial with many succinct programming examples that focus on specific and individual concepts. Also, the focus of the book is on practical .NET security programming rather than on administrative security tasks. This book provides sufficient background information to enable the reader to clearly see why security and cryptography are critically important to modern software development. The goal is to equip the reader to begin building significant applications using the .NET Security Framework. This book is part of The Integrated .NET Series from Object Innovations and Prentice Hall PTR.

Sample Programs

The best way to learn about a significant class library such as the .NET Security Framework is to read and write many programs. This book provides many small programs that illustrate each of the pertinent features of .NET in isolation, which makes them easier to understand. The programs are clearly labeled in the text, and they can all be found in the software distribution that accompanies this book. These sample programs are provided in a self-extracting file on the book's Web site. When expanded, a directory structure is created whose default root is **c:\OI\NetSecurity**. The sample programs, which begin with the second chapter, are in directories **Chap02**, **Chap03**, and so on. All the samples for a given chapter are in individual folders within the chapter directories. The names of the folders are clearly identified in the text.

This book is part of The Integrated .NET Series. The sample programs for other books in the series are located in their own directories underneath **\OI**, so all the .NET examples from all books in the series will be located in a common area as you install them. These programs are furnished solely for instructional purposes and should not be embedded in any software product. The software (including instructions for use) is provided "as is" without warranty of any kind.

Web Site

The Web site for the book series is located at *http://www.objectinnovations.com/ dotnet.htm.*

A link is provided at that Web site for downloading the sample programs for this book.

ACKNOWLEDGMENTS

Peter Thorsteinson

We would like to thank Jill Harry from Prentice Hall for her support in starting this project. Also, we would like to thank the series editor, Robert Oberg, for his valuable help.

G. Gnana Arun Ganesh

I would like to thank my parents G.A. Gnanavel and G.N. Vadivambal for their boundless love, patience, support and inspiration. Also I thank my sister G.G. Saradha for her love, tenderness and companionship. My deepest gratitude goes to my well wisher Dr. Robert J. Oberg who has encouraged me through out this exciting project. My special thanks go out to Mr. Anindo Dey, Mr. Narayana Rao Surapaneni and Mr. Vinod Kumar for their motivation and encouragement. I wish to thank my co-author Peter Thorsteinson for his guidance and assistance. Finally let me thank the Almighty for providing me this opportunity.

We would like to thank Emily Frey, Karen Gettman, and all of our editors for their constructive suggestions to enhance the quality of this book. Also we would like to thank all of the reviewers for their detailed comments which helped a lot in updating the substance.

G. Gnana Arun Ganesh is a Microsoft .NET MVP (Most Valuable Professional), developer, author, and .NET consultant, who leads the .NET Technology Group at Arun Micro Systems, which deals with various phases of .NET technology. He has been working with Microsoft .NET technology since its initial beta version. Arun has a bachelor's degree in electronics and communication engineering from the Bharathiar University, Kongu Engineering College. He is the author and site personality of the *.NET Reference Guide,* published by InformIT. He is one of the authors of *Object Innovations,* which offers training course materials in fundamental software technologies. As a .NET author, he has published more than 50 articles on .NET technology in various top .NET Web sites. As an active member of Prentice Hall's technical review panel, he has performed many technical reviews, beginning with C#: *How to Program,* written by Harvey and Paul Deitel. For more than two years as the administrator of Arun Micro Systems, he has provided online .NET training all over the world.

June 4, 2003

About this Series
Robert J. Oberg, Series Editor

Introduction

The Integrated .NET Series from Object Innovations and Prentice Hall PTR is a unique series of introductory to advanced books on Microsoft's important .NET technology. These books are based on proven industrial-strength course development and application development experience. The authors are expert practitioners, teachers and writers who combine subject matter expertise with years of experience in presenting complex programming technologies. These books *teach* in a systematic, step-by-step manner and are not merely summaries of the documentation. All the books come with a rich set of programming examples, and thematic case studies are woven through several of the books.

From the beginning, these books have been conceived as an *integrated whole* and not as independent efforts by a diverse group of authors. There are three broad categories:

- **NET Programming books.** These books cover both the languages themselves and surveys of the .NET Framework using a particular language.

- **NET Applications and Technology.** These books cover specific areas of .NET technology or application areas. In some cases a specific language is used and, in other cases, the book is about the technology or application without regard to a particular language.

- **.NET Interoperability and Migration.** These books cover fundamental technologies important to .NET's vision of strong interoperability across diverse platforms.

The diagram below gives the reader a broad overview of the entire series.

<table>
<tr><td colspan="4">TITLES IN THE INTEGRATED .NET SERIES FROM OBJECT INNOVATIONS AND PRENTICE HALL PTR</td></tr>
<tr><td rowspan="2">**.NET Programming Books**</td><td>Programming Perl in the .NET Environment</td><td>Introduction to Visual Basic Using .NET</td><td>Introduction to C# Using .NET</td></tr>
<tr><td>.NET Architecture and Programming Using Visual C++</td><td>Application Development Using Visual Basic and .NET</td><td>Application Development Using C# and .NET</td></tr>
<tr><td>**.NET Applications and Technology**</td><td>Fundamentals of Web Applications Using .NET and XML</td><td>.NET Security and Cryptography</td><td></td></tr>
<tr><td>**.NET Interoperability and Migration**</td><td>Migrating to .NET</td><td>The .NET and COM Interoperability Handbook</td><td></td></tr>
<tr><td colspan="4">YOUR AUTHORS ARE EXPERT PRACTITIONERS AND SEASONED INSTRUCTORS</td></tr>
</table>

PRENTICE HALL PTR

.NET Programming Books

These books cover important .NET programming languages. There are also surveys of the .NET Framework from the perspective of particular programming languages.

Introductory .NET Language Books

The first set of books teaches several of the important .NET languages. These books cover their language from the ground up and have no prerequisite other than programming experience in some language. Unlike many .NET language books, which are a mixture of the language and topics in the .NET Framework, these books are focused on the languages, with attention to important interactions between the language and the framework. By concentrating on the languages, these books have much more detail and many more practical examples than similar books.

The languages selected are the new language C#, the greatly changed VB.NET, and the open source language ported to the .NET environment, PerlNET. Visual C++ .NET is covered in our intermediate book, and JScript .NET is covered in *Fundamentals of Web Applications Using .NET and XML*.

Introduction to C# Using .NET

This book gives thorough coverage of the C# language from the ground up. The book is organized with a specific section covering the parts of C# common to other C-like languages. This section can be cleanly skipped by programmers with C experience or the equivalent, making for a good reading path for a diverse group of readers. The book gives thorough attention to the object-oriented aspects of C# and thus serves as an excellent book for programmers migrating to C# from Visual Basic or COBOL. Its gradual pace and many examples make the book an excellent candidate as a college textbook for adventurous professors looking to teach C# early in the language's life cycle.

Introduction to Visual Basic Using .NET

This book gives thorough coverage of the VB.NET language from the ground up. Like the companion book on C#, this book gives thorough attention to the object-oriented aspects of VB.NET. Thus the book is excellent for VB programmers migrating to the more sophisticated VB.NET, as well as programmers experienced in languages such as COBOL. This book would also be suitable as a college textbook.

Programming Perl in the .NET Environment

A very important part of the vision behind Microsoft .NET is that the platform is designed from to support multiple programming languages from many sources, and not just Microsoft languages. This book, like other books in the series, is rooted in long experience in industrial teaching. It covers the Perl language from the ground up. Although oriented toward the ActiveState PerlNET compiler, the book also provides excellent coverage of the Perl language suitable for other versions as well.

Intermediate .NET Framework Survey Books

The second set of books is focused on topics in the .NET Framework, rather than on programming languages. Three parallel books cover the .NET Framework using the important languages C#, VB.NET, and Visual C++. The C# and VB.NET books contain self-contained introductions to the languages suitable for experienced programmers, allowing them to rapidly come up to speed on the new languages without having to plow through an introductory book.

The design of the series makes these books much more targeted than many similar books. The language emphasis is cleanly broken out into introductory books, allowing the intermediate books to cover the important topics of the .NET Framework in greater depth. The series design also makes for flexible reading paths. Less experienced readers can read the language book followed by the intermediate framework book, while more experienced readers can go directly to the intermediate framework book.

Application Development Using C# and .NET

This book covers important topics in the .NET Framework for experienced programmers. The reader does not need prior experience in C#, because there is a self-contained treatment, but the reader should have experience in some object-oriented language such as C++ or Java. A seasoned Visual Basic programmer who has experience working with objects and components in VB could also read the book. A less experienced reader coming from the introductory C# book can skip the chapters on C# and proceed directly to a study of the Framework. The book is practical, with many examples and a major case study. The goal is to equip the reader to begin building significant applications using the .NET Framework.

Application Development Using Visual Basic and .NET

This book is for the experienced VB programmer who wishes to quickly learn the new VB.NET version of VB and then get on to learning the .NET Framework. It is also suitable for experienced enterprise programmers in other languages who wish to learn the powerful RAD-oriented Visual Basic language in its .NET incarnation and go on to build applications. Like the companion C# book, this book is very practical with many examples, and the same case study is implemented in VB.NET.

.NET Architecture and Programming Using Visual C++

This parallel book is for the experienced Visual C++ programmer who wishes to learn the .NET Framework to build high performing applications. Unlike the C# and VB.NET book, there is no coverage of the C++ language itself, because C++ is too complex to cover in a brief space. This book is specifically for experienced C++ programmers. Like the companion C# and VB.NET books, this book is very practical with many examples, and it uses the same case study implemented in Visual C++.

.NET Applications and Technology

These books cover specific areas of .NET technology or application areas. In some cases, a specific language is used and, in other cases, the book is about the technology or application without regard to a particular language.

Fundamentals of Web Applications Using .NET and XML

This book provides thorough coverage of building Web applications using .NET. Unlike other books about ASP.NET, this book gives attention to the whole process of Web application development. The book incorporates a review tutorial on classical Web programming, making the book accessible to the experienced programmer new to the Web world. The book contains significant coverage on ASP.NET Web Forms, Web services, SOAP and XML.

.NET Security and Cryptography

This book is intended to provide the reader with a practical and comprehensive tutorial on implementing both security and cryptography on the .NET platform. It is an effective tutorial, providing a large number of clear and focused code examples, with ample commentary on how the code examples work. Both C# and VB.NET code will be provided for all examples. The book is comprehensive, covering all of the most important concepts and techniques supported by the .NET platform. This book will also provide sufficient background information to enable the reader to clearly see why security and cryptography are critically important to modern software development. Important practical topics that are covered include Code Access Security, Role-based Security, ASP.NET Security, Digital Signatures and Certificate Authorities, as well as Symmetric and Asymmetric Cryptography using the .NET Framework.

.NET Interoperability and Migration

These books cover issues of fundamental technologies important to .NET's vision of strong interoperability across diverse platforms. They also address issues of migrating to .NET.

Migrating to .NET: A Pragmatic Path to VB.NET, Visual C++ .NET, and ASP.NET

This book gives an introduction to the Microsoft .NET platform and covers the basic concepts of migration. It contains a detailed look on various programming languages and technologies (VB.NET, Visual C++ .NET and ASP.NET) and key differences as well as advantages over their predecessors. The book has detailed steps involved in migration, and it also has a rich set of examples and case studies to cover important aspects of migration like Pre Migration and Post Migration. The last section of the book has coverage of issues related to component migration and interoperability.

The .NET and COM Interoperability Handbook

This book explains the .NET Framework from the perspective of a COM/COM+ programmer. It compares COM/COM+ and .NET. It also shows readers how to use their existing COM/COM+ components from .NET and how to call .NET components from their Win32/COM applications. This is not the kind of cursory coverage of COM interoperability that is found in most .NET Framework books. We delve deep into the subject, covering items such as the effect of the COM Apartment threading model, ActiveX controls, late binding and the impedance mismatch between reference counting in COM and garbage collection in .NET. The book also covers how to use the COM+ Services from a .NET application.

.NET Cryptography and Security

*Y*ou do not often see books that discuss both cryptography and security with equal prominence. These two topics seem, at least on the surface, to be entirely separate disciplines, and they are usually discussed independently of one another. After all, how often does a network administrator wonder about cryptographic questions, such as how hard it is to factor a large product of two prime numbers? And how often does a mathematician think about security configuration tasks, such as controlling access to items in the Windows registry or Internet Information Services (IIS) virtual directories? Books on cryptography tend to be quite mathematical and theoretical. In contrast, books on security tend not to be programmer-oriented but very hands-on, dealing with practical issues such as how to set up a certificate server, how to create a new user account, and so on. Between these two extremes, there is the .NET programmer, concerned mainly with problems that are neither administrative nor mathematical in nature.

However, programmers are now becoming increasingly interested in incorporating cryptography and security features into their programs. On the one hand, all security-related functionality is ultimately built on top of cryptographic foundations. In fact, all real-world security protocols and technologies, such as Kerberos, the Windows Encrypted File System, Microsoft Certificate Server, and all the .NET Security Framework classes, are entirely based on cryptographic mathematical primitives at their core. On the other hand, all security-related programming must at some point interact with the underlying security configuration of the platform on which it runs that is ultimately established by an administrator. In this chapter, we take a wide-angle view of .NET cryptography and security, and see how each of these major aspects of security and cryptography fit together into the overall .NET programming picture.

1

In subsequent chapters, we look more closely at the detailed aspects of cryptography and security technologies on the .NET platform.

The Nature of This Book

This book is written specifically for programmers interested in .NET security and cryptography, not for system administrators. Therefore, we do not attempt to describe more than a small fraction of the skills needed by professional system administrators. However, every programmer must have some administrative skills to be effective software developers, and security programming is no exception. Therefore, this book does explore some aspects of administration as it directly relates to the tasks of .NET security programming. This book is also not intended for professional cryptographers[1] or mathematicians, so it does not go too far in that theoretical direction either. However, to gain an appreciation for what goes on under the hood, it can be rather empowering for a programmer to have some understanding of the underlying cryptographic theory and related mathematics, so we provide some light coverage in that direction as well.

As a result, this book takes a blended approach, covering fundamental cryptography theory as well as cryptographic and security programming on the .NET platform. We begin in this first chapter with an introduction to some of the more important overarching concepts of cryptography and security on the .NET platform, providing glimpses of the pieces that work together toward implementing secure .NET applications. In Chapter 2, we look at the theoretical fundamentals of cryptography, starting with the designs and cryptanalysis of some historically significant pencil-and-paper ciphers. Building on that theoretical framework, Chapters 3, 4, and 5 describe practical .NET programming techniques in the three main areas of modern cryptography: symmetric cryptography, asymmetric cryptography, and digital signatures. These three chapters provide extensive example code that demonstrates how to work with the relevant .NET Security Framework classes. Chapter 6 continues to explore encryption and digital signatures, but within the specialized context of XML cryptography. Chapters 7 and 8 show how the main programming techniques work for implementing role-based security and code access security features in .NET programs. Of course, distributed applications and the Internet have made many security issues more important than ever before,

---

1. A *cryptographer* is one who designs and analyzes cryptographic algorithms, not one who merely uses a cryptographic library to incorporate cryptographic and security features into his or her programs.

and Chapters 9 and 10 cover the most important aspects of ASP.NET security and .NET Web services security, respectively.

Risks Are Everywhere

When you start thinking about all the things that can go wrong, you may find yourself wondering if it all becomes a bit silly. The average citizen is, after all, not typically under CIA or FBI investigation (as far as we know) or the target of some espionage plot. If you let your imagination go too far, many of the risks that come to mind may seem rather far-fetched. You may even start to wonder if you should wrap your head in tinfoil just in case the aliens are trying to read your brain waves! Nevertheless, even though it may seem like a paranoid perspective, it is indeed true: Risks are everywhere, and the more important the data is, the more important the data security becomes. It is actually quite surprising how easily and how often dangers can crop up unexpectedly in the world of computing.

THINKING LIKE AN ATTACKER

You may have heard the old angler's advice: To catch a fish, you have to think like a fish. I was never too comfortable with that odd-sounding advice, since it is not at all clear exactly how a fish thinks. However, this advice is very applicable when you apply it to dealing with human adversaries. In particular, to protect yourself from attackers[2] and other such enemies, it pays to put yourself in their shoes and try to think the way they think.

Perhaps one of the biggest problems is that nice folks like you and me have a very hard time thinking ultra-deviously, while the enemy often seems to have an endless supply of brainpower, time, energy, and mischievousness. Often, all we can do is try our best to play catch-up. Unfortunately, it is an uneven playing field in that if a single attacker finds just a single weakness, the algorithm is in jeopardy. In contrast, the weary defender must attempt to anticipate and deal with all potential weaknesses. To get a feel for the kinds of things that the enemy may try, let's look at some examples of the potential risks.

EXAMPLES OF RISKS AND PRESCRIBED REMEDIES

There is probably no limit to the number of ingenious tricks and traps that can be conceived of by our potential enemies. Security pitfalls that garden-variety

---

2. We use the term *attacker* to refer to someone who gains unauthorized access for the purpose of stealing, forging, or destroying data. Such an attacker is often referred to as a cracker. The term *hacker* is often incorrectly used as a synonym for cracker, mainly due to the confusion that is so prevalent in mass media reporting on technical topics. The term *hacker* more correctly refers to a computer expert or enthusiast, often connoting extensive self-taught knowledge and an undisciplined attitude.

email users might experience are conceptually identical to the security pitfalls that programmers must also be able to deal with. For example, most people do not encrypt their email correspondence, which is somewhat analogous to sending an open postcard rather than sending a letter in a sealed envelope. This oversight could be a risk, since it is quite easy to intercept email packets as they are routed through your ISP and through various routers over the Internet. As another example, an email virus could cause you grief by randomly selecting messages from your previously sent email and forwarding copies of them to contacts found in your address book. This could be very embarrassing if not downright costly. If you encrypted your sensitive correspondence, then these problems would be solved. Intercepted email packets would be unintelligible, and the virus just described would send only copies of gibberish to those unintended recipients. There are even email viruses that make file shares on arbitrarily selected folders, unexpectedly exposing large amounts of your information to others on your network. By simply encrypting those folders that contain sensitive information, such unintended file sharing becomes a nonissue. Of course, you should probably have already updated your virus scanner, defensively configured your email client program, and applied any necessary security patches to avoid the virus in the first place. But then, email and file system encryption provides a nice extra layer of security just in case all other up-front efforts fail. These examples prove the importance of using encryption in the world of email. By analogy, it should be clear that encryption is important to use wherever sensitive data may be exposed in the world of programming as well.

Using digital signatures is another way to avoid security risks. Unfortunately, most email users do not have a personal digital ID for signing their important email correspondence. If you do not digitally sign your most sensitive email messages, then someone could send a fraudulent email in your name to someone in an attempt to frame you with bogus evidence or to commit you to some compromising position. If you make a habit of digitally signing all of your sensitive correspondence, then the recipients of your critical messages will expect a signature that they can verify and thus will be able to discern that such a bogus email was not actually from you. This example shows the importance of using digital signatures in the world of email, and by analogy, it shows that it is also important to use digital signatures where appropriate in your own programming.

A FALSE SENSE OF SECURITY

Unfortunately, people often assume that using a computer in a familiar or routine manner is inherently safe, when in fact it is never entirely safe. Here is a startling example: During the summer of 2002, Microsoft accidentally distributed a copy of the Nimda worm in its Korean language version of Visual Studio .NET. Fortunately, as it turned out, the copy of the Nimda worm was included in such a way that it did not in fact result in any realistic risk of infection to anyone's system. But who would have ever thought twice about the security ramifications of installing such an application from such an established and trusted software vendor? This news item was certainly a wake-up call[3] to programmers around the world! There are many other examples in which our implicit trust and assumption of security turns out to be questionable or even dangerously wrong. How often have you heard of newly discovered security vulnerabilities, followed shortly by the announcement of a corresponding security patch? Sadly, this sort of thing happens on a much too frequent basis. The good news is that the .NET Security Framework and the .NET platform can be used to effectively protect applications and data from many of these potential dangers. Unfortunately, security will never be a completely solved problem, but .NET goes a long way in helping us write programs that can protect users better than ever before.

Software vendors, system administrators, programmers, and users all need to become much more vigilant of the myriad risks and aware of their prescribed precautions. Everyone must be on guard against falling into a false sense of security. Clearly, security is an important issue that must be recognized by all computing professionals. This is especially true now that our world has become so heavily dependent on computing in almost all facets of our lives, and our systems have become so thoroughly interconnected by way of the Internet.

The Nature of Cryptography and Security

The major focus of this book is on the theory and practice of .NET cryptography and security. But when you are in the thick of it, it is easy to lose sight of the following two fundamental questions regarding the basic nature of cryptography and security:

- Why are cryptography and security important?
- What can and cannot be done with cryptography and security?

The first question considers why we would want to use it, and the second question considers what we actually accomplish by using it. Let's take a moment now, before we get into all of the technical details in the upcoming chapters, to consider these two fundamental questions in some detail. Then,

---

3. Earlier, in the history of UNIX, there was another very interesting and convincing wake-up call regarding the risk we take when we blindly trust the security of the software that we use. To read more about it, see what Ken Thompson (the father of UNIX) has to say about shaken trust at *http://www.acm.org/classics/sep95/*. As you will see, the story has a fascinating twist.

as you read through the remainder of this book, you might want to keep these two questions in the back of your mind.

Why Cryptography and Security Are Important

Why are cryptography and security important? We have all heard of many examples in business, warfare, and maybe sometimes even personal life where a bit more secrecy could have helped avoid costly problems. In many other cases, severe embarrassment and humiliation could have been avoided with the application of just a bit more discretion. Of course, encryption can help you be much more secure and discrete,[4] at least when the information is in digital form.

There are four main aspects of security that typically present themselves: *secrecy, authentication, integrity,* and *nonrepudiation.* Obviously, secrecy can be very important in many contexts. Of course, secrecy is important whenever sensitive information must be protected from being known by your adversaries. You can also imagine how important it can sometimes be to know exactly whom you are communicating with, which is a problem known as authentication. It can be equally important at times to know that the communicated information you send or receive cannot be somehow manipulated or corrupted during transit or after receipt, which is a problem known as integrity. You may also be concerned with the possibility of someone reneging on an agreement that you have already made with him or her, which is the dastardly act known as repudiation. Security protocols may be devised using digital signatures and digital certificates, as well as symmetric algorithms, cryptographic hashes, and Message Authentication Codes (MACs) that can be used to avoid all of these problems of secrecy, authenticity, integrity, and nonrepudiation.

WHY WORRY IF YOU HAVE NOTHING TO HIDE?

Why should you worry about privacy if you have nothing to hide? This rhetorical question is sometimes posed by people who naively assume that privacy is of interest only to criminals, subversives, and deviants with dirty little secrets to hide. The fallacious argument is that fine upstanding folks should not need much privacy and that aggressively pursuing privacy is evidence of criminality or depravity. It is important to recognize that strong privacy really

---

4. It is obviously illegal in most countries to conceal or destroy evidence that is relevant to a crime or requested by court order, so caution should be exercised where appropriate. Discretion is one thing, but obstruction of justice is another.

is a legitimate concern of all good law-abiding citizens. This is especially true if the authorities that you must deal with are less than perfect.

To shed some light on this question, consider how you would react if you were not permitted any privacy. For example, how would you feel if your government passed legislation that nobody is permitted to enclose postal letters in envelopes and that all medical and banking records must be made publicly open in a national database? How would you feel if you were not permitted to protect your personal information from being hijacked by criminals for fraudulent purposes? How would you like it if all Internet email messages and all Web page access histories were archived in a publicly searchable database hosted by *www.google.com*? Surely, the vast majority of honest and ethical people must agree that privacy is honorable and legitimate, and privacy should be recognized as a fundamental and inalienable human right.

CATEGORIES OF SECURITY ISSUES

There are many examples of specific cases that could be listed, but to avoid going overboard with naming names, let's look instead at some of the broad categories of security issues that have proved to be the downfall of many hapless unfortunates in the past. For each of these, you might be able to think of specific examples that you have heard about in the news or maybe even know about personally.

- Leaks of intellectual property, merger and acquisition plans, and contracts
- Malicious code, such as evil email scripts, logic time bombs, viruses, and trojans
- Unauthorized access programming techniques, such as buffer overrun attacks
- Bogus messages from masqueraders[5]
- Contractual agreement repudiation
- Bugs that corrupt code or data

When properly planned and applied, .NET cryptography and security features go a long way to help avoid all of these issues.

---

5. Bogus messages can take on several forms. One example is the man-in-the-middle attack (also known as TCP hijacking) in which an attacker pulls packets from the network and modifies them in some nefarious way, such as changing an account number or a dollar amount, and then reinserts them back onto the network. Another example is IP spoofing: The attacker forges a bogus source IP address in each packet to impersonate someone else and then sends the spoofed packets over the network. In its crudest and simplest form, a human readable message, such as a fraudulent email, may be sent to swindle an unsuspecting victim in some way.

What Cryptography and Security Can and Cannot Do

Now for the second question: What can and cannot be done with cryptography and security? Although cryptography and security are very important tools, they are not a panacea for all security problems. Knowing what is possible and what is beyond the reach of cryptography and security is important to being able to apply solutions to real-world problems. Let's first look at what cryptography and security can do.

WHAT CRYPTOGRAPHY AND SECURITY CAN DO

Cryptography and security technology can help deal only with risks that relate to software design, not with issues that relate to human character. Just as human error appears to be the most frequent point of failure in traditional tragedies, such as automobile and aircraft accidents, it is the programmer or end user who tends to be the frequent source of security failure in the computing world. Some of the protections that the .NET platform and .NET Security Framework classes can provide include

- Privacy of information
- Authentication of users
- Integrity of information
- Nonrepudiation of agreement
- Access control of resources
- Availability of service

Information privacy can be used to limit access to authorized users by means of encryption. User authentication can be used to ensure that users are who they claim to be by means of password hash comparison or digital signature verification. Information integrity can be used to ensure that only authorized users can create or modify information based on digital signature verification. Nonrepudiation can be used to ensure that the author of a message cannot, after the fact, deny the existence of the message or abrogate an agreement defined in the message that he or she has digitally signed. Access control can be used to ensure that access to information resources are limited in specified ways to authorized users only. Availability of service relates to how available a given server application is when needed. Availability is closely related to issues of reliability (i.e., uptime). It is also related to quota management, which is used to foil denial-of-service (DOS) attacks. Although quota management, which is usually programmatically built into server applications, is not directly supported by any specific .NET feature at the current time, the enhanced reliability made possible by the .NET runtime does help a great deal in improving availability of service.

WHAT CRYPTOGRAPHY AND SECURITY CANNOT DO

Commonly used cryptographic algorithms have been thoroughly analyzed and have stood up rather well in a mathematical sense for their intended purposes over the years. However, real cryptography is done in the real world, not just in a mathematician's head. In the real world, we have a very lovable weak link, affectionately referred to as the user,[6] who is, after all, just a human being. All the cryptography and security that mathematicians, programmers, and administrators can muster cannot protect against the user's human frailties. It is a fact that many security programmers and administrators—who are themselves only human—make the mistake of focusing far too much on the security of this algorithm or that protocol, but the most frequent point of failure results from the imperfections of ordinary folks much like you and me. For example, you can use the strongest cipher ever designed in your application, but if the user writes his or her password on a sticky note attached to the side of a display screen, the battle is lost. Here are some of the types of risk that pertain to human imperfections rather than to the strength of any algorithm design or cryptographic theory.

- Lack of training, diligence, and discipline
- Carelessness, such as exposing keys, poor choice of password, or not encrypting data,
- Inexperience, gullibility, and misplaced trust
- Social engineering attacks and con-artistry
- Bribery, intimidation, and blackmail
- Poor software design and coding bugs

Cryptography and security are like seatbelts. What is the use of having fancy protection if it is not used properly and consistently? Obviously, unencrypted data is not kept secret, and unsigned data can be easily tampered with and repudiated. And what is the point of using a password-protected application if the password is easy to guess? Effective security requires vigilance and discipline. Another concern is misplaced trust. For example, firewalls may not be able to protect against a trusted but disgruntled employee. Proper security policies and procedures as well as effective user training and management are very important for keeping confidential information private.

Social engineering attacks apply psychological or emotional tricks and lies on trusted users to gain access to secure systems. In general, you should be extremely skeptical of anyone who says, "You can trust me," since the people you can really trust rarely need to tell you so. One aspect of this type

---

6. Some rather unkind programmers have a cruel habit of pronouncing the word *user* with an additional leading *l*. We do not condone this arrogant practice, since, after all, if it were not for the user, we programmers would not be paid for our efforts.

of attack that makes it hard to address after the fact is that victims of con-artistry have a hard time admitting that the compromise happened. Denial is attractive—after all, who wants to admit that he or she has been foolish or gullible? So, never let your guard down, and if you do, then don't let your pride get in the way of dealing with the result effectively.

Bribery, intimidation, blackmail, and (heaven forbid) torture is like a social engineering attack on steroids, but on an entirely more evil and illegal level. You may think that this sort of thing doesn't happen except in movies; unfortunately, it also happens in reality if the stakes are high and the participants are vicious. When you think about the economics of cipher cracking, you can see why. Let's say that it would cost $50,000 over three months of CPU time on a multimillion-dollar supercomputer to crack a key for a given cipher. And let's say that it costs only $2,000 to contract a gangster to apply his own persuasive methods to get the same result in a couple of hours. Now, assuming that you have no moral compunctions whatsoever (and such people do exist), which option would you take? Of course, you should stay within the law, watch the company that you keep, and avoid accepting or giving bribes. But as for the more violent possibilities, probably no advice can help you once you are there. Fortunately, torture seems to be exceedingly rare in most democracies, but it is unfortunately a serious human rights problem in many countries around the world.[7]

Of course, we cannot blame everything on the user. There are a few security issues that cryptography and security cannot deal with that are also completely beyond the control of the user. These are physical security and side-channel leakage risks. Physical security pertains to things like how heavy the door is, how big the lock is, how thick the walls are, and the caliber of rifle used. Side-channel leakage relates to any form of information that is unintentionally leaked from the computing premises, which can then be detected and interpreted in exceedingly clever ways.

Physical attacks, such as break-ins, theft, and vandalism, cannot be prevented by any cryptographic algorithm, and it is obviously asking too much of a typical user to mount any defense. Obviously, physical problems need physical solutions. You may not have the same security needs as the NORAD Air Defense Center in the Cheyenne Mountain Complex. But virtually everyone has at least some physical security requirements. Do you care if all your email is read by your babysitter? If nothing else, would you at least be interested in protecting the replacement value of your PC? Probably everyone should have at least password protection and a lockable door between the PC and the outside world.

---

7. For more details on this gruesome problem, you might want to visit *http:// www.amnesty.org/*.

When contemplating protection against physical attacks, keep in mind that theft and vandalism do not come only from perpetrators on the outside. Internal security can be just as important as external security. You should protect your computing facilities according to the value of the resource and the potential threats that you perceive.

Side-channel leakage is a problem where physical side effects of computing may leak sensitive information. Side-channel leakage can come in many surprising forms. For example, what happens to sensitive plaintext data that is left in a swap file or made available as a result of a system crash memory dump? If you are not careful, it is there for the taking. Side-channel leakage can also result from the radio frequency information that computers naturally emanate, which is the focus of Tempest[8] technologies. When you consider the millions of digital switches that are turning on and off within a computer every few microseconds, it is astonishing that anyone can gather any intelligible information in this way. However, it has been demonstrated that data displayed on one computer screen can be replicated on another specialized device based entirely on the emitted electromagnetic radiation. In one widely published case of side-channel leakage, infrared signal crosstalk accidentally shared information between two competing companies via cordless keyboards and PCs in adjacent buildings.

Side-channel leakage also has been shown to occur whenever a computing device encrypts data. Specifically, the execution timings of the cryptographic operations can leak information in some cases. Additionally, power consumption measurements can reveal subtle details about the operations that a computing device performs, right down to the precise sequence of microprocessor instructions being executed! By analyzing these timing and power consumption measurements, an adversary may be able to obtain some critical information about the plaintext being encrypted. Each of these detective techniques is a spectacular example of how incredibly clever and resourceful researchers in this industry can be.

Yet another variety of side-channel leakage occurs in usage and message traffic patterns. Even if you are careful to hide the contents of your sensitive messages, the fact that you are communicating in the first place coupled with the identity of the persons with whom you are communicating may be enough to get you into trouble. Although this is less of a concern in most democratic countries, it can occasionally be relevant even to law-abiding citizens in respectable jurisdictions. If someone wants badly enough to know what you are doing and has substantial resources at her disposal, then you may have a very hard time preventing her from getting that information. In

---

8. *Tempest,* which stands for Transient Electromagnetic Pulse Emanation Standard, refers to a set of classified technologies developed by the U.S. military for analyzing emitted electromagnetic radiation (EMR) produced by analog and digital equipment.

fact, attempting too strenuously to prevent it may itself work against you![9] If you are concerned about side-channel leakage, you should take the necessary steps to block the leaks. A wire mesh cage can be used to shield emanating radio frequency energy, power line filtering can help hide variations in power consumption, and so on.[10] But then your attempts at shielding will probably be detectable. Internet traffic patterns can to some extent be hidden behind services such as anonymous remailers, but such services cannot guarantee absolute anonymity.

We have considered several categories of risk and remedy with the implied assumption that nothing illegal was being committed. however, if crimes have been committed, then the following possibilities may arise. Naturally, there is nothing that cryptography or security can do to help you if you come to this point.

- Testimonial evidence from witnesses or spies
- Behavioral evidence, such as suspicious travel and extravagant lifestyle
- Physical evidence, such as fingerprints, photographs, financial records, and paper trails
- Government investigation[11]

Windows Security Comes of Age

Security and cryptography have always been recognized as important issues in multiuser and enterprise-level computing. Even in the early mainframe systems of the mid-1960s, such as System/360,[12] multiuser operating systems were designed with careful attention given to user authentication, program isolation, auditing, and privacy. Symmetric cryptographic algorithms, such as the Data Encryption Standard (DES), were used heavily in mainframe applica-

---

9. Do you remember hearing about the McCarthy era in your high school history class?

10. These precautions require the skills of a professional electrical engineer with appropriate experience to be done properly.

11. We are the Borg. Resistance is futile. Many governments have computer surveillance tools at their disposal for collecting evidence on criminal and subversive activity. According to numerous reports, the FBI's Carnivore project enables the recording of targeted email messages via a cooperating ISP, and the Magic Lantern project enables inserting a virus onto a suspect's computer to obtain encryption keys used to hide criminal evidence.

12. System/360 was developed by IBM in 1964. The chief architect working on this operating system was Gene Amdahl.

tions by banks and governments by the late 1970s. UNIX[13] systems continued to treat security as a first-class design requirement throughout its history. In the early 1990s, UNIX systems made use of symmetric and asymmetric cryptography in various technologies and protocols, such as Kerberos network authentication.

In contrast, the history of Windows has shown a marked lack of awareness toward issues related to security and cryptography. This is to some degree understandable, considering that for much of its early history, Windows (especially in its 16-bit form) was used primarily as a single-user, non-mission-critical productivity tool and entertainment console. This is not to disparage Windows in any way. Indeed, Windows quickly grew to become a significant industry in its own right, providing the world with effective and affordable computing capabilities. However, the concepts of security, privacy, and authentication were largely unknown to most Windows users, and the vendor simply catered to that market. In contrast to the obsession with security, privacy, and reliability typical of large corporate computing facilities, Windows users have been generally tolerant of security weaknesses and more interested in powerful user-oriented features. This is why, much to the chagrin of mainframe old-timers, Windows has been plagued with malicious code, operating system reliability problems, and information leakage. Fortunately, this is all changing now, for many reasons.

- PC users are now more sophisticated, demanding greater security, privacy, and reliability.
- Corporations recognize the need to extend security policy over the Internet.
- Microsoft has recently stepped up its interest in security and reliability to a strategic level.
- Many secure corporate computing tasks have moved from the mainframe to the PC.
- The Win32 API provides powerful but arcane support for security and cryptography.
- The .NET platform provides powerful and convenient support for security and cryptography.
- Code has become more mobile, making code authentication and verification more important.

---

13. UNIX was initially developed by Bell Labs (then part of ATT) in 1969 and the early 1970s. Ken Thompson wrote the first UNIX system in assembly language, and many other contributors, too numerous to mention, developed it further over the last 30 years. Many vendors contributed to its development, resulting in many competing implementations, including BSD, System V, Solaris, HP-UX, AIX, Linux, and FreeBSD.

- Many experts in the field, including Bruce Schneier, have effectively evangelized security.
- Hardware cost and performance improvements make security and cryptography more practical.
- U.S. export restrictions on strong encryption were dramatically relaxed in January 2000.[14]
- Public awareness of viruses and issues such as buffer overflow[15] vulnerabilities has increased.
- The growth in mission-critical Web services has made security a front-burner concern.

The .NET Framework and the CLR

The .NET Framework and Common Language Runtime (CLR) enable programmers to deal effectively with each of the important security issues described in this chapter. For example, information theft can be avoided by implementing appropriate cryptographic features into your applications. Malicious code can be stifled by defensive programming practices and by configuring appropriate user-based security and Code Access Security (CAS) features. Buffer overrun attacks become virtually impossible to implement given the secure and rigorously managed runtime environment provided by the .NET platform. Bugs resulting from buffer overruns and improper type casting are virtually eliminated by managed code and CLR runtime checks.

The following .NET platform features provide the most important aspects of protection related to security and cryptography.

- Evidence and security policy configuration (administrative control over .NET security)
- CAS (execution control based on evidence and security policy)
- Role-based security (access control based on user identity and role membership)

---

14. High-strength cryptographic products are now generally exportable from the United States without license to most countries. At the time of writing, embargoed countries included Cuba, Iran, Iraq, Libya, North Korea, and a few others. See the Bureau of Industry and Security at *www.bxa.doc.gov* for the most current information on U.S. export regulations.

15. As we shall see later in this book, the buffer overflow is a nasty technique used by the likes of the Code Red Internet worm in which a malicious request overwhelms a server with data that overflows into a sensitive memory area, such as a parameter stack, where it can then take over control of the server and wreak havoc.

- Managed code runtime verification (address range checking and type checking)
- Application domains (lightweight execution isolation)
- Cryptography classes (access to powerful cryptographic algorithms)

How the .NET Framework Simplifies Security

One big problem with security programming using the raw Win32 API was that it was difficult to understand and difficult to use. A ridiculous number of lines of code had to be implemented in order to do the simplest operation, such as obtain a key from the operating system's current cryptographic service provider (CSP) key store. Many developers simply ignored it wherever they could get away with it. Developers who needed to apply security by directly calling the Win32 API often did the best they could with a difficult programming model.

The .NET Framework provides many simplifications by wrapping certain aspects of the underlying Win32 Security API with a powerful and simplified object-oriented interface. Many operations, such as obtaining a key from the CSP key store, now happen automatically using the .NET Security classes where appropriate. In addition, each of the classes in the .NET Security Framework that are entrusted with critical security functionality are declared as sealed classes so that they cannot be hijacked or spoofed into compromising security.

Reliability and the .NET Platform

Before you can reap the benefits of any security or cryptographic technology, you must first have the assurance of application reliability. What is the use of having a well-planned security infrastructure if the underlying application frequently falls apart? The .NET platform goes a long way to help ensure this all-important reliability requirement is satisfied. First, it is important to recognize that .NET applications are not compiled into native code. Instead, they are compiled into an intermediate form known as Microsoft Intermediate Language (MSIL, or just IL for short), much like the bytecode instruction format used on the Java[16]

---

16. There are some truly new contributions that .NET has made to the cause of security, cryptography, and reliability. However, to be fair, it should be acknowledged that many of the most effective of these .NET security-related features were originally made available on the Java platform and in the Java Cryptography Extension (JCE) class library.

platform. This allows the CLR and the .NET Framework to perform many security-related services automatically, including the following:

- Bounds checking performed at runtime prevents memory corruption and stack overruns.
- Datatype checking performed at runtime prevents improper typecasting.
- Stack walks are used to verify permissions granted to calling code.
- Automatic garbage collection effectively addresses memory leak problems.
- Exception handling allows graceful response to abnormal runtime situations.
- Role-based security is used to authenticate and limit actions of the current user.
- Evidence-based security is used to control managed code based on permissions.

Managed Code and Type Safety

Code that can use the services of the CLR is called managed code. The CLR provides a set of services, such as type-safety checking and automatic garbage collection, that enhance application reliability and security. In order to make use of these CLR services, managed code must behave in a predictable, orderly, and consistent manner. Type safety is an important aspect of reliability and security. Type safety is made possible by the fact the CLR knows all the details about each of the managed datatypes. Using this knowledge, the CLR is able to strictly enforce rules of type safety.

For example, all datatypes, including strings and arrays, have consistent layouts and abide by strict behavioral rules. The Common Type System (CTS) defines these rules for each of the managed datatypes as well as the operations that the CLR defines for those datatypes. These restrictive rules are defined by the CTS and are implemented by MSIL. The CTS also defines each of the datatype memory layouts and the operations that are allowed in managed code. It is the CTS that limits class types to single implementation inheritance and prevents unsafe operations, such as casting an integer into a pointer and overflowing the bounds of an array. MSIL code is typically compiled[17] at runtime into the native instruction set of the local hardware after this type checking is complete.

To make this type-safety checking possible, .NET assemblies contain descriptive metadata that define the contained code and data. Managed data is allocated and deallocated automatically by the CLR on the heap. This auto-

---

17. This is known as just-in-time (JIT) compilation.

matic memory management is referred to as *garbage collection*. Garbage collection reduces memory leaks and related reliability problems.

Every object has a type, and therefore every reference to an object refers to a defined memory layout. Since arbitrary pointer operations are not allowed (unless the unsafe keyword is used), the only way to access an object is through its public members. Therefore, it is possible for the CLR to verify an object's safety by analyzing only the object's metadata, which is contained in the assembly. There is no need to analyze all the code that uses the object to verify that it will be used safely. Unsafe code can use pointers, which can be used to subvert the CTS and access arbitrary memory locations.

It is also possible to implement unmanaged code in the C# language using the *unsafe* keyword, but certain languages, such as VB.NET are capable of generating only type-safe managed code. The unsafe keyword is required for working directly with memory pointers. Unmanaged code is useful for calling into legacy DLLs, using the PInvoke facility, but unmanaged code is not verifiably type-safe by the CLR.

MSIL defines a platform-independent[18] instruction set that is used by all .NET compilers. This language implements and enforces the CTS typing rules at runtime. MSIL is then converted into platform-specific native code after the CLR type checking is complete. Type checking is performed by default, but it can be optionally skipped for code that is trusted.

.NET Cryptography Programming

As we shall see in Chapters 3, 4, 5, and 6, there are several cryptography classes available in the .NET Framework. These classes support all of the most important cryptographic algorithms in modern use. We will see these again in much greater detail in the appropriate upcoming chapters, but for now, let's just get a bird's-eye view of the major areas of functionality that are covered by these classes.

- DES, 3DES, and RC2 symmetric encryption
- Cryptographic streams
- RSA asymmetric encryption
- RSA and DSA digital signatures
- Hash algorithms, including MD5, SHA1, SHA-256, and so on
- Message Authentication Codes (MAC)

---

18. Platform independence for .NET CLR is possible in theory. However, it remains to be seen if the CLR is ported to as many platforms as the Java Runtime Environment.

- Keyed hash algorithm
- Pseudorandom number generators[19] (PRNG)
- XML encryption
- XML signatures
- ASP.NET security
- Web services security

.NET Security Programming

As we shall see in Chapters 7 and 8, there are two powerful approaches to security programming supported by the .NET Framework: role-based security and CAS. These two approaches to security programming are then explored further in the context of Internet and distributed applications in Chapters 9 and 10. We shall see these two terms defined more completely with supporting code examples in the relevant chapters to come, but for now, let's take a very brief look at these two major concepts.

Role-Based Security and Principals

Most people have at least an intuitive understanding of users and roles based on their experience using an operating system such as Windows 2000 or Windows XP. The idea is that you can control how certain users can access certain resources, such as files, registry entries, and so on. Thus, role-based security comes down to the two basic questions of *authentication* and *authorization*. The authentication question asks who you are, and the authorization question asks if you are permitted to perform the action you are attempting.

In role-based security programming, the word "you" in these two questions is represented by an object referred to as the *principal*. The principal object contains an *identity* property that represents the user ID that is running the current thread. We shall see in Chapter 7 exactly how to use role-based security to accomplish various security goals in .NET programs.

---

19. The .NET Framework provides a useful class named **Random** in the **System** namespace that can be used for generating pseudorandom number sequences for games, simulations, and most statistical purposes. However, you must never use it for cryptographic purposes, or you run the risk of seriously weakening the security of your application. For cryptographic purposes, be sure to always use a cryptographic strength PRNG, as explained in later chapters.

CAS, Evidence, Policy, and Permissions

Code Access Security (CAS) allows administrative control over the actions that code is permitted to perform. CAS is based on the idea that you can assign levels of trust to assemblies and restrict the actions of the code within those assemblies based on established permissions. CAS is closely related to the concept of *evidence-based* security. *Evidence* is the set of telltale information that is used by the CLR to make decisions about what code group the assembly belongs to and therefore what actions the code is allowed to perform. A piece of evidence might be the location from which the code originated or the digital signature that was used to sign the assembly, and so on.

Security policy is the configurable set of rules that is established by an administrator and used by the CLR to make CAS decisions. Security policy can be set at the enterprise, machine, user, or application domain level. Security policy is defined in terms of permissions. A *permission* is an object that is used to describe the rights and privileges of assemblies that belong to a code group to access various resources or undertake certain actions. In effect, policy maps permissions to evidence.

Assemblies can programmatically or declaratively request to be granted certain permissions. Security policy dictates what permissions will ultimately be granted to a given assembly. Security policy is based on a set of rules that administrators can set, and the CLR uses those rules to enforce the desired policy. The evidence, represented by the identity permissions, is used to determine which policy to apply according to the code group that the assembly belongs to. The CLR determines which permissions are to be assigned to a loaded assembly by evaluating its evidence. Evidence can refer to identity of the assembly, the digital signer of the assembly, and the origin of the assembly, including its URL, site, and Internet Zone. In Chapter 8, we shall see much more detail about how to program using use code access security.

Summary

In this first chapter we learned how cryptography and security differ and how they are related to one another. After a guide to how this book is organized, we looked at the kinds of risk that programmers must learn to deal with as well as the solutions prescribed for dealing with those risks. We also took a bird's-eye view of the broad issues confronting programmers who are interested in implementing cryptography and security features into .NET applications. Finally, we briefly introduced the major .NET-specific programming topics that will be covered in greater depth in subsequent chapters.

Fundamentals of Cryptography

*T*his chapter introduces many of the basic ideas that are required for fully understanding several subsequent chapters. Our purpose is to introduce terminology and concepts, and we consider several simple, classical cryptographic algorithms as examples. These concepts are used in later chapters where more sophisticated algorithms are discussed.

This chapter also gives some interesting historical perspectives on cryptography. The remainder of the book provides a great deal more current, practical information, covering many modern cryptographic and security techniques. Some chapters also delve into the use of the Microsoft .NET Security Framework for implementing many aspects of cryptography and security. Of course, if you are already familiar with basic cryptographic terminology and concepts, you may safely skip this chapter.

The title of this book refers to security and cryptography, which are closely interrelated at a fundamental level. Security comes in many flavors, but the basic idea is always the same: preventing something dangerous or undesirable from happening. For example, you may wish to ensure that only authorized users are permitted to perform certain operations on certain computing resources or to control access to sensitive information. Computer security is ultimately based on the science of cryptography. For example, Kerberos,[1] which is a powerful network security protocol for authenticating users, and .NET evidence-based security, which is used to secure executable code, are both based on strong underlying cryptographic technologies.

---

1. Kerberos is the authentication system of MIT's Project Athena, based on symmetric key cryptography. The Greek name Kerberos (also known by the Latin spelling *Cerberus*) was the name of the three-headed guard dog at the entrance to Hades in Greek mythology. With a name like that, it's got to be secure!

Security and Keeping Secrets

Security is the art of protecting access to information and other computing resources from those whom you do not fully trust. Of course, security is only possible if you are able to keep certain secrets, such as passwords, keys, and so forth. Security is ultimately based on one simple concept: keeping secrets. Indeed, cryptography is the science of keeping secrets. In fact, cryptography is generally nothing more than hiding large secrets (which are themselves awkward to hide) with small secrets (which are more convenient to hide). As we will see in the next section, the large secret is typically referred to as plaintext, and the small secret is referred to as the encryption key.

Basic Cryptographic Terminology

A *cipher* is a system or an algorithm used to transform an arbitrary message into a form that is intended to be unintelligible to anyone other than one or more desired recipients. A cipher represents a transformation that maps each possible input message into a unique encrypted output message, and an inverse transformation must exist that will then reproduce the original message. A *key* is used by a cipher as an input that controls the encryption in a desirable manner. A general assumption in cryptography work is that the key you choose is the critical secret, whereas the details about the cipher design should not be assumed to be secret.[2] A well-designed encryption algorithm produces an encrypted message that is essentially indistinguishable from a randomly generated byte sequence and provides as little information as possible about the original message to an attacker. A *key space* is the set of all possible keys that can be used by a cipher to encrypt messages.

The original message is referred to as *plaintext*. The word plaintext is not meant to imply that the data is necessarily human readable or that it is ASCII text. The plaintext can be any data (text or binary) that is directly meaningful to someone or to some program. The encrypted message is referred to as *ciphertext*. Ciphertext makes it possible to transmit sensitive information over an insecure channel or to store sensitive information on an insecure storage medium. Examples of such applications are Secure Sockets Layer (SSL) and the NTFS Encrypted File System (EFS), respectively. The term *encryption*

---

2. This is known as Kerckhoff's principle, which states that the security of a cipher should depend only on the secrecy of the key and not on the secrecy of the algorithm. The reason for this principle is that it is usually very difficult to keep the algorithm secret, whereas the key can be changed frequently and is therefore much easier to hide. Kerckhoff was a historically significant figure in the science of cryptography in the late 1800s.

refers to the process of transforming plaintext into ciphertext. *Decryption* is the inverse process of encryption, transforming ciphertext back into the original plaintext. Figure 2–1 shows how a symmetric[3] cipher is used to encrypt a confidential message.

A *sender* refers to someone who encrypts a plaintext message and sends the resulting ciphertext to an intended recipient. The intended recipient is referred to as the *receiver.* Anyone who tries to get between the sender and receiver with the intention of obtaining the key and/or the plaintext message is referred to as an *attacker.* An attacker is also known by other names, including *interloper, villain,* and *eavesdropper.* Figure 2–2 shows the relationship between sender, receiver, and attacker. To make a cryptographic

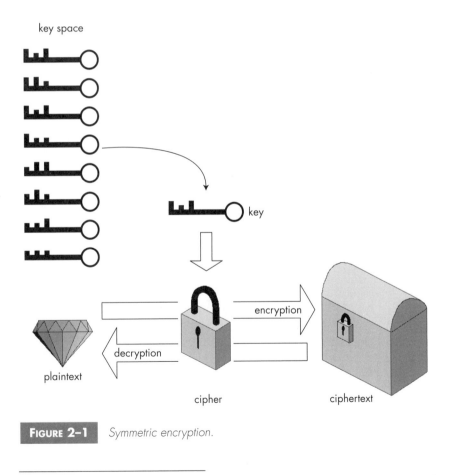

key space

key

encryption

decryption

plaintext

cipher

ciphertext

FIGURE 2–1   *Symmetric encryption.*

3. Symmetric ciphers are discussed in detail in Chapter 3. Another cipher category, known as asymmetric ciphers, is discussed in detail in Chapter 4.

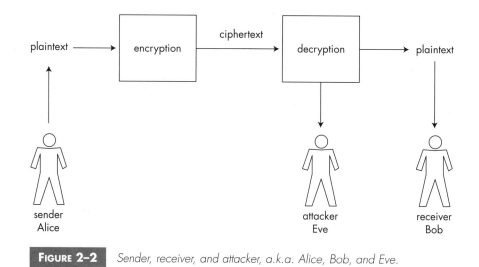

FIGURE 2–2   *Sender, receiver, and attacker, a.k.a. Alice, Bob, and Eve.*

scenario more vivid, these characters are often portrayed in cryptographic literature as protagonists named Alice and Bob, and a villain named Eve. In more complex scenarios, additional characters are often brought into the story. These characters can be very useful for clearly describing complex cryptographic protocols in a familiar manner.

The design and application of ciphers is known as *cryptography,* which is practiced by *cryptographers.* The breaking of ciphers is known as *cryptanalysis.* Because cipher designs must be thoroughly tested, cryptanalysis is also an integral part of designing ciphers. *Cryptology* refers to the combined mathematical foundation of cryptography and cryptanalysis.

A *cryptanalytic attack* is the application of specialized techniques that are used to discover the key and/or plaintext originally used to produce a given ciphertext. As was previously mentioned, it is generally assumed that the attacker knows the details of the cipher and only needs to determine the particular key that was employed.

Another important concept that you should be aware of is represented by the word *break.* When a break has been discovered for a particular algorithm (i.e., the algorithm is said to have been broken), it does not necessarily mean that an effective means has been found to attack the algorithm in practice. A break is a more theoretical concept, which simply means that a technique has been found that reduces the work required for an attack to fall below that of a brute-force approach in which all possible keys are tested. The breaking attack may well still be out of reach given existing computational power in the real world. Although the discovery of such a break does not necessarily imply that the algorithm is vulnerable in the real world, it is generally no longer considered suitable for future usage. After all, why not play it safe?

Secret Keys Versus Secret Algorithms

An important aspect of any effective cipher is the fact that the efficacy of the cipher is entirely based on the secrecy of the key, not on the secrecy of the cipher algorithm.[4] This may seem counterintuitive at first, since it would appear that a secret algorithm would be a great idea. However, it is very hard to keep an algorithm secret and much easier to keep a simple key secret. You could imagine many problems with the secret algorithm approach: What do you do when one person in your trusted group becomes untrusted? It would be easier to change keys than to change algorithms. What if you suspect that your cipher algorithm has been compromised? If your key becomes compromised, you would naturally change to a new key. Changing algorithms would be much more difficult. If you rely on the secrecy of the cipher algorithm, then these scenarios require you to replace your entire cryptographic infrastructure, forcing you to select an entirely new secret algorithm. On the other hand, if only a secret key is compromised, then you simply need to randomly select a new secret key and continue using your existing cryptographic infrastructure.

The idea of depending on the secrecy of an algorithm is often referred to as *secrecy through obscurity,* which is analogous to hiding your valuables in an obscure but insecure location, such as under your mattress. Relying on a well-known but powerful algorithm is a much more secure approach, which is analogous to storing your valuables in a hardened bank vault. Several strong standard algorithms exist, which have been heavily studied and tested. Never use an algorithm that you design yourself (unless you happen to be a world-class cryptographer), and never use a proprietary algorithm offered by the many snake oil vendors out there. If you see any proprietary algorithm advertisement that makes claims such as "perfect security" and "unbreakable," you know that the algorithm is almost certainly weak. Real cryptographers never use such phrases.

By using a respected, well-known, published cipher algorithm, you benefit from the analysis and attacks carried out by the many researchers in the cryptographic community. This goes a long way in helping you gain trust in the cryptographic strength of the cipher you choose to use. Also, there is always a tremendous advantage in adopting standards. This generally reduces costs, increases implementation choices, and improves interoperability. Obviously, if you use a standard cipher algorithm, then the algorithm itself cannot

---

4. By analogy, open-source operating systems may potentially achieve stronger security than proprietary operating systems where source code is kept secret. This is currently an open question and the focus of much heated debate.

be much of a secret! Examples of established cryptographic standards that we discuss in later chapters include

- DES (Data Encryption Standard)
- Triple DES
- AES (Advanced Encryption Standard)
- RSA (Rivest, Shamir, and Adleman)
- DSA (Digital Signature Algorithm)
- SHA (Secure Hash Algorithm)

Note that DES has technically been broken, but it is still considered to be quite strong. We shall see that DES, Triple DES, and AES are symmetric algorithms used for bulk data encryption. RSA and DSA are asymmetric algorithms used for key exchange and digital signature authentication, respectively. SHA is a hashing algorithm used for several cryptographic purposes.

Classical Techniques for Keeping Secrets

Over the course of human history, secret-keeping and secret-breaking technologies have developed in a continuous struggle resembling the game of leap-frog. We now look at a few simple, classical ciphers. Although you would never actually use these techniques today, they are helpful in clearly seeing the big conceptual picture and introducing some of the mathematical concepts.

THE CAESAR CIPHER

To see how some of the terminology is applied to a concrete scenario, we now consider a very simple cipher that is attributed to Julius Caesar. You could imagine that if anyone ever needed cryptography, Caesar most certainly did![5] By modern standards, this cipher is trivial to break, and so it has little real-world application today, but it has the virtue of simplicity, and it will therefore serve us well as a gentle introduction to the topic of ciphers. Starting in the next chapter, we look at much more effective modern ciphers.

---

5. Julius Caesar (100–44 BC) had many secrets to keep. He invaded Britain and Egypt, and most of the land between, so he must have had many military secrets. Being the first true Roman dictator, he had many political enemies, including the republicans Cassius and Brutus, who eventually assassinated him. He also probably wanted to keep confidential a few of the messages he sent to his romantic pal Cleopatra in Egypt. Adding to this intrigue, Cleopatra had intimate relations with Caesar's most powerful general, Mark Antony. Obviously, they all had a few secrets to keep.

In the Caesar cipher, each plaintext letter is shifted by three so that A is replaced with D, B is replaced with E, and so on. This wraps around so that X is replaced with A, Y is replaced with B, and Z is replaced with C. The Caesar cipher shifts each letter by three, but in a generalized sense this cipher can be thought of as a shift by k, where k is an integer that can be considered the cipher's key. In this chapter we refer to this generalized shift cipher as the Caesar cipher without being too concerned with historical accuracy. Because each individual character is replaced by a specific corresponding character, this cipher is a *monoalphabetic* cipher. Figure 2–3 shows the simple mapping that takes place in the Caesar cipher.

To cut our technical teeth, let's look at the definition of the Caesar cipher expressed in mathematical notation. The nice thing about mathematical notation is that it is exceedingly precise and concise. Another good thing about using formal mathematics is that when you have proven a theorem, you know exactly what you have proved, and the result may then be used in proving other theorems. The unpleasant thing about it is that it can give some folks a headache. Although this is such a simple cipher that a mathematical treatment is probably not necessary, more complex ciphers can be understood in their entirety only by devising a rigorous mathematical representation. Therefore, if you want to seriously pursue cryptography, it is recommended that you learn a modicum of several branches of mathematics, including number theory and abstract algebra. In any case, the next page shows the Caesar cipher in mathematical terms.[6]

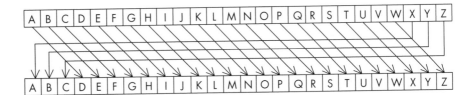

Key:
3

Plaintext:
P = HELLO CAESAR CIPHER

Ciphertext:
C = KHOOR FDHVDU FLSKHU

FIGURE 2-3   *The Caesar cipher.*

---

6. For an explanation of mathematical concepts, see *A Course in Number Theory and Cryptography,* by Neal Koblitz.

Definition: Shift Cipher (Generalized Caesar Cipher)

Given an arbitrary key k, where

$$k \in Z_{26} \text{ (which means an integer where } 0 \le k \le 25\text{)},$$

and an arbitrary plaintext p is a tuple,[7] where

$$p = (p_1, p_2, \dots p_m) \text{ and } p_i \in Z_{26} \text{ for } 1 \le i \le m,$$

let the resulting ciphertext c be represented as a tuple,

$$c = (c_1, c_2, \dots c_m), \text{ where } c_i \in Z_{26} \text{ for } 1 \le i \le m.$$

Then, we define the encryption $E_k(p)$ for the shift cipher as follows:

$$c_i = E_k(p_i) = p_i + k(\text{mod } 26) \text{ for } 1 \le i \le m,$$

and we define decryption $D_k(c)$ as follows:

$$p_i = D_k(c_i) = c_i - k(\text{mod } 26) \text{ for } 1 \le i \le m.$$

Note that a cipher must be invertible, so we must prove the following:

$$D_k(E_k(x)) = x \text{ for all } x \in Z_{26}.$$

You can see that this mathematical definition does not concern itself with real-world details, such as the letters from A to Z that are to be used in the message. Instead, the characters in the plaintext and ciphertext are symbolized by the integers from 0 to 25 rather than a by more realistic choice, such as ASCII or Unicode values. Other details, such as dealing with punctuation and spaces, are also ignored. In this definition E_k is the encryption function, D_k is the decryption function, and k is the encryption key. The standard notation Z_{26} represents the set of integers $\{0,1,2,3,\dots25\}$. The term (mod 26) indicates that we are using modular arithmetic, with a modulus of 26, rather than regular grade-school arithmetic. For a description of modular arithmetic, please see Appendix B on cryptographic mathematics.

If you would like to see a C# implementation of this cipher, look at the **CaesarCipher** code example provided. The implementation is straightforward, so we omit the code listing here; however, you may want to look at the source code provided. If you run this program, you will notice that it can deal with characters in the ranges A to Z plus the space character. It does not accept any lowercase characters or nonalphabetic characters. It prompts you

---

7. The word *tuple* is used in linear algebra to refer to an ordered set of values.

for a key from 0 to 25, and it rejects any value outside of this range. A typical run of the **CaesarCipher** example produces the following output.

```
Enter uppercase plaintext: VENI VIDI VICI[8]
Enter from 0 to 25: 3
Resulting ciphertext: YHQL YLGL YLFL
Recovered plaintext: VENI VIDI VICI
```

If you are a frequent user of Usenet, you may be familiar with an encoding known as ROT13. This is actually the Caesar cipher, but with a key $k = 13$. Because ROT13 is extremely easy to break, it is never used for true encryption. However, Usenet[9] client programs typically provide a ROT13 capability for posting messages that might offend some people or to obscure the answers to riddles, and so on. Anyone can easily decipher it, but it involves an intentional act by the reader to do so. The nice thing about ROT13's key value of 13 is that the same key can be used for encoding and decoding.

BRUTE-FORCE ATTACK: CRACKING THE CAESAR CIPHER

The term *brute-force search* refers to the technique of exhaustively searching through the key space for an intelligible result. To do this on the Caesar cipher, you would start with $k = 1$ and continue toward $k = 25$ until a key is found that successfully decrypts the ciphertext to a meaningful message. Of course, $k = 0$ or $k = 26$ would be trivial, since the plaintext and ciphertext would be identical in those cases. The **CaesarCipherBruteForceAttack** code example shows an implementation of this attack.

```
class CaesarCipherBruteForceAttack
{
    static void Main(string[] args)
    {
...
        //exhaustively test through key space
        for (int testkey=1; testkey<=25; testkey++)
        {
            Console.Write(
                "testkey: {0,2} produced plaintext: ",
                testkey);
```

---

8. The Latin phrase *veni, vidi, vici* means "I came I saw I conquered," which was attributed to Julius Caesar by the second-century Roman historian Suetonius. It is not certain that Caesar ever actually said this phrase, but if he did, it certainly was not one of his secrets!

9. Usenet is the Internet-based bulletin board that provides access to thousands of newsgroups that satisfy virtually every imaginable human interest, including cryptography.

```
        StringBuilder plaintext =
            Decrypt(ciphertext, testkey);
        Console.WriteLine(plaintext);
    }
}
...
  static StringBuilder Decrypt(StringBuilder ciphertext,
     int key)
  {
     StringBuilder plaintext =
        new StringBuilder(ciphertext.ToString());
     for (int index=0; index<plaintext.Length; index++)
     {
        if (ciphertext[index] != ' ')
        {
           int character =
              (((ciphertext[index]+26-'A')-key)%26)+'A';
           plaintext[index] = (char)character;
        }
     }
     return plaintext;
  }
}
```

For example, assume that you have the ciphertext **KHOOR**, and you know that it was encrypted using a Caesar-style shift cipher. The following output from the **CaesarCipherBruteForce** example program shows all possible decryptions for this ciphertext, using each of the 25 possible keys. Note that only the result **HELLO** appears to be meaningful, so the key value $k = 3$ appears to be the correct key. Of course, in an actual brute-force search attack, you would quit as soon as you found the correct key, but we show them all in the following program output listing.

```
Enter uppercase ciphertext: KHOOR
testkey:  1 produced plaintext: JGNNQ
testkey:  2 produced plaintext: IFMMP
testkey:  3 produced plaintext: HELLO
testkey:  4 produced plaintext: GDKKN
testkey:  5 produced plaintext: FCJJM
testkey:  6 produced plaintext: EBIIL
testkey:  7 produced plaintext: DAHHK
testkey:  8 produced plaintext: CZGGJ
testkey:  9 produced plaintext: BYFFI
testkey: 10 produced plaintext: AXEEH
testkey: 11 produced plaintext: ZWDDG
testkey: 12 produced plaintext: YVCCF
testkey: 13 produced plaintext: XUBBE
testkey: 14 produced plaintext: WTAAD
testkey: 15 produced plaintext: VSZZC
```

```
testkey: 16 produced plaintext: URYYB
testkey: 17 produced plaintext: TQXXA
testkey: 18 produced plaintext: SPWWZ
testkey: 19 produced plaintext: ROVVY
testkey: 20 produced plaintext: QNUUX
testkey: 21 produced plaintext: PMTTW
testkey: 22 produced plaintext: OLSSV
testkey: 23 produced plaintext: NKRRU
testkey: 24 produced plaintext: MJQQT
testkey: 25 produced plaintext: LIPPS
```

It may have occurred to you that for some ciphertexts, it is possible that more than one key might result in intelligible plaintext, causing uncertainty about whether or not you have discovered the true key. For example, assume that you have the very short cipher text WZR, and you know that it was produced using the Caesar cipher. If you perform a brute-force key search using the **CaesarCipherBruteForce** program, you will see three plausible plaintext results: TWO (key $k = 3$), RUM (key $k = 5$), and LOG (key $k = 11$). However, keep in mind that as the number of characters in the known ciphertext increases, the probability of finding more than one meaningful plaintext result diminishes quickly. This concept has been mathematically formalized, and it is referred to as the *unicity distance* of the cipher. The unicity distance is a measure of how much ciphertext is needed to reduce the probability of finding spurious keys in a brute-force search, close to zero. It is therefore also an indication of how much ciphertext is required (at least with a hypothetical computer of arbitrary power) to obtain the key from the ciphertext. Unicity distance depends on the statistical characteristics of both the possible plaintext messages and the mechanics of the cipher.

You may be wondering what "meaningful" means in the context of meaningful results. What if the plaintext could be written in any spoken language? Then, all sorts of results could be considered meaningful, making the attack on the cipher more problematic.[10]

What if the plaintext was compressed before it was enciphered? Then, just about nothing would be human readable, and nothing would appear to be meaningful. However, in modern cryptography, we generally assume that the attacker knows all of these details. In real life, this may not always be the case, but for the purposes of analyzing a cipher design, it should be assumed that the

---

10. During World War II, there were only about 50,000 Navajo speakers in the world. At that time, approximately 400 Navajos in the U.S. Marine Corps were trained as "Navajo code talkers." The Germans and Japanese were able to break many of the Allied ciphers; however, the Navajo code talker communications were apparently never cracked. This was indeed a success story. However, a similar approach today would almost certainly be broken very quickly. In modern times, obscurity is not considered to be a reliable means of achieving security.

attacker knows what plaintext would be meaningful. It is also assumed that the attacker knows all the details of the cipher implementation. For example, if the plaintext is compressed before being encrypted, then we should assume that the attacker knows the entire cipher operation, including the compression step. If an obscure language is used, it is assumed that the attacker understands that language as well. In general, we assume that the attacker knows everything except for the secret key and the plaintext he or she is seeking.

You may notice that if you apply the Caesar cipher multiple times, you do not actually increase the strength of the cipher one iota. For example, if you encrypt the text CAT with $k = 6$ to get IGZ, and then encrypt that result with $k = 4$ to get MKD, you have effectively done nothing more than simply encrypt once with $k = 10$, since $4 + 6 = 10$. This is analogous to the fact that if you apply a compression algorithm to a file that has already been compressed, you will typically find that you have not achieved much if any additional compression. Many ciphers experience diminished gains when applied repeatedly in this way; however, Triple DES,[11] described in Chapter 3, is an effective cipher that employs repeated application of the same algorithm (but with different keys) as part of its implementation.

Needless to say, the Caesar cipher is not a very strong cipher by modern standards, but perhaps we should not be asking too much of a 2,000-year-old cipher. A ciphertext-only attack requires just a simple program to exhaustively test the very small key space of 25 keys. In the case of a known plaintext attack, the work is trivial, since the plaintext and its corresponding ciphertext can be compared, and the key that was used becomes visually obvious. We will look at an improved classical cipher named the Vigenère cipher, as well as at some more powerful modern ciphers, later in this chapter. But first, let's look at another simple classical cipher with a much larger key space.

THE SIMPLE SUBSTITUTION CIPHER

The simple substitution cipher was used quite unsuccessfully by Queen Mary[12] of Scotland. In this substitution cipher, each character of the plaintext is replaced by a particular corresponding character in a permuted alphabet,

---

11. DES and Triple DES were designed for efficient hardware implementation and are widely used in ATM machines.

12. Mary Stuart, Queen of Scotland, was born in 1542. Along with several Catholic noblemen, she was accused of plotting to assassinate Queen Elizabeth I of England. She was found guilty and was executed for the crime on February 8, 1587. Mary was very careful to always use a substitution cipher in her correspondence with her conspirators. However, some of her letters were cracked using a frequency analysis attack, providing the crucial forensic evidence against her. It is interesting to note that long before Mary's time, a ninth-century Arab cryptographer named Al Kindi had already discovered the frequency analysis attack. This certainly shows how important it can be to keep your cryptographic skills up to date!

making it (like the Caesar cipher) another type of *monoalphabetic* substitution cipher. This means that there is a one-to-one mapping between the characters of the plaintext and the ciphertext alphabets. This is not a good thing, because this makes the cipher vulnerable to *frequency-analysis* attacks. This attack can be understood if you consider that the relative frequencies of individual characters remain unchanged. Also, common character combinations such as *qu* and *the* (in English) end up as statistically detectable character sequences in the resulting ciphertext. Figure 2–4 shows how a simple substitution cipher works. The key used in this example is one of a large number of possible values.

How many possible values are there for the key *k*? There are 26 factorial[13] permutations on a 26-letter alphabet. That means that this cipher has a key space approximately equivalent to an 88-bit key, since $26! = 403,291,461,126,605,635,584,000,000$, which falls between 2^{88} and 2^{89}. This is much larger than the key space of the Caesar cipher (with only 25 keys), but, as we shall see, this cipher is surprisingly only a very small improvement over the Caesar cipher. The main reason for this is that it is still very easy to attack using the frequency-analysis attack technique. This proves the very important lesson that a large key size is necessary but not sufficient to guarantee security.

To understand how we calculated this large number, imagine that you are given the task of making an arbitrary permutation of the English alphabet. You have to make a sequence of choices. On the first choice you can choose

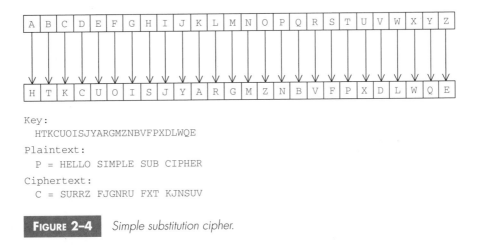

Key:
    HTKCUOISJYARGMZNBVFPXDLWQE
Plaintext:
    P = HELLO SIMPLE SUB CIPHER
Ciphertext:
    C = SURRZ FJGNRU FXT KJNSUV

FIGURE 2–4   *Simple substitution cipher.*

13. In mathematical notation, factorials are represented with the ! symbol, as in 26!, which is the product of all the integers from 1 up to and including 26. This branch of mathematics is known as combinatorics.

any one of the 26 letters in the alphabet for the first letter of the permutation. On the second choice you can choose any one of the remaining 25 letters for the second letter of the permutation. On the third choice you can choose any one of the remaining 24 letters, and so on. On the last choice, there is just one letter remaining. So, in all there are $26 \cdot 25 \cdot 24 \cdot \ldots \cdot 2 \cdot 1$ different ways to make these choices, which is defined as 26! in mathematical notation.

Here is the definition of the simple substitution cipher expressed in mathematical notation.

Definition: Simple Substitution Cipher

Let K be the set of all permutations of the elements in Z_{26}.

$$K = \{(k_1,k_2,k_3,\ldots k_{26}) : k_i \in Z_{26}\}$$

Choose an arbitrary key k, where $k \in K$.
Choose an arbitrary plaintext p, where

$$p = (p_1,p_2,\ldots p_m), \text{ where } p_i \in Z_{26} \text{ for } 1 \le i \le m.$$

Let the resulting ciphertext c be represented as

$$c = (c_1,c_2,\ldots c_m), \text{ where } c_i \in Z_{26} \text{ for } 1 \le i \le m.$$

Then, we define the encryption $E_k(p)$ as follows:

$$c_i = E_k(p_i) = k[p_i] \text{ for } 1 \le i \le m,$$

and we define decryption $D_k(c)$ as follows:

$$p_i = D_k(c_i) = E_k^{-1}(c_i) \text{ for } 1 \le i \le m.$$

The code example **SimpleSubCipher** demonstrates this cipher. Again, the code is fairly simple, so we shall not list it here, but if you are interested, you can look at the C# source code in the provided project. The output of this program is shown as follows.

```
Enter uppercase plaintext: HELLO SIMPLE SUB CIPHER
Enter 26 char key permutation: HTKCUOISJYARGMZNBVFPXDLWQE
Resulting ciphertext: SURRZ FJGNRU FXT KJNSUV
Recovered plaintext: HELLO SIMPLE SUB CIPHER
```

Notice how the double letters LL in HELLO are replaced with the double letters RR in the ciphertext. This is a telltale sign that leads into the next section, describing the statistical type of attack on this cipher, which was used against poor Mary Stuart, Queen of Scots.

FREQUENCY ANALYSIS: CRACKING THE SUBSTITUTION CIPHER

With the simple substitution cipher, you can generally use a *frequency-analysis attack* that employs statistical methods. This takes advantage of the varying probability distribution of letters and letter sequences in typical plaintext. The idea is based on the fact that, for example, in English, the letters E, T, and A are more frequent than other letters. Letter pairs such as TH, HE, SH, and CH are much more common than other pairs, such as TB or WX. Of course, a Q is virtually always followed by a U. This uneven probability distribution indicates that English (or any other natural language) is full of redundancy. Redundancy serves an important purpose: It reduces the probability of transmission errors. Unfortunately, redundancy is also a friend of the attacker.

The code example **SimpleSubCipherFrequencyAttack** demonstrates this attack. The example program is a bit complicated, but the basic idea behind how it works is quite simple. If you try running this program, you will see that it loads a sample file containing English text. Then it loads a plaintext file, generates a random key (i.e., a random permutation of the alphabet), and encrypts the plaintext. The resulting ciphertext is then displayed, and some statistical data for both the sample text and the ciphertext can be used to help you guess at the various letter substitutions in the key. The actual key and plaintext is displayed, but try to use the program to decipher it without looking at the key or plaintext. As you try solving this puzzle, you will find that it is slightly similar to the thought process used for a crossword puzzle or the television game show *Wheel of Fortune*. This program is interactive, it relies on your own intuition, and it is based on displaying a few simple statistics. This program could be enhanced by incorporating more statistical analysis and heuristic decision making to completely automate the attack. This will not be done here, since this cipher is not typically used in modern times. However, the basic concept of frequency analysis that we see being used here is also used in cracking much more powerful ciphers as well. Figure 2–5 shows the frequency attack on the simple substitution cipher in progress.

THE VIGENÈRE CIPHER

With the advent of the telegraph[14] in the mid 1800s, there was an increased interest in cryptography, and it was well known that any monoalphabetic

---

14. An American named Samuel Morse invented the telegraph during the 1830s and was granted a U.S. patent for it in 1840. The telegraph can arguably be described as the precursor of the Internet. The telegraph greatly increased the amount of information being communicated, but it was extremely easy to wiretap without detection. This obviously produced an enormous appetite for improved encryption technology.

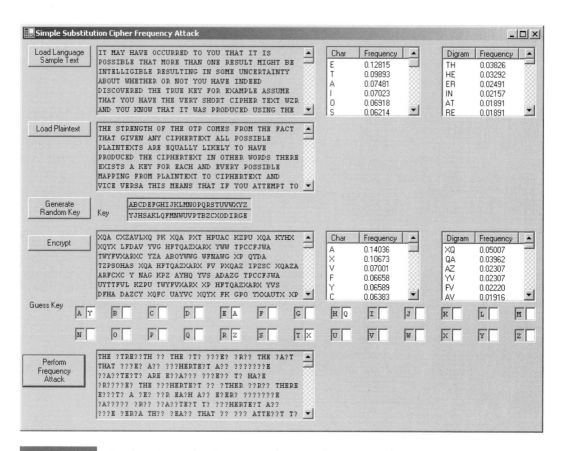

FIGURE 2-5   *Cracking the simple substitution cipher using frequency analysis.*

substitution cipher was too vulnerable to frequency analysis. The Victorian solution to this problem was to adopt the *Vigenère cipher,* which oddly enough had already existed for almost 300 years.[15] This cipher was known in French as *le chiffre indéchiffrable,* which in English means the "undecipherable cipher." This was indeed a formidable cipher for its time. In fact, the Vigenère cipher remained unbroken for almost three centuries, from its

---

15. You may be wondering why it took so long for the Vigenère cipher to gain popularity. The reason is that although Vigenère was more secure, it was also more difficult to use by hand. Remember, they didn't have electronic computers or even complex mechanical devices back then.

invention in 1586[16] until long after its defeat in 1854, when Charles Babbage[17] was finally able to break it.[18] It is interesting to note that this cipher had a very short shelf life once it was applied on a large scale to telegraphy. This seems to show how quickly cryptographic technology can become obsolete once there is a compelling interest in breaking it. This can make one nervous about the security of today's encrypted data. What modern-day Babbage might be lurking out there now?

The Vigenère cipher is a *polyalphabetic* substitution cipher. That means that multiple alphabet mappings are used, thereby obscuring the relative frequencies of characters in the original plaintext. Therefore, unlike the monoalphabetic ciphers (such as Caesar and simple substitution) the Vigenère cipher is immune to simple frequency analysis.

Effectively, the Vigenère cipher changes the mapping of plaintext characters to ciphertext characters on a per-character basis. It is based on the table shown in Figure 2–6. Each row of the table is actually a Caesar cipher shifted by a number according to its row position. Row A is shifted by 0, row B is shifted by 1, and so on.

The Vigenère cipher combines this table with a keyword to encrypt plaintext. For example, assume that you want to encrypt the plaintext GOD IS ON OUR SIDE LONG LIVE THE KING with the key PROPAGANDA. To encrypt this plaintext, you repeat the key as many times as is required to span the length of the plaintext, writing it below the plaintext. Then, each ciphertext character is produced by taking the column determined by the corresponding plaintext character and intersecting it in the table with the row determined by the corresponding keyword character. For example, the first plaintext character G is combined with the first keyword character P, and as you can see in Figure 2–6, the column and row intersect on the resulting first

---

16. It is ironic that the Vigenère cipher was invented in 1586. Queen Mary was convicted and sentenced to death in that same year based on evidence resulting from the use of a much weaker monoalphabetic substitution cipher. Coincidently, Vigenère proposed his new cipher to King Henry III of France, who just happened to be Queen Mary's brother-in-law. If she had used the Vigenère cipher, she would not have lost her head. Perhaps Mary's unpleasant situation prompted Henry to listen very closely to Vigenère's ideas.

17. Charles Babbage, of enormous fame in the history of computer science, is also credited with the invention of the first programmable computer. Babbage's work on cracking the Vigenère cipher was kept secret for more than 100 years. It was only in the late 1900s that the Danish historian Ole Franksen discovered this connection.

18. Although Vigenère was broken by Babbage, this fact was kept secret, and telegraphers continued using it for many decades. It is certain that many people falsely believed that they were communicating securely. This makes one wonder about the ciphers that we use today.

Plaintext Letters

Keyword Letters

	A	B	C	D	E	F	G	H	I	J	K	L	M	N	O	P	Q	R	S	T	U	V	W	X	Y	Z
A	A	B	C	D	E	F	G	H	I	J	K	L	M	N	O	P	Q	R	S	T	U	V	W	X	Y	Z
B	B	C	D	E	F	G	H	I	J	K	L	M	N	O	P	Q	R	S	T	U	V	W	X	Y	Z	A
C	C	D	E	F	G	H	I	J	K	L	M	N	O	P	Q	R	S	T	U	V	W	X	Y	Z	A	B
D	D	E	F	G	H	I	J	K	L	M	N	O	P	Q	R	S	T	U	V	W	X	Y	Z	A	B	C
E	E	F	G	H	I	J	K	L	M	N	O	P	Q	R	S	T	U	V	W	X	Y	Z	A	B	C	D
F	F	G	H	I	J	K	L	M	N	O	P	Q	R	S	T	U	V	W	X	Y	Z	A	B	C	D	E
G	G	H	I	J	K	L	M	N	O	P	Q	R	S	T	U	V	W	X	Y	Z	A	B	C	D	E	F
H	H	I	J	K	L	M	N	O	P	Q	R	S	T	U	V	W	X	Y	Z	A	B	C	D	E	F	G
I	I	J	K	L	M	N	O	P	Q	R	S	T	U	V	W	X	Y	Z	A	B	C	D	E	F	G	H
J	J	K	L	M	N	O	P	Q	R	S	T	U	V	W	X	Y	Z	A	B	C	D	E	F	G	H	I
K	K	L	M	N	O	P	Q	R	S	T	U	V	W	X	Y	Z	A	B	C	D	E	F	G	H	I	J
L	L	M	N	O	P	Q	R	S	T	U	V	W	X	Y	Z	A	B	C	D	E	F	G	H	I	J	K
M	M	N	O	P	Q	R	S	T	U	V	W	X	Y	Z	A	B	C	D	E	F	G	H	I	J	K	L
N	N	O	P	Q	R	S	T	U	V	W	X	Y	Z	A	B	C	D	E	F	G	H	I	J	K	L	M
O	O	P	Q	R	S	T	U	V	W	X	Y	Z	A	B	C	D	E	F	G	H	I	J	K	L	M	N
P	P	Q	R	S	T	U	V	W	X	Y	Z	A	B	C	D	E	F	G	H	I	J	K	L	M	N	O
Q	Q	R	S	T	U	V	W	X	Y	Z	A	B	C	D	E	F	G	H	I	J	K	L	M	N	O	P
R	R	S	T	U	V	W	X	Y	Z	A	B	C	D	E	F	G	H	I	J	K	L	M	N	O	P	Q
S	S	T	U	V	W	X	Y	Z	A	B	C	D	E	F	G	H	I	J	K	L	M	N	O	P	Q	R
T	T	U	V	W	X	Y	Z	A	B	C	D	E	F	G	H	I	J	K	L	M	N	O	P	Q	R	S
U	U	V	W	X	Y	Z	A	B	C	D	E	F	G	H	I	J	K	L	M	N	O	P	Q	R	S	T
V	V	W	X	Y	Z	A	B	C	D	E	F	G	H	I	J	K	L	M	N	O	P	Q	R	S	T	U
W	W	X	Y	Z	A	B	C	D	E	F	G	H	I	J	K	L	M	N	O	P	Q	R	S	T	U	V
X	X	Y	Z	A	B	C	D	E	F	G	H	I	J	K	L	M	N	O	P	Q	R	S	T	U	V	W
Y	Y	Z	A	B	C	D	E	F	G	H	I	J	K	L	M	N	O	P	Q	R	S	T	U	V	W	X
Z	Z	A	B	C	D	E	F	G	H	I	J	K	L	M	N	O	P	Q	R	S	T	U	V	W	X	Y

FIGURE 2-6 *The Vigenère cipher.*

ciphertext character V. Each subsequent ciphertext character is determined in the same way.

```
Plaintext:  GOD IS ON OUR SIDE LONG LIVE THE KING
Keyword     PRO PA GA NDA PROP AGAN DAPR OPA GAND
Ciphertext: VFR XS UN BXR HZRT LUNT OIKV HWE QIAJ
```

To decrypt the ciphertext, write the repeated key below the ciphertext. Each character of plaintext is recovered by taking the row corresponding to the key and finding the column that contains the ciphertext character in that row. Then, take the character at the top of that column, and you have the original plaintext character.

```
Ciphertext: VFR XS UN BXR HZRT LUNT OIKV HWE QIAJ
Keyword:    PRO PA GA NDA PROP AGAN DAPR OPA GAND
Plaintext:  GOD IS ON OUR SIDE LONG LIVE THE KING
```

This procedure is a bit tedious, but it can be accomplished using pencil and paper. You might prefer to run the **VigenereCipher** program example and inspect its code. You will see that it produces the same results as the pencil-and-paper approach described above.

Here is the definition of the Vigenère cipher expressed in mathematical notation.

Definition: Vigenère Cipher

Given an arbitrary key k, where

$$k = (k_1, k_2, \ldots k_n), \text{ where } k_i \in Z_{26} \text{ for } 1 \leq i \leq n,$$

and an arbitrary plaintext p, where

$$p = (p_1, p_2, \ldots p_m), \text{ where } p_j \in Z_{26} \text{ for } 1 \leq j \leq m,$$

let the resulting ciphertext c be represented as

$$c = (c_1, c_2, \ldots c_m), \text{ where } c_j \in Z_{26} \text{ for } 1 \leq j \leq m.$$

Then, we define encryption E_{k_i} as

$$c_j = E_{k_i}(p_j), \text{ where } E_{ki}(p) : p_j \rightarrow p_j + k_i (\text{mod } 26),$$

and we define decryption D_{k_i} as

$$p_j = D_{k_i}(c_j), \text{ where } D_{ki}(c) : c_j \rightarrow c_j - k_i (\text{mod } 26).$$

If you run the **VigenereCipher** program example, you will see that it produces output similar to the following.

```
Enter plaintext:       GOD IS ON OUR SIDE LONG LIVE THE KING
Enter keyword:         PROPAGANDA
Resulting ciphertext:  VFR XS UN BXR HZRT LUNT OIKV HWE QIAJ
Recovered plaintext:   GOD IS ON OUR SIDE LONG LIVE THE KING
```

BABBAGE'S ATTACK: CRACKING THE VIGENÈRE CIPHER

Since a polyalphabetic substitution cipher involves the use of multiple alphabet mappings, this eliminates the one-to-one relationship between each plaintext character and ciphertext character. The result is that there is now a one-to-many relationship between each character and its corresponding character in the ciphertext. Although frequency analysis alone is unable to break this cipher, Babbage found that using a combination of key analysis and frequency analysis did the trick.

How do you proceed with Babbage's attack? First, you perform key analysis to try to determine the length of the key. Basically, you look for periodic patterns of coincidence in the ciphertext. To do this, you shift the ciphertext by one character against itself, and the number of matching characters is counted. It is then shifted again, and matching characters are counted again. This is repeated many times, and the shifts with the largest matching counts are noted. A random shift will give a low number of matching characters, but a shift that is a multiple of the key length will statistically give a higher matching count. This results naturally from the fact that some characters are more frequent than others together with the fact that the key is used many times over in a repeating pattern. Since a character will match a copy of itself that has been encrypted with the same key letter, the match count goes up slightly for shifts that are equal to multiples of the key length. Obviously, this requires a large enough ciphertext to work well, since the unicity distance for this cipher is much larger than that of a monoalphabetic substitution cipher.

Once the key length has been estimated, the next step is to perform frequency analysis. To do this, you segregate the characters of the ciphertext that have been encrypted with the same key letter into their own groups, based on the assumed key length. Each grouping of characters is then treated as a simple Caesar-style shift using either brute-force or frequency analysis techniques. Once these individual groups have been deciphered, they are reassembled into the final recovered plaintext result. When you see how this works, you will realize that it is not all that difficult a concept, and you may be surprised that this cipher was able to stand up against 300 years of cryptanalysis. Other, more sophisticated polyalphabetic ciphers may also be attacked using similar techniques if the key period is not too long.

THE ONLY PROVABLY UNBREAKABLE CIPHER: ONE-TIME PAD

There is only one cipher that is theoretically 100 percent secure, known as the One-Time Pad[19] (OTP). To achieve this perfect security, the OTP has certain stringent requirements: the keys must be truly randomly generated, the keys

---

19. Claude E. Shannon, the inventor of information theory, proved that a perfectly secure algorithm requires, among other things, that the secret key information be at least as great as the information being encrypted. The OTP abides by these requirements. However, for most practical purposes, absolute security is difficult to achieve, and absolute security is abandoned in favor of sufficient security. Therefore, most cryptographic algorithms use keys that are much smaller than the data to be encrypted and are therefore not perfectly secure.

must be kept strictly secret, and the keys must never be reused. Unlike other types of ciphers, the OTP (or any of its mathematical equivalents) is the only cipher that has been mathematically proven to be unbreakable. The OTP boasts perfect security, but the downside is that key management is very problematic. For this reason, the OTP is typically used only in situations where secrecy is of the utmost importance and the bandwidth requirements are low. Examples of this are probably rare, but it has been used in many military, diplomatic, and espionage scenarios.

Let's look at how it works. To use the OTP cipher, you randomly generate a new one-time key that contains the same number of bytes as the plaintext. Then, the plaintext is combined with the key on a bit-by-bit basis, using an invertible operator, such as the exclusive-or operator, to produce the ciphertext. The exclusive-or operator is often abbreviated as XOR and mathematically represented with the $\oplus$ symbol. In C# this operator is represented with the $\wedge$ symbol. Once used, the key is never used for encryption again. It should be recognized that the XOR operator is its own inverse, meaning that $P = ((P \oplus K) \oplus K)$ for any choice of P and K, which is an added convenience. In plain English, this means that if you XOR the plaintext with the key, and then XOR the resulting ciphertext with the same key, you get back the original plaintext. Table 2–1 shows the results of the XOR operator.

TABLE 2-1	*The XOR Operator*	
X	**Y**	**$X \oplus Y$**
0	0	0
0	1	1
1	0	1
1	1	0

The XOR operator is not the only choice for the OTP. Actually, any invertible operator could be used. For example, consider the operator used in the Caesar cipher,[20] adding the corresponding key byte to the plaintext byte, modulo 256. This is basically the same as the Caesar cipher except that instead of using the same key value on every byte in the plaintext, a new, randomly chosen key byte is applied to each individual byte in the plaintext. The slight advantage of using the XOR operator is that it is its own inverse,

---

20. The Caesar cipher used addition modulo 26, but we are extending the idea here to addition modulo 256, since we are now interested in encrypting bytes rather than alphabet letter symbols.

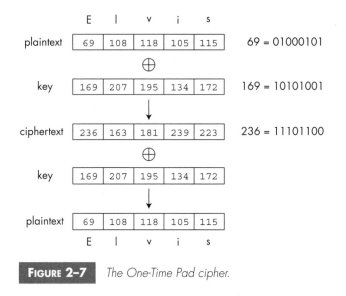

FIGURE 2–7   *The One-Time Pad cipher.*

but mathematically, it can be shown that there is really no significant difference between these two choices.

Figure 2–7 shows how the OTP cipher works. The word *Elvis* is encoded in ASCII as 69, 108, 118, 105, 115 (in base 10). The random key is 169, 207, 195, 134, 172. The result of the XOR operation produces 236, 163, 181, 239, 223. On the right side of the figure, you can see the binary representation of the first bytes of the plaintext, key, and ciphertext.

Mathematically, the OTP cipher is described as follows.

Definition: OTP Cipher

Given an arbitrary key k, where

$$k = (k_1, k_2, \ldots k_m), \text{where } k_j \in \{0,1\} \text{ for } 1 \le j \le m,$$

and an arbitrary plaintext p, where

$$p = (p_1, p_2, \ldots p_m), \text{where } p_j \in \{0,1\} \text{ for } 1 \le j \le m,$$

then we define encryption $E_k(p)$ as follows:

$$E_k(p_i) = p_i \oplus k_i \text{ for } 1 \le i \le m,$$

and we define decryption $D_k(c)$ as follows:

$$D_k(c_i) = c_i \oplus k \text{ for } 1 \le i \le m.$$

Then,

$$c_i = E_k(p_i) \text{ and } p_i = D_k(c_i).$$

The **OTP_XOR** code example shows an implementation of this. The method **EncryptDecrypt** performs both encryption and decryption because XOR is its own inverse.

```
static void Main(string[] args)
{
   Console.Write("Enter plaintext: ");
   StringBuilder plaintext =
      new StringBuilder(Console.ReadLine());

   RandomNumberGenerator rng =
      new RNGCryptoServiceProvider();
   byte[] key = new Byte[100];
   rng.GetBytes(key);

   StringBuilder ciphertext =
      EncryptDecrypt(plaintext, key);
   Console.WriteLine("ciphertext: {0}",
      ciphertext);

   StringBuilder recoveredplaintext =
      EncryptDecrypt(ciphertext, key);
   Console.WriteLine("recovered plaintext: {0}",
      recoveredplaintext);
}
static StringBuilder EncryptDecrypt(
   StringBuilder data_in,
   byte [] key)
{
   StringBuilder data_oput =
      new StringBuilder(data_in.ToString());
   for (int index=0; index<data_in.Length; index++)
   {
      int character =
         ((int)data_in[index] ^ key[index]);
      data_oput[index] = (char)character;
   }
   return data_oput;
}
```

A typical run of the **OTP_XOR** code example produces the following. Each time you run it, you will see a different ciphertext, because the OTP key is randomly generated each time.

```
Enter plaintext: hello
ciphertext: IûE3c
recovered plaintext: hello
```

The strength of the OTP comes from the fact that given any ciphertext, all possible plaintexts are equally likely to have produced the ciphertext. In other words, there exists a key for each and every possible mapping from plaintext to ciphertext, and vice versa. This means that if you attempt to perform a brute-force key-search attack on an OTP ciphertext, you will find that every possible plaintext result will occur in your results. This will include every single possible result, including all those that may appear meaningful. This clearly gets you nowhere. The thing to remember about the OTP is that brute force is futile and irrelevant! The only hope in cracking an OTP encrypted message is if the key is used multiple times on different messages, or the algorithm used to produce the pseudorandom key has predictabilities that you can capitalize on, or you somehow manage to obtain the key through noncryptographic means.

You can convince yourself of this fact by considering the following argument. Assume that your plaintext is just one byte long. Then, according to the definition of the OTP cipher, the key must also be one byte long. Choose any given plaintext from the set of 256 possible 8-bit plaintext messages. If you then XOR each of the 256 possible keys with the chosen 8-bit plaintext, you will produce 256 distinct 8-bit ciphertext messages. The fact that the ciphertext messages are all distinct is because the XOR operator is lossless in an information theoretic sense. This means that by choosing the appropriate key, you can encrypt any 8-bit plaintext into any 8-bit ciphertext. The argument works equally well in the reverse direction, so that by choosing the appropriate key, you can decrypt any 8-bit ciphertext into any 8-bit plaintext. There is simply no way to know which is the correct key.

The OTP does have its problems, however, and if it is not implemented perfectly, it is not completely secure. First, if the same OTP key is ever used more than once, it is no longer 100 percent secure. Second, the security of the OTP is also dependent on the randomness of the key selection. A deterministic algorithm simply cannot generate a truly random sequence of bytes. Even the best deterministic random number generator design cannot produce anything better than pseudorandom numbers. Third, the key length is typically much larger than we would like it to be and must be generated anew for every single message. Since the key is the same length as the message, and the message is of arbitrary length, then the problem of key distribution becomes a significant issue. Key distribution refers to the fact that both the sender and receiver need a copy of the key to effectively communicate with one another. The catch-22 question then arises: If you have a secure enough channel to transmit the new key each time, why can't you just send the actual message via that secure channel? Alternatively, you could ask, If the channel is insecure enough to require encryption in the first place, how can you justify transmitting the OTP keys via that channel?

Well, the answer is that the OTP is occasionally useful in situations where you temporarily have a very secure channel, during which time you quickly exchange as many keys as you expect are needed, and then store them locally in a secure manner.[21] Then, at other times, when you do not have the luxury of a secure channel, you encrypt your messages with your stockpile of OTP keys. The only thing that must be carefully managed is that the sender and receiver must use the keys in the proper order to ensure that they will use the same key for encryption and decryption on each individual message. Historically, the Nazis used the OTP cipher during World War II in diplomatic correspondence.[22] When the Nazi diplomats were back in Berlin, they would have a very secure environment to exchange a large set of new OTP keys. Then, when they were back out in the field, the insecure telegraph, telephone, and radio channels could be used for confidential messages that were encrypted using those keys. The British also made good use of the OTP cipher.[23]

The Enigma Cipher

We have now reviewed some of the most significant classical ciphers and used them to introduce important concepts and fundamental ideas. There are many other interesting classical ciphers, but we will not consider them here, since they will not further us toward our goal of studying cryptography and security in the .NET world. However, the Enigma cipher,[24] used by the German Forces in World War II, is historically fascinating and to a large extent represents the transition from classical cryptography to modern cryptography. We do not discuss the Enigma in this book, but if you are curious about how it worked, there are many Java applet simulations available on the Internet. Many of them even provide the source code so that you can learn about its inner workings. To find these examples, just go to *www.Google.com* and perform a search with the string Enigma java applet.

Brute-Force Attack Work Factor

The amount of work it takes to accomplish a computational goal is referred to as its *work factor*. Calculating the work factor for breaking a cipher is an

---

21. Which typically means that you either physically secure the storage media or (ironically) store them in an encrypted file system.

22. Actually, most major governments have used the OTP heavily for diplomatic correspondence.

23. In 1942 the Nazis had broken the cipher used by the British Royal Navy. This enabled the German U-boats to sink British ships at a phenomenal rate. In late 1942 the Royal Navy switched to using the OTP cipher, and suddenly the losses were drastically reduced.

24. The history of cracking the Enigma cipher is described in *The Codebreakers* by David Khan.

important aspect of analyzing cipher effectiveness. We now briefly look at calculating brute-force attack work factors.

As we have seen, the Caesar cipher is pretty pathetic, since its key space is so tiny—not to mention its other serious weaknesses. With only 25 keys, the key space is equivalent in an information theoretic sense to a tiny, 6-bit key, since 2 to the power of 6 equals 32, which is large enough to represent all 25 key values. Fortunately, there are ciphers with much larger key spaces. The good news for Alice and Bob, and bad news for Eve, is that the brute-force attack work factor grows exponentially as a function of the key size. Mathematically, for an n-bit key, the work factor is $W \propto 2^n$. Of course, if Eve can find an attack that is significantly more efficient than brute force, things could get a bit iffier.

Thus, more powerful ciphers require more sophisticated attacks than the brute-force key search just described. This is because, for very large key spaces, an exhaustive test on each possible key would simply take too long. For example, if a given cipher employs a key that is 128 bits long, then there are 2 to the power of 128 possible keys. This is a horrendously large number of keys! In base 10, this number is represented using 39 digits! Keep in mind that a large enough key is necessary, but not sufficient, to guarantee cipher security.

$2\verb|^|128 = 340,282,366,920,938,463,463,374,607,431,768,211,456$

Ignoring insignificant details, such as leap years, the number of seconds per year is 60 sec/min * 60 min/hr * 24 hr/day * 365 day/year = 31,536,000. If we make the very conservative estimate of the number of CPU clock cycles required for testing each key to be 100, then a 1-GHz machine can test approximately 100,000,000 keys per second. This results in 315,360,000,000,000 keys tested per year. This is a lot of keys, but unfortunately, $2\verb|^|128$ keys will then take 1,079,028,307,080,601,418,897,052 years to test. The universe is believed to be no older than 15 billion years, so the brute-force attack on this cipher would take 71,935,220,472,040 times as long as the age of the universe. Current semiconductor technology is not all that far from the theoretical switching-speed limits imposed on us by quantum mechanics,[25] so we cannot hope to get enough relief by waiting for improved clock speeds.

Trying to solve the problem by distributing the attack over multiple machines is also quite futile. To complete the attack in one year, assuming that you could achieve perfect scalability, you would need to purchase

---

25. Quantum mechanics puts hard limits on how much longer Moore's law (which states that device density grows exponentially, doubling every 18 months) will continue to hold true. For a fixed cost, increased memory capacity and higher CPU speeds are both consequences of this law. Sadly, unless radically innovative computing modalities are developed, Moore's law will probably expire around the year 2015. One hope is that quantum computing may be the solution to this problem.

1,079,028,307,080,601,418,897,052 CPUs. Even at volume discounts, this will cost much more than the entire annual global economy of planet earth. The volume of the moon is approximately 2.2 * 10^25 cubic centimeters. Assuming 1 cubic centimeter per CPU, your custom-built supercomputer would occupy about 5 percent of the volume of the moon. But that is only the volume of the CPUs. The memory and bus interconnect hardware would be the 3D mother of all motherboards, which would easily fill another 20 percent of the moon's volume. This would create enough gravitational force to crush the devices at the center of the computer and would create an enormous list of other moon-sized problems. The questions become absurd: How much would it cost? How long would it take to build? How would we program it? How much power would it consume? Obviously, these are all silly questions, but they do clearly demonstrate that the brute-force key-search attack has its limitations if the key space is large enough.

If you would like to see a program that makes these monstrous calculations, see the C# program example **BigIntegerFun**. The current release of the .NET Framework does not yet support multiprecision arithmetic, so this example is written using GnuMP,[26] which is an open and free software library written in C for arbitrary precision-integer arithmetic, available at *www.gnu.org*.

Arbitrary Precision Arithmetic

Cryptography (especially asymmetric cryptography, described in Chapter 4) often involves the heavy use of arbitrary precision arithmetic. You may never need to use these specialized math capabilities directly. This is because the .NET Framework provides a thorough implementation of most of the cryptographic functionality that you are likely to need. However, there may be situations now and then where you would like to invoke these advanced arithmetic capabilities directly, which would require the use of a specialized math library, such as GnuMP. This can be particularly true if you begin experimenting with your own asymmetric cryptographic algorithm designs. In that case, see Appendix C to see how you can download and install the GnuMP library and use it in your own .NET programs.

Steganography

Steganography is the art of concealing information in such a way that the fact that information is being concealed is itself a secret. Steganography is technically not considered to be a true branch of cryptography, but it can nevertheless

---

26. For instructions, see Appendix C, "Using the GnuMP Library."

be used very effectively for secret communications. The **Steganography** example is a simple program that shows a typical approach to implementing steganography using a graphical image.

We will not go through the details of this example code here, since they do not have much relevance to true cryptography; however, if you are interested, you may choose to look through the source code provided. It makes no use of any specialized .NET Security Framework classes, and is quite easy to follow if you know C# reasonably well. The hardest part is to understand the bit-twiddling that goes on. Basically, each 8-bit byte of the original message is incorporated into a corresponding pixel in the bitmap image. Each pixel is represented by a triplet of bytes containing the red, green, and blue components of that particular pixel. Each byte in the original message is split into a set of 3-bit, 3-bit, and 2-bit fields. These are then used to replace the least significant 3 bits, 3 bits, and 2 bits of the corresponding pixel's red, green, and blue color components, respectively.

The images before and after a short secret message has been inserted are shown in Figure 2–8. Can you see the difference? The difference, which is

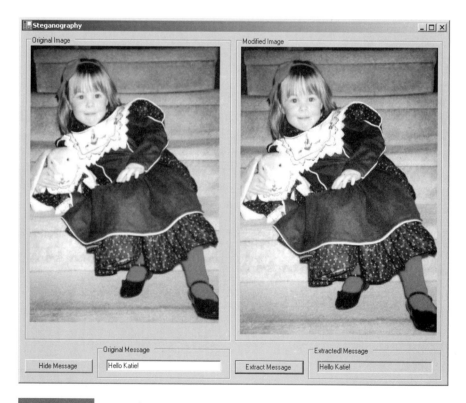

FIGURE 2-8   *A simple steganography example.*

not apparent to the eye, is that the least significant bits of the first few pixels are modified to carry the message. Even if you tried this with a much longer message and with a large percentage of modified pixels, you would still probably not be able to visually detect that the image that carries the message data is different.

This technique works because the least significant bits tend to have little effect on the visual appearance of the image. If you try doing this using the most significant pixel bits, you will see a startling result that looks very psychedelic. In steganography, as in real life, psychedelic effects are best avoided!

The least significant bits in most images tend to be fairly random, so any detectible statistical patterns in these bits could reveal the fact that steganography is being used. Thus, an attacker could do tests on your images to see if those bits are in fact random. To avoid this problem, you can randomize the message bits before inserting them into the image. For example, you could use compression, which not only improves randomness but also improves bandwidth. Alternatively, you could encrypt the message before inserting it, which not only improves randomness but also makes detection and recovery altogether much harder.

When it comes to steganography, the only limitation is that of your imagination. You can carry hidden information in images, audio files, email attachments, Voice over IP, and so forth. In addition, secret-loaded files can be communicated anonymously and in large volumes via newsgroups, email, Web sites, and services such as Napster.

Modern Ciphers

Modern ciphers do not operate on a set of letters such as A through Z, but Caesar was probably unfamiliar with the concept of bits and bytes! Instead, modern ciphers use numbers, sometimes extremely large numbers, to represent keys and plaintext or chunks of plaintext. Arithmetic is used to implement encryption; however, it may not always be the arithmetic you recall from grade school.

Cryptography and the .NET Framework

The .NET Framework class library provides the **System.Security.Cryptography** namespace, which supports the most important symmetric and asymmetric ciphers as well as several secure hash algorithms and a cryptographic-quality random number generator. This cryptography architecture is extensible, allowing third parties to provide alternative implementations and additional algorithms, in the form of cryptographic service providers. The **System.Security.Cryptography.XML** namespace implements the W3C standard for digitally signing XML objects, and the **System.Security.Cryptography.X509Certificates** namespace provides some support for working with public certificates. Here are the major standards implemented by the .NET Framework class library. We review most of these features in more detail in Chapters 3, 4, and 5.

- DES: Digital Encryption Standard (symmetric block cipher)
- 3DES: Triple DES (symmetric block cipher; stronger alternative to DES)
- Rijndael: AES[27] (symmetric block cipher)
- RC2: Cipher design by Ronald Rivest (symmetric stream cipher)
- RSA: Cipher design by Rivest, Shamir, and Adleman (asymmetric algorithm for both encryption and digital signatures)
- DSA: Digital Signature Algorithm (asymmetric algorithm only for digital signatures)
- MD5: Message digest (i.e., a secure hash) algorithm developed by Rivest
- SHA-1, SHA-256, SHA-384, SHA-512: Standard secure hash algorithms developed by NIST (National Institute of Standards and Technology) along with the NSA (for use with the Digital Signature Standard)
- Pseudorandom Number Generator (PRNG)
- XML Signatures: Digital signatures for XML data
- X.509: Public certificates standard

Symmetric Cryptography

Just as the telegraph was a technology in the 1800s that spawned new interest in cryptography, the digital computer, which itself was born out of a need for cryptanalysis in World War II, created an enormous new interest in developing new cryptographic algorithms. From this, the fastest and strongest[28] cryptography in history came into being in the form of modern symmetric block ciphers. The fruits of this came in the form of DES, Triple DES, AES, and several others.

Horst Feistel, working at IBM in the early 1970s, developed symmetric block cipher designs that eventually evolved into the Data Encryption Standard[29]

---

27. The U.S. government selected Rijndael as the AES (Advanced Encryption Standard) encryption standard in October 2000, replacing the DES.
28. You may recall that the OTP is theoretically the strongest cipher possible. However, the OTP is not practical for most realistic scenarios due to the large key size and the difficulty in securely storing and exchanging keys. Therefore, modern symmetric block ciphers are considered to be the strongest practical ciphers available.
29. DES was adopted as a standard by NIST, and it is documented in FIPS PUB 46, published in 1977.

(DES). In DES the same algorithm and the same 56-bit key are used for encrypting and decrypting a message. The DES design is based on repeating 16 rounds, where each round is comprised of a substitution followed by a permutation on a 64-bit input data block. The effect is to introduce confusion and diffusion into the ciphertext in each round, but, of course, in a reversible manner. Substitution adds confusion, since it makes the relationship between plaintext and ciphertext more complex. Transposition results in diffusion, since it rearranges the information, which tends to dissipate statistical redundancies in the plaintext throughout the ciphertext.

Since plaintext data is not typically a multiple of 64 bits, it must first be broken into 64-bit blocks, and then the last partial block must be padded with any required additional bits. Each DES round takes a 64-bit block of input data, which is then partitioned into two 32-bit halves. The right half is encrypted with a specialized encryption function[30] using a subkey unique to the current round, and XORed with the left portion to form the new right portion for the next round. The previous right portion is then substituted into the left portion for the next round. Figure 2–9 shows the basic structure of a single round of DES. We cover DES and other symmetric block ciphers in more detail in Chapter 3.

During the 1990s, DES had probably come to the end of its useful life. To maintain backward compatibility with much hardware and software, many organizations have adopted Triple DES, which is really just regular DES repeated three times with distinct keys. However, DES has recently been formally replaced by a symmetric block cipher called Rijndael as the new AES[31] standard. Rijndael, pronounced "rain doll" or "Rhine doll," was designed by the Belgian cryptographers Joan Daemen and Vincent Rijmen.

The .NET Framework provides the following classes for working with several important symmetric algorithms.

- System.Security.Cryptography.**DES**
- System.Security.Cryptography.**RC2**
- System.Security.Cryptography.**Rijndael**
- System.Security.Cryptography.**TripleDES**

Asymmetric Cryptography

Asymmetric cryptography, which was publicly introduced in the late 1970s,[32] is a relatively new invention in the long history of cryptography. It is actually

---

30. This specialized encryption function is described in Chapter 3.
31. For more information on the new AES standard, please see *http://csrc.nist.gov/encryption/aes/*.
32. There are claims that some form of asymmetric encryption was secretly used by British Intelligence in the 1950s.

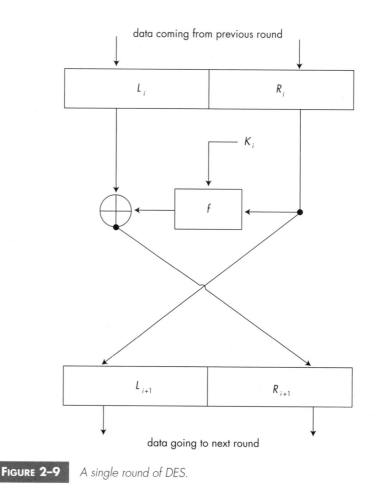

data coming from previous round

L_i R_i

K_i

f

L_{i+1} R_{i+1}

data going to next round

FIGURE 2-9   *A single round of DES.*

quite surprising that it was not invented much earlier, considering that it solves the very long-standing problems of securely exchanging keys and allowing spontaneous secure messaging. These have been vexing problems confronting well-funded governments for centuries and large corporations for decades. What adds to this curiosity is that the mathematics behind asymmetric encryption was well-known for several hundred years. However, it was not until Whitfield Diffie and Martin E. Hellman[33] published the article "New Directions in Cryptography" in 1976 that asymmetric cryptography was born.

Asymmetric cryptography uses modular arithmetic and simple number theory to make it possible to construct two distinct keys. One of the keys is

---

33. Partial credit must also be given Ralph Merkle, who was working independently on closely related ideas.

used for encryption, and the other is used for decryption. Together they form a key pair. Although the two keys are intimately mathematically related to one another, it is exceedingly difficult to determine one by only knowing the other. One of the keys is made publicly known, and the other is retained as a closely guarded secret.

Privacy and confidentiality can be achieved by encrypting with the public key and decrypting with the private key. On the other side of the coin, authenticity, integrity, and nonrepudiation can be achieved by encrypting with the private key and decrypting with the public key.

In every case, asymmetric cryptography is based on the idea of a one-way function that has a trapdoor. The details on what this actually means are clarified in Chapter 4. For now, we can loosely describe a one-way function as any function that is easy to calculate in the forward direction but very hard to calculate in the reverse direction. In other words, given x, it is easy to find $y = f(x)$, but given y, it is very hard to find $x = f^{-1}(y)$. You probably know many analogies to this from everyday life. For example, it is easy to put milk into your coffee, but just try to get it back out!

A trapdoor one-way function is simply a one-way function that suddenly becomes much easier to calculate in the reverse direction if you are provided additional secret information (i.e., a key). A backdoor for getting the milk back out of your coffee would be specialized knowledge of organic chemistry, enabling you to separate the milk using a complex sequence of chemical reagents, followed by filtering and a whirl on the centrifuge. However, I do not think that I would want to drink the result!

Several asymmetric encryption algorithms have been devised, including the RSA, ElGamal, and ECC Cryptosystems.[34] However, by far the most heavily used is RSA. We will go into much more detail on the mechanics of the RSA cipher in Chapter 4, but here is a quick overview of the process. First, Alice decides that she wants to allow Bob to send her a secret message:

1. Alice randomly picks two large prime numbers p and q, which she keeps as the secret key (p,q).

2. Alice multiplies the two large prime numbers to obtain the product $n = p \cdot q$.

---

34. Each of these is based on a different one-way backdoor function resulting from a specific mathematical problem. RSA is based on the integer factorization problem, ElGamal is based on the discrete logarithm problem, and ECC is based on the elliptic curve discrete logarithm problem. Although it has never been mathematically proven, many researchers are now inclined to believe that ECC is the strongest known asymmetric cipher. RSA stands for its inventors, Ron Rivest, Adi Shamir, and Len Adleman. ElGamal is named after its inventor Taher ElGamal. ECC stands for Elliptic Curve Cryptography, which was proposed by Neal Koblitz and Victor Miller in 1985.

3. Alice calculates Euler's totient function $\phi(n) = (p-1)(q-1)$. The function $\phi(n)$ is the number of number of integers less than n that are relatively prime to n.
4. Alice selects an exponent value e such that $1 < e < \phi(n)$ and $\gcd(e, \phi(n)) = 1$.
5. Alice makes the product n and the exponent e available together as the public key (n, e).
6. Alice calculates d as the modular inverse of e such that for any x, then $x = (x^e)^d (\text{mod } n)$.

Then Bob encrypts a message and sends it to Alice:

1. Bob obtains the public key (n, e).
2. Bob creates a plaintext message in the form of a number p.
3. Bob calculates the ciphertext $c = p^e (\text{mod } n)$, and sends it to Alice.

However, Eve is frustrated:

1. Eve obtains c.
2. Since she does not know d, she cannot calculate $p = c^d$.
3. She also cannot calculate d from knowledge of the public key (n, e), since factoring n is too difficult.

But Alice is happy:

1. Alice obtains c.
2. Alice directly calculates the plaintext $p = c^d$.

The .NET Framework provides the following classes for working with various asymmetric algorithms.

- System.Security.Cryptography.**DSA**
- System.Security.Cryptography.**RSA**

Cryptographic Algorithms

Aside from the major symmetric and asymmetric cipher algorithms, there are several important support algorithms, including random number generation and secure hash algorithms. Future chapters go into detail on cipher-specific algorithms, such as DES, RSA, and so forth. However, because PRNGs and secure hash algorithms are generally fundamental to practically all aspects of cryptography, we look at them briefly here. We do not have much more to say about PRNGs beyond our discussion in this chapter; however, we will look more closely at secure hash algorithms in Chapter 5, where we discuss digital signatures and hash authentication codes.

PSEUDORANDOM NUMBER GENERATORS

PRNGs play a very important role in cryptography and security. We have already seen how the OTP cipher critically relies on the randomness of its key to ensure perfect secrecy. In fact, all modern ciphers rely heavily on the randomness of their keys to ensure optimal security strength. If a PRNG-generated number sequence is not sufficiently random, then the numbers sequence may contain analyzable patterns that may be exploited by an attacker. If successful, the attacker may then exploit such a weakness of the PRNG to guess the generated keys that you use, which of course would be a security failure. Symmetric block ciphers typically rely on a PRNG for generating their initialization vector as well as the key.

Unfortunately, it is impossible to generate a truly random number sequence using any deterministic algorithm. Since, without specialized hardware, any computer program is inherently deterministic, all we can hope to achieve is a PRNG. A good quality PRNG is one in which it is very difficult to predict the next number generated based on previously generated numbers. A finite machine executing a deterministic algorithm will inevitably return to the same machine state, resulting in a repeating sequence of numbers, which by definition cannot be a truly random number sequence. PRNGs depend on an initialized value called the *seed*. Starting with a particular seed value, the PRNG then produces the same sequence of numbers. Of course, the same seed should never be used more than once.

If our source of random numbers cannot be perfect, we would at least like it to be very good. A good PRNG should have as flat a probability distribution as possible so that no numbers are significantly more likely than any other numbers over the long term. Also, no particular sequence of numbers should be more frequent than any other number sequence.

If you are willing to go to the extreme, specialized hardware may be used, relying on the assumed randomness of certain physical processes, such as the quantum electronic noise of a resistor or diode, or the radioactive decay detected with a Geiger counter.[35] Fractals and chaotic systems,[36]

---

35. Whether or not any physical process is truly random is still an open question in quantum physics. Heisenberg and others have made convincing arguments that true randomness does exist in nature. However, Einstein made the famous remark, "God does not play dice." In any case, the randomness of quantum noise and radioactive decay is certainly good enough for any cryptographic application for the foreseeable future!

36. Chaos theory is a relatively new branch of mathematics dealing with nonlinear dynamic systems that are deterministic but are nevertheless virtually impossible to predict over the long term. Lava lamps, stock markets, and the human mind are all considered likely to represent chaotic systems. Fractal theory deals with the mathematics of generating huge amounts of information from an initially very small piece of information, which is exactly what a PRNG must be able to do.

such as air turbulence, keyboard typing patterns, and lava lamps, have also been used for this purpose.[37]

PRNG AND THE .NET FRAMEWORK

The random number generators that are typically provided in standard platform APIs, such as Windows and UNIX (i.e., the **srand** and **rand** functions) are not of the high quality required for cryptographic applications. The .NET platform's **Random** class is also not good enough. The **RNGCryptoService-Provider** class provides access to a high-quality PRNG provided by the cryptographic service provider (CSP). However, you may find that you never need to use this class directly, since the .NET Framework cryptographic classes use it internally to generate cryptographic keys.

The abstract base class is **RandomNumberGenerator**, which derives into only one child class named **RNGCryptoServiceProvider**. The **Random-NumberGenerator** class supports the regular **Object** class methods as well as the **GetBytes** and **GetNonZeroBytes** methods, which return an array of bytes containing a cryptographically strong random sequence of values. As indicated by its name, **GetNonZeroBytes** returns a random byte array that contains no zero values. **RandomNumberGenerator** also supports two overloadings of the **Create** method, which creates an instance of a derived concrete implementation of a cryptographic random number generator. Since **RandomNumberGenerator** is abstract, you cannot create an instance of this class, and you cannot call on these methods directly. Instead, you must use the concrete derived class. Let's look at the signature of these functions.

```
public abstract void GetBytes(
   byte[] data //array to fill with random bytes
);

public abstract void GetNonZeroBytes(
   byte[] data //array to fill with non-zero random bytes
);

public static RandomNumberGenerator Create();
   //creates instance of default PRNG implementation

public static RandomNumberGenerator Create(string);
   //creates instance of specified implementation
```

---

37. Either the random number itself or a seed for a PRNG is generated by calculating the cryptographic hash of a continuously changing digital image of a lava lamp.

The concrete **RNGCryptoServiceProvider** class can be created and used directly. The following code snippet demonstrates how to generate an array of 128 random bytes using this class. We use the **RNGCryptoService-Provider** constructor in this example; however, you could use one of the static **Create** methods instead if you wish.

```
byte[] randomBytes = new Byte[128];
RNGCryptoServiceProvider rngcsp =
   new RNGCryptoServiceProvider();
rngcsp.GetBytes(randomBytes); //array gets random bytes
```

CRYPTOGRAPHIC HASH ALGORITHMS

A cryptographic hash algorithm takes an arbitrary amount of input data and reduces it to a fixed-length (typically 128, 160, or 256 bits) output. The output is often referred to as a message digest or a fingerprint, and it is highly characteristic of the input data, just as a fingerprint is a highly characteristic trait of a human. Ideally, a cryptographic hash algorithm satisfies the following requirements:

- It is difficult to determine the input from the output (i.e., it is one-way).
- It is difficult to find an input that will generate a particular output.
- It is difficult to find two inputs that will generate the same output.
- A single bit change on the input changes approximately 50 percent of the output bits.

A hash algorithm is used to generate a highly characteristic fixed-size fingerprint of an arbitrary-size input data. The output of a hash algorithm can be used for the following purposes:

- It can be used in detecting modifications of data.
- It plays a role in implementing digital signature algorithms.
- It can be used to transform a password into a secure representation that can be safely transmitted over a network or stored in an insecure database.
- It can be used to transform a password into an encryption key to be used by a cipher algorithm.

The most commonly used cryptographic hash algorithms are SHA-1 and MD5. The Secure Hash Algorithm (SHA-1) was established by NIST and is specified in the Secure Hash Standard (SHS, FIPS 180-1). SHA-1 produces a 160-bit digest. SHA-1 was followed by SHA-256, SHA-384, and SHA-512, which produce 256-, 384-, and 512-bit digests, respectively. More detailed information is available at *http://csrc.nist.gov/encryption/tkhash.html*. MD5 produces a 128-bit digest, making it faster, but it is not as secure against brute-force attack.[38] MD5 was designed by Ronald Rivest in the early 1990s and was submitted as an RFC, which can be found at *www.rfc.net/rfc1321.html.*

The following classes are provided by the .NET security framework library for secure hash functionality.

- System.Security.Cryptography.**KeyedHashAlgorithm**
- System.Security.Cryptography.**MD5**
- System.Security.Cryptography.**SHA1**
- System.Security.Cryptography.**SHA256**
- System.Security.Cryptography.**SHA384**
- System.Security.Cryptography.**SHA512**

The **KeyedHashAlgorithm** class provides the abstract class from which all classes that implement keyed hash algorithms must derive. A keyed hash is like an ordinary cryptographic hash function except that it takes a key as an additional input. Thus, only individuals who know the key that was used to generate the hash are able to verify the hash. There are two classes that derive from **KeyedHashAlgorithm**: **HMACSHA1** and **MACTripleDES**. **HMACSHA1** accepts a key of any size and generates a 20-byte Message Authentication Code (MAC) result using the SHA-1 hash algorithm. HMAC stands for Keyed-Hash Message Authentication Code, which is a NIST standard (see FIPS PUB 198). **MACTripleDES** generates a MAC using Triple DES as a keyed hash algorithm. It takes a key of 8, 16, or 24 bytes and generates an 8-byte hash. Keyed hash algorithms are most useful in authentication and integrity schemes, providing an alternative to digital signatures.

The other hash classes (implementing the MD5 and SHA hash functions) in the previous list are regular cryptographic hash functions that do not take a key input. They are used in situations where a hash must be used between individuals who have not shared any secret key information.

Cryptographic Protocols

A cryptographic protocol is an agreed-upon convention combining a set of cryptographic algorithms, a sequence of steps, and a group of two or more people to meet a desired security objective.

For example, a simple cryptographic protocol for encrypting and decrypting messages, using both the asymmetric RSA algorithm and the symmetric Tri-

---

38. One tends to think of a cipher as the only target of an attack. It may seem surprising, but hash algorithms and random number generators can also be the targets of attacks. An attack on a hash algorithm can mean determining the input from a given output or finding two inputs that give the same output. An attack on a PRNG means predicting subsequent outputs based on previous outputs. These attacks may play a role in larger attacks, such as cracking a cipher, tampering with digitally signed messages, or masquerading as someone else.

ple DES algorithm, could be the following.[39] Note that the RSA algorithm is too slow to be used for bulk data encryption, so it is only used on the relatively small Triple DES private key. The faster Triple DES algorithm is then used for bulk message encryption.

1. Alice and Bob each generate their own RSA public/private key pair.
2. They each send their public RSA keys to one another but keep their private RSA keys secret.
3. They each generate their own Triple DES private key and encrypt it using the other's public RSA key. The result can only be decrypted with the corresponding private RSA key.
4. They each send their encrypted Triple DES private key to one another.
5. Whenever Alice or Bob want to send a confidential message to the other party, they encrypt their plaintext message using the other party's Triple DES private key and send the resulting ciphertext.
6. The receiving party receives the ciphertext and decrypts it using the private Triple DES key.

As another example, a cryptographic protocol for ensuring that a message originates from a particular person, using the asymmetric RSA algorithm and the secure hash algorithm SHA-1, could be the following. Again, note that the RSA algorithm is too slow to be used for bulk data encryption. Therefore, RSA is used only on the relatively small message hash value. Also note that this protocol is used to verify the identity of the message source, but it does nothing to ensure the privacy of the message. You can probably see how to elaborate on this authentication protocol to include message privacy.

1. Alice and Bob each generate their own RSA public/private key pair.
2. They each send their public RSA keys to one another but keep their private RSA keys secret.
3. Whenever Alice or Bob want to send a message to the other party, they calculate a SHA-1 hash on their message, encrypt the hash with their own private key, and send the plaintext message along with the encrypted hash to the other party.

---

39. The protocol shown here is kept simple for the purpose of demonstrating the intended concept. However, this scheme is vulnerable to certain attacks. One such exploit is known as the "man-in-the-middle attack." This attack has Eve intercepting all traffic between Alice and Bob, substituting her own devious messages to trick and deceive in various ways. Another vulnerability in this protocol is known as the "replay attack," in which Eve records messages flowing between Alice and Bob. Later, Eve replays one or more of these messages, tricking the recipient into thinking she is Alice or Bob. More sophisticated protocols can be devised to deal with these types of attacks.

4. Whenever Alice or Bob receives a message and want to convince themselves that it originated from the other party, they decrypt the SHA-1 hash with the other party's public key. They then recalculate the hash from the received message and compare it with the decrypted hash. If they are identical, then they know it did indeed originate from the other party.

Unlike many of the scenarios we have looked at here, cryptographic protocols may involve people who do not necessarily trust one another but nevertheless want to do business with each other. Financial transactions usually fall into this category, and the banking and retail industries have established industry-specific cryptographic protocols to deal with these situations.

Often, cryptographic protocols have been established as computing standards or conventions. For example, the Kerberos protocol is commonly used to ensure that both parties (i.e., client and server) can know if the other party is who he or she claims to be. Another example is the Code Access Security (CAS) model of the .NET platform, where compiled code is digitally signed by its author for verification purposes. Yet another example is the Secure Sockets Layer (SSL) used for confidential communications over the Internet. Of course, there are many other examples, including PGP (Pretty Good Privacy) for secure email and the Diffie-Hellman key agreement protocol for exchanging session keys over an insecure channel without any prior sharing of secrets. There are several standardized cryptographic protocols that are conveniently implemented for use in the .NET security framework.

Cryptanalytic Attacks

There is an accepted terminology used to categorize the various possible types of cryptanalytic attacks. The following types of attacks are listed in order from hardest to easiest in terms of analytical difficulty, but from most likely to least likely in terms of the probability of the opportunity being presented to the attacker. This is not an exhaustive list, but it gives a basic overview of the most important types of attacks.

- **Ciphertext-only attack:** Attacker has only some randomly selected ciphertext.
- **Known plaintext attack:** Attacker has some randomly selected plaintext and corresponding ciphertext.
- **Chosen plaintext attack:** Attacker has some chosen plaintext and corresponding ciphertext.
- **Chosen ciphertext attack:** Attacker has some chosen ciphertext and the corresponding decrypted plaintext.

- **Adaptive chosen plaintext attack:** Attacker can determine the ciphertext of chosen plaintexts in an iterative manner building on previous calculations. This type of attack is also referred to as a *differential cryptanalysis attack.*

The ciphertext-only attack is the easiest opportunity to imagine. When you first begin your surveillance of messages between a sender and a receiver, you will not likely have much to go on beyond the encrypted packets being sent over the channel. Unfortunately, with so little information to go on, this is the most difficult attack. Then, perhaps over time, you learn about certain plaintext messages that have been encrypted, or perhaps you suspect that certain words or phrases are frequently contained in the plaintext. For example, many of the Nazi secret messages in the first part of World War II contained highly predictable text. This enables a known plaintext attack. The chosen plaintext attack seems a bit more difficult to establish, because you somehow must trick the sender into encrypting and sending a plaintext message that you, the attacker, have chosen. This would be possible if, for example, you pretended to be some trusted party, and you then sent your chosen plaintext message to the sender, convincing the sender to encrypt it and send it to a receiver. By carefully selecting the plaintext message, you can often improve the odds of recovering the key.

Of course, there are rather unsavory, nontechnical alternatives to these attacks, such as physical theft or simply bribing and/or threatening the key owner. Legalities, ethics, and morality aside, these alternatives have practical disadvantages, including the fact that the key owners (i.e., sender and receiver) and perhaps others will know that the key is compromised. This could elicit a change in key or even the transmission of intentionally misleading ciphertext messages. There is an enormous advantage in keeping a secret of the fact that you can crack a cipher.

As was mentioned earlier, a *brute-force search attack* is an exhaustive test of each possible key applied to the ciphertext. When applied to a ciphertext-only attack, the key space is searched until a plausible plaintext is obtained, in which case the success of the search is not entirely certain but often fairly reliable. If the corresponding plaintext is known, then the success of the search is completely certain by direct comparison with the known plaintext. Once the key has been obtained, all other ciphertext encrypted with that key can be easily decrypted.

Issues in Human Interaction and Trust

In a utopian world, security and cryptography would be a complete waste of time and effort. If you could trust everyone, everyone could trust you, and everybody knew that nobody would intentionally do any harm to anyone, then there would be no need to keep secrets, prove identity, or control access. Sadly, this is not reality. Therefore, we must take precautions to protect ourselves from untrustworthy individuals and organizations with conflicting interests.

Risk and Benefit

Whenever we interact with the world, we inevitably encounter both risks and benefits. The obvious strategy is to attempt to take only risks such that the expected benefit outweighs the expected risk. You want to strike a balance in which you gain benefit from communicating with certain individuals but limit how much they and others can know and do. For example, if you want to buy or sell something on *http://www.ebay.com,* you want to be sure that your credit card information is secure. You also want to be sure that you are actually dealing with whom you believe you are dealing with.

This balancing act can come in several flavors. For example, you may be confronted with a very low-probability risk with a huge downside compared against a high-probability benefit of moderate value. This is the type of decision you make every time you drive your car. The converse of this scenario is when you have a very low-probability benefit with a huge upside compared against a high-probability risk (or even a 100 percent certain cost) of low value. If you have ever bought a lottery ticket, then you have encountered this scenario. In some situations, you simply have no good choice. Even where the downside is significant (high probability and high cost) but prevention costs too much or is not possible, then you just have to hope for the best. Death falls into this last category.

These extreme scenarios are intended to get you thinking about weighing risk and benefit. You need to weigh risk and benefit whenever you decide on implementing security or cryptography features into your software or whenever you configure security on your systems. Keep in mind that if you try to be too secure, then users will try to find ways around your plans or worker productivity may be impaired.

Other Important Concepts

Here are several other important concepts related to cryptography and security.

- **Confidentiality** means that sensitive information is protected from disclosure to unauthorized persons. This is closely related to the concept of *privacy.*
- **Integrity** means that data consistency is assured and that the data is tamper-proof.

- **Authentication** is the process of proving the identity of an individual or a system.
- **Nonrepudiation** means that an individual cannot take an action and then deny it later. This is closely related to the concept of *proof of receipt*.
- **Authorization** means that an access policy can be specified that grants or denies specific rights to an individual to perform specific actions on specific resources. This is closely related to the concept of *access control*.
- **Anonymity** means that the identity of an individual can be concealed.
- **Ownership** of a resource represents the right to control the use of that resource.
- **Certification** is the process of endorsement by a trusted authority of a claim made by an individual. This is closely related to the concept of a *Certificate Authority*.
- **Witnessing** means the verification by one individual of an action performed by another individual.
- **Validation** means checking for the validity or truthfulness of a claim made by an individual. It can also mean the process of checking code or data for safety or for compliance with some other desired rules, such as type safety.

Summary

This chapter introduced basic cryptographic terminology, concepts, and mathematical foundations that are required for understanding several upcoming chapters. To accomplish this, several simple classical cryptographic algorithms were reviewed as examples. In the next two chapters, we look more closely at modern symmetric and asymmetric ciphers, which form the basis of secure storage and communications, supporting privacy, confidentiality, authenticity, integrity, and nonrepudiation.

Beyond this chapter, the book takes an applied approach, focusing on specific Windows and .NET platform functionality. Therefore, we will not cover a great deal more on fundamental concepts. For further reading on fundamental concepts, please see the excellent *The Handbook of Applied Cryptography* by Alfred J. Menezes, Paul C. van Oorschot, and Scott A. Vanstone, which is available in Adobe PDF and PostScript formats at *http://www.cacr.math.uwaterloo.ca/hac/*. Another useful book is *Applied Cryptography* by Bruce Schneier. For a wonderful historical (nontechnical) account of classical cryptography, you may want to read *The Codebreakers* by David Kahn.

Symmetric Cryptography

*T*he most basic problems of cryptography have always been confidentiality, integrity, and authentication. The traditional approach to these problems has been to apply solutions based on symmetric cryptographic algorithms. This chapter introduces the concepts of symmetric cryptography and provides examples of how to implement symmetric cryptography solutions using the **System.Security.Cryptography** namespace in the .NET Framework. In particular, we look at the DES, Triple DES, Rijndael, and RC2 symmetric algorithms and how to use them.

Symmetric Ciphers

A symmetric cipher is a cipher in which encryption and decryption use the same key or keys that are mathematically related to one another in such a way that it is easy to compute one key from knowledge of the other, which is effectively a single key. Since the single key is the only secret to encryption and decryption, it is critical that this key be kept strictly private. Otherwise, an interloper could easily encrypt and decrypt messages at will, and we would be leaking information and accomplishing nothing. For this reason, symmetric ciphers are often referred to as private key, secret key, or shared key ciphers. In contrast, asymmetric ciphers involve the use of a pair of keys that are mathematically related, but it is intentionally very difficult to determine one key from knowledge of the other. As we shall see in Chapter 4, this makes it necessary only to keep one private key secret to one individual, and the corresponding public key can then be safely made available to everyone.

Symmetric encryption and decryption are represented mathematically by the following, where E is an encryption function, D is a decryption function, k is the single shared secret key, M is a plaintext message, and C is the corresponding ciphertext message.

Encryption: $C = E_k(M)$

Decryption: $M = D_k(C)$

Figure 3–1 shows how symmetric cryptography works. Note that the sender and receiver (i.e., Bob and Alice) must agree beforehand on what secret key and what algorithm will be used. Along with the algorithm, there are associated details, such as the initialization vector, mode of operation, and padding convention that must also be agreed upon. These associated details are explained shortly.

There are two basic types of symmetric algorithms: block ciphers and stream ciphers. A block cipher processes a block of bytes (usually 64 or 128 bits) at a time. A stream cipher processes a single byte or even a single bit at a time. We shall see that the distinction between block and stream ciphers is somewhat artificial, because certain modes of operation allow a block cipher to behave as a stream cipher.

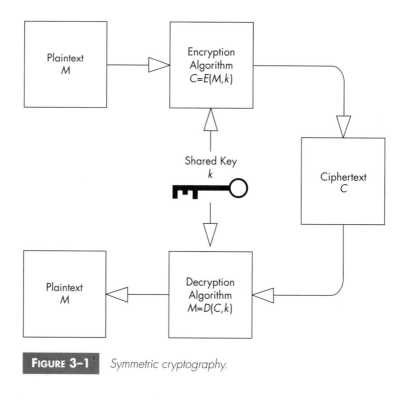

FIGURE 3–1   *Symmetric cryptography.*

As we shall see in the next chapter, asymmetric ciphers solve several significant cryptographic problems; however, they tend to be less secure than symmetric ciphers (for a given key size), and symmetric ciphers tend to be faster, making them more suitable for encrypting large quantities of bulk data. It is important to recognize that symmetric and asymmetric ciphers are used to solve different security problems, and in fact their strengths are often complementary to one another. For this reason, there are several important cryptographic protocols that make use of a combination of both symmetric and asymmetric algorithms to accomplish sets of desirable security goals.

Many symmetric ciphers have been developed throughout history, whereas asymmetric ciphers are a fairly recent invention. Symmetric ciphers improved slowly until just after World War II, when the advent of computers produced a rapid improvement in cipher designs that were developed secretly by several governments. By the late 1970s, private organizations began to discover and use powerful, modern symmetric ciphers that evolved from work done by Horst Feistel in 1967 at IBM.[1] In particular, the Data Encryption Standard (DES) algorithm was adopted as a standard by the U.S. government in 1977 to be used within the federal government for the protection of sensitive but unclassified data. Subsequently, DES was also used in the private sector for many security-related applications, especially in the areas of financial transactions and other banking applications.

DES

DES is documented in the FIPS[2] PUB 46-3 document as well as in ANSI standard X9.32. Although DES is not considered to be ultra-secure[3] by today's standards, it is still heavily used. In fact, every time you use an ATM machine, you are probably using DES. It is still suitable for keeping secrets that are not extremely sensitive and valuable, especially where legacy software is being used, and it is still the most heavily used encryption scheme in commercial use. It was temporarily recommended that DES be replaced as a standard by the more powerful Triple DES algorithm in the 1990s, and subsequently it was formally replaced by the Rijndael algorithm, which is now the current U.S. government standard for symmetric encryption.

---

1. Horst Feistel at IBM developed LUCIFER, the direct ancestor of DES. The NSA was keenly interested in LUCIFER and was closely involved in the final design phase of DES.
2. FIPS stands for Federal Information Processing Standard.
3. DES has been cracked publicly several times now. For example, the Electronic Frontier Foundation (EFF) built a specialized DES cracking machine, costing about $250,000, and won the RSA DES Challenge II contest in 1998 after a 56-hour brute-force attack. The same machine, working with approximately 100,000 PCs on the Internet (*http://www.distributed.net*), cracked DES in just over 22 hours.

DES is a symmetric block cipher that transforms 64-bit data blocks using a 56-bit shared secret key, involving 16 rounds of permutation and substitution. As mentioned in Chapter 2, substitution (replacing bits within the data) adds confusion, since it makes the relationship between plaintext and ciphertext more complex. Transposition (moving bits within the data) results in diffusion, which spreads information throughout the ciphertext data block, making it more random and harder for a cryptanalyst to know if he or she is heading in the right direction when attempting to discover the plaintext.

Mathematically, DES maps the set of all possible 64-bit numbers onto itself in a reversible manner. DES uses the same 56-bit key for both encryption and decryption (making it a symmetric algorithm). The key selects any one of 2^{56} possible invertible mappings (i.e., one-to-one transformations). Selecting a key simply selects one of these invertible mappings.

DES basically deals with 64-bit data blocks; however, since plaintext data is not typically a multiple of 64-bits, it must first be broken into 64-bit blocks, and then the last partial block must be padded with any required additional bits (there are several padding techniques in use). Each DES round takes the 64-bit block of input data, which is then partitioned into two 32-bit halves. The right half is encrypted with a specialized encryption function, using a subset of bits taken from the 56-bit key that is unique to the current round, and XORed with the left portion to form the new right portion for the next round. The previous right portion is then substituted into the left portion for the next round. Figure 3–2 shows the basic structure of a single round of DES.

Figure 3–3 shows the overall structure of the entire 16 rounds of DES. We do not show all of the details involved in the DES algorithm here. For example, the 48-bit subkeys for each round (K1 through K16) are generated from the original 56-bit key in a manner involving several bit manipulations that depend on which round they are applied to. We also do not go into other implementation details here, such as the specialized encryption function used in each round that includes an expansion permutation, an S-box substitution, and a P-box permutation in each round. To use DES in practical situations, these details are not very important; however, if you are interested, you may want to read the FIPS 46-3[4] document for these DES design details.

Modes of Operation

DES is a block cipher, and what we looked at in the previous section is just how DES works at the individual block level. However, arbitrary-length plaintext does not typically fit exactly within a single 64-bit data block. Therefore,

---

4. FIPS 46-3 can be found at *http://csrc.nist.gov/publications/fips/fips46-3/ fips46-3.pdf.*

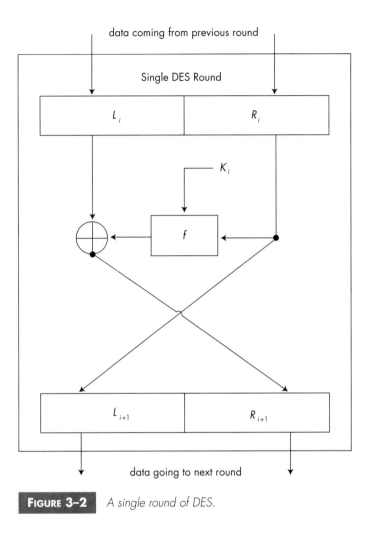

data coming from previous round

FIGURE 3-2 *A single round of DES.*

block ciphers, such as DES and Rijndael, must be able to operate on sequences of input data blocks. To handle sequences of data blocks, these ciphers must operate according to certain agreed-upon rules, as defined by modes of operation. There are four standard DES modes of operation (ECB, CBC, CFB, and OFB) defined by FIPS PUB 81.[5] In addition, the CTS mode was developed for use with the RC5 cipher as defined in RFC 2040, but it can be adapted to other block ciphers as well. These five modes are defined by the **CipherMode**

---

5. This document is titled *DES Modes of Operation*.

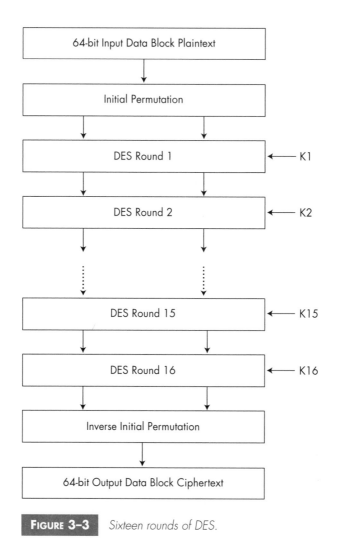

FIGURE 3-3   *Sixteen rounds of DES.*

enumeration in the **System.Security.Cryptography** of the .NET Framework. Here are the full names for each of these modes:

- Electronic Codebook (ECB)
- Cipher Block Chaining (CBC)
- Cipher Feedback (CFB)
- Output Feedback (OFB)
- Cipher Text Stealing (CTS)

It turns out that in the current release of the .NET Framework, only some of these modes are actually available with certain algorithms. ECB, CBC, and CFB currently work with the DES, Triple DES, and RC2 algorithms. Only ECB and CBC currently work with the Rijndael algorithm. OFB and CTS do not work with any algorithm yet; however, their inclusion in the **CipherMode** enumeration seems to imply that they might be supported eventually. It is also interesting to note that CTS was originally intended for use with the RC5 algorithm, which is entirely missing for the current release of the .NET Framework. In spite of some missing pieces, we look at four of these modes of operation in the next several sections in order to gain a more complete picture of operating modes.

We will soon see an actual .NET program that demonstrates how to work with these operating modes. However, let's first look briefly at how these modes work at a conceptual level. In order to understand these details, take note of the following notation:

- M_i is the **i**th 64-bit block of plaintext.
- C_i is the **i**th 64-bit block of ciphertext.
- E_k is the DES encryption function, using the chosen secret key k.
- D_k is the DES decryption function, using the chosen secret key k.
- IV is a 64-bit initialization vector used in certain modes to simulate the previous block for the initial plaintext block.

ECB MODE

The simplest mode, ECB, goes through the 16 Feistel rounds described above for each 64-bit block individually and independently. For a given 56-bit key, ECB mode always results in the same mapping between a given plaintext block and the corresponding ciphertext block, and bit errors are not propagated into subsequent blocks. The fact that blocks are processed independently is why this mode is named ECB, since a (very large) codebook could theoretically be created for each key. ECB has some advantages over other modes. For example, it allows you to randomly encrypt and decrypt blocks of data in a file or a database, since each block is processed independently of all other blocks. ECB also allows encryption and decryption to be performed on multiple blocks concurrently, assuming that you have a hardware implementation that can take advantage of this parallel processing.

Unfortunately, the gains made by ECB in simplicity must be weighed against its slightly reduced security. The security problem with ECB is that an attacker could compile a codebook as plaintext/ciphertext pairs are guessed or discovered. These pairs may be obtained in various ways because of the repeating nature of certain byte sequences, such as message headers or common salutations. The interesting thing about this attack is that the key is never actually needed, but, as the codebook grows, it assists in further cryptanalysis, helping the codebook to grow further, with a snowballing positive-feedback effect. This is like the way a jigsaw puzzle gradually becomes easier as you continue to fit more pieces into the picture. Figure 3–4 shows how ECB mode works.

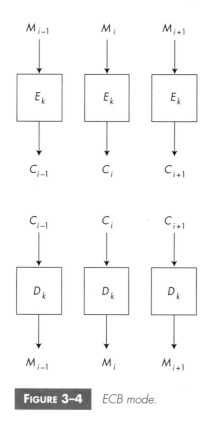

FIGURE 3–4   ECB mode.

As you can see from Figure 3–4, ECB has each block of the plaintext message M_i transformed by the encryption function E_k independently from other blocks. Of course, the decryption in ECB mode also has each ciphertext block C_i decrypted independently of other blocks by the D_k function. Mathematically, the ECB mode can be described as follows.

ECB mode encryption:

$$C_i = E_k(M_i)$$

ECB mode decryption:

$$M_i = D_k(C_i)$$

CBC MODE

CBC is a more secure technique, which does not permit the construction of a codebook. CBC performs an XOR (exclusive-or) operation on each 64-bit plaintext block with the previous ciphertext block prior to going through the

Feistel rounds. The first block is XORed with a random 64-bit initialization vector (IV), since the first plaintext block has no previous ciphertext block. You can think of the IV as nothing more than a dummy ciphertext block to prime the pump for this mode. Interestingly, the IV is not considered to be secret, and it may be safely transmitted in the clear. If this seems surprising, consider that the IV is effectively just another ciphertext block, not a secret key. Figure 3–5 shows how CBC mode works.

As you can see from Figure 3–5, CBC takes each block of the plaintext message M_i, which is first XORed with the previous ciphertext block C_{i-1}, and this result is then transformed by the encryption function E_k to produce the ciphertext block C_i. Decryption in ECB mode first decrypts the ciphertext block C_i with the D_k function, and this result is then XORed with the previous

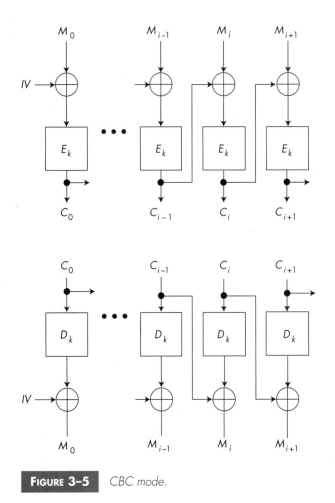

FIGURE 3–5   CBC mode.

ciphertext block C_{i-1} to produce the plaintext block M_i. Mathematically, CBC mode can be described as follows. The symbol $\oplus$ represents the bitwise XOR operation, and IV represents the initialization vector, which is used only for the first block. Here is the mathematical representation of CBC mode.

CBC mode encryption:

$$C_0 = E_k(M_0 \oplus IV)$$

$$C_i = E_k(M_i \oplus C_{i-1})$$

CBC mode decryption:

$$M_0 = D_k(C_0) \oplus IV$$

$$M_i = D_k(C_i) \oplus C_{i-1}$$

CFB AND OFB MODES

There are two other standard DES modes, CFB mode and OFB mode, that allow you to deal with chunks of plaintext data that are less that the full 64-bit block size. This makes these modes useful as stream ciphers in which DES generates pseudorandom bits that are XORed with new plaintext as it becomes available to form new ciphertext data.[6] For example, 8-bit CFB can be used to encrypt and decrypt an ASCII or binary byte stream. ECB and CBC can process only 64-bit chunks at a time, but there are situations where you may need to immediately process smaller data chunks at a time. For example, a radar device may need to transmit individual encrypted bytes, one at a time, to a command and control system in real time, as they are generated. The system may not be able to tolerate waiting an arbitrary amount of time for a full 64-bit block, since it may need to react to information immediately as it is generated. ECB and CBC simply cannot deal with this type of situation satisfactorily, whereas CFB or OFB can.

For a given key, CBC and CFB modes do not result in a fixed mapping between plaintext blocks and ciphertext blocks, since it is affected by previous input blocks as well as by the IV used. This makes cryptanalysis harder, but it also means that a single bit error in a ciphertext block transmission corrupts both the current and the subsequent ciphertext block. For OFB, a single framing error (adding or losing bits in transmission) can corrupt all subsequent ciphertext blocks. An advantage of CFB over OFB is that CFB is self-synchronizing, meaning that even with a temporary loss of framing, it will automatically recover after one block of data.

---

6. The description of CFB and OFB provided here is somewhat simplified to provide general understanding. For fully detailed information on all DES modes, see FIPS PUB 81 at *http://csrc.nist.gov/publications/fips/fips81/fips81.htm*.

Figure 3–6 shows, in a simplified representation, how CFB works. The shift register makes it possible to use a moving subset of the previously generated output bits for XORing with the current input bits, as the algorithm proceeds. Not shown in this diagram is that only the leftmost subset of output bits from each previous stage is XORed with the input of the current stage. In other words, for 8-bit CFB, only the leftmost 8 bits of the previous output is

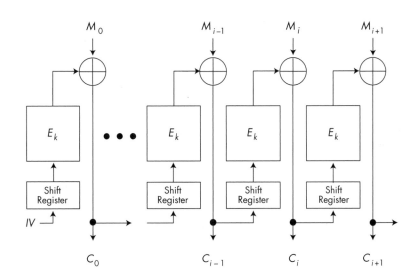

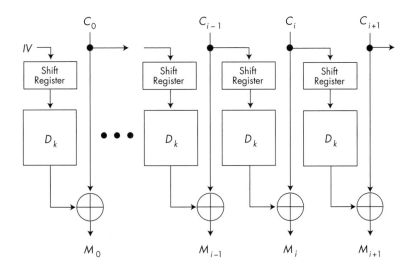

FIGURE 3–6   CFB mode.

XORed with the current 8 bits of the input data. There is nothing special about a step size of 8 bits, and, in fact, any bit size less than the DES block size of 64 bits may be used for each stage. By processing 8 bits at a time, 8-bit CFB effectively transforms DES, which is a block cipher, into a stream cipher.

Mathematically, CFB mode can be described as follows.

CFB mode encryption:

$$C_0 = M_0 \oplus E_k(IV)$$

$$C_i = M_i \oplus E_k(C_{i-1})$$

CFB mode decryption:

$$M_0 = C_0 \oplus D_k(IV)$$

$$M_i = C_i \oplus D_k(C_{i-1})$$

Figure 3–7 shows, in a simplified representation, how OFB mode works. As you can see, the basic idea is almost identical to what we just saw in CFB mode. The only difference is that in CFB mode the input to the shift register comes from bits in the previous stage after they are XORed. In contrast, OFB provides the input to the shift register from bits in the previous stage before they are XORed. Just as in the case of CFB, OFB allows the cipher to work on data in smaller pieces than the 64-bit block size that DES is based on.

Mathematically, OFB mode can be described as follows.

OFB mode encryption:

$$C_0 = M_0 \oplus E_k(IV)$$

$$C_i = M_i \oplus E_k(R_{i-1}),$$

where R_{i-1} comes from the previous stage before the $\oplus$ operation.

OFB mode decryption:

$$M_0 = C_0 \oplus D_k(IV)$$

$$M_i = C_i \oplus D_k(R_{i-1}),$$

where R_{i-1} comes from the previous stage before the $\oplus$ operation.

Triple DES

The banking industry has adopted the ANSI X9.52[7] standard, also known as Triple DES, TDES, or 3DES. Triple DES was used as a more powerful interim alternative to DES. Triple DES is based directly on the basic design of DES

---

7. ANSI and ISO standards are not available freely online, and they must be purchased. See *webstore.ansi.org* for details.

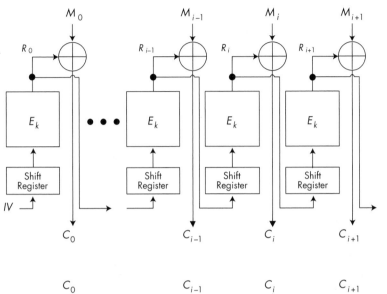

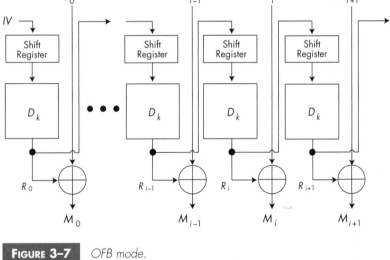

FIGURE 3-7   *OFB mode.*

and is quite backward-compatible with the original DES design and modes. The improvement comes from the fact that each 64-bit block of plaintext is encrypted three times, using the DES algorithm in which three distinct keys are used. Triple DES encrypts each block with the first key, then decrypts the result using the second key, and finally encrypts again using the third key. Triple DES increases the effective key size of DES, but the algorithm takes approximately three times as much time to compute compared to DES.

Triple DES encryption:

$$C = E_{k_3}(D_{k_2}(E_{k_1}(M)))$$

Triple DES decryption:

$$M = D_{k_1}(E_{k_2}(D_{k_3}(C))),$$

where k_1, k_2, k_3 are the three 56-bit keys.

Rijndael

Many experts now feel that DES is near the end of its useful life. In the late 1970s, a 56-bit key would have been viewed by many as sufficient for securing most sensitive commercial data, given the cost and speed of computers available at that time. Unfortunately, this is no longer quite so true, since computers are now much cheaper and faster. In general, you should always use encryption technology that will incur sufficient cost or time for potential attackers to consider it not worthwhile mounting an attack. With the doubling of digital circuit-switching speeds every 18 months, progress made in cryptanalysis research, along with the advent of inexpensive, customizable gate-array hardware and the massive distributed computing model made possible by the Internet, times have certainly changed. Triple DES was a very capable alternative, but it was only intended to be a temporary fix. A replacement for DES has recently gone through an international competition, and the official DES replacement, formerly referred to as AES (Advanced Encryption Standard), is the Rijndael algorithm. The Rijndael specification can be found in FIPS-197,[8] and, like its predecessor, it is intended for use by U.S. government organizations to protect unclassified sensitive information. It is expected that, over time, the Rijndael algorithm will have a huge impact on commercial software security, especially in financial applications.

Unlike the DES algorithm, which uses a fixed 56-bit key size, the Rijndael algorithm is more flexible in that it is able to use key sizes of 128, 192, or 256 bits (referred to as AES-128, AES-192, and AES-256, respectively). Whereas the data block size of DES was fixed at 64 bits, Rijndael can work with 128, 192, or 256 bit data blocks. Rijndael was originally designed to accommodate other key and block sizes, but the AES standard ignores these alternatives. The number of rounds in Rijndael depends on the block and key size. Nine rounds are used if the block and the key sizes are both 128 bits. Eleven rounds are used if either the block or the key size is greater than 128 bits but neither is greater than 192 bits. Thirteen rounds are used if either the block or key size is 256 bits. An additional modified final round is added to the end of the algorithm, so 10, 12, or 14 rounds are actually performed.

---

8. FIPS-197 can be found at *http://csrc.nist.gov/publications/fips/fips197/fips-197.pdf.*

The Rijndael algorithm is much more complex than DES, which was originally designed for simple and efficient digital-circuit hardware implementations. Rijndael involves advanced mathematical concepts, such as algebra on polynomials with coefficients in the Galois field $GF(2^8)$, where the familiar concepts of addition and multiplication take on bizarre new meanings. These details are beyond the scope of this book; however, you are encouraged to read the FIPS-197 document for these details. Fortunately, you do not need to understand these gruesome details to use the Rijndael algorithm in your own .NET programs, since the .NET Framework hides the tough stuff quite nicely!

RC2

RC2 is a registered trademark of RSA Data Security, Incorporated. The RC2 algorithm is a symmetric block cipher designed by Ronald Rivest in 1987, using a 64-bit input data block size. It was designed to be a drop-in replacement for DES, with improved performance, and a variable key size (from one byte up to 128 bytes) that allows for fine-tuning of its cryptographic strength. Effectively, RC2 can be made more or less secure than DES simply by choosing an appropriate key size. One of the strengths of RC2 is that it is designed to be about twice as fast as DES in typical software implementations. According to the folks at RSA Security, RC stands for either Ron's Code or Rivest's Cipher; however, it does not seem all that clear that they have settled the official story on this!

RC2 is licensed for use in several commercial Internet software packages, including Lotus Notes, Microsoft Internet Explorer, Outlook Express, and Netscape Communicator. S/MIME (Secure/Multipurpose Internet Mail Extensions) allows for the choice of using RC2 (along with DES and Triple DES) to provide interoperable, secure email. The security services supported by RC2 in these applications are authentication via digital signatures and privacy via encryption.

RC2 has been submitted to the IETF organization as a Request For Comment. For the detailed RC2 specification, see the RFC 2268 at *http://www.ietf.org/rfc/rfc2268.txt.*

Programming with .NET Symmetric Cryptography

Microsoft initially addressed the issue of data privacy in 1996 with the introduction of the Win32 Cryptography API (CryptoAPI) in Windows NT. Although the CryptoAPI provided thorough support for cryptographic programming, it was very difficult to use. You had to know a great deal about cryptography to make sense out of the many parameters and the large number of APIs. Also, it was not object oriented, since it was a straight C language interface, and you typically had to call many functions to perform even the simplest of operations. Fortunately, the .NET Framework greatly simplifies our work by providing a very elegant set of classes in the **System.Security.Cryptography** namespace.

The Main Cryptography Classes

We look only at asymmetric programming in this chapter; however, since this is our first opportunity to see the .NET Security Framework, we now briefly list the most generally important classes provided in the **System.Security.Cryptography** namespace. The following list contains the classes that are of principal importance, since they are the base classes for each of the main aspects of cryptographic programming. We do not consider any of the classes related to Code Access Security or Role-Based Security here. Security-related classes, which fall into the **System.Security** namespace, are covered in Chapters 7 and 8.

- **SymmetricAlgorithm**-derived classes encapsulate symmetric algorithms such as DES and Rijndael.
- **AsymmetricAlgorithm**-derived classes encapsulate the RSA and DSA asymmetric algorithms.
- **CryptoStream** connects a source data stream to a cryptographic algorithm.
- **CspParameters** encapsulates algorithm-specific parameter information that can be stored and retrieved via a cryptographic service provider (CSP).
- **HashAlgorithm** represents the base class from which all cryptographic hash algorithms are derived.
- **RandomNumberGenerator** represents the base class from which cryptographic pseudorandom number generators (PRNGs) are derived.
- **ToBase64Transform** and **FromBase64Transform** are used to convert between a byte stream and a base-64 representation.
- **CryptographicException** encapsulates error information for various cryptographic operations.

Since these classes reside in the **System.Security.Cryptography** namespace, you should remember to add the **using** statement for this namespace in your programs.

The SymmetricAlgorithm Class

The .NET Framework classes that implement symmetric algorithms are derived from the abstract base class **SymmetricAlgorithm**. The **SymmetricAlgorithm** abstract class has several protected fields, which are not directly accessible to methods of nonderived classes. However, these protected fields can be accessed via public virtual properties that are implemented in concrete derived classes. For example, the protected **int** field **BlockSizeValue** can be accessed via the **BlockSize** public virtual property in a manner that is appropriate, depending on the actual derived class being used. In this way, an attempt to set the block size to a value that is illegal for a particular symmetric algorithm will throw a **CryptographicException**, depending on the actual algorithm (i.e., the particular derived class) being used. In each case the protected field and the corresponding public virtual property have the same datatype, and the names are identical except that the protected fields have the word Value appended to them.

The public virtual properties defined in the **SymmetricAlgorithm** class are shown in Table 3–1.

SymmetricAlgorithm has only one public constructor that takes no parameters. This constructor initializes the new instance with a randomly generated secret key. Of course, **SymmetricAlgorithm** also supports the standard methods **Equals**, **Finalize**, **GetHashCode**, **ToString**, **GetType**, and **MemberwiseClone**, which are defined in the base class **Object**. In addition to these, **SymmetricAlgorithm** supports the public methods shown in Table 3–2.

SymmetricAlgorithm-Derived Classes

You will never work directly with an actual **SymmetricAlgorithm** object, since it is an abstract class, which cannot be instantiated. Instead, you will work with derived concrete classes that implement each of the public properties as well as the abstract and virtual methods of **SymmetricAlgorithm** in an algorithm-specific and polymorphic manner. Figure 3–8 shows the symmetric algorithm class hierarchy.

As you can see from Figure 3–8, the following classes, which are also abstract, are derived from **SymmetricAlgorithm**. We will look at how to program with the concrete classes derived from these abstract classes shortly.

- **DES** is an abstract class that encapsulates the DES symmetric algorithm.
- **TripleDES** is an abstract class that encapsulates the Triple DES symmetric algorithm, which was an effective, backward-compatible alternative to DES, providing much greater security.
- **Rijndael** is an abstract class that encapsulates the Rijndael symmetric algorithm that is the new standard replacing DES.
- **RC2** is an abstract class that encapsulates the RC2 symmetric algorithm that was developed by Ronald Rivest as a potential replacement for DES.

TABLE 3–1	*Public Virtual Properties in the SymmetricAlgorithm Class*
Public Property	**Description**
BlockSize	Gets or sets the block size in bits for the algorithm, which is the amount of data that is encrypted or decrypted in a single operation. Messages that are larger than this are broken into blocks of this size. The final block must be padded to match this block size. Valid block sizes are specified by the **LegalBlockSizes** property for each symmetric algorithm. This property is of type **int**.
FeedbackSize	Gets or sets the feedback size in bits for the algorithm, which is the amount of data that is fed back into successive encryption or decryption operations. This is required in OFB and CFB modes of operation. Valid feedback sizes depend on the symmetric algorithm, but must not be greater than the block size. This property is of type **int**.
IV	Gets or sets the initialization vector for the symmetric algorithm, which is required in CBC mode. This property is of type array of **byte**.
Key	Gets or sets the secret key to be used by the symmetric algorithm for encryption and decryption. This property is of type array of **byte**.
KeySize	Gets or sets the size of the secret key used by the symmetric algorithm in bits. Valid key sizes are specified by the **LegalKeySizes** property for each symmetric algorithm. This property is of type **int**.
LegalBlockSizes	Gets the block sizes that are supported by the symmetric algorithm. This read-only property is of type array of **KeySizes** elements (there is no BlockSizes type). Only block sizes that match an element in this array are supported by the symmetric algorithm.
LegalKeySizes	Gets the key sizes that are supported by the symmetric algorithm. This read-only property is of type array of **KeySizes** elements. Only key sizes that match an element in this array are supported by the symmetric algorithm.
Mode	Gets or sets the mode for operation for the symmetric algorithm. This property is of type **CipherMode**, which may be ECB, which encrypts each block individually; CBC, which introduces feedback; CFB or OFB, which use a shift register to process data in smaller chunks; or CTS, which is a slight variation of the CBC mode of operation.
Padding	Gets or sets the padding mode used in the symmetric algorithm, which is used to fill any remaining bytes of the last block. This property is of type **PaddingMode**, which may be one of three values: **PKCS7**, which indicates that each padding byte is equal to the total number of padding bytes; **Zeros**, which indicates that the padding bytes are all zero; or **None**, which means that no padding is used. For encryption algorithms that specify a specific padding scheme, this property is ignored.

TABLE 3-2	Public Methods in the SymmetricAlgorithm Class

Public Method	Description
Clear	This method calls **Dispose**, which frees resources used by the symmetric algorithm. This method returns **void**.
Create	This overloaded static method is used to create a **SymmetricAlgorithm**-derived object to perform encryption and decryption. This method returns a reference to a **SymmetricAlgorithm** object.
CreateDecryptor	This overloaded method is used to create a symmetric decryptor object using a key and initialization vector that is either implicitly or explicitly provided. This method returns a reference to an **ICryptoTransform** interface that can be used to transform data blocks.
CreateEncryptor	This overloaded method is used to create a symmetric encryptor object using a key and initialization vector that is either implicitly or explicitly provided. This method returns a reference to an **ICryptoTransform** interface that can be used to transform data blocks.
Equals	This overloaded virtual method, inherited from **Object**, is used to compare two **SymmetricAlgorithm**-derived objects for equality. This method returns **bool**.
GenerateIV	This abstract method, when overridden in a derived class, generates a new random initialization vector. This method returns **void**; however, the generated IV becomes the new default IV for the **SymmetricAlgorithm**-derived object.
GenerateKey	This abstract method, when overridden in a derived class, generates a new random key. This method returns **void**; however, the generated key becomes the new default key for the **SymmetricAlgorithm**-derived object.
GetHashCode	This method, inherited from **Object**, produces a hash value of the **SymmetricAlgorithm**-derived object. This method returns **int**.
GetType	This method, inherited from **Object**, is used to get the type of the **SymmetricAlgorithm**-derived object. This method returns **Type**.
ToString	This virtual method, inherited from **Object**, is used to produce a **String** object that represents the **SymmetricAlgorithm** derived object.
ValidKeySize	This method determines whether the specified key size is valid for the current algorithm. This method returns **bool**.

Each of these algorithm-specific abstract classes is further derived into concrete classes that implement each of the supported symmetric algorithms. The .NET Framework provides one such concrete class for each of these algorithms; however, CSPs may choose to implement their own implementation classes to enable proprietary enhancements, or to take advantage of custom encryption hardware, and so on. The public properties and certain of the public methods described previously for the **SymmetricAlgorithm** class are

Namespace: System.Security.Cryptography

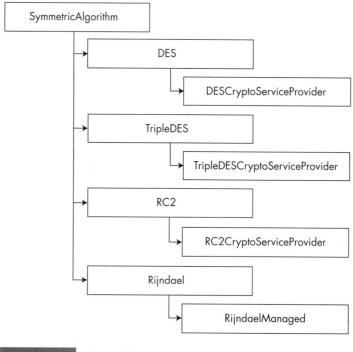

FIGURE 3-8   *The symmetric algorithm hierarchy.*

implemented in each case. For security reasons, each of these concrete classes is sealed, which means that they cannot be inherited from for further customization. The four concrete classes provided out of the box are

- **DESCryptoServiceProvider**[9] is a wrapper class that provides access to the underlying default CSP implementation of DES, which is part of the Win32 CryptoAPI.
- **TripleDESCryptoServiceProvider** is a wrapper class that provides access to the CSP implementation of Triple DES, which is part of the CryptoAPI.

---

9. Classes with names ending in CryptoServiceProvider are wrapper classes that use the underlying Win32 CryptoAPI for their implementation. These are typically older algorithms. Classes with names ending in Managed are entirely new implementations that are written in managed code. These are typically newer algorithms, although a few older algorithms are implemented in both forms.

- **RC2CryptoServiceProvider** is a wrapper class that provides access to the default CSP implementation of RC2, which is part of the CryptoAPI.

- **RijndaelManaged** is a managed class implementation of the Rijndael algorithm. This class is not a wrapper for the underlying unmanaged CryptoAPI.

The SymmetricAlgorithms Example

In this section, we look at the **SymmetricAlgorithms** example program provided for this chapter. This example demonstrates how to encrypt and decrypt with each of the four **SymmetricAlgorithms**-derived concrete class. Figure 3–9 shows the **SymmetricAlgorithms** example being used to encrypt and decrypt a plaintext message.

Now let's look at the code in the **SymmetricAlgorithms** example. This program is somewhat contrived in that it encrypts and then decrypts the data all within a single Form. More realistic scenarios would probably call for transmission or storage of ciphertext; however, for convenience, the purpose of this example is to show the whole story all in one simple, compact form-based example program. To simulate the realistic scenario, five fields have

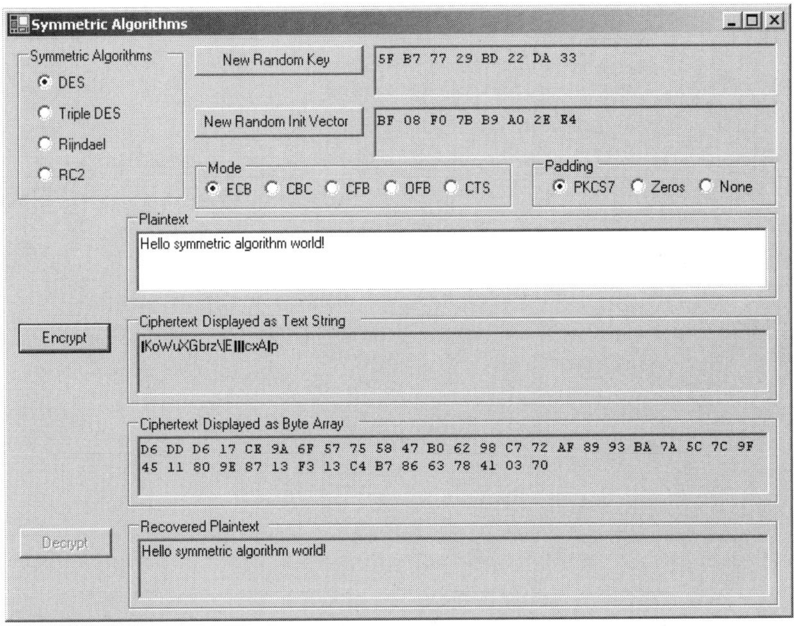

FIGURE 3-9 *The SymmetricAlgorithms example program.*

been added to the **Form**-derived **SymmetricAlgorithms** class, which are used to communicate all the required information from the encryption method to the decryption method. These are fields in this example rather than data to be communicated between participants. In real life, the key, initialization vector, cipher mode, and padding mode would have to be previously agreed upon between the communicating parties. The cipher bytes would of course be sent via some communications channel. These fields are the byte arrays named **Key**, **IV**, **Mode**, **Padding**, and **cipherbytes**:

```
//variables communicated from encrypt to decrypt
byte[] Key;
byte[] IV;
CipherMode Mode;
PaddingMode Padding;
byte[] cipherbytes;
```

When the form initially loads, the following method is called to handle the event. The **Key** and **IV** fields are initialized with new random key and IV byte arrays. The cipher mode and padding convention are established according to the initial state of the associated radio buttons.

```
private void Form1_Load(
   object sender, System.EventArgs e)
{
   //setup initial key, iv, mode, and padding
   GenIV();
   GenKey();
   EstablishMode();
   EstablishPadding();
}
```

There are several methods in the program (including GenIV and GenKey) that need to create a symmetric algorithm object. This functionality is encapsulated in the **CreateSymmetricAlgorithm** method. This method simply creates and returns a **SymmetricAlgorithm**-derived object according to the currently selected radio button choices of RC2, Rijndael, DES, and Triple DES. In each case the corresponding static **Create** method is called to create the desired object.

```
SymmetricAlgorithm CreateSymmetricAlgorithm()
{
   //create new instance of symmetric algorithm
   if (radioButtonRC2.Checked == true)
      return RC2.Create();
   if (radioButtonRijndael.Checked == true)
      return Rijndael.Create();
   if (radioButtonDES.Checked == true)
      return DES.Create();
```

```
   if (radioButtonTripleDES.Checked == true)
      return TripleDES.Create();
   return null;
}
```

The most important methods in the program are those that actually encrypt and decrypt data using the currently selected algorithm with the current values for key and initialization vector fields. These methods are actually handlers for button-click events, with the names **buttonEncrypt_Click** and **buttonDecrypt_Click**. Note that the **CreateSymmetricAlgorithm** method is called again in both the encryption and decryption methods. The **MemoryStream** and **CryptoStream** classes are also used here, which will be briefly described shortly. Here is the code for the encryption method followed by the decryption method.

```
private void buttonEncrypt_Click(
   object sender, System.EventArgs e)
{
   //do UI stuff
   ...

   //establish symmetric algorithm
   SymmetricAlgorithm sa =
      CreateSymmetricAlgorithm();

   //use current key and iv
   sa.Key = Key;
   sa.IV = IV;

   //use current mode and padding
   sa.Mode = Mode;
   sa.Padding = Padding;

   //establish crypto stream
   MemoryStream ms = new MemoryStream();
   CryptoStream cs = new CryptoStream(
      ms,
      sa.CreateEncryptor(),
      CryptoStreamMode.Write);

   //write plaintext bytes to crypto stream
   byte[] plainbytes =
      Encoding.UTF8.GetBytes(textPlaintext.Text);
   cs.Write(plainbytes, 0, plainbytes.Length);
   cs.Close();
   cipherbytes = ms.ToArray();
   ms.Close();

   //display ciphertext as text string
   ...
```

```csharp
    //display ciphertext byte array in hex format
    ...

    //do UI stuff
    ...
}

private void buttonDecrypt_Click(
    object sender, System.EventArgs e)
{
    //establish symmetric algorithm
    SymmetricAlgorithm sa =
        CreateSymmetricAlgorithm();

    //use current key and iv
    sa.Key = Key;
    sa.IV = IV;

    //use current mode and padding
    sa.Mode = Mode;
    sa.Padding = Padding;

    //establish crypto stream
    MemoryStream ms = new MemoryStream(cipherbytes);
    CryptoStream cs = new CryptoStream(
        ms,
        sa.CreateDecryptor(),
        CryptoStreamMode.Read);

    //read plaintext bytes from crypto stream
    byte[] plainbytes =
        new Byte[cipherbytes.Length];
    cs.Read(plainbytes, 0, cipherbytes.Length);
    cs.Close();
    ms.Close();

    //display recovered plaintext
    ...

    //do UI stuff
    ...
}
```

Cryptographic Streams

The Common Language Runtime (CLR) supports a stream-oriented design for cryptographic operations. The class that encapsulates a cryptographic stream is named, not surprisingly, **CryptoStream**. Any cryptographic operations that provide a **CryptoStream** object can be connected with other **CryptoStream** objects. By chaining cryptographic streams together in this way, the output from the one object is passed directly into the input of the next, and no separate storage needs to be provided for the intermediate results.

The **CryptoStream** is a handy class that allows you to read and write data via a cipher stream object just as you would perform simple data input/ output on a file or socket stream object. The **CryptoStream** class can be instantiated for encryption (writing mode) or decryption (reading mode). Since our **SymmetricAlgorithms** example program uses an in-memory byte array to represent plaintext and ciphertext, the **MemoryStream** class is used to enable I/O operations to be performed on these in-memory buffers. Here is the constructor for **CryptoStream**:

```
public CryptoStream(
    Stream stream,
    ICryptoTransform transform,
    CryptoStreamMode mode
);
```

By passing in a freshly created **Stream** object, an **ICryptoTransform** encryptor object associated with the desired symmetric encryption algorithm, and the **CryptoStreamMode.Write** value to indicate I/O direction, we effectively create a **CryptoStream** object that can encrypt all data that is written to it.

```
MemoryStream ms = new MemoryStream();
CryptoStream cs = new CryptoStream(
    ms,
    sa.CreateEncryptor(),
    CryptoStreamMode.Write);
```

Once you have this output **CryptoStream** object established, you can write bytes to it, which are automatically encrypted by the **ICryptoTransform** object and written to the associated **Stream** object (which is a **MemoryStream** object in this example, but it could be a file or socket).

```
    cs.Write(plainbytes, 0, plainbytes.Length);
    cs.Close();
```

By passing in a **MemoryStream** object based on a specified ciphertext byte array, an **ICryptoTransform** decryptor object, and the **CryptoStreamMode.Read** mode, we effectively create a **CryptoStream** object that can decrypt all data read from it.

```
MemoryStream ms = new MemoryStream(cipherbytes);
CryptoStream cs = new CryptoStream(
    ms,
    sa.CreateDecryptor(),
    CryptoStreamMode.Read);
```

Once you have this input **CryptoStream** object established, you can read bytes from the **Stream** object, which are automatically decrypted by the **ICryptoTransform** object and placed into a byte array.

```
cs.Read(plainbytes, 0, cipherbytes.Length);
cs.Close();
```

When you run this example program, you may notice that certain combinations of cipher modes and padding conventions do not work with all symmetric algorithm choices. For example, if you choose the OFB cipher mode along with any of the four algorithm choices, you will see a **CryptographicException** being thrown, with the message *Output feedback mode (OFB) is not supported by this implementation*. This exception is shown in Figure 3–10.

Another example of this type of problem occurs when you try to use Rijndael with either **Zeros** or **None** for the padding value. This results in another **CryptographicException** with the message *Input buffer contains insufficient data*. This is shown in Figure 3–11. It is instructive to see these errors in an example program, but, obviously, these errors should be avoided in actual working programs.

Avoiding Weak Keys

There is a public static method of the **DES** and **TripleDES** classes named **IsWeakKey**, which takes a byte array containing a key as a parameter, and it returns a boolean result. As you can guess by its name, this method can be used to determine if a particular key is weak. As you can also guess, a weak

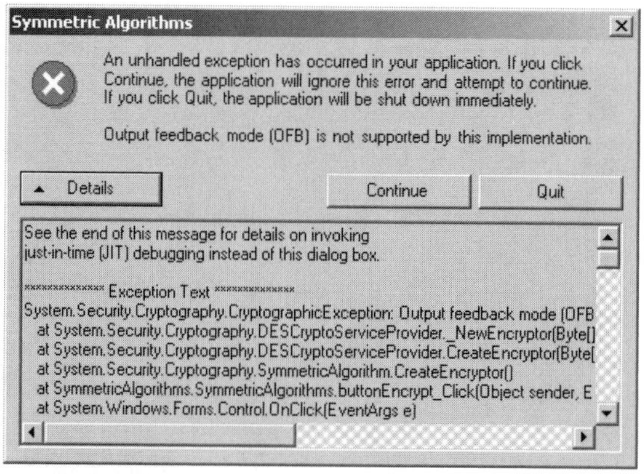

FIGURE 3-10   *OFB is not supported by the current implementation.*

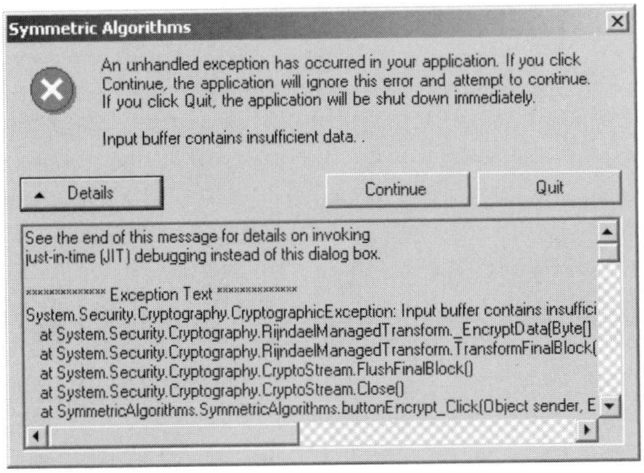

FIGURE 3-11   *Rijndael is incompatible with padding set to Zeros or None.*

key results in a cipher that is easy to break. A weak key has the following characteristic: If plaintext is encrypted with a weak key, then encrypting it again (rather than the normal decrypting) with the same weak key returns the original plaintext.

Because 3DES is based directly on DES, the keys that are weak with respect to DES are also weak when used with 3DES. There are no known weak keys for RC2 and Rijndael algorithms, and therefore, the **RC2** and **Rijndael** classes do not support the **IsWeakKey** method.

There have been four DES keys that have been found to be weak, and, obviously, these weak keys should be avoided. However, it turns out that this whole issue of weak keys is not really much to worry about, since picking a weak key at random is an extremely low probability. Since DES has a 56-bit key there are 2^{56} keys available. The number of weak keys is only four, which is 2^2. That means that the probability of getting a bad key is only 2^{-54}. There are also 12 keys that are considered semi-weak, but that still leaves the probability of using one of these keys so low that we probably do not need to worry about it.

In any case, most programs use the secret key that is generated automatically by the symmetric cipher object's constructor, which will never produce a weak key. If you create a new key by calling the **GenerateKey** method, you are again guaranteed not to get a weak key. In cases where you use a key obtained in some other way, such as from a CSP or another external source, the **DES** and **TripleDES** classes will throw a **CryptographicException** if you try to encrypt with a weak key anyway. In any case, for those of you who tend to worry about such things, you can explicitly test whether any particular key is in fact a weak key using the **IsWeakKey** method.

Key Exchange Issues

One problem with symmetric cryptographic schemes is that distinct keys must be stored on each machine for each communicating pair to enable the sending and receiving of encrypted data. This means that the number of keys that need to be maintained as secrets by all communicating parties grows rapidly as the number of parties increases. If you have N parties, then the maximum number of keys that are potentially needed is the sum of the numbers from 1 to $N - 1$. Figure 3–12 shows how these keys start to proliferate for $N = 1$ and $N = 4$. Note that the number of required keys grows faster than the number of communicating parties. We will see how to solve this problem efficiently in the next chapter, using asymmetric algorithms to reduce the number of keys required by multiple parties so that the number of private keys remains equal to the number of parties.

There is another problem that must be addressed regarding symmetric cryptography. Despite that the symmetric key proliferation problem can be annoying, symmetric algorithms are powerful, fast, and generally more suit-

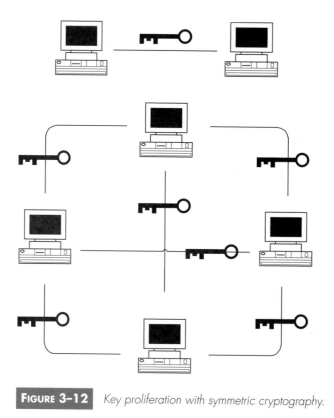

FIGURE 3-12   *Key proliferation with symmetric cryptography.*

able for bulk data encryption than asymmetric algorithms. Therefore, we must be able to exchange symmetric session keys. The problem is that sharing a secret key requires the secure communication of that key from one party to another in order to establish a secure communications channel. This appears to be a catch-22[10] situation, since it seems that you need to be able to communicate securely before you can start to communicate securely! Fortunately, there are reasonable solutions to this riddle.

The **NaiveKeyExchange** program examples (**Sender.exe** and **Receiver.exe**) show a simple-minded approach to exchanging keys by directly writing and reading the key information via an unencrypted disk file. Alternatively, an ordinary socket connection could be used to communicate the keys over a network. The obvious problem with this is that the secret key is not really a secret at all. In fact, it is accessible in the clear, which could be exploited by an interloper if you are not careful. This key exchange scheme works better if special care is taken to ensure that the key was not exposed, such as by encrypting it before being sent. This of course appears to be another catch-22![11] We will see how to solve this key exchange conundrum in the next chapter, using the **RSACryptoServiceProvider** and **CspParameters** classes to encrypt and store the symmetric session key in a very convenient and secure manner.

Encrypted Hash Codes and Message Integrity

The primary concerns in security are confidentiality, integrity, and authentication. We have seen how symmetric encryption can be used to achieve confidentiality, (i.e., keeping data secret from unauthorized parties). Now, what about integrity and authentication? Integrity means preventing, or at least detecting, unauthorized modification of the data. Authentication means determining the true origin or author of the data. It turns out that both symmetric encryption and asymmetric encryption algorithms can be used to ensure integrity and authentication. We now look at how symmetric encryption can be used for these purposes. Chapter 4 explains how to use asymmetric encryption

---

10. If you could send the secret key securely, then you might argue that you wouldn't need the symmetric cryptosystem in the first place, since you could just use that secure channel to send your message instead of the key. Possible solutions to this riddle are to use a temporarily available secure channel, a trusted courier, or an asymmetric key exchange protocol, such as the RSA or Diffie-Hellman key exchange algorithms.

11. This catch-22 results from our need to encrypt the key that will be used to encrypt the data. This implies that for the encrypted key to be secure, we would need to encrypt the key that encrypted the key that encrypted the data, and so on ad infinitum.

techniques, such as RSA and DSA, which can be used for applying digital signatures to data to assure integrity and authentication.

Assume that Alice and Bob are the only people who know the value of a secret shared key. Also, assume that Alice and Bob trust one another to keep the key secret from everyone else. If either one ever receives any encrypted message that can be successfully decrypted into a valid plaintext message, then they can be quite confident that the message did indeed come from the other person who knows the secret key. This is because it would be exceedingly difficult for any other person to successfully create a valid ciphertext without knowing the key.

The only question that remains here is what "valid plaintext message" means in the previous paragraph. The most effective way to prove the validity of a message is to calculate a cryptographic hash value from the message. As long as the message remains unmodified (i.e., valid), its hash function can be recalculated and compared against the original hash value. If the hash value has not changed, the probability that the message has not been altered is exceedingly high.

Of course, it is not really sufficient to just calculate this hash value, since an adversary can also calculate hash functions at will, allowing that person to modify the message along with a brand new hash value. This would not effectively support either integrity or authentication. However, if Alice first calculates the hash value and then encrypts that hash value with a secret key, then this becomes a very effective solution. Alice then sends the message (encrypted or nonencrypted, since we are not discussing confidentiality now) along with the encrypted hash to Bob. Bob can decrypt the received hash and compare it against a freshly recalculated hash on the received message data. If the hashes match, then integrity and authentication are verified to a very high probability. The adversary now has a difficult challenge indeed. If he were to modify the message, he could calculate a new hash value, but he could not encrypt a new hash value without knowing the secret key, and the original hash value would no longer match the modified message data.

There is now a bit of explanation required on exactly what is meant by the term *cryptographic hash*. Let's start by describing a slightly weaker term. A *hash function* is any function that maps an arbitrary-length input data to produce a relatively small, fixed-length data output. The CRC-32 checksum is a simple example of a hash function, which has long been used for data error detection. A cryptographic hash function is basically the same, but it has some additional properties. For example, it must be very difficult to find two distinct inputs that produce the same hash output (which is not true of the CRC-32 checksum). Also, it should be a one-way function, meaning that it is easy to compute the hash value but virtually impossible to reverse-engineer the original data from the hash value. A good cryptographic hash function should also produce many unpredictable bit changes in the hash value even when very small (i.e., single bit) changes are made to the input data. A cryptographic hash is used as manageable-sized data representation that is highly character-istic of the data and very difficult to forge, which makes it quite analogous to a human fingerprint.

The following cryptographic hash classes are provided by the .NET frame-work, all of which are derived from the **HashAlgorithm** abstract class. All of the following classes on the left are abstract classes that are derived into con-crete classes, listed on the right. The MD in MD5 stands for message digest, which is an alternative name for a cryptographic hash. The SHA in SHA-1, SHA-256, and so on stands for Secure Hash Algorithm, which was originally designed by NIST and the NSA for use in the Digital Signature Algorithm (DSA).

- **KeyedHashAlgorithm**, which derives into **HMACSHA1** and **MACTripleDES**
- **MD5**, which derives into **MD5CryptoServiceProvider**
- **SHA1**, which derives into **SHA1Managed** and **SHA1CryptoServiceProvider**
- **SHA256**, which derives into **SHA256Managed**
- **SHA384**, which derives into **SHA384Managed**
- **SHA512**, which derives into **SHA512Managed**

The **EncryptedHash** example program demonstrates how encrypting the cryptographic hash of a message can be used to verify the data's integrity. In this example the plaintext is first hashed using the MD5 hash algorithm, and then that hash value is encrypted using the DES symmetric algorithm. In a realistic scenario, the message and its encrypted hash bytes would be trans-mitted to a separate receiver program that would decrypt and validate the hash value. However, to keep this example simple and compact, all the work that would normally be done by the sending and receiving programs is done in one simple program.

```
...
//Create MD5 hash bytes from plaintext bytes
MD5CryptoServiceProvider md5 =
   new MD5CryptoServiceProvider();
byte[] hashBytes =
   md5.ComputeHash(plaintextBytes);
...
//encrypt hash bytes using DES
SymmetricAlgorithm sa = DES.Create();
MemoryStream msEncrypt =
   new MemoryStream();
CryptoStream csEncrypt = new CryptoStream(
   msEncrypt,
   sa.CreateEncryptor(),
   CryptoStreamMode.Write);
csEncrypt.Write(hashBytes,
   0, hashBytes.Length);
```

```
csEncrypt.Close();
byte[] encryptedHashBytes = msEncrypt.ToArray();
msEncrypt.Close();
...
//decrypt hash bytes using DES
MemoryStream msDecrypt =
    new MemoryStream(encryptedHashBytes);
CryptoStream csDecrypt = new CryptoStream(
    msDecrypt,
    sa.CreateDecryptor(),
    CryptoStreamMode.Read);
byte[] decryptedHashBytes =
    new Byte[encryptedHashBytes.Length];
csDecrypt.Read(decryptedHashBytes,
    0, encryptedHashBytes.Length);
csDecrypt.Close();
msDecrypt.Close();
...
//compare original and decrypted hash bytes
bool match = true;
for (int i=0; i<hashBytes.Length; i++)
{
    if(hashBytes[i] != decryptedHashBytes[i])
    {
        match = false;
        break;
    }
}
if(match)
    Console.WriteLine(
        "The hash values match!");
else
    Console.WriteLine(
        "The hash values do not match!");
```

Keyed Hash Functions and Message Integrity

A keyed hash algorithm is a cryptographic hash function that takes a key as an additional parameter when it is used to hash the data. This means that you do not have to explicitly take the second step of encrypting the hash to ensure data integrity or to prove authenticity, since this effectively happens automatically.

The **KeyedHashAlgorithm** abstract class represents all implementations of keyed hash algorithms. Currently, there are only two derived implementation classes: **HMACSHA1** and **MACTripleDES**. These concrete classes are used to determine if data has been tampered with, based on the assumption that only sender and receiver know the secret key. In this example, the sender computes the HMAC[12] hash for the data, using the secret key, and sends it along with the original data. The receiver recalculates the HMAC hash on the received data, using the same key, and verifies that the data is legitimate. Since virtually any change that might be made to the data produces a mismatched hash value, the message can thus be validated. **HMACSHA1** accepts any key size and produces a 20-byte hash value.

The **HMACSHA1Example** example shows how to calculate keyed hash bytes on a text string entered by the user. Again, no attempt is made here to implement sender and receiver programs. Instead, a simple program is used to show the basic ideas. An actual sender and receiver would simply calculate the keyed hash independently, and the receiver would compare the result with the keyed hash calculated by the sender. If they match, the message is authenticated; otherwise, it is deemed to be corrupt. The only provision that would need to be made is that the sender and receiver must secretly agree beforehand on the key to be used. Then, the sender sends the message, along with the associated keyed hash value to the receiver. The receiver recalculates the keyed hash value with the secret key and compares the result.

```
//get plaintext string from user
Console.WriteLine("Enter a plaintext string:");
String plaintextString = Console.ReadLine();

//Convert plaintext string to byte array
Byte[] plaintextBytes =
    (new UnicodeEncoding()).GetBytes(
    plaintextString);

//Create keyed hash bytes from plaintext bytes
byte[] key = new byte[16];
HMACSHA1 hmac = new HMACSHA1(key);
CryptoStream cs = new CryptoStream(
    Stream.Null, hmac, CryptoStreamMode.Write);
cs.Write(
    plaintextBytes, 0, plaintextBytes.Length);
cs.Close();
byte[] keyedHashBytes = hmac.Hash;
    //display keyed hash bytes
Console.WriteLine(
    "Keyed hash bytes of plaintext string:\n" +
    BitConverter.ToString(keyedHashBytes));
```

---

12. HMAC is a mechanism for message authentication using cryptographic hash functions. See RFC 2104.

Summary

This chapter focused on symmetric algorithms and the .NET Framework classes that implement them. In particular, we looked at the DES, Triple DES, Rijndael, and RC2 algorithms along with related details, such as modes of operation and padding conventions. We also looked at how to make use of the **Symmetric-Algorithm**-derived classes in the .NET Framework to keep secrets. In passing, we also took advantage of the opportunity to introduce the **CryptoStream** class as well as the cryptographic hash classes. Other topics that were touched on include issues related to the symmetric key exchange problem.

Asymmetric Cryptography

*M*odern computing has generated a tremendous need for convenient, manageable encryption technologies. Symmetric algorithms, such as Triple DES and Rijndael, provide efficient and powerful cryptographic solutions, especially for encrypting bulk data. However, under certain circumstances, symmetric algorithms can come up short in two important respects: key exchange and trust. In this chapter we consider these two shortcomings and learn how asymmetric algorithms solve them. We then look at how asymmetric algorithms work at a conceptual level in the general case, with emphasis on the concept of trapdoor one-way functions. This is followed by a more detailed analysis of RSA, which is currently the most popular asymmetric algorithm. Finally, we see how to use RSA in a typical program using the appropriate .NET Security Framework classes.

We focus on the basic idea of asymmetric algorithms, and we look at RSA in particular from the encryption/decryption point of view. In Chapter 5 we explore using the RSA and DSA asymmetric algorithms as they relate to authentication and integrity checking, involving a technology known as digital signatures. For a more thorough discussion of RSA from a mathematical point of view, please see Appendix B.

Problems with Symmetric Algorithms

One big issue with using symmetric algorithms is the key exchange problem, which can present a classic catch-22. The other main issue is the problem of trust between two parties that share a secret symmetric key. Problems of trust may be encountered when encryption is used for authentication and integrity checking. As we saw in Chapter 3, a symmetric key can be used to verify the identity of the other communicating party, but as we will now see, this requires that one party trust the other.

The Key Exchange Problem

The key exchange problem arises from the fact that communicating parties must somehow share a secret key before any secure communication can be initiated, and both parties must then ensure that the key remains secret. Of course, direct key exchange is not always feasible due to risk, inconvenience, and cost factors. The catch-22 analogy refers to the question of how to securely communicate a shared key before any secure communication can be initiated.

In some situations, direct key exchange is possible; however, much commercial data exchange now takes place between parties that have never previously communicated with one another, and there is no opportunity to exchange keys in advance. These parties generally do not know one another sufficiently to establish the required trust (a problem described in the next section) to use symmetric algorithms for authentication purposes either. With the explosive growth of the Internet, it is now very often a requirement that parties who have never previously communicated be able to spontaneously communicate with each other in a secure and authenticated manner. Fortunately, this issue can be dealt with effectively by using asymmetric algorithms.[1]

The Trust Problem

Ensuring the integrity of received data and verifying the identity of the source of that data can be very important. For example, if the data happens to be a contract or a financial transaction, much may be at stake. To varying degrees, these issues can even be legally important for ordinary email correspondence, since criminal investigations often center around who knew what and when they knew it. A symmetric key can be used to check the identity of the individual who originated a particular set of data, but this authentication scheme can encounter some thorny problems involving trust.

---

1. Asymmetric algorithms are also known as public key algorithms, which can be misleading, since there are actually two keys involved; one is public, and the other is private. The term *public key algorithm* is intended to contrast with the idea of symmetric algorithms, where there is no public key but rather only a single secret key.

As you may recall from Chapter 3, in this technique the data is hashed, and the resulting hash is encrypted using a shared secret key with a symmetric algorithm. The recipient, who also knows the secret key, is sent the data along with the encrypted hash value. The recipient then decrypts the hash using the shared key, and the result is verified against a fresh recalculation of the hash value on the data received. This works because only someone who knows the secret key is capable of correctly encrypting the hash of the original data such that it will match the recalculated hash value computed by the recipient. This verifies the identity of the data source. As an added bonus, this technique verifies data integrity in that any individual who is ignorant of the secret key could not have tampered with the data.

This is great if you have the luxury of establishing the shared secret beforehand, but there is an additional problem here. What if you cannot trust the other party with whom you have shared the secret key? The problem is that this scheme cannot discriminate between the two individuals who know the shared key. For example, your pen pal may fraudulently send messages using your shared key, pretending to be you. This would allow your friend to write IOUs to himself in your name, making this scheme useless in any trust-lacking relationship. Other problems could arise if your partner shared the secret key with others without telling you about it. Suddenly, you would have no leg to stand on if certain disputes were to arise. For example, your partner could renege on a contract by claiming that someone else must have obtained the key from you and signed off on a deal in his name. This problem is known as repudiation,[2] and we often need a way to enforce nonrepudiation between untrusting parties. The basic problem with all this is that any symmetric algorithm scheme requires that one party can safely trust the other party, which often is not realistic.

Fortunately, asymmetric algorithms can be used to solve these problems by performing the same basic operations but encrypting the hash using a private key (belonging to an asymmetric key pair) that one individual and only one individual knows. Then anyone can use the associated public key to verify the hash. This effectively eliminates the problems of trust and repudiation.[3]

---

2. The word *repudiation* means refusal to acknowledge a contract or debt. You will frequently encounter its antonym, nonrepudiation, in discussions on digital signatures.

3. Actually, asymmetric algorithms cannot solve all these problems entirely on their own. For a complete solution, we generally need to resort to enlisting the help of a trusted third party, known as a certificate authority, who takes on the formal responsibility of verifying and vouching for the identities of its clients. For the full story on how asymmetric algorithms and certificate authorities together solve these problems, please see Chapter 5.

This technique is called a digital signature, which is the main topic of the next chapter.

The Idea Behind Asymmetric Cryptography

In the 1970s Martin Hellman, Whitfield Diffie, and, independently, Ralph Merkle invented a beautiful cryptographic idea. Their idea was to solve the key exchange and trust problems of symmetric cryptography by replacing the single shared secret key with a pair of mathematically related keys, one of which can be made publicly available and another that must be kept secret by the individual who generated the key pair. The advantages are obvious. First, no key agreement is required in advance, since the only key that needs to be shared with the other party is a public key that can be safely shared with everyone. Second, whereas the security of a symmetric algorithm depends on two parties successfully keeping a key secret, an asymmetric algorithm requires only the party that generated it to keep it secret. This is clearly much less problematic. Third, the issue of trusting the other party disappears in many scenarios, since without knowledge of your secret key, that party cannot do certain evil deeds, such as digitally sign a document with your private key or divulge your secret key to others.

Asymmetric cryptography does not replace symmetric cryptography. Rather, it is important to recognize the relative strengths and weaknesses of both techniques so that they can be used appropriately and in a complementary manner. Symmetric algorithms tend to be much faster than asymmetric algorithms, especially for bulk data encryption. They also provide much greater security than asymmetric algorithms for a given key size. On the down side, symmetric key cryptography requires that the secret key be securely exchanged and then remain secret at both ends. In a large network using symmetric encryption many key pairs will proliferate, all of which must be securely managed. Because the secret key is exchanged and stored in more than one place, the symmetric key must be changed frequently, perhaps even on a per-session basis. Finally, although symmetric keys can be used for message authentication in the form of a keyed secure hash, the full functionality of a digital signature requires asymmetric encryption techniques, such as RSA or DSA. As we shall see in the next chapter, a symmetric keyed secure hash algorithm can be used to implement a MAC (Message Authentication Code), which provides authentication and integrity but not nonrepudiation. In contrast, asymmetric digital signature algorithms provide authentication, integrity, and nonrepudiation, and enable the services of certificate authorities (CAs).

Using Asymmetric Cryptography

To use asymmetric cryptography, Bob randomly generates a public/private key pair.[4] He allows everyone access to the public key, including Alice. Then, when Alice has some secret information that she would like to send to Bob, she encrypts the data using an appropriate asymmetric algorithm and the public key generated by Bob. She then sends the resulting ciphertext to Bob. Anyone who does not know the matching secret key will have an enormously difficult time retrieving the plaintext from this ciphertext, but since Bob has the matching secret key (i.e., the trapdoor information), Bob can very easily discover the original plaintext. Figure 4–1 shows how asymmetric cryptography is used.

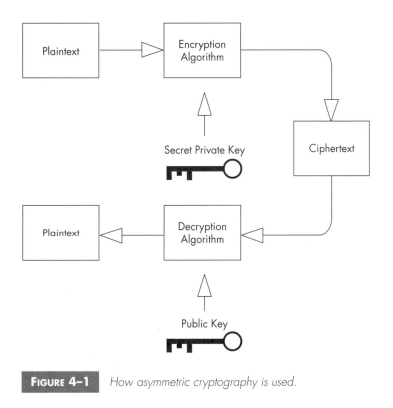

FIGURE 4–1   *How asymmetric cryptography is used.*

---

4. In real life this key pair is generated automatically by a cryptographic application, and the user is typically oblivious to this fact. For example, Microsoft Outlook generates such a key pair, using the underlying Windows CSP (cryptographic service provider), for encrypting and digitally signing secure email messages. PGP (Pretty Good Privacy), which is a freeware tool for secure messaging and data storage, works in a similar manner, but it generates its own keys and works on multiple platforms.

The Combination Lock Analogy

A traditional symmetric cipher is analogous to a lockbox with a combination lock that has one combination used both to open it and close it.[5] The analogy for an asymmetric cipher is a somewhat stranger device: The single lock has two distinct combinations, one for opening it and another for closing it. By keeping one of these combinations secret and making the other combination public, you can effectively control who can place or remove the contents in the lockbox. This added flexibility supports two useful scenarios: confidentiality without prior key exchange and data integrity enforcement.

CONFIDENTIALITY WITHOUT PRIOR KEY EXCHANGE

Here is the first scenario. If you know the public combination for closing the lock but not the private combination for opening the lock, then once you have placed something into the box and locked it, it becomes impossible for anybody who does not know the private opening combination[6] to obtain the contents. This demonstrates spontaneous confidentiality (i.e., keeping a secret without prior key exchange). Hence, we have a solution to the key exchange problem described earlier.

ENFORCING DATA INTEGRITY

The other scenario is if only you know the private combination for closing the lock, and you place contents into the lockbox and then lock it. Then anyone can open the lock, but nobody else can lock other contents into the lockbox, since nobody else knows the private combination for closing the lock. Therefore, nobody else can tamper with its contents and then close the lock again. You might think that this is easy to defeat, since anyone could easily create his or her own key pair and then lock any data into the lockbox. However, only the newly created public key would then work, and the original public key would fail to unlock the lockbox. Therefore, anyone with knowledge of the original public key would not be fooled by such an attack. Since tampering is detectable, this scenario demonstrates how data integrity can be enforced.

---

5. You have to use your imagination just a bit here. Most physical combination locks automatically lock simply by closing them. In this analogy the lock is a bit special in that it requires knowledge of the combination to lock it closed.

6. Even you cannot open it once you have locked it if you do not know the private unlocking combination. Since you placed the contents into the box in the first place, you implicitly know its contents, so this is not often an issue, but this subtle point can occasionally be significant.

Trapdoor One-Way Functions

There are several asymmetric algorithms that make use of this great idea, but all these algorithms have certain mathematical characteristics in common. In each case an asymmetric algorithm is based on a type of function first suggested by Diffie and Hellman that has special properties known as *trapdoor one-way functions*. A trapdoor one-way function, if given some additional secret information, allows much easier computation of its inverse function.

Before discussing what a trapdoor one-way function is, let's look at the broader class of one-way functions.[7] A one-way function is a mathematical function that is highly asymmetric in terms of its computational complexity with respect to its inverse function. Such a function is easy to compute in the forward direction but diabolically difficult to compute in the inverse direction. Such functions are based on *hard* mathematical problems, such as factoring large composites into prime factors, the discrete log problem, and the knapsack problem. The inherent difficulty of such problems falls under the branch of mathematics known as complexity theory, which is beyond the scope of this book. Suffice it to say that the difficulty of these problems grows rapidly in relation to the magnitude of the numbers (which correspond to the key size used in the corresponding cryptographic algorithm) involved.

While finding a solution to the mathematical problem on which a one-way function is based, it is very easy to test if a proposed solution is correct. Imagine yourself working on a large jigsaw puzzle, and you want to find the piece that belongs in a particular position. It might take you a long time to find the correct piece, but at any time that you believe you have good candidate, it takes very little effort to test it out. For a mathematical example, consider the problem of finding all of the prime[8] factors of a large composite number. This is believed to be very difficult,[9] but if you are given the prime factors, testing

---

7. One-way functions are widely believed to exist, and several presumed one-way functions are used heavily in cryptography. Unfortunately, we currently have no formal proofs that they actually do exist!

8. A prime number is a positive integer greater than one that is evenly divisible only by one and itself, such as 2, 3, 5, 7, 11, and so on. A composite number is a positive integer greater than one that is not prime and thus has devisors other than one and itself, such as 4, 6, 8, 9, 10, and so on.

9. Note that this problem is *believed* to be difficult. That is, nobody has yet publicly demonstrated a fast technique for solving this problem, and much evidence indicates that it is very hard. Currently, this is an educated guess, not a proof. But without any hard proof, how confident can we really be? Mathematics is full of examples of clever folks finding devious ways of easily solving problems that appeared to be difficult. According to a story about J. C. F. Gauss, when he was only seven years old, his teacher asked his class to add the integers from 1 to 100. The other children took a very long time, and most did not produce the correct answer. Gauss had the solution 5050 in the blink of an eye, since he realized that it was the sum of 50 pairs, where each pair is equal to 101, or 50*101, which he could do in his head faster than he could write it down.

them is a simple matter of multiplying them together and comparing the result with the original large composite number. To convince yourself of this, imagine trying to find all the prime factors of the composite number 3431 with only pencil and paper to work with. Without the aid of a computer, most people would take several hours to do this. However, if you were asked to test the candidate solution of 47 and 73, you would probably take only a few seconds to show that indeed they do multiply to produce the resulting value of 3431. Now consider that the number 3431 can be represented with a mere 12 bits. What if you tried this experiment with a 1024-bit number? Finding the prime factors is a problem that grows exponentially with bit size (think in terms of billions or trillions of years on a supercomputer), whereas testing a solution grows at a very moderate rate with bit size (microseconds or milliseconds on a personal computer).

The term one-way function is slightly misleading, since by definition, a cipher can only be based on a mathematical function that is invertible, meaning that its inverse function does indeed exist. After all, if a cipher were based on a function that had no inverse, you could encrypt data, but then you could not reliably decrypt that data. However, in practice, the inverse of a one-way function is so difficult to compute that the mere fact that the inverse function exists is of no help whatsoever in computing its value. Such a function is theoretically two-way, but, in practical terms, it is effectively one-way.

Now let's add in the idea of a trapdoor. A trapdoor turns something that is normally very difficult into something that is very easy, provided that you know a powerful little secret. This is analogous to a haunted house where the bookshelf revolves, opening a hidden passageway, but you first need to know that it exists and that the secret to opening it is to pull on the candelabra three times. A one-way function that has the additional property that its inverse function suddenly becomes very easy to compute provided an additional piece of secret information is known (i.e., a private key) becomes a trapdoor one-way function. You can think of a trapdoor one-way function as a haunted mathematical function if you like.

There are many one-way functions to choose from in mathematics, but finding one that allows you to incorporate the all-important backdoor is not so easy. A few candidates have been discovered that are convenient and appear to be secure. Finding those algorithms that are also efficient enough to be practical and use keys of a reasonable size reduces the candidates further. Examples of successful trapdoor one-way functions are the discrete log problem, which forms the basis of the DSA algorithm, and the factoring of large composites into prime factors, which forms the basis of the RSA algorithm.

Advantages of the Asymmetric Approach

With the asymmetric (also known as public key) approach, only the private key must be kept secret, and that secret needs to be kept only by one party.

This is a big improvement in many situations, especially if the parties have no previous contact with one another. However, for this to work, the authenticity of the corresponding public key must typically be guaranteed somehow by a trusted third party, such as a CA. Because the private key needs to be kept only by one party, it never needs to be transmitted over any potentially compromised networks. Therefore, in many cases an asymmetric key pair may remain unchanged over many sessions or perhaps even over several years. Another benefit of public key schemes is that they generally can be used to implement digital signature schemes that include nonrepudiation. Finally, because one key pair is associated with one party, even on a large network, the total number of required keys is much smaller than in the symmetric case.

Combining Asymmetric and Symmetric Algorithms

Since there is no secret key exchange required in order to use asymmetric algorithms, you might be tempted to solve the symmetric key exchange problem by simply replacing the symmetric algorithm with an asymmetric algorithm. However, that would be like throwing the baby out with the bath water. We still want to take advantage of the superior speed and security offered by symmetric algorithms, so, instead, we actually combine the two (and sometimes more than two) algorithms.

For example, Microsoft Outlook and Netscape Communicator implement secure email using the S/MIME (Secure/Multipurpose Internet Mail Extensions) specification. S/MIME is an IETF standard that supports both digital signatures for authentication and encryption for privacy. S/MIME provides bulk message data encryption using any of several symmetric algorithms, including DES, 3DES, and RC2. Secure symmetric key exchange and digital signatures are provided by the RSA asymmetric algorithm as well as either of the MD5 or SHA-1 hash algorithms.

As another example, the popular PGP software (developed by Philip Zimmermann) provides cryptographic services for email and file storage by combining several algorithms to implement useful cryptographic protocols.[10] In this way, message encryption and digital signatures are provided to email clients using an assortment of selected symmetric, asymmetric, and hash algorithms. RSA or ElGamal are used for PGP session key transport. 3DES is one of several alternatives used for bulk PGP message encryption. PGP digital signatures use either RSA or DSA for signing and MD5 or SHA-1 for generating message digests.

There are several other protocols that are built in a hybrid manner by combining asymmetric and symmetric algorithms, including IPSec (IP Security

---

10. For details, see the OpenPGP Message Format RFC 2440 at *http://www.ietf.org/rfc/rfc2440.txt*.

Protocol) and SSL (Secure Sockets Layer). IPSec is an IETF standard that provides authentication, integrity, and privacy services at the datagram layer, allowing the construction of virtual private networks (VPNs). The SSL protocol, developed by Netscape, provides authentication and privacy over the Internet, especially for HTTP (Hypertext Transfer Protocol).

Existing Asymmetric Algorithms

Recall that the only information that needs to be shared before initiating symmetric encryption is the secret key. Since this key is typically very small (typically no greater than 256 bits) compared to the bulk data (which could be megabytes) that must be encrypted, it makes sense to use the asymmetric algorithm to encrypt only the secret symmetric key, and then use this symmetric key for encrypting the arbitrarily large bulk message data. The secret symmetric key is often referred to as a *session key* in this scenario.

There are several asymmetric algorithms in existence today, including RSA, DSA, ElGamal, and ECC. Currently, the most popular is RSA, which stands for Rivest, Shamir, and Adelman, the names of its inventors. RSA is based on the problem of factoring large composite numbers into prime factors. RSA can be used for confidentiality or symmetric key exchange as well as for digital signatures. DSA, which was proposed by NIST in 1991, stands for Digital Signature Algorithm. DSA is somewhat less flexible, since it can be used for digital signatures but not for confidentiality or symmetric key exchange. The ElGamal algorithm, which was invented by Taher ElGamal, is based on the problem of calculating the discrete logarithm in a finite field. EEC stands for Elliptic Curve Cryptography, which was independently proposed in 1985 by Neal Koblitz and V. S. Miller. EEC is not actually an algorithm, but an alternate algebraic system for implementing algorithms, such as DSA, using peculiar mathematical objects known as elliptic curves over finite fields. ElGamal and ECC are not currently supported by .NET out of the box; however, the .NET Framework has been designed to be extensible, making it possible for you or other vendors to provide implementations.

Some asymmetric algorithms, such as RSA and ElGamal, can be used for both encryption and digital signatures. Other asymmetric algorithms, such as DSA, are useful only for implementing digital signatures. It is also generally true that asymmetric algorithms tend to be much slower and less secure than symmetric algorithms for a comparable key size. To be effective, asymmetric algorithms should be used with a larger key size, and, to achieve acceptable performance, they are most applicable to small data sizes. Therefore, asymmetric algorithms are usually used to encrypt hash values and symmetric session keys, both of which tend to be rather small in size compared to typical plaintext data.

RSA: The Most Used Asymmetric Algorithm

The most common asymmetric cipher currently in use is RSA, which is fully supported by the .NET Security Framework. Ron Rivest, Adi Shamir, and Leonard Adleman invented the RSA cipher in 1978 in response to the ideas proposed by Hellman, Diffie, and Merkel. Later in this chapter, we shall see how to use the high-level implementation of RSA provided by the .NET Security Framework. But first, let's look at how RSA works at a conceptual level.

Underpinnings of RSA

Understanding the underpinnings of RSA will help you to develop a deeper appreciation of how it works. In this discussion we focus on the concepts of RSA, and in Appendix B we look at two examples of implementing RSA from scratch. One of these examples is **TinyRSA**, which is a toy version that limits its arithmetic to 32-bit integers, and the other is a more realistic, multiprecision implementation named **BigRSA**. You will probably never implement your own RSA algorithm from scratch, since most cryptographic libraries, including the .NET Security Framework, provide excellent implementations (i.e., probably better than I could do). However, the RSA examples in Appendix B should help you to fully understand what goes on in RSA at a deeper level.

Here is how RSA works. First, we randomly generate a public and private key pair. As is always the case in cryptography, it is very important to generate keys in the most random and therefore, unpredictable manner possible. Then, we encrypt the data with the public key, using the RSA algorithm. Finally, we decrypt the encrypted data with the private key and verify that it worked by comparing the result with the original data. Note that we are encrypting with the public key and decrypting with the private key. This achieves confidentiality. In the next chapter, we look at the flip side of this approach, encrypting with the private key and decrypting with the public key, to achieve authentication and integrity checking.

Here are the steps for generating the public and private key pair.

1. Randomly select two prime numbers p and q. For the algebra to work properly, these two primes must not be equal. To make the cipher strong, these prime numbers should be large, and they should be in the form of arbitrary precision integers with a size of at least 1024 bits.[11]

2. Calculate the product: $n = p \cdot q$.

---

11. In practice, there are other concerns when choosing prime p and q. For example, even if they are large, it turns out to be easy to factor the product if the difference between p and q is small, using a technique known as Fermat's factorization algorithm.

3. Calculate the Euler totient[12] for these two primes, which is represented by the Greek letter ϕ. This is easily computed with the formula $\phi = (p-1) \cdot (q-1)$.

4. Now that we have the values n and ϕ, the values p and q will no longer be useful to us. However, we must ensure that nobody else will ever be able to discover these values. Destroy them, leaving no trace behind so that they cannot be used against us in the future. Otherwise, it will be very easy for an attacker to reconstruct our key pair and decipher our ciphertext.

5. Randomly select a number e (the letter e is used because we will use this value during encryption) that is greater than 1, less than ϕ, and relatively prime to ϕ. Two numbers are said to be relatively prime if they have no prime factors in common. Note that e does not necessarily have to be prime. The value of e is used along with the value n to represent the public key used for encryption.

6. Calculate the unique value d (to be used during decryption) that satisfies the requirement that, if $d \cdot e$ is divided by ϕ, then the remainder of the division is 1. The mathematical notation for this is $d \cdot e = 1 (\text{mod } \phi)$. In mathematical jargon, we say that d is the multiplicative inverse of e modulo ϕ. The value of d is to be kept secret. If you know the value of ϕ, the value of d can be easily obtained from e using a technique known as the Euclidean algorithm. If you know n (which is public), but not p or q (which have been destroyed), then the value of ϕ is very hard to determine. The secret value of d together with the value n represents the private key.

Once we have generated a public/private key pair, we can encrypt a message with the public key with the following steps.

1. Take a positive integer m to represent a piece of plaintext message. In order for the algebra to work properly, the value of m must be less than the modulus n, which was originally computed as $p \cdot q$. Long messages must therefore be broken into small enough pieces that each piece can be uniquely represented by an integer of this bit size, and each piece is then individually encrypted.

2. Calculate the ciphertext c using the public key containing e and n. This is calculated using the equation $c = m^e (\text{mod } n)$.

---

12. The Euler totient, symbolized with the Greek letter phi, represents the number of positive integers less than or equal to n that are relatively prime to n (i.e., have no prime factors in common with n). One is considered to be relatively prime with all integers.

Finally, we can perform the decryption procedure with the private key using the following steps.

1. Calculate the original plaintext message from the ciphertext using the private key containing d and n. This is calculated using the equation $m = c^d(\text{mod } n)$.

2. Compare this value of m with the original m, and you should see that they are equal, since decryption is the inverse operation to encryption.

A Miniature RSA Example

Here is an example of RSA that is almost simple enough to do with pencil and paper. It is similar in scale to the **TinyRSA** code example discussed in this chapter. The bit size of the numbers used in this example is ridiculously small (32-bit integers) and offers no real security whatsoever, but at a conceptual level, this example provides a complete picture of what actually happens in the RSA algorithm. The advantage of studying this tiny paper and pencil example is that with these very small bit sizes, the underlying concepts are much more tangible and easily visualized. After all, not too many people can do 1024-bit arithmetic in their head! Even working with such tiny 32-bit numbers, the exponentiation step of the algorithm will easily overflow this 32-bit capacity if you are not careful about how you implement it.[13]

Following the conceptual steps outlined above, we start off by choosing two unequal prime numbers p and q.[14] Since we intentionally choose very small values, we prevent subsequent calculations from overflowing the 32-bit integer arithmetic. This also allows us to follow along using the Calculator program provided with Windows to verify the arithmetic.

1. Assume that the random values for the primes p and q have been chosen as

$$p = 47$$

$$q = 73$$

2. Then the product n of these two primes is calculated:

$$n = p \cdot q = 3431$$

---

13. To avoid overflow, you must not use the exponentiation operator directly, but rather iterate multiplications in a loop, and in each iteration, you normalize the result to remain within the bounds of the modulus.

14. Again, in real life, end users are oblivious to these steps. The cryptographic application that they are using will automatically choose these two prime numbers and carry out all the required steps listed here. However, as a programmer, you may on rare occasion need to know how to implement a protocol such as this from scratch.

3. The Euler totient ϕ for these two primes is found easily using the following formula:

$$\phi = (p - 1) \cdot (q - 1) = 3312$$

4. Now that we have n and ϕ, we should discard p and q, and destroy any trace of their existence.

5. Next, we randomly select a number e that is greater than 1, less than n, and relatively prime to phi. Of course, there is more than one choice possible here, and any candidate value you choose may be tested using the Euclidian method.[15] Assume that we choose the following value for e:

$$e = 425$$

6. Then the modular inverse of e is calculated to be the following:

$$d = 1769$$

7. We now keep d private and make e and n public.

Now that we have our private key information d and our public key information e and n, we can proceed with encrypting and decrypting data. As you would probably imagine, this data must be represented numerically to allow the necessary calculations to be performed. In a real-life scenario, the plaintext is typically a hash value or a symmetric key, but it could actually be just about any type of data that you could imagine. Whatever form this data takes, it will have to be somehow represented as a sequence of integer numbers, each with a size that will be limited by the key size that you are using. We do not concern ourselves here with the details of encoding and chunking of the data, but instead we focus on the conceptual aspects of RSA. For this reason, this example simply considers a scenario in which the plaintext data is one simple, small integer value.

1. Assume that we have plaintext data represented by the following simple number:

$$\text{plaintext} = 707$$

2. The encrypted data is computed by $c = m^e(\text{mod } n)$ as follows:

$$\text{ciphertext} = 707^{425}(\text{mod } 3431) = 2142$$

---

15. The Euclidian method is an efficient technique for finding the GCD (greatest common devisor) of any two integers.

3. The ciphertext value cannot be easily reverted back to the original plaintext without knowing d (or, equivalently, knowing the values of p and q). With larger bit sizes, this task grows exponentially in difficulty. If, however, you are privy to the secret information that $d = 1769$, then the plaintext is easily retrieved using $m = c^d(\text{mod } n)$ as follows:

$$\text{plaintext} = 2142^{\wedge}1769(\text{mod } 3431) = 707$$

If you compile the following code, you will verify that the results shown above are correct. While you look at this code, keep in mind that a realistic RSA implementation uses a much larger modulus than $n = 3431$, and a realistic message typically contains too many bits to be represented by a tiny number such as $m = 707$.

```
int m = 707;   //plaintext
int e = 425;   //encryption exponent
int n = 3431;  //modulus
int c = 1;     //ciphertext

//encryption: c = m^e(mod n)
for (int i=0; i<e; i++) //use loop to avoid overflow
{
    c = c*m;
    c = c%n; //normalize within modulus
}
//ciphertext c is now 2142

int d = 1769; //decryption exponent
m = 1; //plaintext

//decryption m = c^d(mod n)
for (int i=0; i<d; i++) //use loop to avoid overflow
{
    m = m*c;
    m = m%n; //normalize within modulus
}
//plaintext m is now 707 matching original value
```

Caveat: Provability Issues

Every asymmetric algorithm is based on some trapdoor one-way function. This leads to a critically important question: How do we know for certain that a particular function is truly one-way? Just because nobody has publicly demonstrated a technique that allows the inverse function to be calculated quickly does not actually prove anything about the security of the algorithm.

If somebody has quietly discovered a fast technique to compute the inverse function, he or she could be busily decrypting enormous amounts of ciphertext every day, and the public may never become aware of it. It may seem paranoid, but high on the list of suspicions are major governments, since they employ large numbers of brilliant mathematicians who are outfitted with the most powerful computing resources available, putting them in a better position than most for cracking the trapdoor.

Most reassuring would be a rigorous mathematical proof of the *inherent difficulty* of computing the inverse function without knowledge of the secret key. With such a proof, further attempts at cracking the backdoor would be futile. Currently, rigorous formal proofs on the security of asymmetric algorithms are sorely lacking. Only in a few specialized (and not so useful) cases have any proofs been demonstrated in the public literature.

In spite of this worrisome lack of evidence, most cryptography experts currently believe that popular asymmetric algorithms, such as RSA, are quite secure given that a sufficient key size is used. Note that this is really just a consensus of learned opinion, which falls well short of a rigorous proof. Of course, considering that most ciphers used throughout history were assumed to be secure at the time that they were used, only to be broken using newly discovered attacks, a certain degree of anxiety is warranted.

In the case of RSA, the entire scheme depends on the widely held opinion that there are no techniques known that will allow an attacker to easily calculate the values of $d, p,$ or q given only the public key containing n and e. Of course, this becomes more effective when you use larger values for p and q. C#'s built-in integer types top out at 64 bits for the long data type, which is nowhere near the size that we need for real asymmetric cryptography applications. Instead, we typically want to use integer data types that are represented by 1024-bit or larger words. Another worry is that this technique depends on a critical assumption that is widely believed to be true but has never been mathematically proven. The assumption is that there are in fact no tricks or fast techniques for factoring pq into its prime factors p and q. In fact, it has never been proven that factoring pq into p and q is the only way to attack RSA. If someone was either smart enough or lucky enough to dismantle these assumptions, that person could become the richest person in the world but would likely be a candidate for assassination.

Programming with .NET Asymmetric Cryptography

In this section, we look at the **RSAAlgorithm** and **SavingKeysAsXml** example programs provided for this chapter. These two code examples show how to encrypt and decrypt using the RSA algorithm as well as how to store and retrieve key information using an XML format. The RSA code example uses the concrete **RSACryptoServiceProvider** class. Figure 4–2 shows where this class resides in the class hierarchy, under the abstract **AsymmetricAlgorithm** class. The other concrete class, **DSACryptoServiceProvider**, is discussed in Chapter 5, where we look at digital signatures.

An RSA Algorithm Example

The **RSAAlgorithm** example uses the **Encrypt** method of the **RSACryptoServiceProvider** class. This method takes two parameters, the first of which is a byte array containing the data to be encrypted. The second parameter is a boolean that indicates the padding mode to be used. Padding is required, since the data to be encrypted is usually not the exact number of required bits in length. Since the algorithm requires specific bit-sized blocks to process properly, padding is used to fill the input data to the desired length. If this second parameter is true, then the improved OAEP[16] padding is used. Otherwise, the traditional PKCS#1 v1.5 padding is used. PKCS#1 v1.5 has been traditionally the most commonly used padding scheme for RSA usage. However, it is recommended that all new RSA applications that will be deployed on platforms that support OAEP should use OAEP. Note that OAEP padding is available on Microsoft Windows XP and Windows 2000 with the

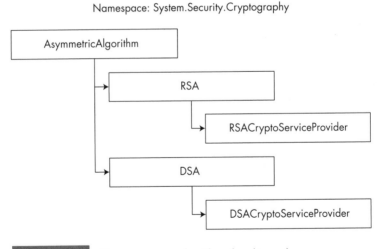

Namespace: System.Security.Cryptography

FIGURE 4–2   *The asymmetric algorithm class hierarchy.*

---

16. OAEP (Optimal Asymmetric Encryption Padding) is a padding technique developed by Mihir Bellare and Phil Rogaway in 1993 for use with RSA. OAEP provides significantly improved security characteristics over the popular PKCS#1 v1.5 padding scheme.

high-encryption pack installed. Unfortunately, previous versions of Windows do not support OAEP, which will cause the **Encrypt** method, with the second parameter set to true, to throw a **CryptographicException**. The **Encrypt** method returns the resulting encrypted data as a byte array. Here is the syntax for the **Encrypt** method.

```
public byte[] Encrypt(
    byte[] rgb,
    bool fOAEP
);
```

The complementary method to **Encrypt** is of course **Decrypt**. You can probably guess how it works. The second parameter is a byte array containing the ciphertext to be decrypted. The second parameter is the same as that in the **Encrypt** method, indicating the padding mode, as described previously. The return value is a byte array that will contain the resulting recovered plaintext. Here is the syntax for the **Decrypt** method.

```
public byte[] Decrypt(
    byte[] rgb,
    bool fOAEP
)
```

Figure 4–3 shows the **RSAAlgorithm** example being used to encrypt and decrypt a plaintext message. You enter the plaintext in the **TextBox** at the top of the form. You then click on the Encrypt button, which fills in all but the last form field, including the resulting ciphertext and RSA parameters that were used. You then click on the Decrypt button, which displays the recovered plaintext in the field at the bottom of the form. Of course, the recovered plaintext should be identical to the original plaintext.

Now let's look at the code in the **RSAAlgorithm** example code. The **buttonEncrypt_Click** method is called when the user clicks on the Encrypt button. This encrypts the contents of the plaintext textbox using the established public RSA key. The public/private RSA key pair is provided by the program automatically when it starts, but it may subsequently be changed using the New RSA Parameters button. There are a few places in the code where user interface elements are being enabled and disabled, which are not germane to our focus on RSA functionality. Therefore, these user interface code sections are ignored here. If you are curious about how these user interface details work, please study the simple code sections following each of the `//do UI stuff` comments.

We first generate the initial RSA parameters by calling the **GenerateNewRSAParams** method in the **RSAAlgorithm_Load** method. The **GenerateNewRSAParams** method is also called each time the user clicks on the New RSA Parameters button, which is handled by the **buttonNewRSAParams_Click** method. The **GenerateNewRSAParams** method is very simple. It just creates

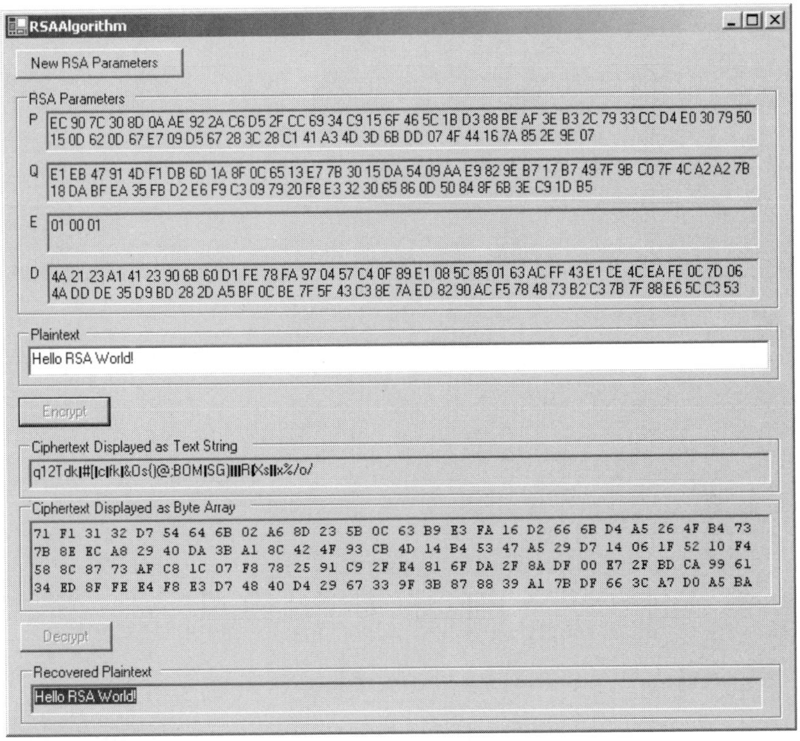

FIGURE 4-3   *The RSAAlgorithm example program.*

an **RSACryptoServiceProvider** class object, stores its public and private RSA parameters by calling the RSA class's **ExportParameters** method, and displays a few of the more important of these parameters in the user interface. These RSA parameters are actually stored in two fields of type **RSAParameters**. The **RSAParameters** field named **rsaParamsExcludePrivate** gets a copy of the public-only RSA parameters (i.e., the modulus and exponent values only), which is required for encryption purposes in the **buttonEncrypt_Click** method. The other **RSAParameters** field, named **rsaParamsIncludePrivate** gets a copy of the combined public and private RSA parameters, which is required in the **buttonDecrypt_Click** method.

Here is the **GenerateNewRSAParams** method. Note that the **Export-Parameters** method is called twice. The first time, the parameter passed into this method is true, and the second time, it is false. Passing true indicates that you want to include all key parameter information, including the private key information. False indicates that only the public key information is to be stored. We separate these cases into two distinct fields to demonstrate how the encryption will use only the public information, but the decryption will use both the public and private key information. This is a crucial point in understanding asymmetric cryptography. This would perhaps be even clearer if we broke the encryption and decryption portions of this example into two separate applications, but this example is provided as a simple monolithic program purely for easy study. You should at some point take a moment to verify that the encryption and decryption functions in this program do indeed use only their own appropriate version of this RSA parameter information, using the corresponding **ImportParameters** method.

```
private void GenerateNewRSAParams()
{
    //establish RSA asymmetric algorithm
    RSACryptoServiceProvider rsa =
        new RSACryptoServiceProvider();

    //provide public and private RSA params
    rsaParamsIncludePrivate =
        rsa.ExportParameters(true);

    //provide public only RSA params
    rsaParamsExcludePrivate =
        rsa.ExportParameters(false);
```

When we create an instance of the **RSACryptoServiceProvider** class, we actually get the RSA implementation provided by the underlying cryptographic service provider (CSP). This class is directly derived from the **RSA** class. The **RSA** class allows other RSA implementations to be implemented as other derived classes; however, the CSP implementation is currently the only one available.

The two fields that store the RSA parameter information when **Export-Parameters** is called are declared as **RSAParameters** type fields, as shown in the following code snippet. The **rsaParamsExcludePrivate** filed will be used for encryption, and the **rsaParamsIncludePrivate** field will be used in decryption in this example.

```
//public modulus and exponent used in encryption
RSAParameters rsaParamsExcludePrivate;

//public and private RSA params use in decryption
RSAParameters rsaParamsIncludePrivate;
```

In the **buttonEncrypt_Click** method we then create a new instance of **RSACryptoServiceProvider** class, and we initialize it with the stored public key information by calling the **RSA** object's **ImportParameters** method, specifying **rsaParamsExcludePrivate** as the parameter. Next, we obtain the plaintext in the form of a byte array named **plainbytes**. Finally, we perform the main function of this method by calling on the **Encrypt** method of the **RSA** object. This returns another byte array, which is an instance field named **cipherbytes**. This is an instance field rather than a local variable, because we need to communicate this byte array to the decryption method, and local variables are not maintained across method calls.

```
private void buttonEncrypt_Click(
   object sender, System.EventArgs e)
{
   //do UI stuff
   ...

   //establish RSA using parameters from encrypt
   RSACryptoServiceProvider rsa =
      new RSACryptoServiceProvider();

   //import public only RSA parameters for encrypt
   rsa.ImportParameters(rsaParamsExcludePrivate);

   //read plaintext, encrypt it to ciphertext
   byte[] plainbytes =
      Encoding.UTF8.GetBytes(textPlaintext.Text);
   cipherbytes =
      rsa.Encrypt(
      plainbytes,
      false); //fOAEP needs high encryption pack

  //display ciphertext as text string
  ...

  //display ciphertext byte array in hex format
  ...

  //do UI stuff
  ...
}
...
//variable communicated from encrypt to decrypt
byte[] cipherbytes;
```

The **buttonDecrypt_Click** method is called when the user clicks on the Decrypt button. Again, an **RSA** object is created. The **RSA** object is repopulated with the information provided by calling the **RSA** object's **ImportParameters** method, but this time, the parameter to this method is the **rsaParamsIncludePrivate**, which includes both public and private RSA key information. The plaintext is then obtained by calling the **Decrypt** method of the **RSA** object. Since a matching set of RSA algorithm parameters were used for both encryption and decryption, the resulting plaintext matches perfectly with the original plaintext.

```
private void buttonDecrypt_Click(
   object sender, System.EventArgs e)
{
   //establish RSA using parameters from encrypt
   RSACryptoServiceProvider rsa =
      new RSACryptoServiceProvider();

   //import public and private RSA parameters
   rsa.ImportParameters(rsaParamsIncludePrivate);

   //read ciphertext, decrypt it to plaintext
   byte[] plainbytes =
      rsa.Decrypt(
      cipherbytes,
      false); //fOAEP needs high encryption pack

//display recovered plaintext
...

//do UI stuff
   ...
}


...
//variable communicated from encrypt to decrypt
byte[] cipherbytes;
```

Saving Keys as XML

You might not always want to transmit the contents of the **ExportParameters** object directly between arbitrary applications, especially between different platforms and cryptographic libraries. After all, the **ExportParameters** class is very Microsoft- and .NET-specific. A much more convenient and generalized format for transmitting a public key is via an XML stream.[17] The **Sav-**

---

17. Transmitting a public key via an **ExportParameters** object or via XML is not a security issue. Of course, you should not make a habit of transmitting private asymmetric keys or symmetric session keys in the clear. To exchange such sensitive key information, you must actually encrypt the encryption key. This may sound a bit like a recursive statement, but it actually makes sense. In Chapter 6 we see how to exchange such encrypted secret key information using established XML cryptography standards.

ingKeysAsXml example program shows how to read and write keys in XML format. This example is almost identical to the **RSAAlgorithm** example we just looked at. The significant difference is that we use XML for storing and transmitting the public key information from the encryption method to the decryption method rather than use an **ExportParameters** object. Another slight difference is that the RSA parameter information is not displayed; the contents of the key XML stream is displayed instead, but that is of course only a user interface detail.

For simplicity and ease of demonstration, this example is again implemented as a single monolithic application. This is purely for ease of demonstration, and it would be straightforward to take this example and break it up into two separate encrypting and decrypting programs. Our purpose here is to show both the sending (encrypting) and receiving (decrypting) code and how the XML data is used to store key information between the two. To make this example somewhat more realistic, the XML data is written to a file rather than stored in a shared field, as was done in the previous example. This simulates the case in a real-world scenario in which you would need to read and write this information to some type of external storage or perhaps via a socket stream. From the programmer's perspective, the most significant change from the previous example is that the calls to the **ExportParameters** and **ImportParameters** methods of the **RSACryptoServiceProvide** class have been replaced with calls to the **ToXmlString** and **FromXmlString** methods of the same class. Once again, a boolean parameter is used to indicate whether private information is included or excluded in the stored key information.

Here is the **GenerateNewRSAParams** method, which serves the same basic purpose as described in the previous program example. The difference is that we are storing the key information in XML format, in two files named **PublicPrivateKey.xml** and **PublicOnlyKey.xml**, by calling the **ToXmlString** method with a boolean parameter. These two files will be used later in the encryption and decryption functions.

```
private void GenerateNewRSAParams()
{
   //establish RSA asymmetric algorithm
   RSACryptoServiceProvider rsa =
      new RSACryptoServiceProvider();

   //provide public and private RSA params
   StreamWriter writer =
      new StreamWriter("PublicPrivateKey.xml");
   string publicPrivateKeyXML =
      rsa.ToXmlString(true);
   writer.Write(publicPrivateKeyXML);
   writer.Close();
```

```
//provide public only RSA params
writer =
   new StreamWriter("PublicOnlyKey.xml");
string publicOnlyKeyXML =
   rsa.ToXmlString(false);
writer.Write(publicOnlyKeyXML);
writer.Close();

//display public and private RSA key
   textBoxPublicKeyXML.Text = publicPrivateKeyXML;

//do UI stuff
...
}
```

Next, let's look at the **buttonEncrypt_Click** method. We create a new **RSACryptoServiceProvider** object and initialize it by calling the **FromXml-String** method with the public key information stored in the **PublicOnly-Key.xml** file. Then we call the **RSA** object's **Encrypt** method to perform the cryptographic transformation on the plaintext.

```
private void buttonEncrypt_Click(
   object sender, System.EventArgs e)
{
   //do UI stuff
   ...

   //establish RSA asymmetric algorithm
   RSACryptoServiceProvider rsa =
      new RSACryptoServiceProvider();

   //public only RSA parameters for encrypt
   StreamReader reader =
      new StreamReader("PublicOnlyKey.xml");
   string publicOnlyKeyXML = reader.ReadToEnd();
   rsa.FromXmlString(publicOnlyKeyXML);
   reader.Close();

   //read plaintext, encrypt it to ciphertext
   byte[] plainbytes =
      Encoding.UTF8.GetBytes(textPlaintext.Text);
   cipherbytes =
      rsa.Encrypt(
      plainbytes,
      false); //fOAEP needs high encryption pack

   //display ciphertext as text string
   ...
```

```
    //display ciphertext byte array in hex format
    ...

    //do UI stuff
    ...
}
```

Finally, the **buttonDecrypt_Click** method creates its own new **RSACryptoServiceProvider** object, but it initializes it by calling **FromXml-String** using the **PublicPrivateKey.XML** file, which contains both public and private key information—a requirement of RSA decryption.

```
private void buttonDecrypt_Click(
    object sender, System.EventArgs e)
{
    //establish RSA using key XML from encrypt
    RSACryptoServiceProvider rsa =
        new RSACryptoServiceProvider();

    //public and private RSA parameters for encrypt
    StreamReader reader =
        new StreamReader("PublicPrivateKey.xml");
    string publicPrivateKeyXML = reader.ReadToEnd();
    rsa.FromXmlString(publicPrivateKeyXML);
    reader.Close();

    //read ciphertext, decrypt it to plaintext
    byte[] plainbytes =
        rsa.Decrypt(
        cipherbytes,
        false); //fOAEP needs high encryption pack

    //display recovered plaintext
    ...

    //do UI stuff
    ...
}
```

Figure 4–4 shows the **SavingKeysAsXml** example being used to encrypt and decrypt a plaintext message. Notice the XML display shows contents of the **PublicPrivateKey.xml** file that is being used by the decryption method. It is a bit difficult to read with all the XML elements running in a single, continuous stream, but if you look closely at it, you should be able to see each of the RSA parameter values used. The encryption method uses only the modulus and exponent elements.

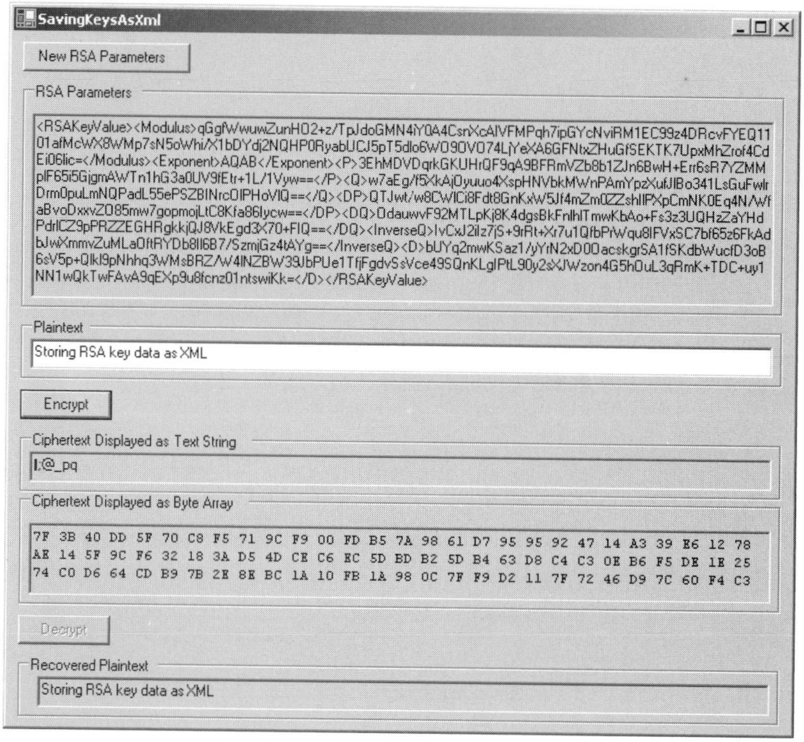

FIGURE 4-4 *The SavingKeysAsXml example program.*

Digital Certificates

In order to make an asymmetric algorithm such as RSA work, you need a way to expose the public key. A public key can be shared manually, but ideally, a CA is used to share a public key that is contained in a digital certificate (also known as a digital ID). A digital certificate is a document that you use to prove your identity in messages or electronic transactions on the Internet. You can obtain a digital certificate from a trusted third party, such as Verisign, or you can set up a locally trusted CA server within your own organization to provide digital certificates. In Microsoft Outlook, you access a CA and generate a digital certificate by selecting the Tools | Options menu item, clicking on the Security tab, and then clicking on the Get Digital ID button.

There are many commercial CAs and many levels of certificates, which differ in cost and levels of trust. To varying degrees, the CA attempts to verify that you are who you claim to be, and, if the CA is convinced of your identity, it will create a document containing the public key that you provide along with other identifying information about you. The CA will then digitally sign that document using its own private key. Of course, nobody other than the CA may ever see the CA's private key, and your private key is never divulged to anyone, including the CA. The resulting signed document is known as a digital certificate, which the CA makes available in a database or directory service to anyone who is interested in dealing with you in either a secure or an authenticated manner. Other parties simply access the database to obtain your digital certificate whenever they need it. Any such party can use the CA's public key to authenticate your digital certificate, and then use the contained public key belonging to you to carry on with whatever encryption or authentication protocol with you that is intended.

Summary

This chapter introduced asymmetric algorithms, particularly the RSA algorithm. We saw how the asymmetric algorithm can be used to solve certain problems with symmetric algorithms by making it unnecessary to share any secret key. We also looked at how RSA works and how to program with the **RSACryptoServiceProvider** class in the .NET Framework. Finally, we looked at how to format RSA parameters into an XML format so that they may be shared with other parties. In the next chapter, we will continue to study asymmetric algorithms, but we will shift our attention to digital signatures, which is the other important aspect of asymmetric algorithms.

Digital Signatures

*I*n the previous chapter we looked at how asymmetric algorithms, particularly RSA, can be used to achieve privacy. It turns out that there is another facet to asymmetric algorithms, known as digital signing, that is used to achieve authentication, integrity, and nonrepudiation. In this chapter, we look at how digital signatures work, and, in particular, we look at how RSA and DSA (Digital Signature Algorithm) are used to implement digital signatures. Both RSA and DSA are fully supported by the .NET Framework, so we look at complete programming examples to demonstrate these two signature techniques.

Digital signatures also require another type of cryptographic primitive, known as cryptographic hash algorithms. The two most commonly used cryptographic hash algorithms are SHA-1 and MD5. SHA-1 produces a 160-bit hash, and MD5 produces a 128-bit hash. For even greater security, SHA-256, SHA-384, and SHA-512 produce hash values with 256, 384, and 512 bits, respectively. All of these hash algorithms are supported by .NET out of the box. Since these hash algorithms are a prerequisite for working with digital signatures, we look at them first. Then, once we have seen how to build programs that make use of digital signatures, we look at how to generate, store, import, and export keys.

Hash Algorithms

As we shall see, cryptographic hash functions are used in digital signatures, since they can be efficiently used for detecting message tampering. A hash is a function that maps an arbitrary-length binary data input to a small, fixed-length binary data output, often referred to as a *message digest* or *finger print*.

Good Hash Function Characteristics

A good hash function should have the property that it is a very low probability that two distinct inputs collide, producing the same hash value result. This allows the smaller, more manageable hash to be used effectively to represent or identify the larger data object. This is analogous to using a human fingerprint, which is a small and manageable, yet highly characteristic piece of information that can be used to identify or authenticate its owner. The fact that for any particular hash value, it is exceedingly difficult to find another distinct input message that would produce the same hash output is precisely what protects a digitally signed message from being tampered with.[1]

Simple hash functions have many uses in computing outside of the specialized discipline of cryptography, such as for error detection and quickly searching for objects in a hash table. The **GetHashCode** virtual method of **Object** is an example of a simple hash function not intended for cryptographic purposes. How does a cryptographic hash function differ from an ordinary hash function such as **GetHashCode**? A cryptographic hash function is a hash function with some additional characteristics that are required for cryptographic purposes, such as password hashing or digital signing. For example, for a cryptographic hash function, it should be infeasible to compute a valid input data from knowing only the output hash value. It should also be infeasible, given one input data, to discover an alternate input data that would produce the same hash value.

Additionally, it is also highly desirable that a hash function be efficient to compute. There is a clear tradeoff here, since achieving greater security comes at the expense of a penalty in performance. Fortunately, MD5, SHA-1, as well as SHA-256, SHA-384, and SHA-512 are all quite efficient designs that provide choice and balance in their security/performance tradeoff. Of these, MD5 is the fastest, but, of course, it is also the least secure.

It is also desirable that a small number of bit changes on the input data should produce a large number of unpredictable bit changes in the resulting output hash value. This makes it more difficult to reverse-engineer the input from the output. In summary, an ideal cryptographic hash function has the following properties:

- Input data can be of arbitrary length.
- Output data is of small, fixed length, defined by the algorithm.

---

1. Currently, no collisions have been discovered for MD5, SHA-1, SHA-256, SHA-384, or SHA-512. MD5, which at 120 bits is the weakest of these, given current publicly known techniques, would take a work factor that is proportional to a 2^64 brute-force search, which is well beyond all but the most powerful adversaries today. For SHA-1, with 160 bits, the work factor is proportional to 2^80, which is probably completely out of reach at this time. What about SHA-256, SHA-384, and SHA-512? These are most likely to be secure for a very long time indeed!

- Fast to compute.
- Hard to invert (i.e., a one-way function).
- Produces few collisions.

The last point mentioned means that it is hard to find two distinct inputs that produce the same output. This may seem odd at first glance. If you can have input data that is of any arbitrary length, then there are an infinite number of possible inputs. If the hash output has a fixed size, then there are only a finite number of possible outputs. Thus, it is obvious that there must be an infinite number of inputs that do in fact produce a collision of identical outputs. It may seem paradoxical, however, that even though there are an infinite number of colliding inputs for any given output, it is still extraordinarily difficult to find even just two such colliding inputs! Thus, the fact that collisions are hard to find is not due to the fact that few collisions exist, since there are many. Rather, collisions are hard to find because such collisions are interspersed with a very much larger number of message pairs that do not collide. The security of the hash results from the extreme difficulty in finding any of these infinitely numbered colliding input pairs!

Hash Algorithms Provided by .NET

The two most commonly used cryptographic hash functions are SHA-1 (Secure Hash Algorithm published by NIST in the mid 1990s) and MD5 (Message Digest algorithm designed by R. Rivest in the early 1990s). In addition, several important new versions of SHA have recently been published. Keyed hash algorithms are also important for certain message authentication–related purposes. These are all supported by the .NET Framework in the form of the classes derived from **HashAlgorithm**:[2]

- **MD5**
- **SHA1**
- **SHA256**
- **SHA384**
- **SHA512**
- **KeyedHashAlgorithm**

Figure 5–1 shows the hash algorithm class hierarchy. The **Object**-derived abstract class **HashAlgorithm** sits at the top of this hierarchy. The derived abstract classes **KeyedHashAlgorithm**, **MD5**, **SHA1**, **SHA256**, **SHA384**, and **SHA512** represent each of the most commonly used cryptographic hash

---

2. It should be noted that the method **GetHashCode** of the **Object** class produces a 32-bit hash of an object, but this hash function is not intended for cryptographic purposes. Rather, it is intended for more mundane purposes, such as allowing an object to be used in an efficient hash table lookup, and so forth.

Namespace: System.Security.Cryptography

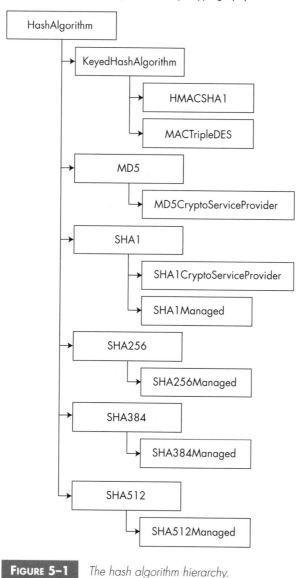

FIGURE 5-1   *The hash algorithm hierarchy.*

algorithms in use today. Since these are all abstract classes, they cannot be instantiated or directly used. Derived from each of these are the concrete implementation classes that can be directly used. Those class names that end in the word CryptoServiceProvider are implemented using the underlying unmanaged CryptoAPI functionality provided by the operating system. Those that end with the word Managed are implemented entirely from scratch in managed C# code, independently of the CryptoAPI.

The **HMACSHA1** class produces a keyed hash (Keyed-Hash Message Authentication Code, or HMAC) using the SHA-1 hash function. The **MACTripleDES** class produces a keyed hash HMAC using Triple DES[3] encryption as a hash function. An HMAC is similar to a digital signature in that it can be used to verify message authenticity and integrity; however, it differs in that it is not suitable for enforcing nonrepudiation: Whereas a digital signature is an asymmetric scheme in which one key is held private, an HMAC is a symmetric scheme in which both the sender and receiver use the same secret key for applying and verifying the MAC. Since the key is known by more than one individual, there is no way to prove to a third party which of those individuals applied the hash. Also, MACs are smaller and more efficient to compute than digital signatures.

Although the .NET framework is very extensible, allowing proprietary hash algorithms to be implemented as classes derived from **HashAlgorithm**, it is highly recommended that you do not attempt to design your own cryptographic algorithms! To be considered secure, a cryptographic algorithm must be analyzed intensively by many experts in the field over a prolonged period. It is a widely held opinion that any gains in security that may result from the obscurity of a proprietary design is far outweighed by the likelihood that such a design is dangerously flawed. Rather, it is much better to use an existing trusted algorithm such as MD5 or one of the SHA variants.

Beyond those supported by .NET, there are no other cryptographic hash algorithms that are currently in significant use in the industry.[4] The underlying Microsoft Windows CryptoAPI and CSP (cryptographic service provider) support three hash algorithms: MD4, MD5, and SHA-1. The .NET Framework does not support MD4, since MD5 is an improvement over MD4, which has critical weaknesses that have been fixed. The .NET Framework does support SHA-256, SHA-384, and SHA-512, which are not supported by the underlying CryptoAPI, since these are relatively new standards.

The HashAlgorithm Class

The **HashAlgorithm** class has a public property named **Hash**, which is a byte array containing the resulting hash value. The public property **HashSize** gets

---

3. Some cryptographic hash algorithms, such as MD5 and SHA-1, have been designed from scratch, whereas others have been built on the bases of an existing PRNG (pseudorandom number generator) or a symmetric algorithm. The **MACTripleDES** class is an example of a hash that is based on the Triple DES symmetric algorithm. Unfortunately, Triple DES is a fairly slow technique for generating a hash.

4. There are many cryptographic algorithms that have been proposed, including GOST, HAVAL, RIPE-MD, SNERFU, and TIGER. However, none of these alternatives are as widely used or thoroughly analyzed as MD5 or SHA-1.

the size of the hash code in bits. The most important public method of the **HashAlgorithm** class is **ComputeHash**, which returns the hash value as a byte array for the input data provided as a byte array parameter. The following code shows how the **HashAlgorithm** class is used, along with the concrete derived class that encapsulates the SHA-1 algorithm. This example assumes that the input message **messageByteArray** has been previously instantiated as a byte array.

```
HashAlgorithm sha1 = new SHA1CryptoServiceProvider();
byte[] sha1Hash = sha1.ComputeHash(messageByteArray);
```

The MD5 and SHA Classes

The **MD5** class encapsulates the MD5 algorithm, which takes an input of arbitrary length and produces a 128-bit hash result. The MD5 message digest algorithm is defined in RFC 1321.[5] This algorithm was originally designed for digital signature applications, where the hash (i.e., message digest) is encrypted with a private key in the RSA public key cryptosystem. The MD5 algorithm is an extension of the MD4 message digest algorithm (published by Rivest in 1990), but, while slightly slower, it provides more security.

The **SHA1** class encapsulates the SHA-1 algorithm. SHA-1 can take any message up to 2^{64} bits in length and produce a 160-bit hash output. This message digest can be fed into the DSA,[6] as we shall see shortly. The SHA-1 algorithm has been adopted as the NIST standard known as the SHS (Secure Hash Standard), which is published in FIPS PUB 180-1.[7] It is interesting to note that the FIPS 180-1 document states that SHA-1 is based on principles similar to those used in the design of the MD4 message digest algorithm. Therefore, the two most heavily used hash functions, MD5 and SHA-1, are related to one another.

The **SHA256**, **SHA384**, and **SHA512** classes encapsulate a closely related set of hash algorithms, which produce hash sizes of 256, 384, and 512 bits. These new algorithms, defined in FIPS PUB 180-2[8] in 2002, are closely related to SHA-1, but, since the original publication of FIPS PUB 180-1 in 1993, concerns have been raised over whether 160 bits provide sufficient security for highly sensitive applications over the long term. Whereas a brute-force attack on an *n*-bit symmetric encryption algorithm represents a work

---

5. See *http://www.faqs.org/rfcs/rfc1321.html* for details.
6. DSA is based on the discrete logarithm problem originally proposed by Schnorr and ElGamal.
7. See *http://csrc.nist.gov/publications/fips/fips180-1/fip180-1.pdf* for details.
8. See *http://csrc.nist.gov/publications/fips/fips180-2/fips180-2.pdf* for details. FIPS 180-2, which covers SHA-1 as well as the new 256, 384, and 512 bit versions, supersedes FIPS 180-1 as of February 1, 2003.

factor that is proportional to 2^n, an attack on an *n*-bit cryptographic hash algorithm is only $2^{n/2}$. This is because a birthday attack[9] on the hash is considered successful if any two inputs are found that produce the same hash output. Therefore, the work factor for attacking the 160-bit SHA-1 algorithm is actually only on the order of 2^{80}. This is still probably beyond the reach of almost all existing adversaries, but probably not sufficient for extremely high security requirements over the very long term.

It is interesting to note that the newly selected AES symmetric encryption standard, known as Rijndael, comes in three flavors based on key size: AES-128, AES-192, and AES-256. You may notice that the bit sizes of the new SHA algorithms are 256, 384, and 512, which are exactly double that of the corresponding 128, 192, and 256 bit sizes for AES. This effectively makes the new AES and SHA algorithms of equivalent strength, since a hash is vulnerable to a birthday attack, which cuts the work factor by two. This is an important point if you are constructing a security protocol that involves both symmetric encryption and secure hashing. This is because the security of the entire protocol is only as strong as the weakest link. For example, if you use a very high-security symmetric algorithm, and combine that with a relatively weak hash algorithm (or vice versa), then your adversary will simply attack the weaker of the two. In effect, you will have wasted processing power and performance for zero gain in overall security. In contrast, if you combine algorithms of equivalent strength, then all processing overhead effectively contributes equally towards the desired level of security.

The KeyedHashAlgorithm Class

The **KeyedHashAlgorithm** class is an interesting variation on the basic hash algorithm concept in that it calculates a hash output that is based on both the message data fed into it as well as an additional piece of information used as a key input. Such a keyed hash algorithm is therefore a key-dependent, one-way hash function. This is handy for message authentication purposes, since only someone who knows the correct key can apply or verify the hash. Keyed hash algorithms therefore provide both integrity and authenticity checking between trusting parties that have exchanged key information. The **KeyedHashAlgorithm** class is abstract, which is implemented by the concrete derived

---

9. The term *birthday attack* refers to a brute-force search for a hash function collision, where two input messages hash to the same output. The term originates from a probability theory scenario, known as the Birthday Problem, which involves the calculation of the probability of finding any two people in a group of individuals who celebrate their birthday on the same day. Although it may seem intuitively too low, the smallest number of people needed for there to be at least a 50 percent chance for a birthday collision is only 23 individuals.

HMACSHA1 and **MACTripleDES** classes, These classes encapsulate keyed hash algorithms based on the SHA-1 and Triple DES algorithms respectively.

Object Identifiers

Sometimes, programmers need a systematic naming convention that allows each of the hundreds of standard and proprietary protocols, algorithms, and data formats to be efficiently and uniquely identified. ASN.1[10] OIDs (Object Identifiers) are defined and managed by a number of organizations, including ANSI (American National Standards Institute), for the purpose of uniquely identifying computing formats in a logical and hierarchical manner. There are a large number of OIDs that identify specific protocols, algorithms, and data formats. In particular, most encryption algorithms that are recognized by ANSI have also been assigned a unique OID. For example, the OIDs for the most commonly used cryptographic hash algorithms are shown in Table 5–1. We shall see that these OIDs must be specified in certain .NET Security Framework class methods, such as the **SignHash** and **VerifyHash** methods of the **RSACryptoServiceProvider** and **DSACryptoServiceProvider** classes.

TABLE 5–1	ASN.1 OIDs for Commonly Used Cryptographic Hash Algorithms
Cryptographic Hash Algorithm	**OID**
MD5	1.2.840.113549.2.5
SHA-1	1.3.14.3.2.26
SHA-256	2.16.840.1.101.3.4.2.1
SHA-384	2.16.840.1.101.3.4.2.2
SHA-512	2.16.840.1.101.3.4.2.3

The following code snippet shows an example of using an OID as a parameter to the **SignHash** method of the **RSACryptoServiceProvider** class. Of course, it is assumed that the **hashbytes** variable is a byte array that has already been created by calling the **ComputeHash** method of the **SHA1** class.

```
//create  RSA object using default key
RSACryptoServiceProvider rsa =
   new RSACryptoServiceProvider();
```

---

10. ASN.1 stands for Abstract Syntax Notation number One, which is an international standard for specifying data used in communication protocols.

```
//sign hash using OID for SHA-1
signaturebytes =
    rsa.SignHash(hashbytes, "1.3.14.3.2.26");
```

How Digital Signatures Work

Figure 5–2 shows an overall picture of how a digital signature is applied to a message. In the upper left corner of this diagram, we take the original message and create a 160-bit message digest by applying the SHA-1 hash algorithm on the message. The message digest is then encrypted using the private key known only to the private key owner (i.e., the sender). Note that this is not a secretive encryption, since the sender is using his or her own private key, not the public key, to encrypt. This means that absolutely anyone can decrypt the message digest, using the associated public key, and retrieve the hash. In fact, as we will see next, this is exactly what the receiver will do with the signed message.

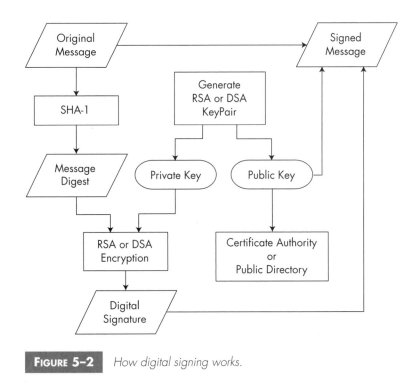

FIGURE 5–2   *How digital signing works.*

The result of this encryption is called the digital signature. No other party can create this particular digital signature, even if that party has access to the original message, since he or she does not know the private key that was used. By the same argument, nobody could change this message or make up a different message and sign it with this private key.

In the upper right corner of the diagram, the signed message is formed by concatenating the original message with the unique digital signature and the public key that is associated with the private key that produced that signature. This entire signed message is then sent to the desired recipient. This diagram also shows that the public key should be made available to the public in an effective way. For improved trust, using a recognized certificate authority (CA) is a good way to do this.

The other side of this story is shown in Figure 5–3, which shows how a digitally signed message is verified by the receiving party. The receiver is interested in determining whether the signed message came from the authen-

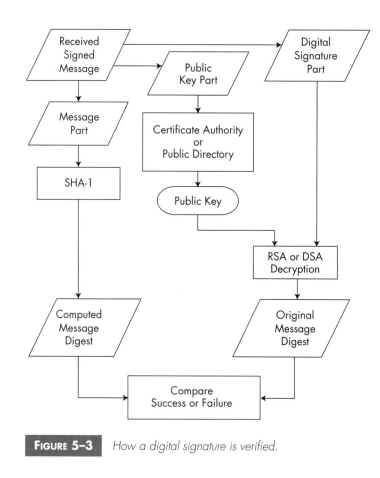

FIGURE 5–3　*How a digital signature is verified.*

tic sender or from someone else pretending to be that sender. The receiver is also interested in whether the message might have been altered in any way by an unauthorized party between the time the message was signed by the legitimate sender and the time it was received.

In the top left corner of the diagram, the received signed message is broken into its three components: the original message, the public key, and the digital signature. For comparison against the hash of the original message, it is necessary to compute the hash of the received message. If the message digest has not changed, then you can be very confident that the message itself has not changed. On the other hand, if the message digest has changed, then you can be quite certain that the received message has been corrupted or tampered with.

Now that the hash of the received message has been found, the hash of the original message must be obtained. In the upper right corner of the diagram, we have the digital signature that was encrypted with the private key of the sender. The receiver then has to decrypt this digital signature using the associated public key to obtain the original hash. The receiver therefore takes the provided public key and checks that it is valid, which is generally done—at least the first time—using the services of a trusted third-party CA. If the public key checks out okay, then it is used to decrypt the original message digest, which is then compared against the message digest calculated on the received message. If these hashes match, then the message has been authenticated and has not been tampered with. Assuming that the sender has been successful in keeping the private key secret, this also can be used to hold the signer responsible for signing the message (i.e., nonrepudiation).

The Digital Signature Standard (DSS), defined in document FIPS PUB 186-2,[11] defines three signature algorithms: Digital Signature Algorithm (DSA), RSA (as specified in ANSI X9.31), and Elliptic Curve DSA. Since Elliptic Curve DSA is the only one of these algorithms that is not currently supported directly by the .NET Security class library, we only consider the DSA and RSA cases here.

RSA Used as a Digital Signature Algorithm

The RSA algorithm can be used for both privacy and digital signing. In Chapter 4, we saw how RSA can be used for keeping secrets, and especially for sharing secret symmetric keys. In this chapter, we look at RSA digital signatures, which is the flip side of the coin. Whereas privacy is achieved by encrypting with the public key and decrypting with the associated private key, digital signing is achieved the other way around, by encrypting with the private key and decrypting with the matching public key.

---

11. See *http://csrc.nist.gov/publications/fips/fips186-2/fips186-2-change1.pdf* for details.

For digital signatures, it turns out that it is not actually necessary to encrypt the entire original message. It is entirely sufficient, as well as much more efficient, to generate a hash of the original message, and then just encrypt that smaller hash value with the private key. Anyone with the matching public key (i.e., everybody) can then decrypt that hash with the public key for verification purposes. If the decrypted hash matches the recalculated hash of the actual message received, then the receiver can be quite confident that the original message that generated the hash must also match the received message. This comes from the fact that it is extremely difficult to find any two inputs that produce the same hash output.

An RSA Signature Example Program

The **RSASignature** example program demonstrates how to create and verify an RSA digital signature for a message. Figure 5–4 shows the **RSASignature** example program generating and verifying a digital signature. If you create the digital signature for the message by clicking the Create Signature button, and then, without modifying the original message, you test the signature by clicking the Verify Signature button, you will see a dialog box display the fact that the verification succeeded. If you click the Create Signature button, but

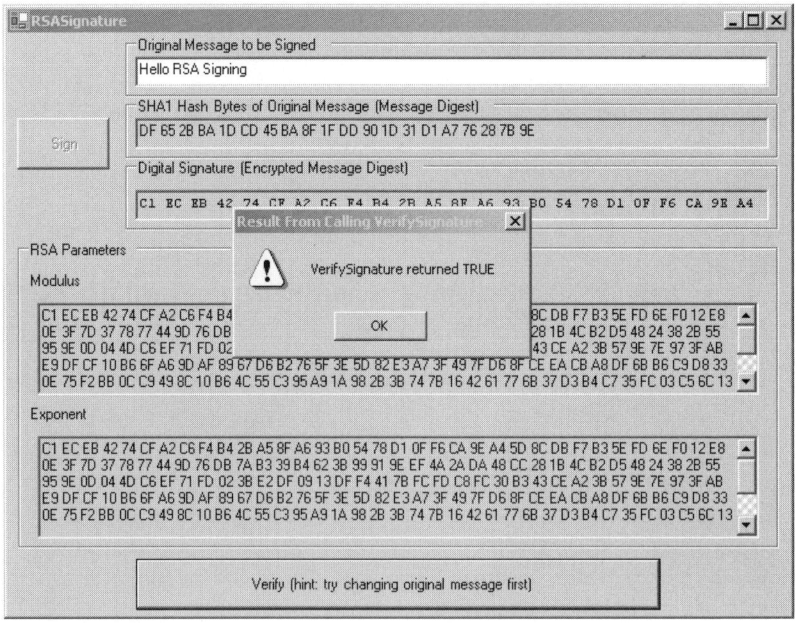

FIGURE 5–4   *The RSASignature example program.*

then modify the message in the **TextBox** control before clicking the Verify Signature button, the dialog box indicates that verification fails. Thus, the program detects that the message has been tampered with.

This example is somewhat contrived, since the digital signing and signature verification are all done within a single program window. This is done this way in the example purely for convenience, so that the overall effect of working with digital signatures can be demonstrated in a compact manner. A real-world example involving digital signatures would more likely be a client/server or distributed application scenario, such as an email client or Internet-based banking.

The **buttonSign_Click** method that performs the digital signing on the message data is shown next. User interface code is ignored here so that we can focus on the cryptographic aspects of the program.

```
private void buttonSign_Click(
   object sender, System.EventArgs e)
{
   //get original message as byte array
   byte[] messagebytes = Encoding.UTF8.GetBytes(
      textOriginalMessage.Text);

   //create digest of original message using SHA1
   SHA1 sha1  = new SHA1CryptoServiceProvider();
   byte[] hashbytes =
      sha1.ComputeHash(messagebytes);

   //display hash bytes in hex format
   ...

   //create RSA object using default key
   RSACryptoServiceProvider rsa =
      new RSACryptoServiceProvider();

   //sign hash using OID for SHA-1
   signaturebytes =
      rsa.SignHash(hashbytes, "1.3.14.3.2.26");

   //provide RSA parameters to verification
   rsaparams = rsa.ExportParameters(false);

   //display digital signature in hex format
   ...

   //display RSA parameter details in hex format
   ...

   //do UI stuff
   ...
}
```

The previous code listing shows a message hash being generated, which is then digitally signed by calling the **SignHash** method of the **RSA** object. The **ExportParameters** method is then used to store only the public key information in an **RSAParameters** object to be used later for verification. The verifier needs to know only the public key information, not the private key information, and only the signer needs to know the entire key, including both public and private parts.[12] This is why the signer creates the **RSACryptoServiceProvider** object, and then exports only the public key information by calling the **ExportParameters** method with a false parameter.

Now let's look at the **buttonVerify_Click** method that verifies the digital signature on the message. The hash is recalculated on the message, since it might have been tampered with, which is exactly what we are attempting to detect. Then a new **RSA** object is created, but, this time, the automatically generated public key information is replaced by calling **ImportParameters** on the same **RSAParameters** object established earlier in the signing method. This ensures that the RSA parameters that were used in the signing of the message are identical to those to be used now in the verification of the signature. Although the user interface code is not shown here, the program then displays the result of the call to **VerifyHash** in a message box.

```
private void buttonVerify_Click(
   object sender, System.EventArgs e)
{
   //get possibly modified message as byte array
   byte[] messagebytes = Encoding.UTF8.GetBytes(
      textOriginalMessage.Text);

   //create digest of original message using SHA1
   SHA1 sha1  = new SHA1CryptoServiceProvider();
   byte[] hashbytes =
      sha1.ComputeHash(messagebytes);

   //create RSA object using parameters from signing
   RSACryptoServiceProvider rsa =
      new RSACryptoServiceProvider();
   rsa.ImportParameters(rsaparams);

   //do verification on hash using OID for SHA-1
   bool match = rsa.VerifyHash(
      hashbytes, "1.3.14.3.2.26", signaturebytes);
```

---

12. Recall how encryption for privacy was described in Chapter 4 as the opposite of this scenario.

```
    //show message box with result of verification
    ...

    //do UI stuff
    ...
}
```

In order to communicate the necessary information from the signing method to the verification method, we provide two fields. The first one is an **RSAParameters** object mentioned earlier. This object encapsulates public key parameter information for the algorithm, such as the RSA key pair information. The second is a byte array that will contain the digital signature when it is generated from the message in the signing method. Although the actual text message does need to be communicated between the signing code and the verifying code, it is not stored as a field in this program. Instead, the message is stored and retrieved directly from a textbox in the user interface, allowing the user to modify it. This allows the user to see the effect of tampering with the message between the operations of signing and verification. This helps in visualizing how it works and allows you to interact with it by tampering with the signed data, but in a realistic scenario, it would probably be transmitted between distinct applications.

```
//variables communicated from signing to verifying
RSAParameters rsaparams;
byte[] signaturebytes;
```

The Digital Signature Algorithm

DSA is a NIST federal standard, used along with the Secure Hash Standard, to attach digital signatures to data. NIST published the first version of the DSA algorithm as part of the DSS (Digital Signature Standard, FIPS 186) in May 1994. DSA is based on the discrete logarithm problem, which is described in the next two sections.

Recall from Chapter 4 that an asymmetric algorithm is always based on some one-way function. The one-way function upon which DSA is based is known as the discrete logarithm problem. The discrete logarithm problem involves an area of abstract algebra known as group theory. A group is actually a sophisticated and somewhat generalized concept that transcends familiar elementary school arithmetic. However, for our purposes, it is sufficient for us to understand the concept of group theory from an elementary point of view. Let's look briefly at what group theory is, and then move on to the discrete logarithm problem before we do any .NET DSA programming.

Some Mathematical Background: Group Theory

In a simplistic sense, a group can be thought of as a nonempty set that we call G, combined with a binary operation, that we conventionally call multiplication. By definition, a group G must satisfy the following four axioms:

- Closure: If a and b are elements in G, then $a \cdot b$ is also an element in G.
- Associative: $(a \cdot b) \cdot c = a \cdot (b \cdot c)$ holds true for any elements a, b, c in G.
- Identity: G contains a unique element, conventionally represented as 1, such that $(a \cdot 1) = (1 \cdot a) = a$ for each element a in G. The element 1 is known as the identity element.
- Inverse: For each a in G there exists an element a^{-1} in G such that $a \cdot a^{-1} = a^{-1} \cdot a = 1$. The elements a and a^{-1} are known as multiplicative inverses.

The above axioms may strongly remind you of the elementary arithmetic of rational numbers,[13] and, indeed, the set of rational numbers taken together with multiplication does constitute a group according to the above definition. But notice that elementary integer arithmetic does not constitute a group, since the axiom regarding the existence of an inverse does not hold true. For example the inverse of the integer 3 is 1/3, which is not in the set of integers. The existence of the inverse is critical for constructing encryption algorithms, because decryption is the inverse of encryption. Without the existence of an inverse, you would be able to encrypt but not reliably decrypt, which of course would be entirely useless.

All is not lost for the integers, however! If you make a slight modification to the idea of an integer such that it is constrained to a finite range of values, and if you tweak the idea of multiplication such that resulting numbers beyond this finite range are wrapped around at the beginning of the range, then it is possible to construct a finite group of integers. This is known as modular arithmetic.

The discrete logarithm problem involves a finite group on which we perform repeated multiplications using modular arithmetic. Specifically, we use a multiplicative group of the integers modulo a prime number. The reason for the modulus being a prime is simply to guarantee that a unique multiplicative inverse exists for each and every element in the group. If you choose a modulus that is not a prime, then there will be some elements that invert to the same number, resulting in a collision that must be avoided.

---

13. Note that we are talking about the rational numbers of mathematics here, not the float or double-datatypes used in programming languages to approximate rational and real numbers. Unfortunately, float and double-datatypes do not form a group, making them useless for cryptographic purposes.

The following shows the multiplication table for a modulus of 7, which happens to be prime. Note that every row after the first one is a permutation, meaning that no product is the same as any other product in the same row. This means that a unique multiplicative inverse exists for every number in the group. Of course, this is just an example and does not prove anything about the existence of the inverse for an arbitrary prime modulus. We will not provide the proof here, since that would require too much background material; however, if you are interested, many textbooks on abstract algebra or number theory provide a proof.

All we are concerned with here is that if the modulus is prime, the multiplicative inverse does indeed exist for all elements in the group. This is important because this inverse must exist if we are going to try to use such a scheme as a cryptographic one-way function. Recall that although a one-way function is hard to invert, the inverse must actually exist for it to be useful to us.

```
*|0 1 2 3 4 5 6 (modulus is 7, which is a prime)
-+--------------
0|0 0 0 0 0 0 0
1|0 1 2 3 4 5 6
2|0 2 4 6 1 3 5
3|0 3 6 2 5 1 4
4|0 4 1 5 2 6 3
5|0 5 3 1 6 4 2
6|0 6 5 4 3 2 1
```

As a complementary example, consider the multiplication table for a modulus that is composite (i.e., not prime). Here we see the case where the modulus is 8, which of course is not a prime number. If you look at some of the rows in this table, you will see that some products are repeated within some rows. This indicates that multiplication does not have a unique inverse defined for some of these values and therefore cannot be used as the basis of an asymmetric algorithm. Bold text is used to show the numbers that are repeated in their row. These repeats indicate that the row is not a permutation, and therefore the inverse is not unique.

```
*|0 1 2 3 4 5 6 7 (modulus is 8, which is not a prime)
-+----------------
0|0 0 0 0 0 0 0 0
1|0 1 2 3 4 5 6 7
2|0 2 4 6 0 2 4 6
3|0 3 6 1 4 7 2 5
4|0 4 0 4 0 4 0 4
5|0 5 2 7 4 1 6 3
6|0 6 4 2 0 6 4 2
7|0 7 6 5 4 3 2 1
```

The Discrete Logarithm Problem

You may recall from elementary mathematics that the repeated multiplication of a number on itself is called a power or an exponentiation, and the inverse operation is known as a logarithm or a log. For example, the following arithmetic expressions show the inverse relationship between power and logarithm operations. Consider the expressions *10 to the power of 2 is 100* and *the logarithm to base 10 of 100 is 2.* In mathematical notation, we would write

$$10^2 = 100$$

$$\log_{10}100 = 2$$

You can probably already get a sense for the one-way nature that will emerge out of this scheme: Calculating a power is easy, since it is just a number of repeated multiplications, which is rather simple to compute. The calculation of logarithms is clearly the more complex direction to work in. It turns out that the ratio of difficulty between these two directions becomes even more pronounced when dealing with larger numbers. In the branch of mathematics known as complexity theory, we say that the work factor of the power operation is polynomial-time, and the work factor of the logarithm is exponential-time. As the number of bits of the problem is scaled up, you always reach some point where the difficulty of an exponential-time problem grows explosively relative to a polynomial-time problem. Voila! You have a one-way function.

Let's discuss the problem algebraically in terms of an unknown quantity x. One would say, "Ten to the power of x equals 100. Find x." In mathematical notation, the problem would be stated as

$$10^x = 100$$

The solution for this problem would then be expressed as

$$x = \log_{10}100$$

Now let's look at these operations being performed on elements in a finite modular arithmetic group, denoted as Z_p,[14] (containing the integers from 0 to $p - 1$) with the implied modulo p arithmetic, where p is a prime number. Any element g chosen from Z_p taken to the power x is represented using the traditional notation: g^x, which means g is multiplied modulo p by itself x times. The number g is called a generator of the group, because all members of the group can be obtained by taking g to some appropriate power. The discrete logarithm problem is then, given the elements a and b in Z_p, find an integer x

---

14. We previously referred to a group in a very general sense as the set G, but the notation Z_p more specifically refers to a finite modular arithmetic group of integers. There are many other groups that do not fall into this category.

such that $a^x = b$. For example, let $p = 19$, $a = 5$, and $b = 7$, then find x given the following:

$$5^x = 7(\text{mod } 19)$$

The solution for x would then be expressed as

$$x = \log_5 7(\text{mod } 19)$$

The above equation expresses x as a modular logarithm. Although this example uses tiny numbers, in the case where the bit size is large, there is no known way to solve it in any fast and direct manner. The fastest known methods of solution all have work factors that grow exponentially as a function of the bit size of the problem.

In the example above, you could just use a brute-force search, going through each of the possibilities for x, ranging from 0 to 18, and substituting each of these candidates back into the equation $5^x = 7(\text{mod } 19)$ to see if it becomes true. After going through this attack for a short while, you will discover the solution is 6, because indeed $5^6 = 7(\text{mod } 19)$. The brute-force attack in this example is not much work, since a modulus of 19 is very small, and therefore the number of candidates to test is tiny. After all, a modulus of 19 can be represented as a 5-bit number, but what if the modulus was hundreds of bits in size? Then, consider the fact that DSA allows key sizes ranging from 512 to 1024 bits. The work factor of such a brute-force attack doubles with each additional bit, providing us with a comfortable margin of safety.

Although it has never yet been formally proven, the discrete logarithm problem appears to be an effective one-way function. Therefore, just as the prime-factoring problem is used in RSA, the discrete logarithm problem is used as the one-way function in DSA. This parallel is not quite complete, because, unlike RSA, which can be used for both privacy and digital signatures, DSA can be used only for digital signatures.

Note that since the private key is known only to its owner, and the private key is used to digitally sign messages, signatures can be generated only by the owner of that private key. Since the corresponding public key is available to anyone who is interested, anyone can successfully verify the digital signature.

The details of the DSA algorithm are a bit confusing,[15] but in essence the signature is computed by raising the original message, which is really just an arbitrary precision number, to a power that is kept secret. Verification is then the inverse operation, which calculates the modular logarithm from the signature, using a secret key that speeds the process. Since the sender then

---

15. The basic idea of the discrete logarithm problem as a one-way function is quite simple. What makes DSA confusingly difficult is that additional mechanisms are incorporated that are necessary to provide the backdoor to this one-way function, making a secret key possible.

sends the original message along with the signature, the receiver has all the information to make the comparison, thus allowing the receiver to detect any message tampering that may have occurred.

Just as we saw in the case of RSA signing, when we want to sign a long message, it is inefficient and unnecessary to sign the entire message. Therefore, we first create a message hash (i.e., a digest), and sign this hash rather than the entire message. This is viable because it would be very difficult to forge the message such that the resulting hash would match the original message hash.

How DSA Works

An overview of the gory details of how DSA works is provided here. As you can see, there is a bit more to it than just the discrete logarithm problem discussed earlier. We won't go into an explanation of why each step is necessary or why they work the way they do. Instead, this description is intended only as an outline of the scheme, which can be used as a basis for an actual DSA implementation. From these details, you can see that the implementation of DSA is not trivial, and we are rather fortunate that cryptographic libraries, such as the .NET Framework, provide this implementation for us!

GENERATING THE KEY

1. Choose a prime p with a bit size of 512, 576, 640, 704, 768, 832, 896, 960, or 1024.
2. Choose a 160-bit prime q that evenly divides $p - 1$.
3. Choose numbers g and h such that $g = h\wedge((p - 1)/q) \bmod p > 1$ and $1 < h < p - 1$.
4. Randomly choose a private key x in the range $0 < x < q$.
5. Calculate $y = g\wedge x \bmod p$.
6. The resulting public key is the set of numbers (p,q,g,y).
7. The resulting private key is the number x.

SIGNING THE MESSAGE

1. Obtain the plaintext message m to be signed.
2. Choose a random value s such that $1 < s < q$.
3. Calculate $r = (g\wedge s \bmod p) \bmod q$.
4. Calculate $s = (H(m) - r * x)s\wedge-1 \bmod q$, where $H(m)$ is the SHA-1 algorithm.
5. The resulting signature is the set of numbers (r,s).

VERIFYING THE SIGNATURE

1. Calculate $w = (s)\wedge-1 (\bmod q)$.
2. Calculate $u1 = H(m) * w (\bmod q)$.

3. Calculate $u2 = r * w(\mathrm{mod}\ q)$.
4. Calculate $v = (g^{\wedge}u1 * y^{\wedge}y\,2\ \mathrm{mod}\ p)\ \mathrm{mod}\ q$.
5. The signature is valid if and only if $v = r$.

The Asymmetric AlgorithmHierarchy Class Hierarchy

The asymmetric algorithm class inheritance hierarchy, which is located in the **System.Security.Cryptography** namespace, is shown in Figure 5–5. Not shown in this figure is that **AsymmetricAlgorithm** derives from the **Object** class. Recall from Chapter 4 that the **AsymmetricAlgorithm** class is abstract and derives into the **DSA** and **RSA** classes, which are also abstract. The **RSA** and **DSA** classes further derive into the **RSACryptoServiceProvider** and **DSACryptoServiceProvider** classes, which provide concrete implementations of the RSA and DSA algorithms. These are both based on the underlying CryptoAPI support provided by the Windows operating system. Other implementations of RSA and DSA may be implemented by either yourself or other vendors; however, in most cases the implementation provided by .NET is recommended.

Now let's consider the public methods and properties of the **DSACryptoServiceProvider** class. As is the case with all of the symmetric and asymmetric algorithms, this class's constructor automatically generates its own key information at creation time.

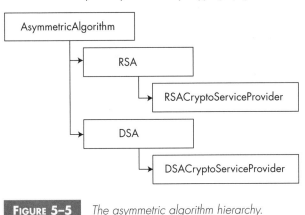

Namespace: System.Security.Cryptography

FIGURE 5–5   *The asymmetric algorithm hierarchy.*

The DSACryptoServiceProvider Class

The public properties of the **DSACryptoServiceProvider** class are the following:

- **KeyExchangeAlgorithm** gets the name of the key exchange algorithm.
- **KeySize** gets the size of the key in bits.
- **LegalKeySizes** gets the key sizes that are allowed.
- **PersistKeyInCsp** determines whether or not the key should be persisted in the CSP.
- **SignatureAlgorithm** gets the name of the signature algorithm.

DSACryptoServiceProvider also has several public methods that you may be interested in using. There is some overlap in the provided functionality, which means that you can often accomplish the same effect in multiple ways. The most important public methods of the **DSACryptoServiceProvider** class are the following:

- **CreateSignature** creates the DSA signature for the provided message data.
- **VerifySignature** verifies the DSA signature for the provided message data.
- **SignData** calculates the hash of the message data and digitally signs the resulting hash value.
- **VerifyData** verifies the provided signature with the signature calculated on the provided data.
- **SignHash** calculates the signature for the specified hash value.
- **VerifyHash** verifies the provided signature with the signature calculated on the provided hash.
- **ToXmlString** creates and returns an XML representation of the current DSA object.
- **FromXmlString** reconstructs a DSA object from an XML representation.
- **ExportParameters** exports DSA parameters to a **DSAParameters** object.
- **ImportParameters** imports DSA parameters from a **DSAParameters** object.

A DSA Programming Example

The **DSAAlgorithm** example program demonstrates how to create and verify a DSA digital signature. You should see many similarities between this example and the **RSASignature** example we looked at earlier in this chapter. After all, even though DSA and RSA are implemented using different algorithms, they are both used for the same purpose when it comes to digital signing. Figure 5–6 shows the **DSAAlgorithm** example program generating and verifying a digital

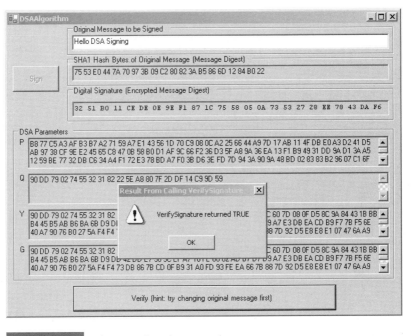

FIGURE 5-6   *The DSAAlgorithm example program.*

signature for a message. As you can see, this example's user interface works in exactly the same way as the previous **RSASignature** example program. You enter a message, create a digital signature, and, after either modifying or not modifying the original message, you verify the signature. A dialog box will display whether or not the message has been tampered with.

The **buttonSign_Click** method, which performs the digital signing on the message data, is shown next. Again, user interface code is ignored here so that we can focus on the cryptography. This DSA code example performs the same basic logic seen in the previous RSA digital signature example.

```
private void buttonSign_Click(
   object sender, System.EventArgs e)
{
   //get original message as byte array
   byte[] messagebytes = Encoding.UTF8.GetBytes(
      textOriginalMessage.Text);

   //create digest of original message using SHA1
   SHA1 sha1  = new SHA1CryptoServiceProvider();
   byte[] hashbytes =
      sha1.ComputeHash(messagebytes);
```

```
//display hash bytes in hex format
...

//create DSA object using default key
DSACryptoServiceProvider dsa =
    new DSACryptoServiceProvider();

//sign hash using OID for SHA-1
signaturebytes =
    dsa.SignHash(hashbytes, "1.3.14.3.2.26");

//provide DSA parameters to verification
dsaparams = dsa.ExportParameters(false);

//display digital signature in hex format
...

//do UI stuff
...
}
```

The **buttonVerify_Click** method performs the digital signature verification on the message. Again, this is very similar to the logic shown in the RSA programming example shown earlier. Once the hash has been performed on the received message, the **VerifyHash** method is used to verify that this hash is valid.

```
private void buttonVerify_Click(
    object sender, System.EventArgs e)
{
    //get possibly modified message as byte array
    byte[] messagebytes = Encoding.UTF8.GetBytes(
        textOriginalMessage.Text);

    //create digest of original message using SHA1
    SHA1 sha1  = new SHA1CryptoServiceProvider();
    byte[] hashbytes =
        sha1.ComputeHash(messagebytes);

    //create DSA object using parameters from signing
    DSACryptoServiceProvider dsa =
        new DSACryptoServiceProvider();
    dsa.ImportParameters(dsaparams);

    //do verification on hash using OID for SHA-1
    bool match = dsa.VerifyHash(
        hashbytes, "1.3.14.3.2.26", signaturebytes);
```

```
    //show message box with result of verification
    ...

    //do UI stuff
    ...
}

//variables communicated from signing to verifying
DSAParameters dsaparams;
byte[] signaturebytes;
```

We have just seen in the **DSAAlgorithm** and **RSASignature** examples that working with digital signatures via the **DSACryptoServiceProvider** and **RSACryptoServiceProvider** classes is virtually identical. Such consistency is what you would expect from a well-designed class library such as .NET. You simply call the **SignHash** method to sign the message hash, and then you call the **VerifyHash** method to check the signature for validity, in exactly the same manner, regardless of whether you are using RSA or DSA.

If the message has been tampered with since it was signed, the **VerifyHash** method detects the problem. In addition, if the private key, which was automatically generated by the call to **SignHash**, does not match with the public key, used in the call to **VerifyHash**, then again, **VerifyHash** method detects the problem. In this way, the digital signature ensures that the message is coming from the authentic private key owner.

When you look at the code in these two examples, you may notice that there is nothing that explicitly generates the key pair or transmits the public key. Actually, the key pair is automatically produced when the **DSACryptoServiceProvider** or **RSACryptoServiceProvider** class is instantiated. The public key is then transmitted from the sender to the receiver via the calls to the **ExportParameters** and **ImportParameters** methods of the **DSACryptoServiceProvider** or **RSACryptoServiceProvider** classes.

These two example programs show only one of several techniques for accomplishing the same basic result. For example, rather than explicitly creating a hash byte array and then calling **SignHash** and **VerifyHash**, you could accomplish the same effect by simply calling **SignData**, which automatically generates a new hash, followed by a call to **VerifyData**. **SignData** and **VerifyData** do not require a preexisting hash, and they do not require an OID, but rather take a simple string name, such as "**SHA1**" or "**MD5**" to indicate the hash algorithm to be used.

Yet another approach is available in the case of DSA by calling the **CreateSignature** method, which creates a digital signature byte array directly from a hash byte array. Then a subsequent call to the **VerifySignature** method, passing in the original hash byte array along with the signature byte array, returns a boolean result indicating success or failure.

There are two small differences between RSA and DSA to note here. Unlike the **DSACryptoServiceProvider** class, the **RSACryptoServiceProvider** class does not support the **CreateSignature** and **VerifySignature** methods. The second difference results from the fact that the DSA algorithm does not support true encryption/decryption and therefore can be used only for signatures, not for privacy. Therefore, **DSACryptoServiceProvider** does not support the **Decrypt** and **Encrypt** methods, which are supported by **RSACryptoServiceProvider**. Other than these small differences, the two classes have identical public methods and fields.

Summary

This chapter introduced digital signatures, which are based on cryptographic hash and asymmetric encryption algorithms. In particular, the RSA and DSA digital signature algorithms were discussed. The mathematical foundations of these two algorithms were briefly reviewed, followed by working program examples showing how to use the **DSACryptoServiceProvider** and **RSACryptoServiceProvider** classes. In Chapter 6 we continue the study of digital signatures, but we focus on how XML cryptography is used in combination with digital signatures.

XML Cryptography

*E*xtensible Markup Language[1] (XML) has recently become perhaps the most ubiquitous new technology in the computing industry. It has found its way into every imaginable aspect of programming, from document-publishing software to SOAP-based distributed transaction-processing applications. In fact, XML has proven to be useful in virtually every situation in which data must be structured in a standardized format. In each of these applications, XML allows independence of programming language and platform. In essence, XML enables data interoperability and allows the development and use of reusable software libraries for processing structured data.

Since cryptography and security can also be useful in practically every conceivable type of application that sends or receives structured data, it is not surprising that there is a significant overlap of interest between cryptography and security on the one hand and XML on the other. The obvious idea is therefore to apply cryptographic algorithms, such as encryption and signatures, to XML data. The result of this combination has produced two new important World Wide Web Consortium (W3C) standards, referred to as *XML encryption* and *XML signatures*, which are the topics of this chapter.

---

1. This chapter assumes that you are already somewhat familiar with XML. For your reference needs, please see the *www.xml.org* Web site. For a more complete and rigorous reference, please see the W3C Recommendation XML 1.0, which can be found at *http://www.w3.org/TR/REC-xml*.

XML Encryption

Just one of the many nice features of XML is that it tends to be rather human readable when compared to most traditional proprietary or legacy binary data formats. Just open an Excel spreadsheet in Notepad and try to figure out what is meant by all the proprietary formatting codes. In XML, all those human-meaningful tags sprinkled throughout the document tend to visually jump out and help you to interpret the underlying meaning. This can go a long way in helping you sort your way through the complex morass that is so typical of most structured data that is processed by complex applications. The readability of XML can therefore often be a great benefit to programmers, who must frequently read XML input and output to help guide them during software development and testing. Of course, human readability is an advantage only if you in fact do intend for people to make visual sense of your data. Frequently, that is not the case, especially after the application is deployed and used for processing real-world sensitive data. Fortunately, XML encryption can be selectively applied to the sensitive elements contained within your XML documents. In this way, you can ensure that those parts of your data that need to be kept private are made unintelligible to unauthorized individuals.

XML Encryption Versus SSL/TLS

There already exist Internet encryption and security protocols, such as Secure Sockets Layer (SSL), Transport Layer Security (TLS),[2] and IPSec,[3] which can be used to protect privacy and ensure data integrity between two communicating applications. There are two aspects of XML encryption that contrast with these encryption protocols. The first difference is that with XML encryption, you can selectively encrypt those XML elements that actually require it, and other non-sensitive elements may be intentionally left unencrypted. The second difference is that XML encryption can be used for encrypting data that is either transmitted directly to another application or accessed by many applications via stored media, such as a disk file or database record. In contrast, protocols such as SSL, TLS, and IPSec encrypt the entire connection as a whole, allowing it to be used between two communicating applications, but it is not as useful for encrypted data storage purposes. XML encryption does not replace these existing security protocols, but instead solves an entirely different type

---

2. The SSL protocol was developed by Netscape to provide privacy and data integrity between two communicating applications. SSL formed the basis for the TLS protocol, which is defined in RFC2246. SSL and TLS are basically the same protocol, referred to collectively as SSL/TLS.

3. The IPSec protocol provides packet-level security, which essentially implements a VPN protocol.

of security problem. The two major issues that are specifically addressed by XML encryption are the following:

- Encrypting only specific subsets of structured data.
- Encrypting structured data storage that is accessible to multiple parties.

The XML Encryption Specification

For the full details on the XML encryption specification, you can review the official XML Encryption Syntax and Processing specification.[4] This specification provides an overview with examples, as well as a complete XML schema[5] definition of XML encryption syntax. At the time of writing, the status of this specification was at the Proposed Recommendations[6] stage, meaning that it could potentially undergo changes. In fact, the .NET Framework does not yet provide any specialized support for this specification. We therefore, for the time being, need to write our own code to support this specification where necessary.

It would be an undertaking of major proportions to design and code an entire .NET class library to fully support this specification, which we will not attempt here. Instead, we implement modest and makeshift functionality inline where necessary to demonstrate in a simple example program how to encrypt a portion of a simple XML document. We do this using the currently available XML and cryptography classes provided by the .NET Framework. Fortunately, as we will see later in this chapter, the XML signature specification has completed its standardization process, and .NET therefore provides much more complete support for that standard.

What XML Encryption Provides

XML encryption provides a standardized means for encrypting structured data and representing the result in a standard XML format. This allows you to encrypt any data, whether it is an entire XML document, just specific elements within an XML document, or arbitrary, externally referenced data that is not even necessarily in XML format. The result is then represented as an XML encryption element that can either directly contain the encrypted data

---

4. This W3C specification can be found at *http://www.w3.org/TR/xmlenc-core/*.
5. More information on the XML schema specification can be found in two parts located at *http://www.w3.org/TR/2001/REC-xmlschema-1-20010502/* and *http://www.w3.org/TR/2001/REC-xmlschema-2-20010502/*.
6. A W3C Proposed Recommendation is a draft that meets all requirements established by the associated Working Group, but it is not yet appropriate for widespread deployment. It is considered to be a work-in-progress and may be updated, replaced, or made obsolete at any time.

or indirectly reference the externally encrypted data. In either case the resulting representation allows the encrypted data to be conveniently accessed for processing by applications that use powerful, familiar, and platform-independent XML programming techniques.

The general cryptographic concepts that we have already seen in previous chapters regarding symmetric and asymmetric algorithms remain the same when dealing with XML encryption. The only difference here is that we make use of a standardized XML tag syntax for representing relevant information such as key information, algorithm, and, of course, the actual encrypted data that is contained or referenced within the resulting XML document.

XML Encryption Syntax

XML encryption syntax is defined clearly and completely by the W3C specification, so we will not provide a lengthy duplication of that information here. Rather than exhaustively discussing each tag and processing rule, we instead provide a brief overview of some of the key aspects of XML encryption syntax along with a simple example to help you get started in understanding the specification.

THE XML ENCRYPTION NAMESPACE

Namespaces[7] are used in XML for much the same reason that they are used in many programming languages, such as C#, Java, and C++. Namespaces solve the problem of name collisions by providing universal names that extend beyond the scope of individual XML applications.

Each XML syntax specification defines a set of tags (i.e., elements and attributes), which are referred to as the syntax's markup vocabulary. But applications often must work with many XML documents that originate from multiple syntax specifications, each with its own distinct markup vocabularies. The problem can therefore arise where name collisions occur between conflicting markup vocabularies. By defining each markup vocabulary within its own distinct namespace, such collisions are avoided. For this reason, the XML encryption specification defines the following namespace:

```
xmlns:xenc='http://www.w3c.org/2001/04/xmlenc#'
```

In addition to providing syntactic scope, the namespace is used as a prefix for algorithm identifiers referred to in the specification. Here are some examples of algorithm identifiers that are defined in the specification. You

---

7. More information on XML namespaces can be found at *http://www.w3.org/TR/1999/REC-xml-names-19990114/*.

should recognize each of the algorithms being identified, such as RSA, 3DES, SHA-1, and so on.

- *http://www.w3.org/2001/04/xmlenc#rsa-1_5*
- *http://www.w3.org/2001/04/xmlenc#tripledes-cbc*
- *http://www.w3.org/2001/04/xmlenc#aes128-cbc*
- *http://www.w3.org/2001/04/xmlenc#aes256-cbc*
- *http://www.w3.org/2001/04/xmlenc#aes192-cbc*
- *http://www.w3.org/2001/04/xmlenc#rsa-1_5*
- *http://www.w3.org/2001/04/xmlenc#rsa-oaep-mgf1p*
- *http://www.w3.org/2000/09/xmldsig#sha1*
- *http://www.w3.org/2001/04/xmlenc#sha256*
- *http://www.w3.org/2001/04/xmlenc#sha512*
- *http://www.w3.org/2001/04/xmlenc#ripemd160*

THE XML ENCRYPTION ELEMENTS

The EncryptedData element is the main syntactic component used in XML encryption. All other XML encryption elements are children of the Encrypted-Data element. This section provides a brief overview of the XML encryption elements, including the EncryptedData element and each of its children.

- The **EncryptedData** element is the outermost element that encloses (contained or referenced) encrypted data as well as related information needed for decryption, such as private session key information and the encryption algorithm used. If this element is the document's root element, then the entire document is encrypted. A single document may contain multiple occurrences of this element, but no such element can be a parent or child of another EncryptedData element.
- The **EncryptionMethod** element is a child of the EncryptedData element that describes the encryption algorithm used, using one of the algorithm identifiers listed in the previous section. If this element is not provided, then the encryption algorithm must be somehow shared or implicitly known by the participating applications.
- The **ds:KeyInfo** element is a child of the EncryptedData element that provides the symmetric session key used to encrypt and decrypt the data. If this element is not provided, then the session key must be somehow shared or implicitly known by the participating applications. The ds:KeyInfo element may be used in the EncryptedData element of an encrypted XML document, but it can also be used in the EncryptedKey element in a standalone key-exchange document. The XML schema for the ds:KeyInfo element is defined in the separate XML signatures specification.
- The **EncryptedKey** element is a child of the ds:KeyInfo element that is used to exchange a symmetric session key. The EncryptedKey

element is similar to the EncryptedData element except that the data encrypted is always a session key rather than arbitrary data.

- The **AgreementMethod** element is a child of the ds:KeyInfo element that is used to establish an application-defined method for sharing a secret session key. If this element is absent, then key agreement must be handled in some way by the applications involved.
- The **ds:KeyName** element is a child of the ds:KeyInfo element that is optionally used to access a secret session key by way of a human-readable name.
- The **ds:RetrievalMethod** element is a child of the ds:KeyInfo element that can provide a URI link to another EncryptedKey element that contains the private session key.
- The **CipherData** element is a mandatory child element of the EncryptedData element, which contains or references the actual encrypted data. If it contains the encrypted data, a child CipherValue element is used. If it references encrypted data, a CipherReference element is used. This is the only child element of EncryptedData that is not optional. This makes sense, since it would be silly to have an EncryptedData element that provided no encrypted data.
- The **CipherValue** element encloses the raw encrypted data.
- The **CipherReference** element encloses a reference to externally encrypted data.
- The **EncryptionProperties** element provides additional application-specific information that may be useful, such as the origin, date, time of the encryption operation, and so on.

Let's now look at how all these elements are used together in an encrypted XML document. EncryptedData is the outermost element, which can contain any of its optional child elements: EncryptionMethod, ds:KeyInfo, and EncryptionProperties. It must also contain its one mandatory CipherData element. The ds:KeyInfo element can contain any of its optional elements that make session key information available. The CipherData element may contain either one of its optional elements, CipherValue or CipherReference. The EncryptedData element syntax has the following structure, where ? denotes zero or one occurrence and * denotes zero or more occurrences.[8]

```
<EncryptedData Id? Type? MimeType? Encoding?>
  <EncryptionMethod/>?
  <ds:KeyInfo>
    <EncryptedKey>?
    <AgreementMethod>?
    <ds:KeyName>?
```

---

8. Although it is not needed in this particular syntactic description, the specification uses + in other syntactic descriptions to denote one or more occurrences.

```
   <ds:RetrievalMethod>?
   <ds:*>?
 </ds:KeyInfo>?
 <CipherData>
   <CipherValue>?
   <CipherReference URI?>?
 </CipherData>
 <EncryptionProperties>?
</EncryptedData>
```

To help make this more concrete, let's take a look at how the Encrypt-edData element is used in an actual example. This is the same simple XML document that we will see in the upcoming XML encryption example program. Let's now look at this XML document before and after encryption. Here is the content of the original document, before encryption is performed.

```
<invoice>
   <items>
      <item>
         <desc>Deluxe corncob pipe</desc>
         <unitprice>14.95</unitprice>
         <quantity>1</quantity>
      </item>
   </items>
   <creditinfo>
      <cardnumber>0123456789</cardnumber>
      <expiration>01/06/2005</expiration>
      <lastname>Finn</lastname>
      <firstname>Huckleberry</firstname>
   </creditinfo>
</invoice>
```

As you can see, we have a simple invoice containing the information on the list of items purchased, which is not considered sensitive data in this example. But we also have credit information that is clearly in need of encryption. The following document shows the new contents after the encryption of the credit information.

```
<invoice>
<items>
   <item>
      <desc>Deluxe corncob pipe</desc>
      <unitprice>14.95</unitprice>
      <quantity>1</quantity>
   </item>
</items>
<EncryptedData Type="http://www.w3.org/2001/04/
                     xmlenc#Element">
```

```
    <ds:KeyInfo xmlns:ds="http://www.w3.org/2000/09/
                          xmldsig#">
        <KeyName>My 3DES Session Key</KeyName>
    </ds:KeyInfo>
    <CipherData>
        <CipherValue>tu7ev6nuRCYUgZpN0ZABz+VJvL...
        </CipherValue>
    </CipherData>
  </EncryptedData>
</invoice>
```

This document is the same as the original except that the creditinfo element has been entirely replaced with the EncryptedData element. The Cipher-Value element contains the encrypted data representing the entire creditinfo element of the original document. The ds:KeyInfo element contains the name of the encrypted session key that must be used to decrypt the contents of the CipherValue element to recover the original credit information.

If you look at the tail end of the Type attribute in the EncryptedData element, you will see that we are specifying #Element rather than #Content. This means that we want the entire creditinfo element, not just the content of that element, to be encrypted. You must decide for yourself which of these effects is desirable in your own applications. You must decide if you want only the content of the element to be hidden or if you want the entire element to be hidden, obscuring the fact that the information even exists in the document. It is of course a more secure approach to encrypt the entire element, since that helps to prevent an attacker from even noticing or taking an interest in the first place. However, it may be necessary for the type of element to be in the clear to make processing by your applications more convenient, in which case you should encrypt only the element contents.

It is important to recognize that the credit information is not the only data that must be encrypted in the above example. The credit information is encrypted with a secret symmetric key, but that key must be asymmetrically encrypted with a public key so that only the intended recipient who has the matching private key can decrypt that session key and then use it to decrypt the credit information. We could have incorporated the encrypted session key data directly into the invoice document. To do that, we would have placed a CipherValue element containing the encrypted session key into the Encrypt-edData element. Instead, we included only information on the name of the key within the invoice document. In this example we provide the encrypted session key data its own dedicated key exchange document, as shown in the following listing. Notice that this key exchange document uses EncryptedKey rather than EncryptedData as the top-level element.

```
<EncryptedKey CarriedKeyName="My 3DES Session Key">
  <EncryptionMethod Algorithm="...xmlenc#rsa-1_5" />
```

```
<ds:KeyInfo xmlns:ds="http://www.w3.org/2000/09/
                      xmldsig#">
    <KeyName>My Private Key</KeyName>
</ds:KeyInfo>
<CipherData>
    <CipherValue>bYgmKUZIXzwt2te9dmONF7Mj...
    </CipherValue>
</CipherData>
</EncryptedKey>
```

How XML Encryption Works

As is the case with most general-purpose encryption schemes, XML encryption makes use of a combination of symmetric and asymmetric algorithms. The symmetric algorithm is used for bulk encryption of XML data elements, and the asymmetric algorithm is used to securely exchange the symmetric key. Here is the typical scheme used by the sender and receiver of encrypted XML data messages.

1. The receiver generates an asymmetric key pair, making one key public and the other key private. This makes it possible for anyone to use the public key to encrypt data that then can be decrypted only by the owner of the private key.
2. The sender obtains the receiver's public key by direct, nonsecure means or by way of a certificate authority if it is necessary to authenticate the public key.
3. The sender generates a secret symmetric key.
4. The sender encrypts the desired elements in the XML document using the symmetric key.
5. The sender encrypts the symmetric key using the recipient's public key.
6. The sender incorporates the encrypted data and encrypted symmetric key, along with optional information such as algorithm parameters, to produce a new encrypted XML document. This is done in accordance with the standard syntactic rules defined in the XML encryption specification.
7. The sender sends the encrypted XML document to the receiver.
8. The receiver extracts the encrypted data, the encrypted symmetric key, and any additional optional information that it might need.
9. The receiver decrypts the symmetric key using the appropriate asymmetric algorithm and the receiver's own private key.
10. The receiver decrypts the encrypted elements within the document using the decrypted symmetric key.

Classes Used in XML Encryption

Although the .NET Framework does provide high-level support for the XML signatures specification, which is covered later in this chapter, there is currently no high-level support for the XML encryption specification. Instead, we make do with our own approach to implementing the necessary functionality using the available classes found in the **System.Xml** and **System.Security.Cryptography** namespaces. These namespaces provide general-purpose XML parsing capabilities and cryptographic functionality, respectively.

We will not exhaustively study these two namespaces here. We have already seen the main cryptography namespace classes in action in previous chapters, and we will also not get sidetracked by all the powerful parsing capabilities in the XML namespace, which is beyond the scope of this book. Instead, we look at just a few methods in some of these classes that will be useful in the upcoming XML encryption program example.

THE XMLDOCUMENT CLASS

The **XmlDocument** class enables the navigation and editing of an XML document as defined by the W3C Document Object Model[9] (DOM). The **XmlDocument** class, defined in the **System.Xml** namespace, supports a large number of methods and properties. The **XmlDocument** class inherits from **XmlNode**, from which it derives many of its members. The fact that the document is an element that can contain subelements makes sense, since an XML document is inherently hierarchical.

The following paragraphs describe the methods that are particularly useful in understanding the upcoming XML encryption program example.

There are four overloaded versions of the **Load** method, each of which loads an XML document from a specified source. One of these **Load** methods takes a string parameter, representing the URL for the file containing the XML document to load. In the upcoming example program, this parameter is simply the name of a disk file.

```
public virtual void Load(
   string filename
);
```

The **LoadXml** method is similar to the Load method, except that it loads the XML document directly from the contents of the specified string. We will pass a literal string containing the desired XML data.

```
public virtual void LoadXml(
   string xml
);
```

---

9. The DOM specification is available at *http://www.w3.org/TR/2002/WD-DOM-Level-3-Core-20021022/*.

There are three overloaded versions of the **CreateElement** method. In each case these methods create and add a new XML element with the specified name to the XML document. We will use the following two overloadings.

```
public XmlElement CreateElement(
   string name
);

public virtual XmlElement CreateElement(
   string prefix,
   string localName,
   string namespaceURI
);
```

The **AppendChild** method, inherited from **XmlNode**, adds the specified node to the end of the child list of the current node. We will use this to add child nodes to the XML document.

```
public virtual XmlNode AppendChild(
   XmlNode newChild
);
```

The **CreateAttribute** method has three overloadings that are used to create an XML attribute with a specified name. We will use only the one that takes a single string parameter.

```
public XmlAttribute CreateAttribute(
   string name
);
```

The **SelectSingleNode** method, inherited from **XmlNode**, has two overloadings. We will use the overloading that takes a single string parameter.

```
public XmlNode SelectSingleNode(
   string xpath
);
```

The **Save** method saves the XML document to the specified location. There are four overloadings available for this method. We will use the one that takes a string parameter, which represents the name of the file to which the XML document is saved.

```
public virtual void Save(
   string filename
);
```

THE XMLELEMENT CLASS

The **XmlElement** class, defined in the **System.Xml** namespace, represents an XML element within a document. The **XmlElement** class is derived from **XmlLinkedNode**, which in turn is derived from **XmlNode**. **XmlElement** supports many methods and properties, but we will use only the **Append-Child** method and **InnerText** property.

The **AppendChild** method, inherited from **XmlNode**, adds the specified node to the end of the child list of the current node. We will use this to add child nodes to an XML element. This method is identical to the method of the same name in the **XmlDocument** class described earlier.

```
public virtual XmlNode AppendChild(
   XmlNode newChild
);
```

The **InnerText** property is used to get or set the concatenated string representing the node and all its children.

```
public override string InnerText
   {get; set;}
```

THE XMLATTRIBUTE CLASS

The **XmlAttribute** class, defined in the **System.Xml** namespace, supports many useful properties and methods. We will use only the **Value** property, which is used to get or set the value of the node.

```
public override string Value
   {get; set;}
```

THE RSACRYPTOSERVICEPROVIDER CLASS

We have already seen how to use the **RSACryptoServiceProvider** class in Chapters 4 and 5. You may recall from those previous discussions that this class is defined in the **System.Security.Cryptography** namespace. We will use the familiar **Encrypt** and **Decrypt** methods. We will also use the two methods **FromXmlString** and **ToXmlString**. The **Decrypt** method decrypts data using the RSA algorithm.

```
public byte[] Decrypt(
   byte[] rgb,
   bool fOAEP
);
```

The **Encrypt** method encrypts data using the RSA algorithm.

```
public byte[] Encrypt(
    byte[] rgb,
    bool fOAEP
);
```

The **ToXmlString** method creates and returns an XML string object that represents the RSA object. The **includePrivateParameters** parameter is used to control whether or not private key information is stored. If this parameter is true, both public and private information is stored in the XML output.

```
public override string ToXmlString(
    bool includePrivateParameters
);
```

The **FromXmlString** method recreates the RSA object from an XML string representation.

```
public override void FromXmlString(
    string xmlString
);
```

THE CONVERT CLASS

When dealing with encryption, we generally must work a great deal with data that is in the form of an array of bytes. However, when dealing with XML data processing, we invariably work with data that is in the form of text strings. To bridge this gap, we often must convert between these two datatypes. To do this, we make use of the **ToBase64String** and **FromBase64String** static methods provided by the **Convert** class. **ToBase64String** converts an array of 8-bit unsigned integers to its equivalent string representation consisting of base64 digits.

```
public static string ToBase64String(
    byte[] inArray
);
```

The **FromBase64String** method converts a string representing a sequence of base64 digits to the corresponding array of 8-bit unsigned integers.

```
public static byte[] FromBase64String(
    string s
);
```

Communicating Asymmetric Key Information

You do not need to do anything special to generate an asymmetric key pair, since each asymmetric algorithm class (i.e., RSA and DSA) automatically generates a random key pair each time that it is instantiated. Since the sender and receiver will each need to create a distinct instance of their own RSA object, the resulting public and private key information will obviously not automatically match between the two parties. This problem can be solved simply by communicating the public key information between the two parties. In the case of RSA the public key information is limited to the modulus and exponent.

This can be accomplished using the method pairs **ToXmlString** and **FromXmlString** or **ExportParameters** and **ImportParameters**. **ToXmlString** and **FromXmlString** allow you to store and retrieve an asymmetric algorithm object in XML format in a way that is reminiscent of traditional object serialization. **ExportParameters** and **ImportParameters** allow you to get much the same result, but rather than storing the asymmetric algorithm object in an XML format, an **RSAParameters** object is used for storage instead. Working with XML has an appealing simplicity about it, but since the **RSAParameters** class is serializable, it is also a workable solution for communicating key information. For example, if the receiver creates an RSA instance, then he or she can save the public key information and send it to the sender, unencrypted. The sender obtains the public key information and uses it to encrypt the sensitive data, which is then sent back to the receiver. The receiver obtains the encrypted data, and uses the associated private key information to decrypt the sensitive data.

We will see the **ToXmlString** and **FromXmlString** methods of the **RSA** class in the upcoming program example. But first, let's look at the somewhat similar **ExportParameters** and **ImportParameters** methods. The **ExportParameters** method has the same parameter as **ToXmlString**, named **includePrivateParameters**, which is used to control whether or not private key information is stored. If this parameter is true, both public and private information is stored. If it is false, only public key information is stored. This parameter is handy, since the key information you will want to share with other parties should always contain only the public key information. Private key information may sometimes be stored for local usage, but then you must be sure that it is stored in a secure manner, such as in an Encrypted File System (EFS) file.[10] As an alternative, the private key information can be stored in

---

10. This may seem to be a never-ending story. A symmetric session key used for secure transmission is encrypted using an asymmetric key that the application created, and the asymmetric key itself may be stored in an operating system-encrypted (i.e., EFS) file. This file is encrypted by yet another symmetric session key maintained by the operating system, which is in turn encrypted using an asymmetric key that is associated with an encrypted version of your logon password. Nobody ever said that cryptography and security was simple!

the CryptoAPI (CAPI) keystore. One of the **RSACryptoServiceProvider** constructors takes a **CspParameters** object as a parameter. That **CspParameters** class contains a field named **KeyContainerName**, which can be used to store and retrieve your key pair.

The following shows the syntax for the **ExportParameters** and **ImportParameters** methods of the **RSA** and **DSA** algorithm classes. Instead of storing the key information in XML format, it stores the information in an algorithm-specific object, **RSAParameters** for **RSA** and **DSAParameters** for **DSA**. The **includePrivateParameters** parameter is provided in each of these **ExportParameters** methods and serves exactly the same purpose as that previously described for the **ToXmlString** method.

```
public abstract RSAParameters ExportParameters(
   bool includePrivateParameters
);

public abstract void ImportParameters(
   RSAParameters parameters
);

public abstract DSAParameters ExportParameters(
   bool includePrivateParameters
);

public abstract void ImportParameters(
   DSAParameters parameters
);
```

The XmlEncryption Example

The **XmlEncryption** example program demonstrates how to encrypt and decrypt XML data. The source code for this entire example program is shown in the following code listing. As you can see, the program starts out in the Main method by creating a sender and receiver object. This models the typical scenario where one sending program encrypts data and transmits the result to a receiving program. To keep things simple and self-contained in this example, we represent these two communicating entities as two distinct classes; however, in a real-world scenario, these would almost certainly be distinct program instances.

The program then has the receiver establish the RSA parameters that will be used to secure the symmetric algorithm session key by calling the **EstablishXmlRsaParameters** method. This is typically what is done in a real-life scenario, since it is the receiver who must establish the asymmetric key pair before any sender can use the public key to encrypt the session key that will be sent to the receiver.

Then, by calling the **CreateOriginalXmlDocument** method, the sender creates the original XML document that will be encrypted.

```
//XMLEncryption.cs

//NOTE: must add a project reference to System.Security

using System;
using System.IO;
using System.Text;
using System.Xml;
using System.Security.Cryptography;
using System.Security.Cryptography.Xml;

class XMLEncryption
{
    static void Main(string[] args)
    {
        //create participants
        Sender sender = new Sender();
        Receiver receiver = new Receiver();

        //establish public and private RSA key information
        receiver.EstablishXmlRsaParameters(
            "RsaIncludePrivateParams.xml",
            "RsaExcludePrivateParams.xml");

        //create original XML document to be encrypted
        sender.CreateOriginalXmlDocument(
            "OriginalInvoice.xml");

        //create session key and encrypt via RSA public key
        byte [] IV = sender.CreateAndEncryptXmlSessionKey(
            "RsaExcludePrivateParams.xml",
            "SessionKeyExchange.xml");

        //encrypt original XML document with session key
        sender.EncryptOriginalXmlDocument(
            "OriginalInvoice.xml",
            "RsaExcludePrivateParams.xml",
            "SessionKeyExchange.xml",
            "EncryptedInvoice.xml");

        //encrypt XML document with session key
        receiver.DecryptXmlDocument(
            "EncryptedInvoice.xml",
            "RsaIncludePrivateParams.xml",
            "SessionKeyExchange.xml",
            "DecryptedCreditInfo.xml",
            IV);
    }
}
```

```
class Sender
{
    public void CreateOriginalXmlDocument(
        String originalFilename)
    {
        //establish the original XML document
        XmlDocument xmlDoc = new XmlDocument();
        xmlDoc.PreserveWhitespace = true;
        xmlDoc.LoadXml(
            "<invoice>\n" +
            "    <items>\n" +
            "        <item>\n" +
            "            <desc>Deluxe corncob pipe</desc>\n" +
            "            <unitprice>14.95</unitprice>\n" +
            "            <quantity>1</quantity>\n" +
            "        </item>\n" +
            "    </items>\n" +
            "    <creditinfo>\n" +
            "        <cardnumber>0123456789</cardnumber>\n" +
            "        <expiration>01/06/2005</expiration>\n" +
            "        <lastname>Finn</lastname>\n" +
            "        <firstname>Huckleberry</firstname>\n" +
            "    </creditinfo>\n" +
            "</invoice>\n");

        //write original XML document to file
        StreamWriter file =
            new StreamWriter(originalFilename);
        file.Write(xmlDoc.OuterXml);
        file.Close();

        //let the user know what happened
        Console.WriteLine(
            "Original XML document written to:\n\t" +
            originalFilename);
    }

    public byte [] CreateAndEncryptXmlSessionKey(
        String rsaExcludePrivateParamsFilename,
        String keyFilename)
    {
        //obtain session key for 3DES bulk encryption
        TripleDESCryptoServiceProvider tripleDES =
            new TripleDESCryptoServiceProvider();

        //store IV and Key for sender encryption
        IV = tripleDES.IV;
        Key = tripleDES.Key;
```

```
//fetch public only RSA parameters from XML
StreamReader fileRsaParams = new StreamReader(
   rsaExcludePrivateParamsFilename);
String rsaExcludePrivateParamsXML =
   fileRsaParams.ReadToEnd();
fileRsaParams.Close();

//RSA encrypt session key
RSACryptoServiceProvider rsa =
   new RSACryptoServiceProvider();
rsa.FromXmlString(rsaExcludePrivateParamsXML);
byte[] keyEncryptedBytes =
   rsa.Encrypt(tripleDES.Key, false);

//store encrypted 3DES session key in Base64 string
String keyEncryptedString = Convert.ToBase64String(
   keyEncryptedBytes);

//create XML document for 3DES session key exchange
XmlDocument xmlKeyDoc = new XmlDocument();
xmlKeyDoc.PreserveWhitespace = true;

//add EncryptedKey element to key XML
XmlElement xmlEncryptedKey =
   xmlKeyDoc.CreateElement("EncryptedKey");
xmlKeyDoc.AppendChild(xmlEncryptedKey);
XmlAttribute xmlCarriedKeyName =
   xmlKeyDoc.CreateAttribute("CarriedKeyName");
xmlCarriedKeyName.Value = "My 3DES Session Key";
xmlEncryptedKey.Attributes.Append(
   xmlCarriedKeyName);

//add the EncryptionMethod element to key XML
XmlElement xmlEncryptionMethod =
   xmlKeyDoc.CreateElement("EncryptionMethod");
xmlEncryptedKey.AppendChild(xmlEncryptionMethod);
XmlAttribute xmlAlgorithm =
   xmlKeyDoc.CreateAttribute("Algorithm");
xmlAlgorithm.Value =
   "http://www.w3.org/2001/04/xmlenc#rsa-1_5";
xmlEncryptionMethod.Attributes.Append(
   xmlAlgorithm);

//add KeyInfo element to key XML
XmlElement xmlKeyInfo =
   xmlKeyDoc.CreateElement(
   "ds",
   "KeyInfo",
   "http://www.w3.org/2000/09/xmldsig#");
xmlEncryptedKey.AppendChild(xmlKeyInfo);
```

```
        //add KeyName element to key XML
        XmlElement xmlKeyName =
            xmlKeyDoc.CreateElement("ds", "KeyName", null);
        xmlKeyName.InnerText = "My Private Key";
        xmlKeyInfo.AppendChild(xmlKeyName);

        //add CipherData element to key XML
        XmlElement xmlCipherData =
            xmlKeyDoc.CreateElement("CipherData");
        xmlEncryptedKey.AppendChild(xmlCipherData);

        //add CipherValue element to key XML
        XmlElement xmlCipherValue =
            xmlKeyDoc.CreateElement("CipherValue");
        xmlCipherValue.InnerText = keyEncryptedString;
        xmlCipherData.AppendChild(xmlCipherValue);

        //save key XML information
        xmlKeyDoc.Save(keyFilename);

        //let the user know what happened
        Console.WriteLine(
            "Encrypted Session Key XML written to:\n\t" +
            keyFilename);

        return IV; //needed by receiver too
    }

    public void EncryptOriginalXmlDocument(
        String originalFilename,
        String rsaExcludePrivateParamsFilename,
        String keyFilename,
        String encryptedFilename)
    {
        //load XML document to be encrypted
        XmlDocument xmlDoc = new XmlDocument();
        xmlDoc.PreserveWhitespace = true;
        xmlDoc.Load(originalFilename);

        //get creditinfo node plaintext bytes to encrypt
        XmlElement xmlCreditinfo =
            (XmlElement)xmlDoc.SelectSingleNode(
            "invoice/creditinfo");
        byte[] creditinfoPlainbytes =
            Encoding.UTF8.GetBytes(xmlCreditinfo.OuterXml);

        //load XML key document
        XmlDocument xmlKeyDoc = new XmlDocument();
        xmlKeyDoc.PreserveWhitespace = true;
        xmlKeyDoc.Load(keyFilename);
```

```
//get encrypted session key bytes
XmlElement xmlKeyCipherValue =
   (XmlElement)xmlKeyDoc.SelectSingleNode(
   "EncryptedKey/CipherData/CipherValue");
byte[] xmlKeyCipherbytes =
   Convert.FromBase64String(
      xmlKeyCipherValue.InnerText);

//create 3DES algorithm object for bulk encryption
TripleDESCryptoServiceProvider tripleDES =
   new TripleDESCryptoServiceProvider();

//establish crypto stream using 3DES algorithm
MemoryStream ms = new MemoryStream();
CryptoStream cs = new CryptoStream(
   ms,
   tripleDES.CreateEncryptor(Key, IV),
   CryptoStreamMode.Write);

//write creditinfo plaintext to crypto stream
cs.Write(
   creditinfoPlainbytes,
   0,
   creditinfoPlainbytes.Length);
cs.Close();

//get creditinfo ciphertext from crypto stream
byte[] creditinfoCipherbytes = ms.ToArray();
ms.Close();
String creditinfoCiphertext =
   Convert.ToBase64String(
      creditinfoCipherbytes);

//create EncryptedData in XML file
XmlElement xmlEncryptedData =
   xmlDoc.CreateElement("EncryptedData");
XmlAttribute xmlType =
   xmlDoc.CreateAttribute("Type");
xmlType.Value =
   "http://www.w3.org/2001/04/xmlenc#Element";
xmlEncryptedData.Attributes.Append(xmlType);

//add KeyInfo element
XmlElement xmlKeyInfo =
   xmlDoc.CreateElement(
   "ds",
   "KeyInfo",
   "http://www.w3.org/2000/09/xmldsig#");
xmlEncryptedData.AppendChild(xmlKeyInfo);
```

```
        //add KeyName element
        XmlElement xmlKeyName =
            xmlDoc.CreateElement("ds", "KeyName",null);
        xmlKeyName.InnerText = "My 3DES Session Key";
        xmlKeyInfo.AppendChild(xmlKeyName);

        //add CipherData element
        XmlElement xmlCipherData =
            xmlDoc.CreateElement("CipherData");
        xmlEncryptedData.AppendChild(xmlCipherData);

        //add CipherValue element with encrypted creditinfo
        XmlElement xmlCipherValue =
            xmlDoc.CreateElement("CipherValue");
        xmlCipherValue.InnerText = creditinfoCiphertext;
        xmlCipherData.AppendChild(xmlCipherValue);

        //replace original node with the encrypted node
        xmlCreditinfo.ParentNode.ReplaceChild(
            xmlEncryptedData, xmlCreditinfo);

        //save XML to encrypted file
        xmlDoc.Save(encryptedFilename);

        //let the user know what happened
        Console.WriteLine(
            "Encrypted XML document written to:\n\t" +
            encryptedFilename);
    }

    //information sender needs across method calls
    static byte [] IV;
    static byte [] Key;
}

class Receiver
{
    public void EstablishXmlRsaParameters(
        String rsaIncludePrivateParamsFilename,
        String rsaExcludePrivateParamsFilename)
    {
        //create RSA object with new key pair
        RSACryptoServiceProvider rsa =
            new RSACryptoServiceProvider();

        //store public and private RSA key params in XML
        StreamWriter fileRsaIncludePrivateParams
            = new StreamWriter(
            rsaIncludePrivateParamsFilename);
```

```
      fileRsaIncludePrivateParams.Write(
         rsa.ToXmlString(true));
      fileRsaIncludePrivateParams.Close();

      //store public only RSA key params in XML
      StreamWriter fileRsaExcludePrivateParams =
         new StreamWriter(
         rsaExcludePrivateParamsFilename);
      fileRsaExcludePrivateParams.Write(
         rsa.ToXmlString(false));
      fileRsaExcludePrivateParams.Close();

      //let the user know what happened
      Console.WriteLine(
         "RSA parameters written to:\n\t" +
         rsaIncludePrivateParamsFilename + "\n\t" +
         rsaExcludePrivateParamsFilename);
   }
   public void DecryptXmlDocument(
      String encryptedFilename,
      String rsaIncludePrivateParamsFilename,
      String keyFilename,
      String decryptedFilename,
      byte [] IV)
   {
      //load encrypted XML document
      XmlDocument xmlDoc = new XmlDocument();
      xmlDoc.PreserveWhitespace = true;
      xmlDoc.Load(encryptedFilename);

      //get creditinfo node ciphertext bytes to decrypt
      XmlElement xmlEncryptedData =
         (XmlElement)xmlDoc.SelectSingleNode(
         "invoice/EncryptedData");
      XmlElement xmlCipherValue =
         (XmlElement)xmlEncryptedData.SelectSingleNode(
         "CipherData/CipherValue");
      byte[] creditinfoCipherbytes =
         Convert.FromBase64String(
            xmlCipherValue.InnerText);

      //load XML key document
      XmlDocument xmlKeyDoc = new XmlDocument();
      xmlKeyDoc.PreserveWhitespace = true;
      xmlKeyDoc.Load(keyFilename);

      //get encrypted session key bytes
      XmlElement xmlKeyCipherValue =
         (XmlElement)xmlKeyDoc.SelectSingleNode(
         "EncryptedKey/CipherData/CipherValue");
```

```
byte[] xmlKeyCipherbytes =
   Convert.FromBase64String(
      xmlKeyCipherValue.InnerText);

//fetch public only RSA parameters from XML
StreamReader fileRsaParams = new StreamReader(
   rsaIncludePrivateParamsFilename);
String rsaIncludePrivateParamsXML =
   fileRsaParams.ReadToEnd();
fileRsaParams.Close();

//RSA decrypt 3DES session key
RSACryptoServiceProvider rsa =
   new RSACryptoServiceProvider();
rsa.FromXmlString(rsaIncludePrivateParamsXML);

byte[] keyPlainBytes =
   rsa.Decrypt(xmlKeyCipherbytes, false);

//create 3DES algorithm object for bulk encryption
TripleDESCryptoServiceProvider tripleDES =
   new TripleDESCryptoServiceProvider();

//establish crypto stream using 3DES algorithm
MemoryStream ms = new MemoryStream(
   creditinfoCipherbytes);
CryptoStream cs = new CryptoStream(
   ms,
   tripleDES.CreateDecryptor(keyPlainBytes, IV),
   CryptoStreamMode.Read);

//read creditinfo plaintext from crypto stream
byte[] creditinfoPlainbytes =
   new Byte[creditinfoCipherbytes.Length];
cs.Read(
   creditinfoPlainbytes,
   0,
   creditinfoPlainbytes.Length);
cs.Close();
ms.Close();

String creditinfoPlaintext =
   Encoding.UTF8.GetString(creditinfoPlainbytes);

//write decrypted XML node to file
StreamWriter fileplaintext =
   new StreamWriter(decryptedFilename);
fileplaintext.Write(creditinfoPlaintext);
fileplaintext.Close();
```

```
         //let the user know what happened
         Console.WriteLine(
            "Decrypted XML credit info written to:\n\t" +
            decryptedFilename);
      }
   }
}
```

When you run the **XmlEncryption** program, you will see the following output displayed in the console window. From this output, you can see the various XML files that are produced.

```
RSA parameters written to:
         RsaIncludePrivateParams.xml
         RsaExcludePrivateParams.xml
Original XML document written to:
         OriginalInvoice.xml
Encrypted Session Key XML written to:
         SessionKeyExchange.xml
Encrypted XML document written to:
         EncryptedInvoice.xml
Decrypted XML credit info written to:
         DecryptedCreditInfo.xml
```

Let's now take a look at the contents of each of these XML files. Here is the listing of the **OriginalInvoice.xml** file. As you can see, it is quite simple. It represents an invoice, which contains a list of items purchased and some credit card information. In this example we assume that the item list is not sensitive information, but the credit information must be hidden from view by unauthorized parties.

```
<invoice>
   <items>
      <item>
         <desc>Deluxe corncob pipe</desc>
         <unitprice>14.95</unitprice>
         <quantity>1</quantity>
      </item>
   </items>
   <creditinfo>
      <cardnumber>0123456789</cardnumber>
      <expiration>01/06/2005</expiration>
      <lastname>Finn</lastname>
      <firstname>Huckleberry</firstname>
   </creditinfo>
</invoice>
```

Here is the **RsaExcludePrivateParams.xml** file, slightly reformatted to allow for the width of the printed page. As you can see, the only parts of the

RSA key information that are made publicly available are the RSA modulus and exponent parameters.

```
<RSAKeyValue>
    <Modulus>1x6LG6Hv3cf87U0n+3E2OZtxJAEZI...</Modulus>
    <Exponent>AQAB</Exponent>
</RSAKeyValue>
```

Here is the **RsaIncludePrivateParams.xml** file, reformatted to allow for the width of the printed page. You can see that several other private pieces of information, including the very sensitive parameters P, Q, and D, are contained in this XML file, so it is critical that this XML file never be exposed in the clear. This file must never be made available to others, so it should probably be stored in a password-protected, encrypted directory.

```
<RSAKeyValue>
    <Modulus>1x6LG6Hv3cf87U0n+3E2OZtxJAEZIjzKkk9hDmg...
    </Modulus>
    <Exponent>AQAB</Exponent>
    <P>7vMj9Ji4CR+ObULD8q1sFgJwHiVLVJK4LKO9zA5KvFTtV...</P>
    <Q>5ngYdhg+0fxhv4Pu/Wl9eh/BvRzavGFRsPYl9AROD8UuA...</Q>
    <DP>5mGwkfzIu6scNEYCDLGeG55gIQCOH82SGyAIN3y0G96...</DP>
    <DQ>pmVtG86ThJ6YoGKMKXCBhKvrADQWBU6qYX7GljCJf79...</DQ>
    <InverseQ>1KGPyuuUOa3A7iNA00Ocsg4zwSZS3sb...</InverseQ>
    <D>kRNyMVKG2AVVmBweyL5TGYqxRNzQvHxPCVk1tJPOdYAdo...</D>
</RSAKeyValue>
```

Here is the **SessionKeyExchange.xml** file, reformatted to allow for the width of the printed page. You can see the encryption method is based on RSA, and the key name is provided as well. The most important piece of information is contained in the CipherValue tag, which provides the ciphertext representing the encrypted symmetric session key that is being exchanged.

```
<EncryptedKey CarriedKeyName="My 3DES Session Key">
    <EncryptionMethod Algorithm="http://...
                            /xmlenc#rsa-1_5" />
    <ds:KeyInfo xmlns:ds="http://www.w3.org/2000/09/
    xmldsig#">
        <KeyName>My Private Key</KeyName>
    </ds:KeyInfo>
    <CipherData>
        <CipherValue>Uqth0M4Cu6vcRSGIiI9rzg/Hk...
        </CipherValue>
    </CipherData>
</EncryptedKey>
```

Here is the **EncryptedInvoice.xml** file, slightly reformatted to allow for the width of the printed page. You can see here that the original creditinfo tag has been replaced with the EncryptedData tag. The actual encrypted credit-card information is contained in the CipherValue tag.

```
<invoice>
   <items>
      <item>
         <desc>Deluxe corncob pipe</desc>
         <unitprice>14.95</unitprice>
         <quantity>1</quantity>
      </item>
   </items>
   <EncryptedData Type="http://www.w3.org/2001/04/
                        xmlenc#Element">
      <ds:KeyInfo xmlns:ds="http://www.w3.org/2000/09/
                           xmldsig#">
         <KeyName>My 3DES Session Key</KeyName>
      </ds:KeyInfo>
      <CipherData>
         <CipherValue>IrdwslX+xx3Ej2BYvDd3gFfuKw...
         </CipherValue>
      </CipherData>
   </EncryptedData>
</invoice>
```

Now, here is the final result. The decrypted data for the credit information is shown in the file named **DecryptedCreditInfo.xml**. As can be seen in the following listing, its contents match with the original data representing the credit-card information in the original file named **OriginalInvoice.xml**.

```
<creditinfo>
   <cardnumber>0123456789</cardnumber>
   <expiration>01/06/2005</expiration>
   <lastname>Finn</lastname>
   <firstname>Huckleberry</firstname>
</creditinfo>
```

XML Signatures

XML signatures define a powerful new technology that is used for digitally signing data that is represented in an XML format. XML has become such an important standard that it is now used in practically every conceivable programming scenario where the exchange of data takes place between applications. In many of these scenarios where data must be exchanged there may also be requirements for ensuring data integrity, authentication, and/or non-repudiation.

Recall from previous chapters that in public key encryption, the original data is encrypted with the public key and decrypted with the private key. In digital signatures, only a message digest of the original data is encrypted with the private key and decrypted with the public key. Then, the message digest is recalculated and checked to see if the data was tampered with.

To make use of this new technology, you must learn two distinct aspects of XML signatures. The first is the XML signature syntax and processing rules as defined in the specification. The second is how to program with XML signatures on the .NET platform using the classes defined in the **System.Security.Cryptography.Xmlnamespace**.

The XML signature specification is sometimes referred to as XMLDSIG and is defined by W3C. The specification provides the syntax and semantics of XML signature in the form of an XML schema[11] and Document Type Definition (DTD) as well as the associated processing rules.

The XML Signature Specification

For all of the nitty-gritty details, you may want to read through the official W3C XML Signature Syntax and Processing specification found at *www.w3.org/TR/xmldsig-core/*. You can also learn about this technology in the request for comment found at *www.ietf.org/rfc/rfc3275.txt*. The status of the XML signature specification is now at the Recommendation stage, meaning that it is stable and may now be used as an implementation reference for widespread deployment.

What XML Signatures Provide

XML signatures can be applied to arbitrary data that may be located within or external to a given XML document. XML signatures support the following capabilities for data:

- Integrity assures that the data has not been tampered with or corrupted since it was signed.
- Authentication assures that the data originates from the signer.
- Nonrepudiation assures that the signer is committed to the document contents.

---

11. XML schema is a standardized language (which is itself represented in XML) that is used to define XML syntax. XML schema improves and extends upon traditional DTD language. For more information on the XML schema definition language, see *http://www.w3.org/TR/xmlschema-1/*.

XML Signature Syntax

Data objects are hashed and encrypted into a digest, which is then placed into an element, together with related information, which is then cryptographically signed. XML digital signatures are represented with the **Signature** element, which has the following layout. Again, the character ? denotes zero or one occurrence, + denotes one or more occurrences, and * denotes zero or more occurrences.

```
<Signature ID?>
   <SignedInfo>
       <CanonicalizationMethod/>
       <SignatureMethod/>
       (<Reference URI? >
          (<Transforms>)?
          <DigestMethod>
          <DigestValue>
       </Reference>)+
   </SignedInfo>
   <SignatureValue>
(<KeyInfo>)?
(<Object ID?>)*
</Signature>
```

THE XML SIGNATURE ELEMENTS

The **Signature** element is the main syntactic component used in XML signatures. All other XML signature elements are children of the Signature element. This section provides a brief overview of the XML signature elements, including the Signature element and each of its children.

- The **Signature** element is the outermost element (i.e., root element) of an XML signature that encloses the signed data.
- The **SignedInfo** element contains the canonicalization and signature algorithm elements, and one or more reference elements. The SignedInfo element can also specify an optional ID attribute that can be referenced by other signature elements.
- The **CanonicalizationMethod** element specifies the algorithm that is applied to the SignedInfo element prior to performing the signature operation. Canonicalization means to make the data conform to an established standard format, which is necessary for consistent digital signature results. This allows for crossplatform differences, such as the code representing a carriage return and so on.
- The **SignatureMethod** element specifies the algorithm that is used to convert the canonicalized SignedInfo element into the corresponding SignatureValue element. This element represents a combination of

digest algorithm (such as SHA-1), encryption algorithm (such as RSA), and possibly a padding algorithm.

- The **SignatureValue** element contains the computed value of the digital signature, which is base64 encoded.
- The **KeyInfo** element is optional, and it provides information that can be used to obtain the key for validating the signature. The KeyInfo element may contain public key-exchange information such as key name or certificate information.
- The **Object** element is optional and may occur one or more times. It may contain any arbitrary data.

It might be helpful to look again at a before and after picture to help make this syntax more concrete. The following invoice document is the same one that we saw in the XML encryption example earlier in this chapter.

```
<invoice>
    <items>
        <item>
            <desc>Deluxe corncob pipe</desc>
            <unitprice>14.95</unitprice>
            <quantity>1</quantity>
        </item>
    </items>
    <creditinfo>
        <cardnumber>0123456789</cardnumber>
        <expiration>01/06/2005</expiration>
        <lastname>Finn</lastname>
        <firstname>Huckleberry</firstname>
    </creditinfo>
</invoice>
```

Now, after the signature is applied to this XML document, we obtain the following. The entire invoice element, along with its purchased items and credit information, is all wrapped up in a rather complex Signature element, which contains all the details needed to verify the RSA signature that is contained.

```
<Signature xmlns="http://.../xmldsig#">
    <SignedInfo>
        <CanonicalizationMethod Algorithm="..." />
        <SignatureMethod Algorithm="http://...
                                /xmldsig#rsa-sha1" />
        <Reference URI="#MyDataObjectID">
            <DigestMethod Algorithm="http://...
                                /xmldsig#sha1" />
            <DigestValue>fFyEpmWrhIwMjnrBZOOGmATvvG8=
            </DigestValue>
        </Reference>
```

```
    </SignedInfo>
    <SignatureValue>V2tW6tmZnOnuvKi8cZBXp...
    </SignatureValue>
        <KeyInfo>
            <KeyValue xmlns="http://www.w3.org/2000/09/
                            xmldsig#">
                <RSAKeyValue>
                    <Modulus>rJzbWtkPyhq+eBMhRdimd...</Modulus>
                    <Exponent>AQAB</Exponent>
                </RSAKeyValue>
            </KeyValue>
        </KeyInfo>
    <Object Id="MyDataObjectID">
        <invoice xmlns="">
            <items>
                <item>
                    <desc>Deluxe corncob pipe</desc>
                    <unitprice>14.95</unitprice>
                    <quantity>1</quantity>
                </item>
            </items>
            <creditinfo>
                <cardnumber>0123456789</cardnumber>
                <expiration>01/06/2005</expiration>
                <lastname>Finn</lastname>
                <firstname>Huckleberry</firstname>
            </creditinfo>
        </invoice>
    </Object>
</Signature>
```

DETACHED, ENVELOPING, AND ENVELOPED SIGNATURES

There are three ways in which a signature may be defined within an XML document.

- Detached signature is calculated over a data object that is external to the XML Signature element. In this scenario, the data object is identified via a URI or a transform. The Signature element and data object may reside either in separate XML documents or in separate tags within the same XML document.
- Enveloping signature is calculated over data content defined within an Object element of the actual signature itself. The Object element, or its content, is identified via a Reference element via a URI fragment identifier or transform.
- Enveloped signature is calculated over the XML content that contains the Signature element.

Classes Used in XML Signatures

Let's take a brief look at the classes that we will be working with in the upcoming XML signature example program. These classes are defined in the **System.Security.Cryptography.Xml** namespace. We will not have to do as much work as we did in the previous section on XML encryption, because the .NET library provides more complete support for XML signatures.

THE DATAOBJECT CLASS

The **DataObject** class encapsulates an XML element that holds the data to be signed. We will use the **Data** property, which gets or sets the data of the **DataObject**, and the **ID** property, which gets or sets the ID of the **DataObject**.

```
public XmlNodeList Data
   {get; set;}

public string Id
   {get; set;}
```

THE SIGNEDXML CLASS

The **SignedXml** class encapsulates the core XML signature object for a signed XML document. This class has several methods and properties that we will use in the upcoming program example. The **SigningKey** property gets or sets the asymmetric algorithm key used for signing the XML element.

```
public AsymmetricAlgorithm SigningKey
   {get; set;}
```

The **AddObject** method adds a new **DataObject** to the list of objects to be signed.

```
public void AddObject(
   DataObject dataObject
);
```

The **AddReference** method adds a Reference element to the list of references that are to be hashed and signed.

```
public void AddReference(
   Reference reference
);
```

The **KeyInfo** property gets or sets the KeyInfo element of the SignedXml object.

```
public KeyInfo KeyInfo
   {get; set;}
```

The **ComputeSignature** method performs the actual signature operation on the XML element. There are two overloaded versions of this method. We will use the one with no parameter.

```
public void ComputeSignature();

public void ComputeSignature(
   KeyedHashAlgorithm macAlg
);
```

The EnvelopingXmlSignature Example

The **EnvelopingXmlSignature** example program demonstrates how to sign and validate an XML signature. The entire source code for this simple program is shown in the following code listing.

The first thing that the program does in the **Main** method is call the **CreateXMLDocument** method, which creates an XML file that contains a simple invoice document named **OriginalInvoice.xml**. Next, the program calls the **PerformXMLSignature** method that computes an XML signature for the invoice and then writes the resulting signed invoice to a file named **SignedInvoice.xml**. Then, the **VerifyXMLSignature** method is called, which verifies that the signature in **SignedInvoice.xml** is valid, and it displays the fact that it is indeed valid in the console window. Next, in order to show the effect of tampering with a signed XML document, the **TamperSignedXMLDocument** method is called, which takes the valid **SignedInvoice.xml** file and modifies the credit-card number in the invoice, and then writes the modified result to the file named **TamperedInvoice.xml**. This tampered file contains the original invoice data but with a forged credit-card number and the original signature, which is no longer valid due to the tampered data. Finally, the **VerifyXMLSignature** method is called once again, but, this time, it attempts to verify the signature in **TamperedInvoice.xml**, and the negative result is then displayed in the console window. Take a look through the following source code listing to understand how these operations work, and then study the console output and the three resulting XML files that follow. Here is the source code.

```
//EnvelopingXMLSignature.cs

//NOTE: must add a project reference to System.Security
```

```csharp
using System;
using System.IO;
using System.Xml;
using System.Security.Cryptography;
using System.Security.Cryptography.Xml;

class EnvelopingXMLSignature
{
    static void Main(string[] args)
    {
        //create participants
        Sender sender = new Sender();
        Receiver receiver = new Receiver();
        Tamperer tamperer = new Tamperer();

        //show the effects of signing and tampering
        sender.CreateXmlDocument("OriginalInvoice.xml");
        sender.PerformXmlSignature(
            "OriginalInvoice.xml", "SignedInvoice.xml");
        receiver.VerifyXmlSignature("SignedInvoice.xml");
        tamperer.TamperSignedXmlDocument(
            "SignedInvoice.xml", "TamperedInvoice.xml");
        receiver.VerifyXmlSignature("TamperedInvoice.xml");
    }
}

class Sender
{
    public void CreateXmlDocument(String originalFilename)
    {
        //establish the original XML document
        XmlDocument xmlDoc = new XmlDocument();
        xmlDoc.PreserveWhitespace = true;
        xmlDoc.LoadXml(
            "<invoice>\n" +
            "   <items>\n" +
            "      <item>\n" +
            "         <desc>Deluxe corncob pipe</desc>\n" +
            "         <unitprice>14.95</unitprice>\n" +
            "         <quantity>1</quantity>\n" +
            "      </item>\n" +
            "   </items>\n" +
            "   <creditinfo>\n" +
            "      <cardnumber>0123456789</cardnumber>\n" +
            "      <expiration>01/06/2005</expiration>\n" +
            "      <lastname>Finn</lastname>\n" +
            "      <firstname>Huckleberry</firstname>\n" +
            "   </creditinfo>\n" +
            "</invoice>\n");
```

```
    //write original XML document to file
    StreamWriter file =
        new StreamWriter(originalFilename);
    file.Write(xmlDoc.OuterXml);
    file.Close();

    //let the user know what happened
    Console.WriteLine(
        "Original XML document written to\n\t:" +
        originalFilename);
}
public void PerformXmlSignature(
    String originalFilename, String signedFilename)
{
    //load the XML document
    XmlDocument xmlDoc = new XmlDocument();
    xmlDoc.PreserveWhitespace = true;
    xmlDoc.Load(originalFilename);

    //create signature wrapper with default RSA key
    RSA key = RSA.Create();
    SignedXml signedXml = new SignedXml();
    signedXml.SigningKey = key;

    //create data object to hold the data to be signed
    DataObject dataObject = new DataObject();
    dataObject.Data = xmlDoc.ChildNodes;

    //set data object id for URI ref from elsewhere
    dataObject.Id = "MyDataObjectID";

    //add data object to be signed to signature wrapper
    signedXml.AddObject(dataObject);

    //create reference object to ref data object
    Reference reference = new Reference();
    reference.Uri = "#MyDataObjectID";

    //add reference object to signature wrapper
    signedXml.AddReference(reference);

    //add key information to signature wrapper
    KeyInfo keyInfo = new KeyInfo();
    keyInfo.AddClause(new RSAKeyValue(key));
    signedXml.KeyInfo = keyInfo;

    //generate the XML signature
    signedXml.ComputeSignature();
```

```
        //apply XML signature to XML document
        XmlElement xmlSignature = signedXml.GetXml();
        xmlDoc = new XmlDocument();
        xmlDoc.PreserveWhitespace = true;
        XmlNode xmlNode = xmlDoc.ImportNode(xmlSignature,
                          true);
        xmlDoc.AppendChild(xmlNode);
        xmlDoc.Save(signedFilename);

        //let the user know what happened
        Console.WriteLine(
            "Signed XML document written to\n\t:" +
            signedFilename);
    }
}

class Receiver
{
    public void VerifyXmlSignature(String signedFilename)
    {
        //load signed XML document
        XmlDocument xmlDoc = new XmlDocument();
        xmlDoc.PreserveWhitespace = true;
        xmlDoc.Load(signedFilename);

        //create signature wrapper from signed XML file
        SignedXml signedXml = new SignedXml(xmlDoc);

        //get <Signature> node (assume only one exists)
        XmlNodeList nodeList = xmlDoc.GetElementsByTagName(
            "Signature",
            "http://www.w3.org/2000/09/xmldsig#");
        signedXml.LoadXml((XmlElement)nodeList[0]);

        //let the user know what happened
        if (signedXml.CheckSignature())
            Console.WriteLine(
                signedFilename + " signature is VALID");
        else
            Console.WriteLine(
                signedFilename + " signature is NOT VALID");
    }
}
class Tamperer
{
    public void TamperSignedXmlDocument(
        String signedFilename, String tamperedFilename)
    {
```

```
//load signed XML document
XmlDocument xmlDoc = new XmlDocument();
xmlDoc.PreserveWhitespace = true;
xmlDoc.Load(signedFilename);

//tamper signed XML document and write to file
XmlNodeList nodeList =
    xmlDoc.GetElementsByTagName("cardnumber");
XmlNode xmlOldNode = (XmlElement)nodeList[0];
XmlNode xmlNewNode = xmlOldNode.Clone();
xmlNewNode.InnerText = "9876543210";
xmlOldNode.ParentNode.ReplaceChild(
    xmlNewNode, xmlOldNode);
xmlDoc.Save(tamperedFilename);

//let the user know what happened
Console.WriteLine(
    "Tampered signed XML document written to\n\t" +
    tamperedFilename);
    }
}
```

If you run the preceding program, you will see the following console window output. In particular, notice that the file named **SignedInvoice.xml** contains a valid XML signature, but the file named **TamperedInvoice.xml** does not contain a valid XML signature. These two files are identical except that the credit-card information was modified after the signature was generated. Since only the rightful owner of the private key used to generate the signature knows the value of that key, it is impossible for nonauthorized individuals to modify the document in an undetectable manner. This is because nonauthorized individuals do not know the correct value of this private key.

Of course, in this simple example the code that does the tampering happens to be the same program that does the signing, which is a bit unrealistic if not downright silly. Nobody would intentionally tamper with data that they themselves have produced. This example is only intended to prove the concept that, by signing a document, you can detect if it has been modified by someone else after signing has taken place.

```
Original XML document written to OriginalInvoice.xml
Signed XML document written to SignedInvoice.xml
SignedInvoice.xml signature is VALID
Tampered signed XML document written to TamperedInvoice.xml
TamperedInvoice.xml signature is NOT VALID
Press any key to continue
```

Now, let's look at the three XML files that this program has generated: **OriginalInvoice.xml**, **SignedInvoice.xml**, and **TamperedInvoice.xml**. First, here is **OriginalInvoice.xml**. Notice that the credit-card number is set to 0123456789. We will see what happens if we try tampering with this card number shortly.

```
<invoice>
   <items>
      <item>
         <desc>Deluxe corncob pipe</desc>
         <unitprice>14.95</unitprice>
         <quantity>1</quantity>
      </item>
   </items>
   <creditinfo>
      <cardnumber>0123456789</cardnumber>
      <expiration>01/06/2005</expiration>
      <lastname>Finn</lastname>
      <firstname>Huckleberry</firstname>
   </creditinfo>
</invoice>
```

Now, let's look at the **SignedInvoice.xml** file. Several parts of the file have been shortened using ellipses, and a few carriage returns have been added to make it more legible and to fit it within the confines of this printed page. As you can see, the signed version of this file contains information on both the signature and the public aspects of the key that corresponds with the private key used to used sign the file.

```
<Signature xmlns="http://www.w3.org/2000/09/xmldsig#">
   <SignedInfo>
      <CanonicalizationMethod Algorithm="..." />
      <SignatureMethod Algorithm="..." />
      <Reference URI="#MyDataObjectID">
         <DigestMethod Algorithm="..." />
         <DigestValue>...</DigestValue>
      </Reference>
   </SignedInfo>
   <SignatureValue>...</SignatureValue>
   <KeyInfo>
      <KeyValue xmlns="...">
         <RSAKeyValue>
            <Modulus>...</Modulus>
            <Exponent>...</Exponent>
         </RSAKeyValue>
      </KeyValue>
   </KeyInfo>
   <Object Id="MyDataObjectID">
      <invoice xmlns="">
         <items>
            <item>
               <desc>Deluxe corncob pipe</desc>
```

```
            <unitprice>14.95</unitprice>
            <quantity>1</quantity>
        </item>
    </items>
    <creditinfo>
        <cardnumber>0123456789</cardnumber>
        <expiration>01/06/2005</expiration>
        <lastname>Finn</lastname>
        <firstname>Huckleberry</firstname>
    </creditinfo>
  </invoice>
 </Object>
</Signature>
```

We will not bother showing the entire contents of the **TamperedIn-voice.xml**, since it is identical to the **SignedInvoice.xml** file in every way except that the credit-card number is changed from 0123456789 to 9876543210, as shown in the following snippet. You can verify that this is the only difference by comparing these two files using a tool such as **Windiff.exe**.

```
<Signature xmlns="http://www.w3.org/2000/09/xmldsig#">
    <SignedInfo>
        ...
        <creditinfo>
            <cardnumber>9876543210</cardnumber>
            <expiration>01/06/2005</expiration>
            <lastname>Finn</lastname>
            <firstname>Huckleberry</firstname>
        </creditinfo>
      </invoice>
    </Object>
</Signature>
```

Combining XML Signing and XML Encryption

It is possible to combine the two cryptographic operations of XML signing and XML encryption. If you encrypt and sign an XML document, then the order of those cryptographic operations makes a big difference. An application must distinguish between the case where encryption was performed before signing and the other case where encryption is performed after signing. If encryption was performed before signing, then it requires that the document must not be decrypted before verifying the signature. This is because decryption will corrupt the unencrypted signature, and verification becomes impossible. Conversely, if encryption was performed after signing, then the document must be decrypted before the signature can be validated. See *http://www.w3.org/TR/2002/PR-xmlenc-decrypt-20021003* for details.

Summary

In this chapter we looked at the two major cryptographic operations that can be applied to XML data. The first half of this chapter focused on XML encryption, and the second half focused on XML signatures.

.NET User-Based Security

*I*n its simplest form, the purpose of security is to prevent people and programs from doing things that an administrator or a programmer is not willing to allow. In this chapter we look at the first of two major aspects of .NET security programming, known as user-based security.[1] In the past, security has always focused on managing user permissions that allow you to restrict actions based on the identity of the current user. Thus, traditionally, you have been able to control how specific users can access certain resources, such as files, registry entries, and so forth. If you have already worked with security-related programming in Windows or UNIX, you are probably familiar with this traditional concept of user-based security.

Before discussing .NET security programming, we study the big picture of how the security model works on the .NET platform. Then we drill down on most of the classes in the .NET Framework that are related to user-based security. After that, we look at several programming examples that demonstrate how to use these classes in various ways. Finally, we consider a few general rules of thumb that you should keep in mind whenever you are involved in security programming.

In Chapter 8 we look at the very different and new concept in security programming known as Code Access Security (CAS).[2] In contrast to user-based security, CAS allows you to restrict actions based on the identity of the executing code rather than on the identity of the user who runs that code.

---

1. User-based security is also often referred to as role-based security.
2. CAS is also known as evidence-based security.

Authentication and Authorization

Before we can get anywhere in this chapter or the next, we must first come to grips with the questions of *authentication* and *authorization*. The central issue in both cases is that security must be able to ensure that only authenticated entities are permitted to carry out authorized actions. This issue therefore is resolved into two distinct questions:

- Authentication: Who are you?
- Authorization: Are you permitted?

Who are you?[3] can refer to either the identity of the user currently executing the code or the identity of the assemblies[4] that contain the code being executed. In fact, this distinction is the key difference between user-based security and CAS. In the case of user-based security, the question of authentication deals with the current user's identity, which is represented by the **Principal** and **Identity** classes. In the case of CAS, the question of authentication deals with the identity of the executing assemblies, which is represented by the **Evidence** class. This evidence can be used to discriminate on various aspects of the assembly, such as who digitally signed it and where it originated from. There may also be additional custom-assembly evidence that programmers may have defined.

Are you permitted? addresses the issue of whether or not the current user or currently executing assemblies are authorized to do what it is being attempted. This question takes the answer to the first question (identity or evidence), and then makes a decision according to the currently established security policy.[5] As we shall see in more detail later, security policy is based on permissions that have been programmatically or administratively established.

There are several types of permissions, which are represented by the many classes that implement the **IPermission** interface. For user-based security, the **PrincipalPermission** class is used to check against the identity of

---

3. This authentication question was made famous by Pete Townshend and Roger Daltrey in 1978.
4. The word *assemblies* is plural here because at any given moment, the currently executing method is actually performing work on behalf of all the method calls currently in the call stack. Since one method in one assembly may call another method in a different assembly, there are generally multiple assemblies that must be evaluated simultaneously according to the current security policy.
5. Security policy is the configurable set of rules used by the CLR to make security decisions. Security policy is usually set by administrators. Security policy can be set at the enterprise, machine, user, or application domain levels.

the current user (i.e., the user attached to the calling thread). For CAS, the many **CodeAccessPermission**-derived classes are used to check against the individual permissions that have been granted or denied to all the callers of the currently executing method.

.NET Security Model

The .NET security model is layered on top of the operating system's security model, and it can also interact with the security features of various server applications, such as SQL Server and Internet Information Services (IIS). Therefore, the security characteristics of a .NET application result from several factors, including how .NET security is configured, how the application components are programmed, as well as various security features that may be configured in Windows,[6] the network,[7] and other applications.

Figure 7–1 shows how the .NET security model works on top of the Windows security subsystem. An administrator sets up user accounts and manages security policy on Windows using various Microsoft Management Console (MMC) snap-ins. An administrator is also responsible for managing .NET security configuration. Subsequently, when a user logs onto the operating system and then runs a .NET-managed application, the CLR authenticates the user and authorizes the actions of the program, and then passes those operations on to the security monitor of the operating system.

As an example of how .NET security can interact with the operating system, consider the fact that code always runs under some user identity. When you log on, you provide your username along with your password as proof that you are who you claim to be. Once your identity has been established, as a general rule, every action that you undertake when running any program is performed under your user identity. The result is that if an administrator has established an ACL (Access Control List) that denies you the right to read or write on a particular file, you will be unable to do so.

As we go through examples of securing objects in various ways throughout this chapter, it is important to recognize that regardless of what permissions may have been established using .NET security permissions, such a file may still be protected at the operating system level, which falls outside of the jurisdiction of the .NET platform.

---

6. Throughout this chapter, the underlying operating system is assumed to be Windows 2000 or Windows XP.
7. For example, you can restrict access to your system from other IP addresses using IPSec (Internet Protocol Security).

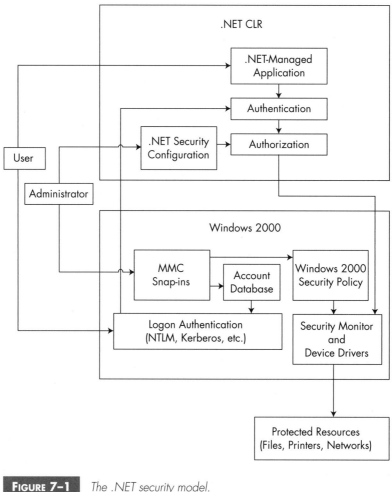

FIGURE 7-1   *The .NET security model.*

Administrating Windows Security

At a basic level, the underlying operating system has its own security infrastructure. The system administrator can configure operating system security, and programmers can use various security objects to accomplish just about any desirable security goals. An administrator can configure security at the enterprise level, using Active Directory, or at the other extreme can simply configure security at the level of individual files using NTFS (New Technology

File System) and EFS (Encrypted File System).[8] At a more mundane level, an administrator can also create new user accounts and groups and set passwords on the local machine or the domain.

Defining Users and Roles on Windows

You can easily define new users and groups on Windows. Each user or group established by an administrator corresponds to one user or role from the perspective of the security programmer. To define a user or group, you can use the Computer Management[9] MMC snap-in. To add a new user, under Local users and groups, select the Users node, and select the Action | New User menu item. To add a new group, select the Groups node instead, and select the Action | New Group menu item. The resulting New User and New Group dialog boxes appear as shown in Figures 7–2 and 7–3.

Defining Shared Folder Permissions on Windows

An administrator can also establish what individual users and members of specific groups are permitted to do with various operating system resources. For example, an administrator can control who can do what with the folders and files on storage media.

For example, you can set shared folder permissions, which apply to all files and subfolders in a specified shared folder. Figure 7–4 shows how to do this on a shared folder named **MyCodeExamples**. To do this using Windows Explorer, right-click the folder that you wish to share and select the Sharing menu item. Select the Sharing tab, and select the Share this folder radio button. Click on the Permissions button, and in the resulting Permissions dialog box, you can add or remove users and groups, and allow or deny the desired shared folder permissions. Note that the effect of this is quite limited, since shared folder permissions are effective only when the folder is accessed via the network. If you log on as a different user on the local machine, your access rights

---

8. NTFS supports file and directory access security within the confines of the host operating system. However, NTFS by itself provides no real protection if there is no physical security (such as a locked room). This is because an attacker may access the disk in nefarious ways, such as by booting from a floppy. Even if floppy boot is password protected, an attacker may physically remove the disk and perform offsite analysis. This NTFS weakness exists because there are file system drivers such as NTFSDOS that understand NTFS disk structure but ignore NTFS access security. The EFS device driver solves this problem, because it actually encrypts the data, using a combination of RSA and DESX (a fortified version of DES). EFS therefore solves the problem of file system security without physical security, which is very useful, especially for laptops!
9. To do this, click Start | Programs | Administrative Tools | Computer Management.

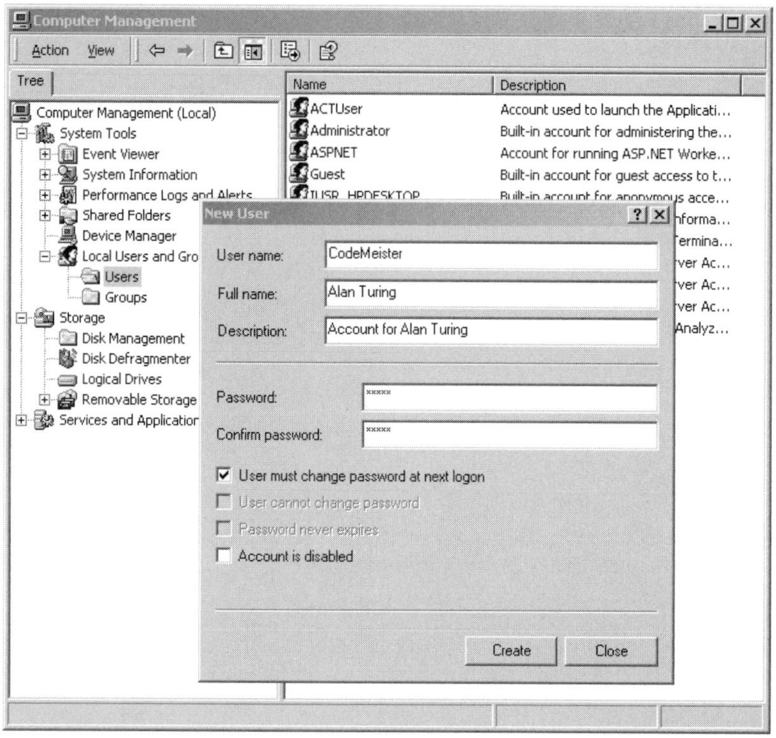

FIGURE 7-2   Creating a new user.

to the shared folder are completely unaffected by any shared folder permissions that may have been established.

Defining NTFS Security on Windows

As was just pointed out in the previous section, shared folder permissions are effective only when the folder is accessed via the network (or locally if you use the UNC name). Therefore, shared folder permissions provide no protection on local folders accessible to the user logged onto the local machine. In order to protect folders on the local computer, you must use NTFS permissions, which of course requires that you have set up an NTFS disk partition on your disk. There are several ways to establish an NTFS file system. For example, you may choose NTFS when you originally install Windows, or you may use the **Convert.exe** utility to convert an existing FAT drive to NTFS. To be safe, please read the documentation carefully to choose the best approach

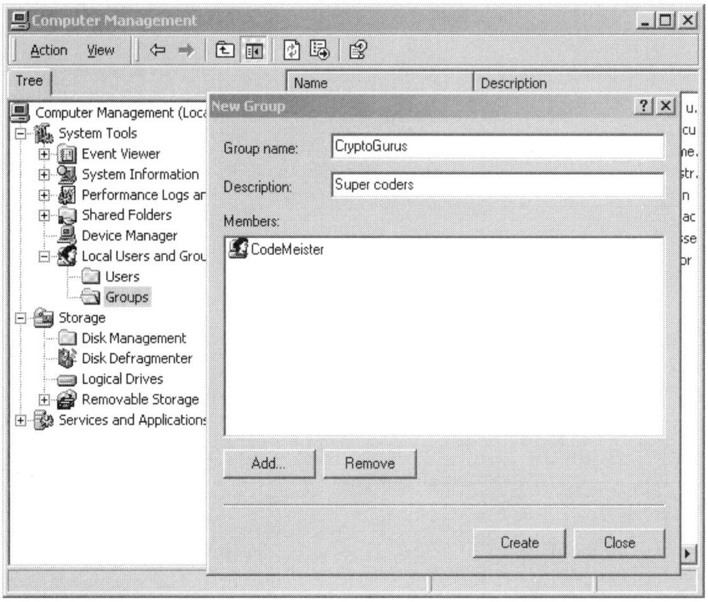

FIGURE 7-3   *Creating a new group.*

for your circumstances, and make sure that you understand the consequences of any such procedure before attempting it on a disk that contains important data.

ESTABLISHING NTFS FOLDER PERMISSIONS

Here are the steps for establishing NTFS permissions on a folder. First, you right-click on the folder in Windows Explorer and select the Security tab on the Folder Properties dialog box that appears. If you are using some disk format other than NTFS, this Security table will not appear. Figure 7–5 shows this being done with a folder named **EncryptedFiles**. The name of the folder in this example is purely arbitrary, and it is certainly not necessary that the folder must be encrypted for NTFS permissions to be established. Note that the Security tab on the Folder Properties dialog box allows you to allow or deny various permissions for each user or group that you have in the Name list. The Add button allows you to add users and groups to the Name list, and the Remove button allows you to remove them. The Permissions list that you can choose from includes such items as Modify, Read, Write, and so on. The Advanced button provides access to additional permissions that can be allowed or denied, including Create and Delete permissions.

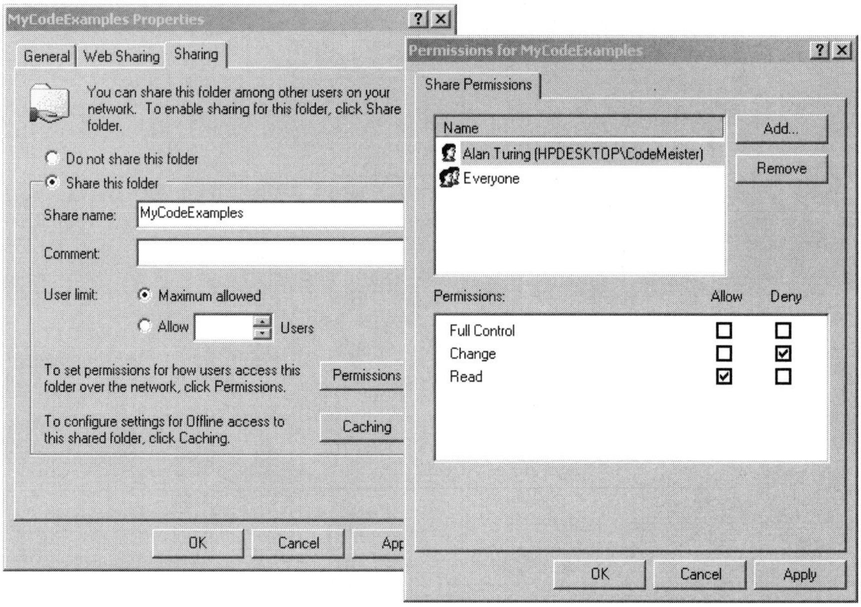

FIGURE 7–4   *Managing shared folder permissions.*

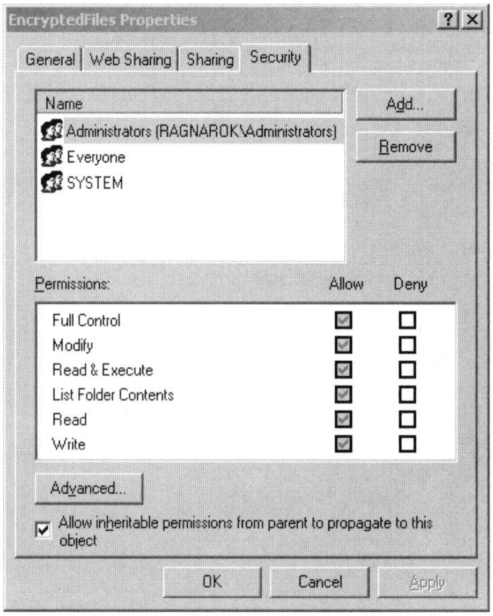

FIGURE 7–5   *Managing file system security.*

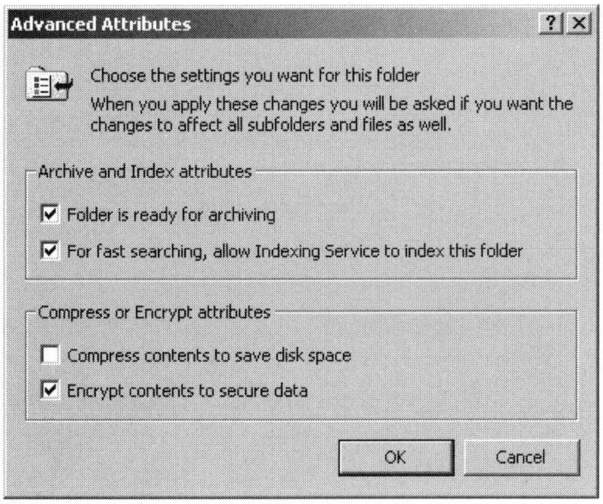

FIGURE 7-6   *Encrypt an NTFS folder.*

ENCRYPT AN NTFS FOLDER

Although it is purely optional, you can indeed encrypt any folder if you are using NTFS. To do this, click the Advanced button on the General tab of the Folder Properties dialog box. This brings up the Advanced Attributes dialog box shown in Figure 7–6. This dialog box allows you to encrypt the folder and its contents using the Encrypted File System driver. All you have to do is check the Encrypt contents to secure the data check box, and then click OK. By doing this, you do not have to worry about divulging the information in the folder, even if someone is able to somehow obtain a physical copy of the folder contents. Without the cryptographic key, the contents are unintelligible.

Administrating .NET Security

Figure 7–7[10] shows the .NET Admin Tool, which is used to configure various .NET-related security features. To start this tool, open the Control Panel and select Administrative Tools. Then, double-click the Microsoft .NET Framework Configuration node. From there, open the Runtime Security Policy node. We look more closely at using this tool in Chapter 8.

---

10. To do this, click Start | Programs | Administrative Tools | Microsoft .NET Framework Configuration.

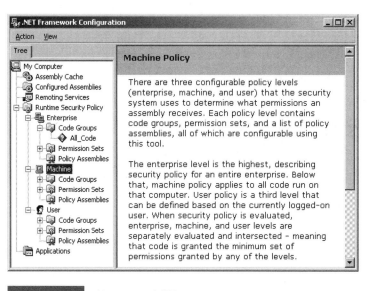

FIGURE 7-7   *Managing .NET security.*

Permissions

User-based security and CAS are the two major branches of the .NET security story, and they both require an understanding of a common concept known as permissions. For user-based security, the **PrincipalPermission** class is used to check against the identity of the current user of the calling thread. For CAS, the many **CodeAccessPermission**-derived classes are used to check against the individual permissions that have been granted or denied to all threads executing the current method. We bring up the concept of permissions in this chapter because this is where we first use the concept. In the next chapter on CAS, we make heavier use of permissions; however, this discussion of the permission concept will not be repeated there, so please read this prerequisite material before moving on.

Permissions are objects that describe sets of operations that can be permitted or denied for securing specific resources based on existing security policy. For CAS permissions (but not for user permissions), the .NET CLR uses a stack-walking mechanism to determine if all calling stack frames[11] have

---

11. By convention, the call stack is represented as growing downward, so methods higher in the call stack call methods lower in the call stack, and the current stack frame is therefore at the very bottom of the stack.

been granted a specified permission. A permission object contains specific permission information. If a permission reference is set to null, then it is treated in the same way as a permission object with the state **Permission-State.None**, meaning that it provides no permissions. Permissions are typically used in the following ways:

- Code can define the permissions it needs to carry out its tasks.
- The security system policy may grant or deny permissions requested by code.
- Code can demand that its calling code has a required permission using the **Demand** method.
- Code may override the security stack checking using the **Assert**, **Deny**, or **PermitOnly** methods.

It is also possible to work with permission sets, which are collections that can contain many different types of permission objects. This is accommodated by the **PermissionSet** class, which allows a permission set to be managed as a group of permissions.

The IPermission Interface

The **IPermission** interface encapsulates the fundamental idea of permission. The **IPermission** interface supports the following public methods:

- **Copy** creates an identical copy of an existing permission object.
- **Demand**[12] causes a **SecurityException** to be thrown if any callers higher on the call stack have not been granted the permission specified by the permission object. This method is used defensively to prevent other code from tricking the current code into doing inappropriate actions.
- **Intersect** creates a permission object that contains the intersection (i.e., overlapping set) of permissions of two existing permission objects.
- **IsSubsetOf** determines whether or not a permission object contains a subset of the permissions contained in another specified permission object.
- **Union** creates a permission object that contains the union (i.e., combined set) of permissions of two existing permission objects.

---

12. For many people, the word *demand* might imply a guarantee of success. Since the **Demand** method can fail with an exception, perhaps it should have been named something a little more modest, such as Request or Attempt. Oh well, it's too late now!

THE IPERMISSION DEMAND METHOD

Probably the most important member of the **IPermission** interface is the **Demand** method, which takes no parameters, returns void, and can throw a **SecurityException**. Here is its signature.

```
void Demand();
```

The **Demand** method checks that all callers of the current method have permission to access a specified resource in a specified way and throws its exception if this check fails. The particular type of resource that is being protected depends on the specific type of **IPermission** interface-implementing derived class that is being used. For example, the **FileIOPermission** class protects disk files, and the **RegistryPermission** class protects registry entries.

Of course, before the **Demand** can be used, the permission object must first be established, specifying the resource to be protected and the type of access being considered. In the case of file IO permissions, a **FileIOPermission** object must be established that specifies the file to be protected and the type of file access being considered, such as read, write, and append operations. This can be established using the appropriate constructor, and the **Copy**, **Intersect**, and **Union** methods may be used to tailor new objects from existing ones.

It is not all that intuitive, but it is important to remember that the permissions of the code that call the **Demand** method are not checked. The checking begins with the immediate caller on the call stack and continues on up the call stack. Obviously, **Demand** succeeds only if no exception is raised.

THE IPERMISSION COPY, INTERSECT, UNION, AND ISSUBSETOF METHODS

The methods for manipulating a permission object are **Copy**, **Intersect**, and **Union**. The method for testing a permission object is **IsSubsetOf**. Here are the syntax signatures for these four methods.

```
IPermission Copy();

IPermission Intersect(
    IPermission target
);

IPermission Union(
    IPermission target
);

bool IsSubsetOf(
    IPermission target
);
```

The IPermission Inheritance Hierarchy

The **IPermission** interface has only two derived implementation classes: **PrincipalPermission** and **CodeAccessPermission**. **PrincipalPermission** allows security checks to be made against the current, active principal object, which is the basic idea behind user-base security. The principal associated with the current thread or application domain is determined at logon time, and a specific principal object may be defined declaratively or imperatively in the application code. We will postpone a discussion of the **CodeAccessPermission** class until Chapter 8, which describes how to program using CAS.

Figure 7–8 shows the **IPermission** inheritance hierarchy. Individual namespaces are not shown in this figure, but you should know that these permission classes are defined in several different namespaces. The most commonly used namespace for permission classes is **System.Security.Permissions**.

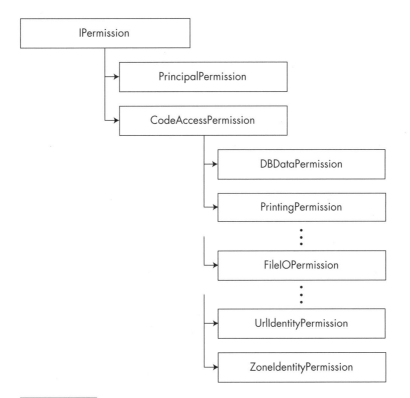

FIGURE 7-8   *The IPermission inheritance hierarchy.*

The PrincipalPermission Class

As we have just seen, the **PrincipalPermission** class implements the **IPermission** interface. As we will see in the **PrincipalPermission** program example later in this chapter, the **PrincipalPermission** class is used to check against the current principal object for user verification purposes. For a full understanding of what the **PrincipalPermission** class represents, you probably need to know more about what a principal object is, which we have not yet discussed in detail. For now, however, it is sufficient to know that a principal object represents a logged on user that you would like to discriminate on for security purposes. We provide a deeper explanation of what a principal object is shortly. Now, with the **IPermission** inheritance still fresh in our minds, let's look at some of the more important members of the **PrincipalPermission** class.

The **Demand** method, which has the same syntax as we saw in the **IPermission** inheritance, determines whether the current principal matches the specified **PrincipalPermission** object. The **SecurityException** is thrown if the check fails. Again, this method is used to enforce that the identity of the active principal is authorized to proceed without exception.

```
public void Demand();
```

The other methods of **IPermission** work for **PrincipalPermission** as expected, including the **Copy**, **Intersect**, and **Union** methods. For a brief example of how to use just one of these methods, consider the following code snippet. This code shows how to combine two principal permission objects using the **Union** method. After the call on **Union**, the subsequent call on **Demand** will succeed only if the principal object **pp** represents a user that is either the user Abbott in the role of StraightMan or the user Costello in the role of FunnyMan.

```
String user1 = "Abbott";
String role1 = "StraightMan";
PrincipalPermission PrincipalPerm1 =
   new PrincipalPermission(user1, role1);
String user2 = "Costello";
String role2 = "FunnyMan";
PrincipalPermission pp =
   new PrincipalPermission(user2, role2);
PrincipalPermission.Union(pp).Demand();
```

THE PRINCIPALPERMISSION CONSTRUCTORS

To create a **PrincipalPermission** object with a specified **PermissionState** enumeration, use the following constructor. The **PermissionState** enumeration specifies either a permission with all access (**PermissionState.Unrestricted**) or no access (**PermissionState.None**) to the protected resource.

```
public PrincipalPermission(
   PermissionState state
);
```

To create a **PrincipalPermission** object with a specified name and role, use the following constructor.

```
public PrincipalPermission(
   string name,
   string role
);
```

To create a **PrincipalPermission** object with a specified name and role and authentication status, use the following constructor:

```
public PrincipalPermission(
   string name,
   string role,
   bool isAuthenticated
);
```

THE FROMXML, TOXML, AND ISUNRESTRICTED METHODS

Beyond the methods defined by **IPermission**, such as **Copy** and **Demand**, and those methods defined by **Object**, such as **Equals** and **GetHashCode**, the **PrincipalPermission** class also defines the following three additional methods.

- **FromXml** reconstructs a permission object from a specified XML representation.
- **ToXml** creates an XML representation of the current state of the permission object.
- **IsUnrestricted** returns a boolean indicating whether the permission is unrestricted. An unrestricted **PrincipalPermission** will match any principal whatsoever.

Here are the syntax signatures of these three new methods. Note that a **SecurityElement** is used as the parameter in the **FromXml** method and as the return value in the **ToXml** method. The **SecurityElement** class represents a simple XML object model for encoding security objects as a set of tags, attributes, child nodes, and text elements.

```
public void FromXml(
   SecurityElement elem
);

public SecurityElement ToXml();

public bool IsUnrestricted();
```

User-Based Security

User-based security is the traditional form of security programming, which has been with us since the first version of Windows NT and the Win32 Security API. The .NET Security Framework supports user-based security in the form of classes, interfaces, enumerations, and so forth, which encapsulate the access control underlying Win32 Security API. These existing Win32 APIs, together with ACL, SA (Security Attribute), and SID (Security Identifier) objects have been, and still are, very effective, but they have now been complemented by new .NET security programming features.

Principal and Identity Objects

Principal and identity objects are used to represent users. A principal object encapsulates the current user. A principal object contains an identity object, which encapsulates identity information about that particular user. By definition, an identity object is an instance of a class that implements the **IIdentity** interface, and a principal object is an instance of a class that implements the **IPrincipal** interface.

The IIdentity Interface

The **IIdentity** interface has only three public read-only properties: **AuthenticationType**, **IsAuthenticated**, and **Name**.

- **AuthenticationType** is a string that indicates the type of authentication that was used on the current user. This authentication may be provided by the operating system or by some other authentication provider such as IIS. It may even be a custom authentication scheme. Examples of standard authentication types are Basic authentication, NTLM, Kerberos, and Passport.
- **IsAuthenticated** is a boolean that indicates whether or not the user has been authenticated.
- **Name** is a string that provides the username of the current user. The username originates from an authentication provider, such as the operating system.

Here are the syntax signatures of these three read-only properties. As you can see, **AuthenticationType** returns a string, **IsAuthenticated** returns a boolean, and **Name** returns a string.

```
string AuthenticationType {get;}

bool IsAuthenticated {get;}

string Name {get;}
```

IIdentity Implementation Classes

There are four classes that implement **IIdentity** interface: **FormsIdentity**, **GenericIdentity**, **PassportIdentity**, and **WindowsIdentity**. The **WindowsIdentity** class is used when you rely on standard Windows authentication. The simplified **GenericIdentity** class can be used in your own custom authentication logon scenarios. Generic principals therefore represent a concept of users that are entirely independent of Windows users. The **FormsIdentity** and **PassportIdentity** classes are used in ASP.NET and Passport authentication scenarios, respectively. You can also derive your own custom identity classes from **GenericIdentity** that provide your own additional specialized user authentication information.

- **GenericIdentity** represents a simplified identity object for a user that can be authenticated in custom logon scenarios.
- **WindowsIdentity** represents the identity of an ordinary Windows user that has logged onto the underlying Windows operating system.
- **FormsIdentity** provides an identity class for ASP.NET applications that use forms authentication.
- **PassportIdentity** provides an identity class for use within Passport-enabled applications. You must install the Passport SDK in order to use this class.

The GenericIdentity Class

The **GenericIdentity** class is quite simple, and it is not associated with any specific authentication protocol. Instead, it is intended for use with custom logon mechanisms. For example, an application could independently prompt a user for a name and password. Then, the application could check against a custom database containing records of established usernames and passwords. The password would of course be encrypted! If the username and password were valid, then the application would create the appropriate generic principal object and an associated identity object, based on the matching record in the database.

The **GenericIdentity** class provides no additional members beyond the three **IIdentity** interface-defined properties named **AuthenticationType**, **IsAuthenticated**, and **Name** that we saw earlier. This class does, however, provide two constructors. One constructor takes a string parameter that specifies the username. The other constructor takes two parameters: The first parameter is a username string, and the second parameter is an arbitrary authentication type string.

```
public GenericIdentity(
    string name
);
```

```
public GenericIdentity(
   string name,
   string type
);
```

We will not go into detail about how to use the **GenericIdentity** class just now. For now, we simply provide the following code snippet that shows how to use the two available constructors to create instances of the **GenericIdentity** class. Later, when we look at the **GenericPrincipal** class, we will see more fully how to use **GenericIdentity** objects in an actual program.

```
IIdentity genericIdentity1 =
   new GenericIdentity("JoeUser");

IIdentity genericIdentity2 =
   new GenericIdentity(
      "JoeUser", "MyAuthenticationProtocol");
```

The WindowsIdentity Class

Of the classes that implement the **IIdentity** interface, in this chapter we are mainly interested in the **GenericIdentity** class, which we have just discussed, and the **WindowsIdentity** class. The **FormsIdentity** and **PassportIdentity** classes will not be considered further in this chapter. The **WindowsIdentity** class is used to represent the user that has logged onto Windows.

THE WINDOWSIDENTITY CONSTRUCTORS

There are several constructors for creating a **WindowsIdentity** object representing a specified user. The simplest constructor takes a single parameter that takes an **IntPtr** type parameter, which refers to a Windows user account token. The **IntPtr** datatype is generally used to refer to platform-specific datatypes that represent either a memory pointer or a handle. In this case the **IntPtr** parameter refers to a Win32 handle that represents a 32-bit user account token. This token is usually obtained via a call to an unmanaged Win32 API, such as **LogonUser**. For information on the available Win32 APIs and how to call unmanaged code, please see the appropriate Microsoft Visual Studio .NET documentation.

Each of the other constructors take this same initial **IntPtr** parameter, followed by one or more of the following additional pieces of information: an authentication type, a Windows account type, and an authentication status. Here are the syntax signatures of each of these constructors. Note that the

WindowsAccountType parameter must take one of the **WindowsAccount-Type** enumeration values, **Anonymous**, **Guest**, **Normal**, or **System**.

```
public WindowsIdentity(
    IntPtr userToken
);

public WindowsIdentity(
    IntPtr userToken,
    string authType
);

public WindowsIdentity(
    IntPtr userToken,
    string authType,
    WindowsAccountType acctType
);

public WindowsIdentity(
    IntPtr userToken,
    string authType,
    WindowsAccountType acctType,
    bool isAuthenticated
);
```

THE WINDOWSIDENTITY PUBLIC PROPERTIES

Naturally, the **WindowsIdentity** class exposes the three read-only properties defined in the **IIdentity** interface: **AuthenticationType**, **IsAuthenticated**, and **Name**. This class also exposes a few additional properties. The following list describes all of these **WindowsIdentity** properties.

- **AuthenticationType** gets the type of authentication on the user.
- **IsAnonymous** gets a boolean indicating whether the user account is an anonymous account on the operating system.
- **IsAuthenticated** gets a boolean indicating whether the user has been authenticated on the operating system.
- **IsGuest** gets a boolean indicating whether the user account is a Guest account on the operating system.
- **IsSystem** gets a boolean indicating whether the user account is a System account on the operating system.
- **Name** gets the user logon name in the form of Domain\User.
- **Token** gets the account token for the user.

The three properties **AuthenticationType**, **IsAuthenticated**, and **Name** were all defined in the **IIdentity** interface, which are thus implemented here in the **WindowsIdentity** implementation class. In addition to these, this class also implements several new properties, as shown in the previous list. Here are the syntax signatures of all these properties.

```
public virtual string AuthenticationType {get;}
public virtual bool IsAnonymous {get;}
public virtual bool IsAuthenticated {get;}
public virtual bool IsGuest {get;}
public virtual bool IsSystem {get;}
public virtual string Name {get;}
public virtual IntPtr Token {get;}
```

THE WINDOWSIDENTITY PUBLIC METHODS

Beyond the obvious methods defined in the **Object** class, the **WindowsIdentity** class also exposes the **GetAnonymous**, **GetCurrent**, and **Impersonate** methods. **GetAnonymous** and **GetCurrent** are static methods, whereas the **Impersonate** method comes in both static and instance flavors.

- **GetAnonymous** returns a **WindowsIdentity** object that represents an anonymous user.
- **GetCurrent** returns a **WindowsIdentity** object that represents the current user.
- **Impersonate** allows code to temporarily impersonate a different user.

Both the **GetAnonymous** and **GetCurrent** return a **WindowsIdentity** object. The instance version of the **Impersonate** method takes no parameters and returns a **WindowsImpersonationContext** based on the **WindowsIdentity** that you called the method on. The static version of this method takes an **IntPtr** parameter, which is a handle to a Windows account token, as described earlier. In either case, the **WindowsImpersonationContext** class is used to represent a Windows user that you wish to impersonate. Impersonation is useful for server applications that must reduce their permissions to a lower (i.e., safer) level corresponding to the user account of the client accessing the server. Here are the syntax signatures of these methods.

```
public static WindowsIdentity GetAnonymous();
public static WindowsIdentity GetCurrent();

public virtual WindowsImpersonationContext Impersonate();

public static WindowsImpersonationContext Impersonate(
    IntPtr userToken
);
```

Principal Objects

A principal object is an instance of a class that implements the **IPrincipal** interface. A principal object is used to represent the user in user-based security scenarios. The **System.Security.Principal** namespace contains several types of principal object classes that encapsulate the security context under which application code may run. These principal objects contain information that is used to represent the identity of a user. Access to resources can therefore be protected based on the credentials that were supplied for a particular user. We shall soon see an example in which the username and role are checked to determine whether or not to allow a particular execution path to proceed based on the user's identity and role membership.

OBTAINING THE CURRENT PRINCIPAL OBJECT

Each thread has associated with it a principal object. This principal object contains the identity object representing the user that is running the current thread. The **Thread** class has a static property named **CurrentPrincipal** that returns this principal object, and is typically used in the following manner.

```
IPrincipal ip =
   Thread.CurrentPrincipal;
```

The IPrincipal Interface

The **IPrincipal** interface has only one public property named **Identity** and one public method named **IsInRole**.

- The **IIdentity** property references an **IIdentity** object that is associated with the principal object.
- The **IsInRole** method takes a string containing the name of a role as a parameter and returns a boolean that indicates whether the principal object belongs to the specified role.

Here are the syntax signatures for these members of the **IPrincipal** interface.

```
IIdentity Identity {get;}

bool IsInRole(
   string role
);
```

You may implement your own custom principal classes; however, the following two classes are the only predefined .NET Framework classes that implement the **IPrincipal** interface. We concern ourselves mainly with the **WindowsPrincipal** class and only look briefly at the **GenericPrincipal** class.

- **GenericPrincipal** represents a generic principal object for a logged on user.
- **WindowsPrincipal** represents a principle for a logged on Windows user.

The GenericPrincipal Class

The **GenericPrincipal** class is used in conjunction with the **GenericIdentity** class to represent a custom authenticated user. Once you have created a **GenericIdentity** object, as described earlier, you can create an instance of the **GenericPrincipal** class. The **GenericPrincipal** constructor allows you to initialize it with a previously created **GenericIdentity** object along with an array of strings that represent the roles to be associated with the new principal object.

To get an idea of how custom authentication can work, look at the following code snippet, which is taken from the **CustomLogon** method in the **GenericPrincipal** example. It creates a **GenericIdentity** object and then creates an encapsulating **GenericPrincipal** object using an array of strings that represent associated roles. The **GenericIdentity** object is constructed with the provided username, and the custom authentication type arbitrarily named **MyAuthenticationType**. This authentication type is therefore a homegrown alternative to Kerberos or NTLM. To keep this example simple, roles are ignored, so this array is null. Once the **GenericPrincipal** object is established, it is attached to the current thread so that it can later be used for validating the current user.

```
//create a generic identity object
IIdentity myGenericIdentity =
   new GenericIdentity(
      strUserName, "MyAuthenticationType");

//create a generic principal object
String[] roles = null; //not used in this example
GenericPrincipal myGenericPrincipal =
   new GenericPrincipal(myGenericIdentity, roles);

//attach generic principal to current thread
Thread.CurrentPrincipal = myGenericPrincipal;
```

At the start of this example program, it prompts for a username before creating the **GenericIdentity** object shown above.[13] For simplicity, it is hard-coded to accept only two possible usernames, which are TrustedUser and UntrustedUser. All other usernames are rejected as invalid. Also, for simplicity, no password is requested. Of course, prompting for a password and comparing it against an encrypted password database would be necessary in a realistic scenario, but that would tend to clutter this example too much. These additional complicating issues are fairly easy to implement, but because they have nothing to do with the actual .NET security programming that we are interested in here, we will not concern ourselves further with them. Another simplification in this example is that the issue of role membership is completely ignored. Realistically, roles associated with particular users should also come from a query on a custom user database and be passed as a string array in the second parameter of the **GenericPrincipal** constructor.

The program then proceeds to call a method named **AttemptCodeAsUser** twice to demonstrate both possible cases. The first time, the user logs on as TrustedUser and calls the **AttemptCodeAsUser** method. Then the user logs on as UntrustedUser and calls the **AttemptCodeAsUser** method again. The following code snippet shows how the username is obtained from the principal object and compared against the hardcoded name TrustedUser. If the name matches, it works normally; otherwise, it throws an exception.

```
//get current principal object
IPrincipal principal = Thread.CurrentPrincipal;

if (!principal.Identity.Name.Equals("TrustedUser"))
{
   throw new SecurityException(
      strUserName + " NOT PERMITTED to proceed.\n");
}
Console.WriteLine(
   strUserName + " is PERMITTED to proceed.\n");
```

The following console output shows the result of running this program. As you can see, the program allows you to log on as a particular user and then discriminate on the basis of who you are.

```
Logon as TrustedUser
Enter username: TrustedUser

User name: TrustedUser
Authenticated: True
```

---

13. This is not suitable for ASP.NET applications, since the users are remote. Instead, ASP.NET applications should use the **HttpContext.User** property.

```
Authentication type: MyAuthenticationType
TrustedUser is PERMITTED to proceed.

Logon as UntrustedUser
Enter username: UntrustedUser

User name: UntrustedUser
Authenticated: True
Authentication type: MyAuthenticationType
UntrustedUser NOT PERMITTED to proceed.
```

The main thing to note in this example is that this program has a completely independent custom logon facility. Despite that the actual logon mechanism is grossly simplified and not all that realistic, it does demonstrate the key aspects of programming with the **GenericIdentity** and **GenericPrincipal classes.**

The WindowsPrincipal Class

We have recently seen that the **WindowsPrincipal** class is one of two classes that implement the **IPrincipal** interface. We have also seen how simple the **IPrincipal** interface is, exposing little more than one property named **Identity** and one method named **IsInRole**. Of course, **WindowsPrincipal** inherits the standard method of **Object**, and it implements the two members of **IPrincipal**, but it does not bring much of anything else new to the table. It does provide a single constructor, and its implementation of the **IsInRole** method is overloaded three ways, but that is about all it adds.

THE WINDOWSPRINCIPAL CONSTRUCTOR

There is only one constructor for the **WindowsPrincipal** class, which creates a **WindowsPrincipal** object from an existing **WindowsIdentity** object. We discussed the **WindowsIdentity** class earlier in this chapter.

```
public WindowsPrincipal(
    WindowsIdentity ntIdentity
);
```

Here is an example of how you can use this constructor to create a **WindowsPrincipal** object from a **WindowsIdentity** that represents the current user. A convenient way to get a **WindowsIdentity** object to pass into the **WindowsPrincipal** constructor is to call on the **WindowsIdentity.GetCurrent** static method.

```
WindowsIdentity wi = WindowsIdentity.GetCurrent();
WindowsPrincipal wp = new WindowsPrincipal(wi);
```

THE IDENTITY PROPERTY

The **Identity** property of the **WindowsPrincipal** class has the following syntax.

```
public virtual IIdentity Identity {get;}
```

THE WINDOWSPRINCIPAL.ISINROLE METHOD

The **WindowsPrincipal** class has three overloadings for the **IsInRole** method. The first overloading takes an integer representing a user group as a RID, which is a relative identifier.[14] RID values are defined in the Platform SDK header file Winnt.h, found in the ...\Microsoft Visual Studio .NET\Vc7\PlatformSDK\Include folder. The second overloading takes a string representing a user group name in the form of MachineName\GroupName. For example, HPDESKTOP\CodeGurus represents the group of users that belong to the CodeGurus group defined on the machine named HPDESKTOP. This must be modified slightly in the case of built-in groups, such as Administrators. In that case the group name would not be HPDESKTOP\Administrators; it would be BUILTIN\Administrators. This may seem odd and unintuitive, and so for built-in groups, it is probably better to just use the third constructor overloading, which is provided specifically for working with built-in types. This third overloading takes a **WindowsBuiltInRole** enumeration, which may take on values such as **Administrator**, **Guest**, and **User**. The following shows the syntax for each of these three overloadings of the **IsInRole** method.

```
public virtual bool IsInRole(int);
public virtual bool IsInRole(string);
public virtual bool IsInRole(WindowsBuiltInRole);
```

Here is the list of all the values defined for the **WindowsBuiltInRole** enumeration to be used with the third overloading of the **IsInRole** method.

- **AccountOperator**—Manage user accounts on computer or domain.
- **Administrator**—Have unrestricted access to computer or domain.
- **BackupOperator**—Perform backup and restore operations on file system.
- **Guest**—Like users, but with more restrictions.
- **PowerUser**—Almost like administrators, but with some restrictions.
- **PrintOperator**—Perform printer operations.

---

14. A RID is defined as a well-known domain-relative subauthority ID. Winnt.h defines RIDs for several well-known users, including DOMAIN_USER_RID_ADMIN and DOMAIN_USER_RID_GUEST. It also defines RIDs for several well-known groups, including DOMAIN_GROUP_RID_ADMINS, DOMAIN_GROUP_RID_USERS, and DOMAIN_GROUP_RID_GUESTS.

- **Replicator**—Perform file replication within domain.
- **SystemOperator**—Manage computer.
- **User**—Prevented from making dangerous or systemwide changes.

Two Approaches to User-Based Security

There are two major approaches to working with user-based security in .NET. The first way is known as the *imperative* approach, which involves explicit decision making in code. The second way is known as the *declarative* approach, which involves the use of attributes.

There are actually two slightly different styles that can be used in the imperative approach. The old-style imperative approach is basically the same as that used in conventional Win32 security programming, where you determine who the user is and explicitly choose the execution path using an **if** statement. Typically, the decision is made between two execution branches, where one is successful and the other throws a **SecurityException**. Although this technique is quite familiar to many programmers, the additional code required makes it slightly cumbersome.

In the new-style imperative approach, you create a **PrincipalPermission** object representing the user or role that you wish to discriminate on, and then you call on that **PrincipalPermission** object's **Demand** method to test it against the current user. The **Demand** method automatically makes the security decision and throws the **SecurityException** for you if there is no match. The advantage of doing it this way is that the code is a little more simple and clean looking, since there is no visible **if** statement and exception-throwing code.

Alternatively, you can implement user-based security using the declarative approach. In general, the difference between imperative and declarative programming is that in the imperative case, you write explicit code that makes things happen. In declarative programming, you passively define attribute data that will, at runtime, have an effect on the behavior of the program. In the case of declarative user-based security programming, the desired behavior is produced by applying the **PrincipalPermission** attribute to the desired method. Let's now look at two examples that demonstrate these imperative and declarative approaches to user-based security programming.

Imperative User-Based Security

As you are probably aware, Windows defines several built-in users, such as Administrator and Guest, and groups, such as Administrators, Users, and Guests. The administrator typically defines many others as well. The **ImperativeUserBasedSecurity** code example demonstrates how simple it is to implement security decisions that are based on the identity or role membership of these users and role. Near the top of the **ImperativeUserBasedSecurity.cs** source file, you will find the following **using** statements that enable the use of short names for the required security- and thread-related classes that are used in the program.

```csharp
using System.Security;
using System.Security.Principal;
using System.Threading;
```

This simple example program has two **Button** controls. The Test On User Name button demonstrates how to make a security decision based on a username that you provide in a **TextBox** control. The Test On Role button works in a similar manner except that it makes its security decision based on the role that you have selected with the Guest, User, and Administrator **RadioButton** controls. Let's first look at the **buttonTestOnUserName_Click** method.

```csharp
private void buttonTestOnUserName_Click(
    object sender, System.EventArgs e)
{
    //set default principal for appdomain threads
    AppDomain appdomain = AppDomain.CurrentDomain;
    appdomain.SetPrincipalPolicy(
        PrincipalPolicy.WindowsPrincipal);

    //get current principal object
    WindowsPrincipal principle =
        (WindowsPrincipal)Thread.CurrentPrincipal;

    //get specified user name string
    string userName = textUserName.Text;

    //execute code according to specified user name
    if (!principle.Identity.Name.Equals(userName))
    {
        throw new SecurityException(
            "Specified user is " +
            userName +
            ".\n" +
            "Therefore current user " +
            principle.Identity.Name +
            " is NOT permitted to proceed.");
    }
    MessageBox.Show(
        "Specified user is " +
        userName +
        ".\n" +
        "Therefore current user " +
        principle.Identity.Name +
        " is permitted to proceed.");
}
```

SetPrincipalPolicy Throws SecurityException

This example program calls the **SetPrincipalPolicy** method, which throws a **SecurityException** if the code does not have the permission to manipulate the **AppDomain** object's security policy. To keep things simple in this example, we do not concern ourselves with the possibility of this exception being thrown; we simply call **SetPrincipalPolicy** without any precaution. In your own programs, you should probably check for this permission before attempting to call **SetPrincipalPolicy**. The following code snippet checks for this by calling the **Demand** method on a specially constructed **SecurityPermission** object. The **SecurityPermission** class controls "metapermissions" that govern the CLR security subsystem. We talk more about permission objects and the **Demand** method shortly.

```
SecurityPermission sp = new SecurityPermission(
   SecurityPermissionFlag.ControlPrincipal);
try
{
   sp.Demand();
}
catch(SecurityException se)
{
   ...//cannot call SetPrincipalPolicy
}
//can call SetPrincipalPolicy
```

The first thing this example code does is call **SetPrincipalPolicy**, which sets the type of principal that is to be associated with the current application domain to be a **WindowsPrincipal** type of principal object. This is necessary because only a **WindowsPrincipal** object carries the required information about the current user that was authenticated by the Windows logon facility.[15] Without this information, we would not be certain about whom we are dealing with. Next, the current principal object is obtained by calling the **Thread.CurrentPrincipal** static method.

```
//set default principal for appdomain threads
AppDomain appdomain = AppDomain.CurrentDomain;
appdomain.SetPrincipalPolicy(
   PrincipalPolicy.WindowsPrincipal);
```

---

15. If we did not call **SetPrincipalPolicy** to specify that we want a **WindowsPrincipal**, we would get a **GenericPrincipal** by default, which would not contain the user information that we are interested in. Since the user was authenticated by the Windows logon facility, the user's name and role are provided by a **WindowsPrincipal** but not by a **GenericPrincipal**.

```
//get current principal object
WindowsPrincipal principle =
    (WindowsPrincipal)Thread.CurrentPrincipal;
```

Next, the program gets the specified username from the user interface. Finally, this string is compared against the **Identity** object's **Name** property to see if the specified username matches the actual user's name. If it matches, then the program permits the desired action. Otherwise, the action is avoided by throwing an exception. This program is only for demonstration purposes, so the action is just simulated by displaying an appropriate message box.

```
//get specified user name string
string userName = textUserName.Text;

//execute code according to specified user name
if (!principal.Identity.Name.Equals(userName))
    ... //throw exception
```

The **buttonTestOnUserName_Click** method we have just looked at makes its security decision on a specified username. Users may belong to one or more groups, which can greatly simplify matters, allowing us to make decisions on the generalized characteristics of a set of users rather than on individuals. Let's now look at the **buttonTestOnRole_Click** method, which makes its security decision on a specified group.

```
private void buttonTestOnRole_Click(
    object sender, System.EventArgs e)
{
    //set default principal for appdomain threads
    AppDomain appdomain = AppDomain.CurrentDomain;
    appdomain.SetPrincipalPolicy(
        PrincipalPolicy.WindowsPrincipal);

    //get current principal object
    WindowsPrincipal principal =
        (WindowsPrincipal)Thread.CurrentPrincipal;

    //get specified role
    WindowsBuiltInRole role = 0;
    if (radioButtonGuest.Checked == true)
        role = WindowsBuiltInRole.Guest;
    if (radioButtonUser.Checked == true)
        role = WindowsBuiltInRole.User;
    if (radioButtonAdministrator.Checked == true)
        role = WindowsBuiltInRole.Administrator;

    //execute code according to specified role
    if (!principal.IsInRole(role))
    {
```

```
        throw new SecurityException(
            "Specified role is " +
            role +
            ".\n" +
            "Therefore current user " +
            principle.Identity.Name +
            " is NOT permitted to proceed.");
    }
    MessageBox.Show(
        "Specified role is " +
        role +
        ".\n" +
        "Therefore current user " +
        principle.Identity.Name +
        " is permitted to proceed.");
}
```

This method starts off the same way, establishing the type of principle object that we need to work with by calling **SetPrincipalPolicy**. Again, we do this to specify that we want a **WindowsPrincipal** type of principal object. Then, we make a security decision, but this time it is based on the role of the user rather than the name of the user. The specified role is obtained from the user interface, and then the **IsInRole** method is used to choose between performing the desired action and throwing an exception.

```
//execute code according to specified role
if (!principle.IsInRole(role))
    ... // throw exception
```

Figures 7–9 and 7–10 show the two possible results for this example program. These results assume that the currently logged on user is named Administrator, who is in the roles of Administrators and Users, but not in the role of Guests. You should substitute the appropriate machine and domain name accordingly when you do this on your own system.

USING PRINCIPALPERMISSION IN IMPERATIVE USER-BASED SECURITY

The **ImperativeUserBasedSecurity** example that we just looked at is slightly cumbersome in that it uses an **if** statement and it explicitly throws an exception. This program could be slightly simplified by using the **PrincipalPermission** class instead. The test of the specified user against the actual current user can be replaced with code that uses the **PrincipalPermission** class. For example, notice how the following code taken from the **PrincipalPermission** example creates a **PrincipalPermission** object with the desired username and/or role, and then calls on the **Demand** method. Just like the previous **ImperativeUserBasedSecurityexample**, this **PrincipalPermission** example

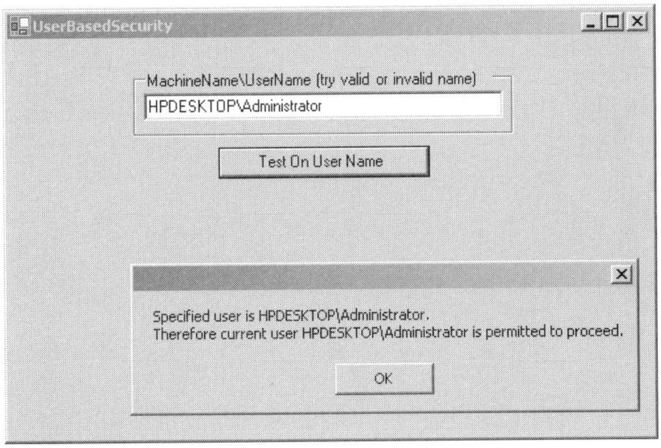

FIGURE 7-9   Valid username Administrator is permitted.

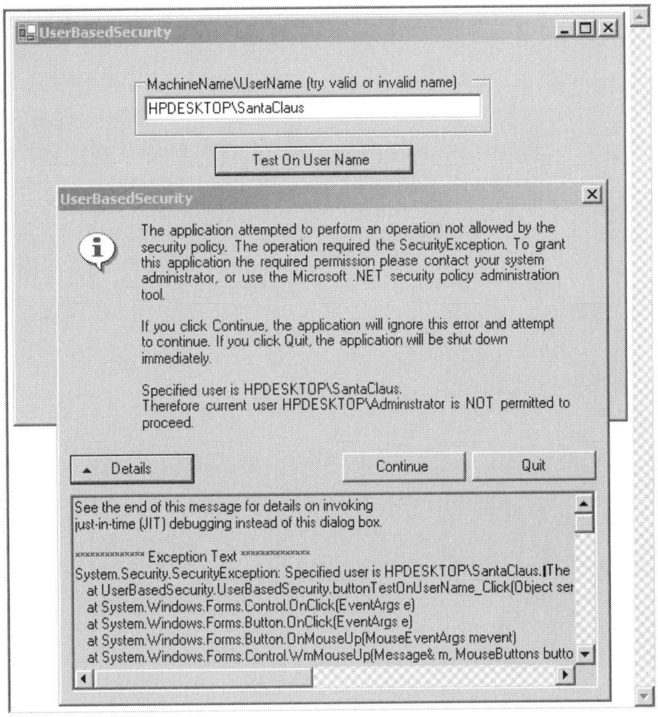

FIGURE 7-10   Invalid username SantaClaus is not permitted.

is also considered to be an imperative rather than a declarative approach to user-based security.

```
PrincipalPermission pp =
    new PrincipalPermission(
        strUserName, strUserRole);

//can throw SecurityException if wrong user
pp.Demand();

//if we got this far, then user is OK
MessageBox.Show(
    "Specified user matches current user." +
    "User permitted to proceed.");
```

The two string parameters to the **PrincipalPermission** constructor, which represent the username and role that you want to test against, are of course established beforehand. If either of these parameters is null, it is ignored for security comparison purposes. Then, in place of the **if** statement used in the previous example, you simply call the **Demand** method, which performs the comparison and automatically throws a **SecurityException** if the specified user does not match properly.

PrincipalPermission Not Derived from CodeAccessPermission

Like other permissions, **PrincipalPermission** does implement the **IPermission** interface, but, unlike other permissions, it does not derive from **CodeAccessPermission**. This is because **PrincipalPermission** is not based on the identity of the executing assembly (i.e., not used for CAS). Instead, it is based on the identity of the current user. We will look at permissions in more detail in Chapter 8.

Declarative User-Based Security

The **DeclarativeUserBasedSecurity** example shows how to accomplish user-based security in a declarative manner. As you can see, the code is very simple here, because there is no code that explicitly tests against the identity of the current user. By applying the **PrincipalPermission** attribute to the method as a whole, the method can simply go directly about its business without any security concerns whatsoever. If the current user is not consistent with that described by the **PrincipalPermission** attribute, a **SecurityException** is automatically thrown.

```
[PrincipalPermission(
    SecurityAction.Demand,
    Name="HPDESKTOP\\Administrator")]
```

```
private void buttonTest_Click(
    object sender, System.EventArgs e)
{
    MessageBox.Show(
        "Specified user is permitted to proceed.");
}
```

The square brackets in the preceding code declare a **PrincipalPermission** attribute for the method **buttonTest_Click**. This attribute specifies the Demand action, and the HPDESKTOP\\Administrator username. For more information on this attribute, please see the documentation on the **PrincipalPermissionAttribute** class, which encapsulates this attribute.

If you run this program, depending on whether or not you are logged on as HPDESKTOP\\Administrator, you will get one of the results shown in Figure 7–11 and Figure 7–12.

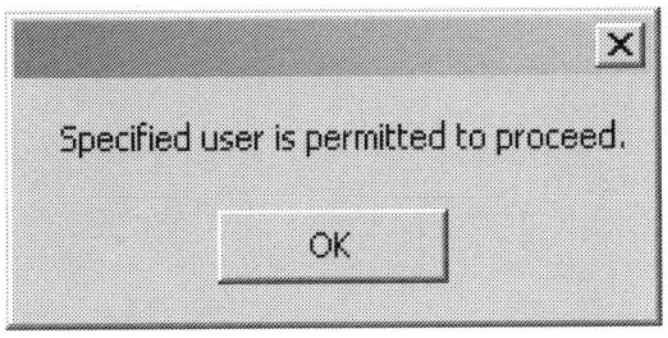

FIGURE 7-11   *PrincipalPermission: Valid user is permitted.*

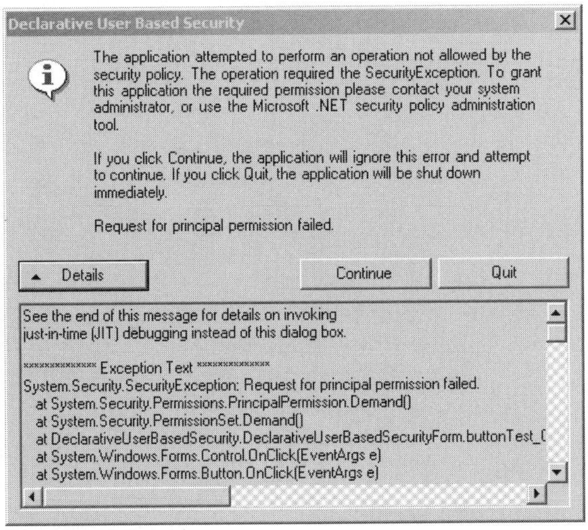

FIGURE 7-12   *PrincipalPermission: Invalid user is not permitted.*

Note that it is too much trouble to log out and back in again to test this program with different usernames. Instead, you can go to a command prompt and use the **runas** command, as shown in the following command lines to accomplish this. When you do this, you will be prompted for the password associated with the username that you provide.

```
C:\...>runas /user:HPDESKTOP\Administrator
  DeclarativeUserBasedSecurity.exe

C:\...>runas /user:HPDESKTOP\CodeMeister
  DeclarativeUserBasedSecurity.exe
```

When using declarative security, we still need to establish **Windows-Principal** as the principal for the application domain, just as we did in the case of imperative security. However, because the **PrincipalPermission** attribute is being applied to the method as a whole, it is too late to call **SetPrincipalPolicy** within that actual method. For this reason, the **DeclarativeUserBasedSecurity** example establishes this beforehand with the following code, found in the **Main** method. Note that this time, we do not actually have to obtain the current principal object from the **Thread** class. That will be done automatically from the effect of using the **PrincipalPermission** attribute on the **buttonTest_Click** method.

```
static void Main()
{
   //set default principal for appdomain threads
   AppDomain appdomain = AppDomain.CurrentDomain;
   appdomain.SetPrincipalPolicy(
      PrincipalPolicy.WindowsPrincipal);

   Application.Run(new DeclarativeUserBasedSecurityForm());
}
```

Credentials

Recall that in user-based security, the authentication question centers on the *identity* of the user. *Credentials* are used to prove who the user is. A credential might be a password, a smart card, or a biometric device. Credentials are verified by some security authority, such as Windows or ASP.NET.

In certain cases it may be justifiable to provide unverified access to certain resources. This is known as anonymous access, which is often used for public access to ASP.NET resources.

In user-based security, the authorization question centers on whether or not the identity can perform the attempted action. The principal is then compared to a list of rights to determine whether the access is permitted. For example, at the file-system level, when you access a file, the username is compared against an ACL for the desired action to determine whether the file access is granted.

In a multitier architecture, the identity under which the server executes is often very powerful, and you want to restrict the ability of the client that makes requests to some subset of privileges that the server has. In this case the server can *impersonate* the client, effectively reducing the privileges to a safer level. In the case of anonymous access, the server does not even know who the actual client is. In this case it makes sense to use a specially devised user account for anonymous access, with special care taken in the determination of rights assigned to the anonymous user.

Network Credentials

Credentials can be obtained from an authentication service over the network. The **ICredentials** interface, which is defined in the **System.Net** namespace, has one method named **GetCredential**, which is used for this purpose. The **GetCredential** method takes a first parameter containing a URI that specifies the location of an authentication service on the network. The second parameter is a string that provides the type of authentication that is desired. The **GetCredential** method returns a **NetworkCredential** instance that contains the credentials associated with the specified URI and authorization scheme. When no credentials are available, the **GetCredential** method returns a null reference.

```
NetworkCredential GetCredential(
    Uri uri,
    string authType
);
```

There are only two classes that implement the **ICredentials** interface: **CredentialCache** and **NetworkCredential**. **CredentialCache** provides storage for a set of multiple credentials.[16] **NetworkCredential** provides credentials for password-based authentication schemes such as NTLM and Kerberos. The following code snippet gives a general idea of how this technique works.

```
NetworkCredential nc = new NetworkCredential(
    "JoeUser","MyPassword","SomeDomain");
CredentialCache cc = new CredentialCache();
cc.Add(new Uri("www.xyz.com"), "Basic", nc);
WebRequest wr = WebRequest.Create("www.xyz.com");
wr.Credentials = cc;
```

---

16. You can use **CredentialCache.DefaultCredentials** to use the current thread context for credentials based on NTLM and Kerberos.

Security Discipline

There are a couple of basic rules of thumb that should be followed when either configuring or programming security. The first is the principle of least privilege, which is primarily a conservative guideline that helps avoid unforeseen risks. The other rule of thumb is that you should try to plan ahead by establishing security policy early in the project life cycle.

Principle of Least Privilege

Many programmers recommend that you do not run a development tool such as Visual Studio .NET under administrative privileges. In situations where you temporarily need greater privileges, you can use the **runas** utility, which allows you to specify a username and password for an individual command line.

This is the *principle of least privilege,* which dictates that you should work with only the minimal set of necessary privileges required to perform the application's task, and no more. The argument is that you should be aware of the security restrictions that will be in effect when the application is deployed. Fortunately, you don't need to be an administrator to run Visual Studio .NET and debug your .NET applications.

Unfortunately, this can be very awkward during development, so you may prefer to work as an administrator during the development phase only. Then, during the testing and debugging phases, which require that you much more closely simulate the realistic runtime environment of the deployed application, revert to a more limited set of privileges. Of course, when the application is deployed, it should run strictly under minimal privileges according to the principal of least privilege.

Establish Security Policy Early

It is important that security issues are understood and designed into the application early in the life cycle of the project. It can be very difficult to add security as an afterthought to an existing project.

Summary

In this chapter we have explained the basics of user-based security programming on the .NET platform. We have looked at most of the major .NET classes involved in user-based security programming and at several programming examples that demonstrate the main techniques. The other major flavor of security programming, Code Access Security, is the topic of the next chapter.

.NET Code Access Security

*T*raditionally, security models have been purely logon-oriented and process-centric. This approach on its own is not sufficiently flexible for dealing with the new component-oriented world of mobile code. *Code Access Security* (CAS) deals with this new challenge by layering a flexible component-oriented security model over the user-based security model provided by the operating system.

Chapter 7 introduced the first part of the .NET security story, but we focused only on user-based security techniques. In this chapter we continue our study of .NET security programming by investigating its other major aspect, known as CAS. In contrast to user-based security, CAS allows you to restrict actions based on certain characteristics of the assemblies that are executing rather than on the identity of the current user. As we shall see, there are several characteristics of a loaded assembly, collectively known as *security evidence,* which together with *security policy* may be used by the CLR to make code access decisions for your programs. We will also investigate security policy management and the use of several of the code access permission classes, as well as how to implement both imperative and declarative CAS.

The Need for Code Access Security

Back in the old days, before the Internet was mainstream, a user or administrator typically installed all software into fixed locations on desktop machines, servers, and local network shares. Most organizations with significant investments at stake made certain that the administrator understood the relevant security issues. Corporate security standards, auditing procedures, disaster recovery planning, as well as end-user training helped reduce the risk further. Even in that relatively closed and controlled environment, there were a few notable security risks. On the desktop the threats came mainly in the form of boot sector viruses, executable file viruses, and trojan horses. These nasty executables spread primarily via relatively slow manual means (i.e., via diskette over the so called "sneaker net") or over isolated local area networks. Servers were used in isolated client/server configurations that were relatively free from attack, but the risk was not zero there either. For example, a disgruntled employee with a powerful account could leave a time bomb behind that could do substantial damage to a server.

Now, with virtually every computer attached to every other computer over the Internet, threats come in many new forms, including executable downloads, remote execution, email attachments, and buffer overrun attacks. Unfortunately, the Internet has created several new opportunities for nasty code to proliferate. First, the speed at which rogue code can travel has increased due to higher bandwidth and interconnectivity. Second, because of the much larger number of services and protocols that now exist, the number of vulnerable targets has grown tremendously. Third, an enormous amount of how-to information is available on the Internet in the form of hacker Web sites and newsgroups that enable a much wider audience of potential attackers. Gone are the days when you had to be a genius evildoer to figure out how to mount a cyber attack. Sadly, you now only have to be an evildoer of average-intelligence!

Cost Versus Risk

How far should one go with implementing security? This is of course a purely economic question. The amount of effort or money you expend on protection should be dictated by the value of your data or, more precisely, the cost to your organization if the data were to be destroyed or compromised. For higher risk scenarios, senior management is concerned with mission-critical issues such as system recovery and business continuity, which might entail considerably high expense. In the most extreme case, the tradeoff is between the cost of total annihilation versus the cost of a mainframe housed in a nuclear bomb-hardened bunker. However, the programmer is typically concerned with more mundane risks and costs, where the question might be whether or not a particular assembly should be allowed to read a particular environment variable or the files in some directory. Nevertheless, even in this less extreme situation, the same tradeoff question must be considered: How much security effort (i.e., cost) should be expended given the perceived risk?

It may seem on the surface that the cost of implementing mundane security logic into a program is negligible; however, that is certainly not the case. Software development incurs significant additional costs during the design, coding, testing, and maintenance phases for every additional feature that you implement. Unfortunately, security features must compete against every other desirable application feature. That security represents a real and significant cost is attested to by the fact that many software developers tend to implement as many nifty features as possible at the expense of critical security features. In the past, Microsoft, Oracle, and others have been criticized by some security experts[1] for focusing too much on bells, whistles, and ease-of-use features at the expense of solid security. It is my opinion that this is now improving across the industry. The choice is yours. If you want your code to be more than just fancy whiz-bang Swiss cheese, you cannot focus entirely on cool features and ignore security.

The Range of Risks

Unfortunately, there is an enormous range of possible risks to be considered for systems and data, including rogue code, password cracking, packet sniffing, and denial-of-service attacks. Even physical attacks, such as theft or destruction of media, as well as espionage and con artistry are possibilities. In extreme cases, you may need to consider dealing with natural disasters and terrorist attacks. Although many attacks are possible, and they should all be considered, in this chapter we focus only on rogue code attacks, since it is the only type of attack that .NET security can effectively address.

Let's consider some of the main threats in the rogue code category. Stack-overrun[2] attacks have proven to be a serious risk, especially on the server side.

---

1. Some top security experts feel that because the marketplace has rewarded cool features over security, software vendors have not treated security seriously enough. They even claim that major software vendors have treated major security holes as nothing more than public relations problems. Some are proponents of the full-disclosure movement in which the security community makes discovered vulnerabilities public. Full disclosure is a double-edged sword, since it motivates software vendors to fix security issues quickly, but it also arms hoodlums with information that can help them in their malicious efforts. It is hard to say whether full disclosure was the only factor in play, but it does seem that Microsoft is now truly committed to security. This is evidenced by the fact that .NET has such great security programming support. To read one of the many fascinating articles by Bruce Schneier on the issue of features versus security, see *http://www.counterpane.com/crypto-gram-0202.html*.

2. The Code Red II Worm is an example of a stack-overrun attack, exploiting a stack-overflow bug in the IIS indexing service. An unchecked buffer in the URL handling code in the Index Server ISAPI extension DLL (**Idq.dll**) is the key vulnerability in this case. The unchecked buffer is used to overwrite the call stack with specially crafted code, and the target application is then tricked into executing it. By sending a specially constructed URL request to IIS (unpatched versions 4.0 or 5.0 with Indexing services enabled), an attacker can thereby execute arbitrary code on that server machine. Compounding this risk is the fact that Index Server runs under the powerful System account, giving the rampaging attacker a great deal of power over the server.

If you are interested in seeing a demonstration of how a stack-overrun attack actually works, see the **Win32ProjectBufferOverflow** example program in Appendix A. Clients send requests to servers, and those requests, if cleverly constructed, may be able to exploit certain types of careless sloppy code in the server. Unmanaged C/C++ code is notoriously prone to buffer overrun and type-casting bugs that can be exploited by evil client programs. The most famous example of this was the Morris Internet worm.[3]

It is very easy to accidentally introduce such security holes into traditional unmanaged C and C++ code, and extraordinary care must be taken to avoid all the possible pitfalls. Code that is written for a managed runtime environment, such as C# or Java,[4] is inherently much safer[5] and takes no special vigilance on the part of the programmer. This is because managed languages generate code that automatically ensures that data is properly initialized, buffer overruns are automatically detected and prevented at runtime, and unsafe type casting is disallowed at compile time. Of course, C was the language used to build virtually all the traditional Internet host programs. As more server code in the future is written as managed code using languages such as C#, VB.NET, and Java, a great deal more protection against this type of attack will exist.

---

3. A Worm is a program that automatically duplicates and propagates itself to other host computers on the Internet. The first and most famous example is the Morris worm, written by a computer science graduate student at Cornell University. It was released on November 2, 1988, quickly infecting approximately 10 percent of all Internet hosts and bringing them to their knees. This worm took advantage of several security holes in certain BSD UNIX programs, including a buffer overflow bug in the finger daemon. Interestingly, there is evidence that the worm's author was only interested in researching the worm concept, and he may have not intended the enormous damage that resulted. The code contained intentional self-limiting features designed to reduce the potential damage, but, unfortunately, there was a bug in his code that prevented this safety feature from working properly. The good news is that this proves that even brilliant minds write bugs, which should be comforting to us mere mortals!

4. The Java language has mostly the same security features as C#, including type safety and bounds checking. The Java runtime environment, known as the Java Virtual Machine (JVM), also supports the same basic security features as the .NET CLR, including code verification and managed code execution. The Java class library also supports a set of security classes that are somewhat similar in concept and functionality to the .NET Framework security classes.

5. It may be argued that it is possible to avoid buffer overruns in C/C++ by avoiding a few high-risk API functions, and some C/C++ compilers can generate stack boundary checking code for each function call. However, using a managed runtime environment such as .NET or Java provides these protections automatically without the need for any heroic programmer vigilance.

Internet-mobile code, such as email[6] attachments and scripts and ActiveX controls, has also been a major source of risk on the client side. These threats come in several forms, including trojans,[7] logic bombs,[8] the traditional virus,[9] and even good old-fashioned bugs. Fortunately, by using CAS in the development of your applications, you can achieve effective protection from these forms of malicious code as well. Managed code obviously helps clientside code to be more reliable, secure, and bug-free as well.

Assembly Trustworthiness

The fundamental question that CAS addresses is this: What code should you trust and to what degree should you trust it? The problem is that code can now originate from many sources, representing varying degrees of risk. This becomes an issue wherever there is a concern that a particular piece of code may either maliciously or accidentally do some type of damage to your system or data, or leak confidential information in some way. For example, you

---

6. The Nimda worm primarily infects email, but it can also attack IIS via the backdoor left behind by the Code Red II worm, as well as any unprotected file shares that it may discover. Nimda is an HTML email with an executable attachment. IE is tricked into executing the attachment automatically when the HTML is rendered. Unfortunately, just opening the email can infect the machine, even if the user never explicitly opens the attachment. The worm is propagated from an infected machine by sending copies of itself to other machines via email. Unpatched IE versions 5.01 and 5.5 and IIS 4.0 and 5.0 are vulnerable.

7. A trojan is a program that purports to be beneficial or useful, but in fact performs an additional hidden and possibly malicious action. Unlike viruses and worms, a trojan does not typically replicate itself programmatically. There are many examples of trojans, but probably the most interesting of all is described by Ken Thompson (known as the father of UNIX) in his article "Reflections on Trusting Trust," found at *http://www.acm.org/classics/sep95/*. He describes how he built a C compiler that installs a trojan login backdoor into a UNIX build. The cool thing that he points out is that he did it in such a way that there is no trace of the trojan in any of the source code in either the C compiler or the UNIX system. That means you can't be completely certain about any software, even if you have the source code! Scary, huh?

8. A logic bomb is a secretly deployed time-activated program that either causes severe damage to its host or quietly provides a backdoor for future system access. One of the most notorious cases involved an employee who was demoted after 11 years as chief programmer at a defense contractor company in New Jersey. The disgruntled employee retaliated by quickly deploying a logic bomb that deleted much of the company's most critical data after he left.

9. A virus is a code fragment that inserts itself into other programs, modifying them in a way that causes further virus replication. Some viruses infect ordinary executable program files. Other viruses infect sensitive operating-system disk sectors, such as the system boot record. Examples of famous viruses are Brain, Stoned, and Michelangelo.

might trust code that you have written to have certain access privileges that you would not entrust to code written by some other software developers. Or, you may trust an assembly to carry out certain limited actions if it was written by a particular company, but not if it was written by some other company. You probably also have varying degrees of trust based on where the code physically originated, trusting locally deployed assemblies that have been installed by a trusted administrator over assemblies that are installed by a mere user or automatically deployed via a Web browser.

This problem becomes more complex when you consider that a single application may contain a combination of assemblies, which fall into varying degrees of trustworthiness. With many assemblies working together in a single application, it could happen that a trusted component is tricked or coerced into doing evil by less trusted components.[10]

CAS enables these kinds of risk assessments to be made on the basis of many factors concerning the trustworthiness of individual assemblies. CAS also allows you to customize your level of trust at a finer level of granularity than was possible in traditional programming environments. For example, you can choose your degree of trust at the assembly level, class level, or even at the individual method level.

The need for CAS becomes especially clear when you consider that code can be used to perform many different tasks, and it is not obvious to users, administrators, or even programmers exactly what operations a particular assembly may attempt. Clearly, a security model that provides access control based only on user accounts, as described in the previous chapter, is insufficient to deal with these new problems. This has become especially true in the modern era of mobile code, remote method invocation, and Web services.

Risks of Calling into Unmanaged Code

It is important to note that for CAS to do its work at all, the executing code must be verifiably type-safe managed code. That means that the CLR must be able to verify the assembly's type safety when it is loaded into memory. Using PInvoke to call into legacy Win32 DLLs is a security risk because we are then on our own, and the CLR cannot help us in any way. Obviously, only highly trusted code should be permitted to use PInvoke, but if the DLL being called uses the Win32 Security API effectively, or if you are calling a clearly harmless Win32 API such as **GetSystemTime**, then you may decide to allow it. But you must always keep in mind that if you call into unmanaged native code, you are opening a potential security hole. For this reason, calling into unmanaged code requires you have the unmanaged code permission. If you have ever programmed in C or C++, then you probably know all too well how easy

---

10. This is known as the luring attack, which CAS is particularly well suited to deal with.

it is to get into trouble with uninitialized variables, invalid pointers, out-of-bounds array indexing, incorrect type casts, memory leaks, and the use of inherently unsafe functions such as **strcpy**, **gets**, **strcat**, and **sprintf**.

The need to call legacy native code is, however, a fact of life for the foreseeable future, so it is important to architect your applications to limit native code calls to a minimal number of fully trusted assemblies. Then, you can configure security or call the **Deny** method to disable PInvoke in the majority of your code and use the **Assert** method to enable PInvoke in the few methods where it is needed. We will talk more about the **Deny** and **Assert** methods later. We will see in the upcoming **PInvoke** example how to configure security policy to enable or disable the permission to call into unmanaged code.

Security, Managed Code, and the CLR

At its most fundamental level, the security of the entire .NET platform is based on two things: the type safety of managed code and the vigilance of the Common Language Runtime (CLR). Type-safe managed code ensures that bounds checking is performed on all datatypes, including arrays and strings. It also does not permit inappropriate or dangerous type conversions or direct memory manipulations via pointers. In effect, type-safe code can access only memory locations that it is justifiably permitted to access, and those memory locations are accessible only in the intended legitimate manner. For example, type-safe managed code cannot directly access or modify the memory containing an object's fields or a class's executable code. It can access fields and methods only in a responsible and well-behaved manner.

The upshot of all this is that type-safe managed code effectively prevents buffer overruns and arbitrary code insertion. Effectively, this means that it is extremely difficult to trick a managed program into executing arbitrary attacker-provided code. Although, when talking about security, you should probably never say never, type safety does practically eliminate the possibilities of virus code fragment insertion and stack-overrun attacks. But even if it were somehow possible to inject such malicious code into a loaded assembly, further protection is provided by the CLR by applying administrator-defined security policy, limiting the possible actions to only those permissions that are actually granted to the code. On top of this protection, by digitally signing an assembly, programs that use that assembly can detect any masquerading or tampering of the assembly contents that may have occurred prior to assembly load time. Digital signatures and certificates also allow you to know who provided the assembly so that if any damage were caused by it, you would be in a better legal position in the case of litigation. That should make the disgruntled employee think twice before leaving any time-bomb program!

Microsoft Intermediate Language

Managed .NET code is initially compiled only to an intermediate level language, known as MSIL (Microsoft Intermediate Language). MSIL is sometimes called IL for short. MSIL contains nonnative managed code along with the associated metadata describing the contents and attributes of the assembly. This means that each assembly, which is typically in the form of an EXE or DLL file, is self-contained, requiring no external metadata to be placed in the system registry. MSIL is then dynamically converted to native code on the fly at runtime by the .NET platform's JIT (just-in-time) compiler.

The JIT compiler performs code verification,[11] which attempts to determine that the code is indeed type-safe and checks for any illegal operations, such as direct memory manipulation. It does this by examining intermediate language of each method and the metadata to see what risky operations may exist and what specific operations are explicitly denied. This means that even if a rogue compiler was used to generate the assembly, or if someone managed to insert a virus fragment into an unsigned assembly, it will be detected and prevented[12] at runtime. Type-safe managed code is secure because it is not permitted to directly manipulate memory or call into unmanaged (i.e., native) code unless it has been intentionally given the specific permission to do so.

Verifiably Type-Safe Code

Security policy, which we discuss in more detail later, can be applied only to verifiably type-safe code. It is important to recognize that not all .NET languages necessarily generate type-safe managed code, and not even all type-safe code is necessarily verifiably type-safe according to the JIT's code verification efforts. Visual Basic .NET always produces verifiably type-safe managed code.[13] Visual C# generates verifiably type-safe managed code unless you use the **unsafe** keyword. Unsafe C# code is handy but risky when you need to pass arrays and pointers as parameters into unmanaged legacy C/C++ code via PInvoke. Visual C++ .NET can produce type-safe or non-type-safe managed code, or even native code; however, it cannot generate any code that is verifiably type-safe according to the JIT code verification efforts. For

11. If the code has been granted the **SkipVerification** security permission, then it is possible to bypass this verification step.
12. Because of technical limitations and performance constraints, there is no guarantee that all type-safety issues will be detected at JIT compile time (i.e., at application runtime). The JIT compiler does, however, make a terrific effort to catch most type-safety issues.
13. Unlike C#, VB.NET does not allow you to work with memory pointers. C# allows direct memory manipulation via pointers, but this requires the use of the **unsafe** keyword.

other languages, you must check with the provided documentation to see if and under which conditions verifiably type-safe managed code is generated.

When using languages, such as C#, that can generate verifiably type-safe managed code only when you avoid certain language features, you can use the **PEVerify.exe** utility to test whether the generated code is verifiably type-safe. Assemblies that are not verifiably type-safe are permitted to run only if they are fully trusted. According to default security policy, assemblies that originate from the local machine are fully trusted. Fully trusted code is allowed to request the **SkipVerification** permission, allowing it to bypass verification, which is necessary for managed C++ code as well as C# compiled with the /unsafe option.

Denying and Demanding Permissions

Another powerful security feature is that code can request permissions that it expects it will need in carrying out its duties. In that case the CLR applies the currently configured security policy to determine whether or not it will grant a requested permission. In this way an assembly can determine upfront whether it has all the needed permissions before starting the first of several steps that could run into trouble partway through. It is far cleaner to deal with the security exception at the outset than to wait until you are halfway through a complex sequence of operations that are difficult to back out of cleanly. We shall see how to request a permission imperatively, using the **Demand** method, and how to request a permission declaratively, using the **PermissionSetAttribute** attribute and **SecurityAction** enumeration, which can be applied to constructs such as assemblies, classes, and methods.

Code can also specify to the CLR those permissions that it does not need and specifically does not want to have. This can be an effective defense tactic that limits risk, ensuring that the code will not be lured into performing unintended actions on behalf of a malicious client code. We will see how to specify permissions imperatively, using the **Deny** method, and how to specify permissions declaratively by applying the **PermissionSetAttribute** attribute and **SecurityAction** enumeration to program constructs.

How CAS Is Used

CAS provides a very useful security model, which is quite distinct from, but complementary to, user-based security.[14] Let's look at some of the ways that

---

14. Unlike CAS, user-based security does not seem to be referred to in the literature by an acronym.

CAS can be used to solve security problems that are not effectively handled with user-based security techniques alone.

Flexible Security

CAS provides a flexible security layer over user-based security that allows for varying degrees of trust. This is somewhat similar to the Internet Explorer concept of security zones but is much more configurable and extensible. CAS minimizes the amount of code that must be fully trusted, and it takes into account the fact that trust is not always an all-or-nothing proposition.

As described in the previous chapter, user-based security is great for situations where you have a manageable number of users and groups that you can effectively evaluate in terms of trustworthiness. But what if there is no limit to the number of users? For example, what about implementing a secure public Web service? What about developing a reusable library that might be called upon by hundreds of programs written by unknown programmers that could then be executed by virtually anyone anywhere? It would not be practical to create a user account or role and assign individual privileges for an arbitrarily large number of users. The traditional solution was to use a special anonymous account to represent unknown users, allowing you to broadly define anonymous user privileges. The Web server then temporarily impersonates the anonymous user to service the request. This is fine in many cases, but sometimes you may need finer control over the privileges granted to anonymous users, in a way that might vary, depending on the nature of the code that is being executed. This is another situation where CAS can provide greater flexibility.

The Luring Attack and Walking the Stack

User-based security by itself is also problematic in situations where an evildoer lures innocent users running trusted programs into unintentionally doing nasty things. If you are the parent of a teenager, you are perhaps familiar with the need for limiting certain permissions that are not motivated by a lack of trust in your child but rather by your mistrust of your child's peers. In the same way, whenever you are executing trusted code that interacts with code that originates from unknown sources, you may need to manage the risk by controlling the privileges of the trusted code as well. You should always try to limit what can be done to the smallest set of actions that you expect may be legitimately required. This works well for code security, but of course for teenager security, your mileage may vary!

Since a less trusted assembly has reduced permissions granted to it, it probably cannot do much damage on its own. More trusted code is typically granted greater permissions, so it should somehow check on its callers before doing anything that could be potentially dangerous. The CLR provides a nifty, built-in feature called *stack walking* that makes this security check on the caller possible. Whenever you call a method that demands a request for a particular permission, the CLR performs a stack walk, first checking the immediate caller and then continuing up the call stack until it is satisfied that all callers have been granted the specified permission. If security policy does not permit the action, or if any callers have denied the permission, then a security exception is thrown, and the action is prevented.

Managing Security Policy with Code Groups

Security becomes a major challenge when dealing with mobile code and third-party components. For example, you probably want to restrict macros and assembly components from accessing anything other than the document or application that contains them. You may even want to protect your system from bugs in software from trusted vendors. To handle these situations, CAS allows security policy to be enforced on assemblies according to established rules of code group membership. This means that security decisions can be applied to individual assemblies that are used in combination within an application such that each assembly is treated in a specific and appropriate manner according to the trust level of the code group to which it belongs.

It would be too difficult to manage security policy on an assembly-by-assembly basis. Since there could potentially be thousands of assemblies on a given machine, it would be far too labor-intensive to fiddle with them all individually. Instead, you manage code groups by specifying the criteria that is used to determine code group membership for entire categories of assemblies. You can think of a code group as a set of assemblies that represent a common degree of trust. Then, security policy is defined in terms of the permission set granted to each specific code group rather than to each individual assembly.

The Basic Concepts of Security Policy Management

There are three configurable security policy levels: Enterprise, Machine, and User. Enterprise is the highest level, and User is the lowest level. There is also a fourth security policy level, which is the lowest, known as the AppDomain level,[15] but it is only programmatically managed within a given application

---

15. An application domain, often referred to as an AppDomain, provides CLR-controlled memory isolation within a program. It is similar in concept to an operating system process in that it provides safety through isolation, but it is much more lightweight and scalable. Multiple AppDomains can exist within a single operating system process. As you may have guessed, only verifiably type-safe code can be managed within an AppDomain. AppDomain-level policy is not configurable, but instead is established by calling the **AppDomain.SetAppDomainPolicy** method, which is effective only if the **SecurityPermission** has been granted.

and not administratively managed. Each level is used to define code access security policy, but lower security policy levels cannot grant more permission than that defined by higher security policy levels. Each policy level contains a hierarchy of code groups. Each code group specifies a membership condition that determines which assemblies belong to that particular code group. Strangely, it is possible to define membership conditions that result in an assembly falling into more than one code group.

Each code group has a named permission set associated with it. A permission set specifies the actions that the CLR will permit code in that code group to perform. As you can guess from its name, a permission set contains a set of permissions. Each of these permissions defines exactly what resource access or program action is being permitted. Permissions are determined for an assembly at each policy level, and the resulting permissions are determined by evaluating the intersection of the permissions for policy levels.

Ultimately, permissions are determined according to code group membership, which in turn is based on host and assembly evidence. Therefore, you can think of security policy as a mapping from security evidence to a permission set. By manipulating permission sets and code groups membership criteria, the administrator can determine what permissions are ultimately granted to individual assemblies. The .NET platform provides the following two tools for managing .NET security policy:

- The .NET Framework Configuration tool, Mscorcfg.msc
- The code access security policy utility, Caspol.exe

The .NET Framework Configuration tool can be used to administer local machine security policy, and it can also be used to create policy deployment packages that target the enterprise using SMS (System Management Server) and Active Directory Group Policy. The **Caspol** command-line utility is not as easy to use manually, but it is more suitable for automated scripting of policy administration.

Using the .NET Framework Configuration Tool

The .NET Framework Configuration tool runs as an MMC (Microsoft Management Console) snap-in. This tool is used for many configuration purposes, but in this chapter we focus on using it for .NET security policy configuration. You can start this tool by double-clicking on the **Mscorcfg.msc** file, or you can select Start | Settings | Control Panel menu, and then select Administrative Tools | Microsoft .NET Framework Configuration.

Within this tool, you open the Runtime Security Policy node, as shown in Figure 8–1. As you can see, there are three subnodes named Enterprise, Machine, and User, which are the three configurable security policy levels we talked about earlier. Under each of those policy levels, there are three subnodes named Code Groups, Permission Sets, and Policy Assemblies. Each of

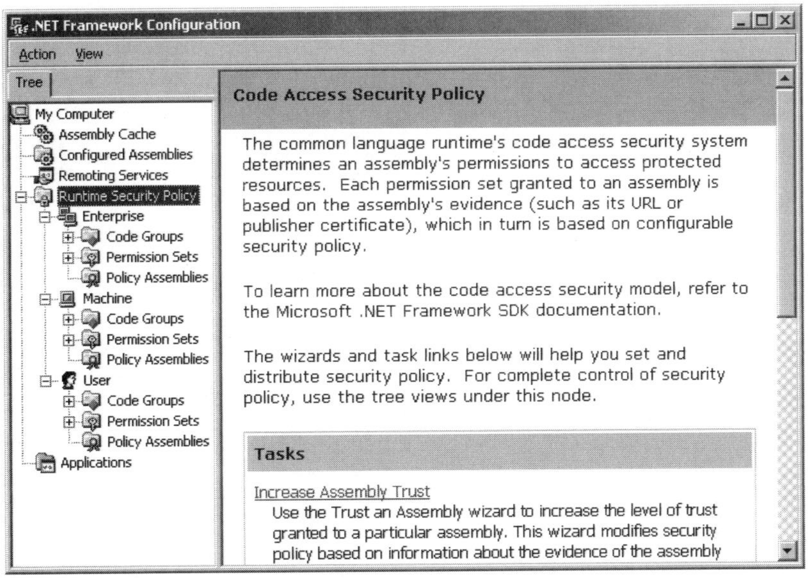

FIGURE 8-1   *Runtime security policy in the Microsoft .NET Framework Configuration tool.*

these subnodes contains further subnodes, which we discuss in more detail shortly. For now, it is sufficient to understand that the Code Groups node contains criteria for categorizing groups of assemblies with common security requirements, the Permission Sets node contains named sets of security permissions, and the Policy Assemblies node contains fully trusted assemblies that implement classes that define security objects that represent code group membership conditions and code access permissions.

Actually, policy assemblies are very special. Policy assemblies define permissions and membership conditions that are used by the security engine during permission evaluation. If you add a custom permission or custom membership condition to your security policy, you must first add the assembly implementing the custom security object and all the assemblies it depends on to the list of policy assemblies. The policy system will then grant the required full trust to those assemblies for use in evaluating the security policy that is defined using those custom security objects. Policy assemblies must be fully trusted, digitally signed, and deployed in the global assembly cache before they can be added to the list of policy assemblies. Since policy assemblies enter the inner sanctum of security management, it is obvious that you must be absolutely certain that they are completely trustworthy, or your entire security infrastructure will be compromised!

The highest of the configurable security policy levels is the Enterprise level, which is used to define policy for an entire organization. The second security policy level is the Machine level, which defines policy for all code that is run on the local computer. The third level is User, which defines security policy for the currently logged-on user. Table 8–1 shows the purpose of each of these three policy levels.

TABLE 8-1	*Configurable Security Policy Levels*
Configurable security policy level	**Purpose**
Enterprise	Defines security policy for an entire enterprise.
Machine	Defines security policy for code on the local computer.
User	Defines security policy for the currently logged-on user.

At runtime, when the CLR loads an assembly, it first determines which code group (or groups) the assembly belongs to according to the supporting evidence provided by the assembly, and then it evaluates the appropriate security policy according to its code group membership. The security policy is determined by evaluating all of the three security policy levels, and the result is formed by the intersection of the permissions granted by all three levels. In other words, it requires a unanimous vote so that if an assembly lacks a given permission at any of these levels, then it is not granted that permission.

Figure 8–2 shows the hierarchy of code groups defined under the machine level. At each code group node, you can edit the code group membership properties, and you can also create child code groups. The hierarchy allows you to loosely define group membership near the root node, and as you go further down the tree, you typically define more restrictive membership constraints. Every code group has a single permission set associated with it, and it also has a set of criteria that is used to determine if any given assembly belongs to that code group.

If you select a particular code group, and then click on the Edit Code Group Properties link, you will see the Code Group Properties dialog. With this dialog, you can edit the code group name, description, membership condition, and permission set. This is shown in Figures 8–3, 8–4, and 8–5 for the preexisting My_Computer_Zone Code Group.

As we have just seen, every code group has a single permission set. However, a single permission set can contain a number of permissions. A single permission represents the right to take some action or access some resource in some way. There are several preexisting permission sets, and it turns out that the .NET Framework Configuration tool also allows you to construct your own new named permission sets.

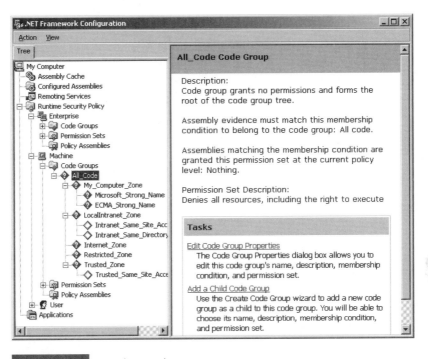

FIGURE 8-2   Machine code groups.

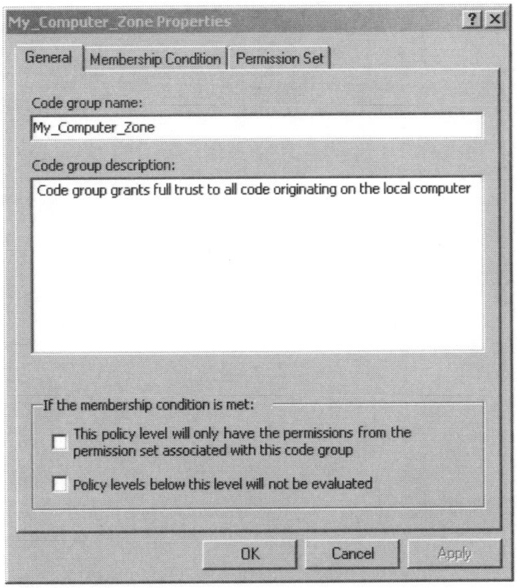

FIGURE 8-3   Code Group Properties general tab.

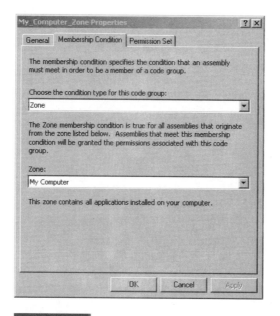

FIGURE 8-4   Code Group Properties membership condition tab.

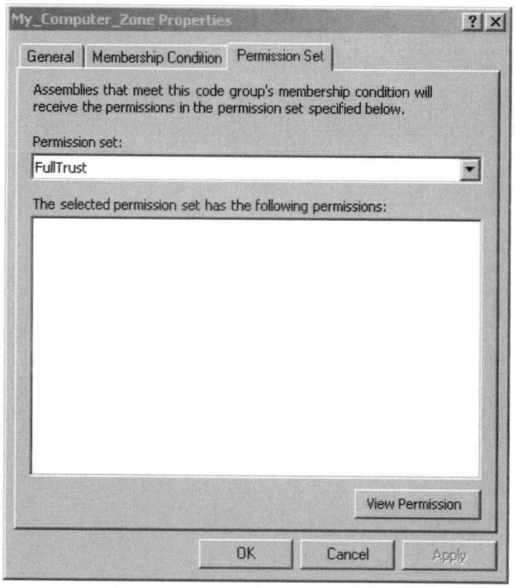

FIGURE 8-5   Code Group Properties permission set tab.

There are also several preexisting code group membership conditions that are provided by the .NET Framework. Just as was the case for code access permissions, each of the code group membership conditions is also implemented as a class defined in a policy assembly. Also, just as you can create your own custom code access permission classes, you can also create your own code group membership condition classes. The key concept here is simply that a code group membership condition determines whether the membership condition is satisfied by an assembly's evidence. Table 8–2 shows the name and purpose of the prebuilt code group membership conditions along with the evidence used in determining membership.

TABLE 8–2	*Code Group Membership Criteria*
Code group	**Evidence used in making membership determination**
All code	Matches all code regardless of evidence.
Application directory	Application installation directory.
Hash	MD5 or SHA1 hash.
Publisher	Public key of digital signature (X.509 certificate).
Site	Web or FTP site hostname.
Strong name	Digital signature.
URL	The entire originating URL.
Zone	The originating zone (MyComputer, LocalIntranet, Internet, Restricted, or Trusted).

THE PINVOKE EXAMPLE: DEFINING A NEW CODE GROUP

There are several general-purpose predefined code groups, such as My_Computer_Zone and LocalIntranet_Zone, with associated default permission sets. However, there are times when you need to modify existing code groups or define your own new code groups. Let's go through the steps of a typical example where the .NET Framework Configuration Tool is used to define a new code group with specific code access permissions.

The **PInvoke** example is a simple program that attempts to call into the two Win32 APIs **GetComputerName** and **GetLastError**. If you run this program under the original default security policy, you will see that it works properly even though it takes the risk of calling into unmanaged code. This is because it is run on the local machine, and, according to default security policy, the MyComputer security zone is fully trusted, as shown in Figure 8–6.

We will soon see how we can change this so that the PInvoke program is no longer permitted to call into unmanaged code, but, first, let's look at the source code for the program. As you can see, there is no hint of any

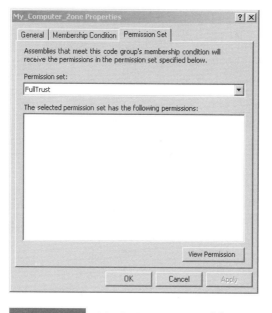

FIGURE 8-6 *My_Computer_Zone is fully trusted.*

security-related code whatsoever. This is because we are not interested in security programming at this point. Instead, we want to focus on the administrative business of managing security policy. When you run this program under default security policy, it simply displays the name of the local machine.

```
//PInvoke.cs

using System;
using System.Text;
using System.Runtime.InteropServices;
using System.Security;

public class Test
{
    [DllImport("kernel32.dll", CharSet=CharSet.Ansi)]
    public static extern bool GetComputerName(
        StringBuilder name, out uint buffer);
    [DllImport("kernel32.dll")]
    public static extern uint GetLastError();

    public static int Main(string[] args)
    {
```

```
bool result = true;
uint error = 0;
StringBuilder name = new StringBuilder(128);
uint length = 128;
Console.WriteLine(
    "Attempting to call GetComputerName");
result = GetComputerName(name, out length);

if (result == true)
    Console.WriteLine(
        "GetComputerName returned: " +
        name);
else
{
    error = GetLastError();
    Console.WriteLine(
        "Error! GetComputerName  returned: " +
        error);
}

Console.Write("Press Enter to exit...");
Console.Read();
return 0;
    }
}
```

Here is the output from the program. Note that this is before we make any changes to the default security policy. Naturally, the name of your machine will appear differently.

```
Attempting to call GetComputerName
GetComputerName returned: HPDESKTOP
```

Of course, the **PInvoke** program does not actually do any real damage; otherwise, you would not want to try running it as a demonstration example! But let's pretend for a moment that you are an administrator and you do not have its source code. Since you do not know what it might attempt to do, you might want to configure security such that it cannot do any harm.

To do this, you first define a new code group with membership criteria that includes the **PInvoke.exe** assembly. Start the .NET Framework Configuration Tool, and then open the Code Groups node under the Machine policy level. You could have just as easily chosen the Enterprise or User level, but in this example you will be working under the Machine policy level. Under the Code Groups node, click on the All_Code node and then click on the Add a Child

Code Group link.[16] In the resulting Create Code Group wizard, enter the name My_Own_Zone and a description for the new zone, as shown in Figure 8–7.

Click Next to go to the next step of the wizard to choose the code membership condition. In the condition type combo box, choose URL, and in the URL field, enter **file://C:/OI/NetSecurity/Chap8/PInvoke/bin/Debug/***, as shown in Figure 8–8. This will make any assembly found in that directory a member of the My_Own_Zone code group.

Click Next to proceed to the third step of the wizard, where you will assign a permission set to the new code group. In the Use existing permission set combo box, select the Execution permission, as shown in Figure 8–9.

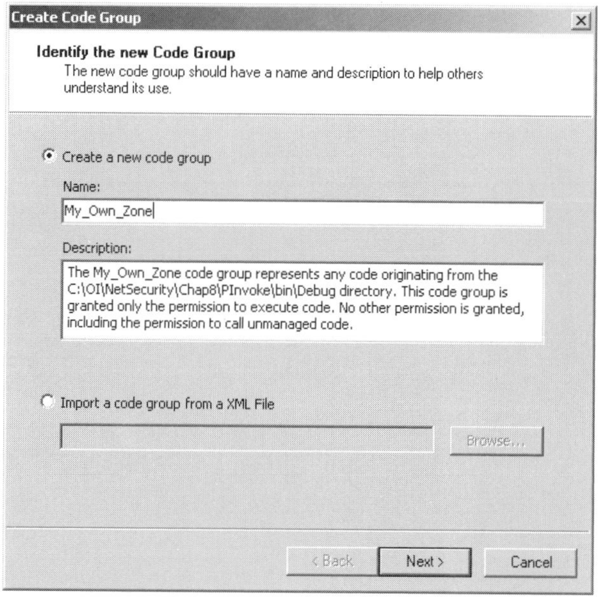

FIGURE 8-7   Creating My_Own_Zone step 1.

---

16. We will be adding and changing several aspects of security policy in this section. This can mess things up quite badly if you are not careful. Fortunately, once you are finished experimenting with security policy, you can revert everything back to its original default. To do this, simply right-click on the Runtime Security Policy node, and select Reset All from the context menu. Of course, if you have previously made great effort to establish an intricate policy that you would like to keep intact, then you might want to carefully back out of your changes manually rather than revert back to the defaults. Alternatively, you may want to construct a batch file that uses **Caspol.exe** to automatically reestablish your baseline security policy configuration.

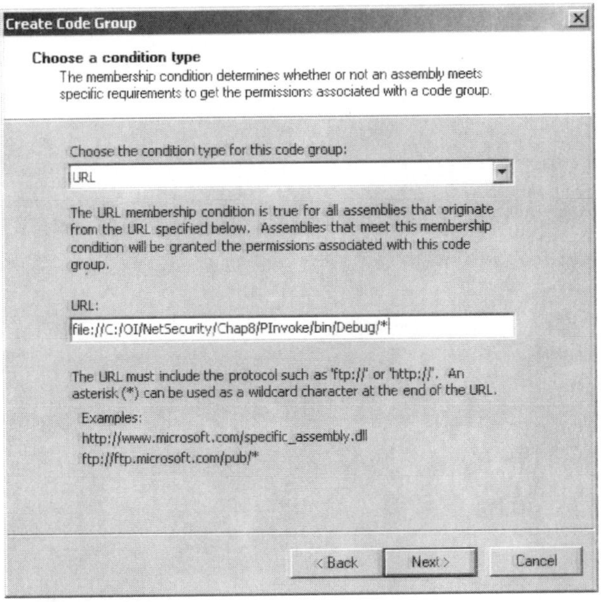

FIGURE 8-8   Creating My_Own_Zone step 2.

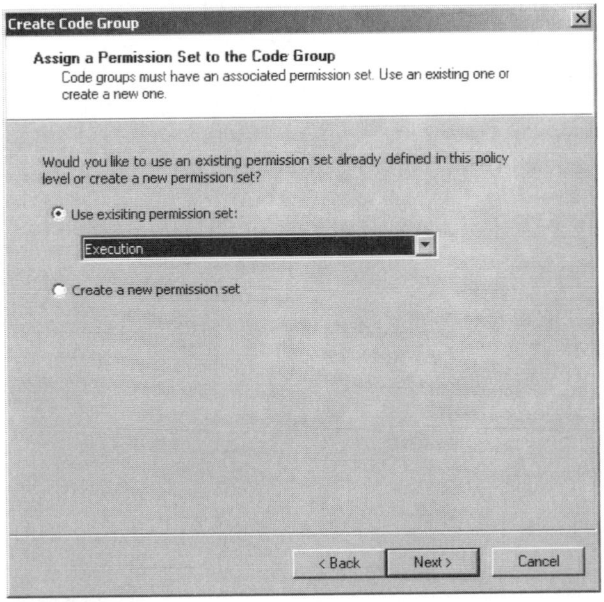

FIGURE 8-9   Creating My_Own_Zone step 3.

Finish the wizard by clicking Next and Finish. The new code group will then appear in the .NET Configuration Tool, as shown in Figure 8–10. Notice that the name My_Own_Zone appears in the code group hierarchy, and the description and membership condition appear in the right-hand pane.

Now, click on the Edit Code Group Properties link to see the My_Own_Zone code group properties dialog. On the General tab, select the checkbox that specifies that this policy level will only have the permissions from the permission set associated with this code group, as shown in Figure 8–11.

On the Permission Set tab, you can see what permissions are granted by the Execute permission set. As you can see in Figure 8–12, the Execute permission set contains a single permission named Security.

If you now select the Security permission in the list box, and then click on the View Permission button, you can see the details of this Security permission. Figure 8–13 shows that this permission allows code execution, but it disallows every other possible aspect of the Security permission.[17] In particular,

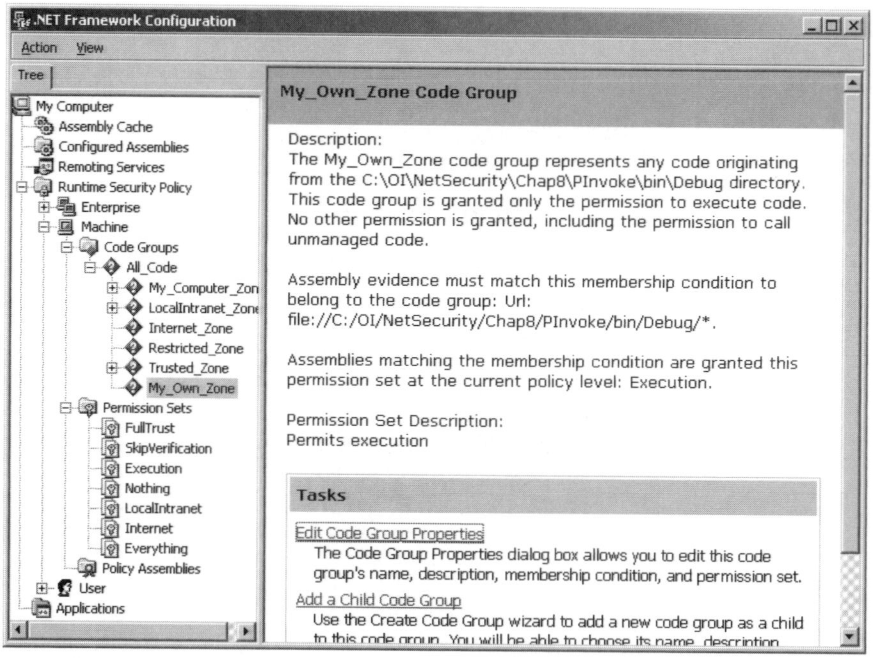

FIGURE 8–10   *My_Own_Zone created.*

---

17. If you take a look at the documentation for the **SecurityPermission** class, you will see each of these Security permission aspects in the form of the **Flags** property, which takes on values defined by the **SecurityPermissionFlag** enumeration.

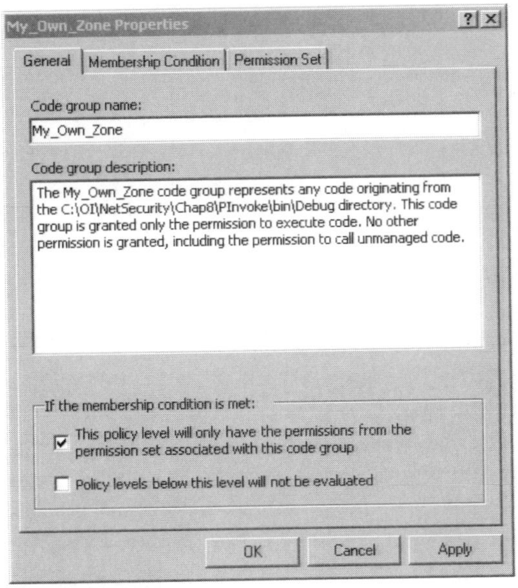

FIGURE 8-11 *My_Own_Zone properties general tab.*

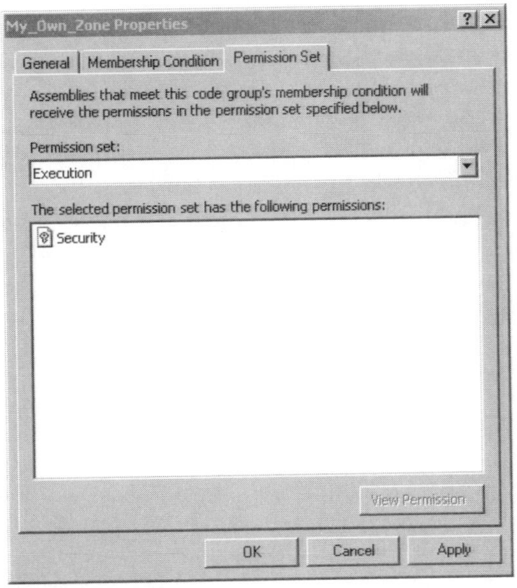

FIGURE 8-12 *My_Own_Zone properties permission set tab.*

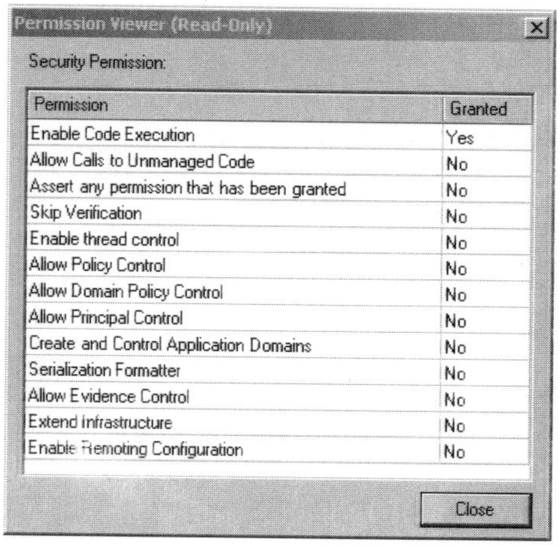

FIGURE 8-13   My_Own_Zone permission viewer.

notice that the permission to call unmanaged code is not granted. Since the permission set contains no permissions other than the Security permission, it is clear that the My_Own_Zone code group is rather severely restricted.

Next, close the Permission Viewer window and click OK to close the Code Group Properties dialog. Now that you have finished creating your own code group and established its membership criteria and associated permission set, you can try running the PInvoke program again. Previously, this program simply displayed the current machine name. But now, it throws an exception, as shown in the following output. There is no point in trying to catch this exception within the PInvoke program's **Main** method, since it is actually thrown when an attempt is made to call the **Main** method. This is because of the **DllImport** attribute that is applied to the **Main** method.

```
Unhandled Exception: System.Security.SecurityException:
  System.Security.Permissions.SecurityPermission
    at Test.Main(String[] args)

The state of the failed permission was:
  <IPermission class=
    "System.Security.Permissions.SecurityPermission,
    mscorlib, Version=1.0.3300.0, Culture=neutral,
    PublicKeyToken=b77a5c561934e089"
            version="1"
            Flags="UnmanagedCode"/>
```

DEFINING A NEW PERMISSION SET

We have just seen how to add a new code group and associate it with a permission set. However, we just used a predefined permission set named Execution, which has a rigidly defined set of permissions contained within it. Recall that the Execution permission set contains a single permission named Security, and that permission has only the one enabled capability to execute code. What if you want a Security permission that will enable code execution and thread control but disable all other possibilities, such as calling unmanaged code and application domain creation? You may even want to define a new permission set that contains a combination of permissions, such as Security, User Interface, and File IO permissions, each with a customized set of options enabled. For these situations, you need to create a new permission set.[18]

To define a new permission set, start the .NET Framework Configuration Tool and open the desired policy level. In this example choose the Machine policy level, and then open the corresponding Permission Sets node. Click on the Create New Permission Set link in the right-hand pane, and in the resulting Create Permission Set wizard, enter the name MyPermissionSet and provide a description for the new permission set, as shown in Figure 8–14.

Click Next to move to the second step of the wizard, where you construct the permission set contents. You select permission items in the left list box, and click the Add button to move them to the right list box. Figure 8–15 shows what this dialog looks like before any permission has been added.

For each of the items that you move to the right list box, you are provided a permission-specific dialog where you can make detailed decisions about exactly what options the permission entails. This is shown in Figure 8–16 in the case of the File IO permission and in Figure 8–17 in the case of the Security permission.

After you have added the desired permissions to your new permission set, you can click Finish to close the Create Permission Set wizard. The final result is shown in Figure 8–18.

Now that you have created the new permission set, you can associate it with a code group in the same way we saw earlier with a predefined permis-

---

18. In fact, you can go one step further by programmatically defining a completely customized permission class that controls access to application-specific functionality. This involves several steps, including the definition of a class derived from **CodeAccessPermission** in an assembly that must be digitally signed, deployed to the global assembly cache, and fully trusted. An XML representation of the permission is also required, and the resulting assembly is then added under the Policy Assemblies node in the .NET Framework configuration tool. Once that is all completed, the new permission may be added to a permission set and used in configuring code group security policy.

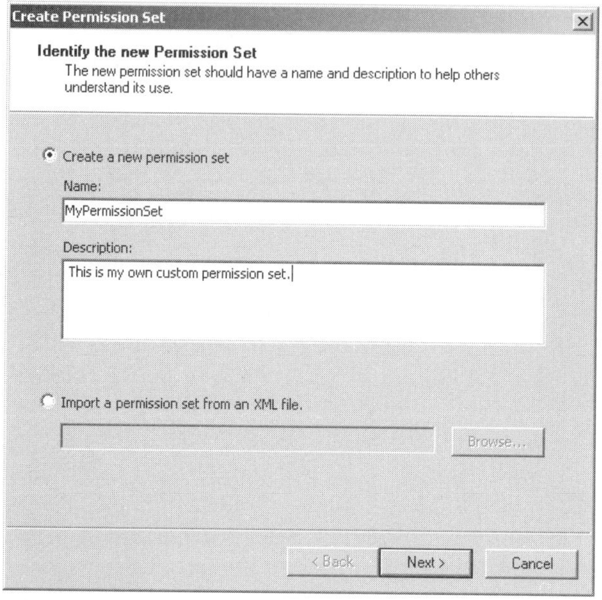

FIGURE 8-14   Create MyPermissionSet step 1.

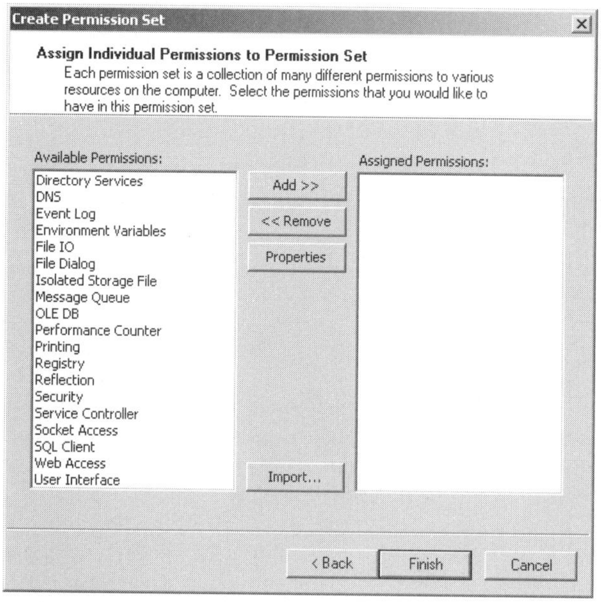

FIGURE 8-15   Create MyPermissionSet step 2.

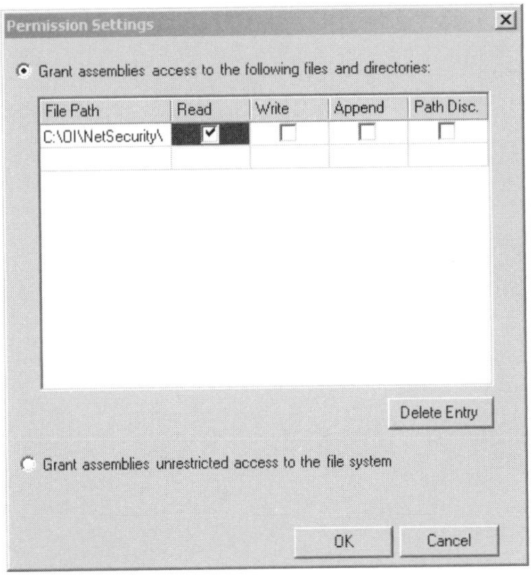

FIGURE 8-16   *File IO permission settings.*

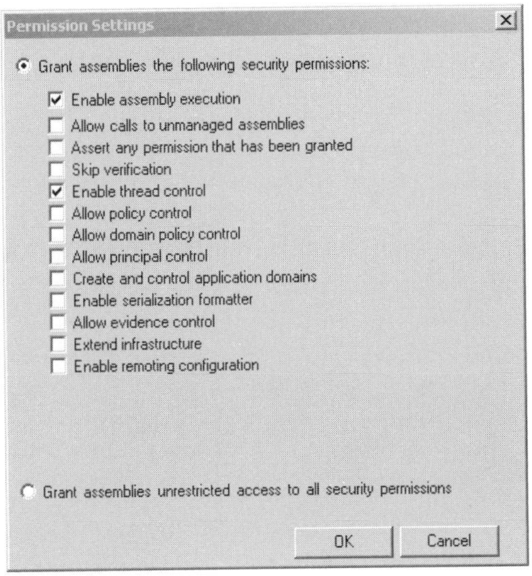

FIGURE 8-17   *Security permission settings.*

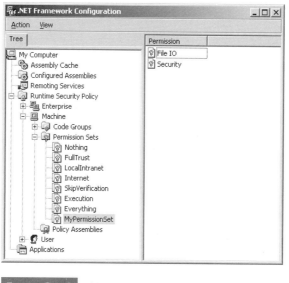

FIGURE 8-18   *MyPermissionSet created.*

sion set. In particular, you should notice that the newly created permission set will now automatically appear in the Create Code Group wizard and the Edit Code Group Properties dialog that we saw earlier.

Using the Caspol.exe Utility

There is a command-line alternative to the .NET Configuration tool, named **Caspol.exe**.[19] Generally, people prefer to use a nice GUI interface, especially when first learning about the concepts. However, command-line tools are more useful when batch file scripts and programs are used to automate the configuration process.

The command-line options supported by **Caspol** are numerous, and we will not go into them in exhaustive detail here. Instead, let's just look at a few examples of the types of work that can be done with this utility. Table 8–3 shows some of the more commonly used command-line options. Abbreviations for command-line arguments and target operands are not shown here. Please see the **Caspol** documentation for further details.

---

19. **Caspol** stands for code access security policy.

TABLE 8-3	*The Caspol Command-Line Options*
Caspol command line	**Purpose**
caspol -help	Display the Caspol command-line documentation.
caspol -machine	Make subsequent commands act on the machine level.
caspol -user	Make subsequent commands act on the user level.
caspol -enterprise	Make subsequent commands act on the enterprise level.
caspol -addgroup ...	Add code group to policy level.
caspol -remgroup ...	Remove code group to policy level.
caspol -listgroups	List code groups.
caspol -addpset ...	Add named permission set to policy level.
caspol -rempset ...	Remove a named permission set from the policy level.
caspol -listpset	List permission sets.
caspol -addfulltrust ...	Add full-trust assembly to policy level.
caspol -remfulltrust ...	Remove a full-trust assembly from the policy level.
caspol -listfulltrust	List full-trust assemblies.
caspol -resolvegroup ...	List code groups that assembly belongs to.
caspol -security ...	Turn security on or off.
caspol -reset	Reset a policy level to its default state.

Imperative Versus Declarative CAS

Just as we saw in the previous chapter on user-based security, CAS can also be implemented in either an imperative or a declarative manner. We will also see shortly that, just as was the case in user-based security, imperative CAS can be implemented using two slightly different approaches.

The first of these imperative approaches involves the explicit use of the **Evidence** class. This approach is sometimes referred to as explicit evidence-based security, because you explicitly evaluate host and assembly security evidence in making programmatic decisions. The other imperative approach makes use of various permission classes, derived from **CodeAccessPermission**, that automatically throw a **SecurityException** where appropriate. In a later section, we will also see how to implement CAS in a declarative way by making use of permission attributes applied to methods, classes, and assemblies.

Evidence-Based Security

To learn about imperative CAS, and particularly about evidence-based security, let's begin by looking at the **Evidence** class. We will then see how to obtain an **Evidence** class object of the currently running application domain. Finally, we will see how to enumerate its contents and then make imperative programming decisions based on the discovered evidence.

The Evidence Class

Before we look at the **ImperativeCASComponent** example, we should have a good understanding of the **Evidence** class itself, since it is the crucial ingredient in that code example. The **Evidence** class, found in the **System.Security.Policy** namespace, encapsulates the set of evidence information that can be used to enforce security policy decisions.

Terminology: Evidence and Security Policy

Evidence is the set of security characteristics associated with running code, such as an assembly's digital signature, zone, and site of origin. Evidence is used to categorize assemblies into code groups to which permissions are granted or denied based on established security policy.

Security policy is the set of rules established by an administrator that grants or denies permissions for managed code, effectively determining what operations an assembly is allowed to perform.

For security reasons, the **Evidence** class is sealed, meaning that it cannot be used as the superclass for any new derived classes. Just imagine the skullduggery you could unleash if you were able to trick the CLR into substituting your own derived class in place of the highly trusted **Evidence** class!

The types of evidence that can be obtained via an **Evidence** object may include digital signature, point of origin, or even custom evidence information that may be useful in explicitly making imperative CAS decisions.

The **Evidence** class implements the two interfaces **ICollection** and **IEnumerable**. As we will see shortly, the **ICollection** interface specifies members for containing a collection of objects, and the **IEnumerable** interface provides access to those objects via the **IEnumerator** interface. In the case of the **Evidence** class, the contained objects represent distinct pieces of host evidence and assembly evidence. Here is the declaration for the **Evidence** class.

```
public sealed class Evidence :
    ICollection, IEnumerable
```

Terminology: Host Evidence and Assembly Evidence

When evaluating code access permissions, security policy can make use of two sources of evidence, known as host evidence and assembly evidence.

Host evidence is evidence provided by the host computer that provided the assembly. This evidence provides information about the origin (i.e., the URL, site, and zone) of the assembly as well as the identity of the assembly (i.e., hash or, in the case of a signed assembly, a digital signature or certificate).

Assembly evidence is additional evidence contained within the assembly itself and may be incorporated into security policy by an administrator or programmer. Assembly evidence extends the set of evidence available for making security policy decisions. The default security policy ignores assembly evidence, but security policy can be configured to make use of it.

EVIDENCE CONSTRUCTORS

There are three constructors in the **Evidence** class. The **Evidence** constructor, which takes no parameters, initializes a new empty instance of the **Evidence** class. Of course, an **Evidence** object that contains no evidence information is not too useful. However, we shall see that the **Evidence** class provides methods for adding evidence. The constructor that takes a single **Evidence** parameter provides a shallow copy. The third constructor takes two **Object** array parameters, which are used to initialize the new **Evidence** instance with two arrays of host and assembly evidence objects.

```
public Evidence(); //initialize a new empty instance

public Evidence(
    Evidence evidence //shallow copy

);

public Evidence(
    object[] hostEvidence, //host evidence array
    object[] assemblyEvidence //assembly evidence array
);
```

EVIDENCE PROPERTIES

In the **Evidence** class, there are five public properties named **Count**, **Locked**, **IsSynchronized**, **SyncRoot**, and **IsReadOnly**. Strangely, only the two properties **Count** and **Locked** are of any actual use. As we previously mentioned, the **Evidence** class implements the **ICollection** interface, which specifies the public properties **Count**, **IsSynchronized**, and **SyncRoot**, as well as the public method **CopyTo**. Since the **Evidence** class encapsulates a set of evidence information objects, it makes sense that **Count** is a read-only property that represents the number of these pieces of contained evidence.

The **IsSynchronized** method is normally used on collections to determine if the collection is thread-safe.[20] In the case of the **Evidence** class, **IsSynchronized** always returns false, since thread-safe evidence sets are not supported. This actually makes sense, since it would be quite difficult to imagine why threads would be messing around with sensitive, security-related operations at the same time using the same evidence. In any case the **IsSynchronized** property is effectively useless and therefore is not used.

The **SyncRoot** property normally provides an object on which you can synchronize access to a collection. However, since synchronization of evidence collections is not supported, **SyncRoot** only returns **this**. Therefore, the **SyncRoot** property is also of no practical use and is not used. In spite of being useless, both **IsSynchronized** and **SyncRoot** are defined by the **ICollection**, and therefore the **Evidence** class must expose them even if they serve no useful purpose!

The **IsReadOnly** property always returns **false**, because read-only evidence sets are not supported. Since this return value is a forgone conclusion, **IsReadOnly** is also a useless property, and it is therefore not used.

The **Locked** property gets or sets a true or false value indicating whether the evidence is currently locked. If this property is set to false, then the contained evidence can be modified by calling the **AddHost** or **Merge** methods, which we discuss shortly. If the **Locked** property is set to true, however, then a **SecurityException** exception is thrown by the **Merge** or **AddHost**[21] methods, unless the code has been granted the **ControlEvidence** security permission. In fact, it turns out that you need the **ControlEvidence** security permission to set the **Locked** property to a new value in the first place. The default value for the **Locked** property is false. If you are not planning to add or merge evidence information to an **Evidence** object, then you can simply ignore the **Locked** property altogether.

The following list briefly describes each of these **Evidence** properties. Again, note that three of them are of no use because they return hardwired results, and also note that **Count** is read-only, but **Locked** is read/write.

- **Count** gets the number of items in the evidence collection (read-only).
- **Locked** gets or sets a value indicating whether the evidence collection is locked (read/write).

---

20. A thread-safe collection can keep its cool while multiple threads add, remove, and modify its elements simultaneously. If a collection is not thread-safe, then accessing it from simultaneous threads can lead to data corruption or exceptions being thrown.

21. Strangely, this is true for the **Merge** and **AddHost** methods, but not for the **AddAssembly** method.

- **IsSynchronized** indicates whether the collection is thread-safe (always returns false).
- **SyncRoot** is normally used to synchronize access to the collection (always returns this).
- **IsReadOnly** indicates whether the evidence is read-only (always returns false).

EVIDENCE METHODS

In the **Evidence** class there are seven[22] public methods: **GetEnumerator**, **CopyTo**, **AddAssembly**, **AddHost**, **GetAssemblyEnumerator**, **GetHost-Enumerator**, and **Merge**. The basic operations that these methods support are enumerating and copying, as well as adding and merging evidence information.

One of these methods, **GetEnumerator**, originates in the **IEnumerable** interface. The **GetEnumerator** method simply returns an **IEnumerator** interface that can be used to walk through the evidence collection via its **Current** property and the **MoveNext** and **Reset** methods. Another method, **CopyTo**, originates in the **ICollection** interface. The **CopyTo** method simply copies the elements of the evidence collection to an **Object** array, starting at a particular index position. The remaining six methods are specific to the **Evidence** class itself.

- **GetEnumerator** provides access to all the contained host and assembly evidence.
- **CopyTo** copies evidence to an **Object** array.
- **AddAssembly** adds specified assembly evidence to the collection.
- **AddHost** adds specified host evidence to the collection.
- **GetHostEnumerator** provides access to the host evidence.
- **GetAssemblyEnumerator** provides access to the assembly evidence.
- **Merge** combines the two evidence collections into a single evidence collection.

Obtaining the Current Application Domain Evidence

Although the **Evidence** class does provide constructors, you typically want to obtain a ready-made **Evidence** object that reflects the current runtime situation. The way to get such an **Evidence** object is to access the **Evidence** property of the current application domain object. The **AppDomain.CurrentDomain**

---

22. The **Evidence** class has seven public methods, not including those originating from the **Object** superclass. All classes inherit, and frequently override, these **Object** class public methods named **Equals**, **GetHashCode**, **GetType**, and **ToString**, as well as the protected methods **Finalize** and **MemberwiseClone**.

static property provides the current application domain for the current thread. This is shown in the following code.

```
Evidence evidence =
    AppDomain.CurrentDomain.Evidence;
```

Enumerating Evidence

You can walk through the available evidence by enumerating the contents of the current application domain **Evidence** object. If you do that, you will find security zone and URL information, which is determined by the physical origin of the assembly. You will also find hash code information, which provides identity evidence relating to the binary contents of the assembly itself. If, and only if, the assembly has been digitally signed, you will also find cryptographically strong name evidence. A strong name allows the signer to be mathematically verified and ensures that the assembly cannot be forged, tampered with, or repudiated. To be effective, these guarantees depend on a trusted certificate authority that vouches for the digital signature.

These types of evidence are represented by the following classes, all of which are defined in the **System.Security.Policy** namespace:

- **Zone** specifies a security zone, such as **MyComputer**, **Internet**, and so on.
- **Url** specifies the protocol and path information that specifies the assembly's origin.
- **Hash** contains the SHA1 and MD5 hash values for the assembly.
- **StrongName** contains, if digitally signed, the name, version, and public key of the assembly.
- **Site** specifies, if loaded via an Internet protocol, the site from which the assembly originated.

Once you have the current application domain's **Evidence** object, you can obtain an **IEnumerator** interface on it and walk through the evidence information, making any appropriate security decisions that you deem necessary. To do this, simply call on the **Evidence** object's **GetEnumerator** method and enter a while loop that calls **MoveNext** in each iteration.

```
//walking thru the evidence
IEnumerator enumerator = evidence.GetEnumerator();
while (enumerator.MoveNext())
{
    object item = enumerator.Current;
```

```
        //make decisions based on evidence item
        if (...)
        {
            ...
        }
}
```

The WalkingThruEvidence Example

Let's look at the **WalkingThruEvidence** example to see how this can be done in practice. This program obtains the current **Evidence** object and then displays the evidence information that it contains. In this example we have a digitally signed assembly, so we can see the additional **StrongName** evidence that is produced by the presence of a digital signature.

How to Sign an Assembly

The **WalkingThruEvidence** example is a digitally signed assembly. There are two ways to digitally sign an assembly. One way is to use **Al.exe** (Assembly Linker) to add the signature to an existing assembly. The other way is to use either the **AssemblyKeyFileAttribute** or the **AssemblyKeyNameAttributeassembly** attribute to define the signature directly in your source code.

In any case you must first generate a public/private key pair before you can sign an assembly with either of these techniques. Since we are interested in authentication rather than secrecy, we must digitally sign the assembly with the private key and then make the assembly and the associated public key publicly available. You can create this key pair using **Sn.exe** (Strong Name utility). For example, the following command line creates a new key pair file called **MyKeyPair.snk**. **Sn.exe** can also write the resulting keys to a named key container managed by a CSP (cryptographic service provider). Check the tool's documentation for details.

```
sn -k MyKeyPair.snk
```

The resulting file contains both public and private keys, but it must be kept secret, since it does contain the private key. To expose only the public key in the key pair file, you must extract and copy it to a separate file. The following command line extracts the public key from **MyKeyPair.snk** and places it into **MyPublicKey.snk**.

```
sn -p MyKeyPair.snk MyPublicKey.snk
```

To sign a DLL or an EXE assembly, you can use the Assembly Linker utility **Al.exe**. The following command line specifies that the **WalkingThruEvidence.exe** assembly is to be signed and the **MyKeyPair.snk** key pair file that contains the private key is to be used for

How to Sign an Assembly *(continued)*

the digital signature. The Assembly Linker utility looks for the key pair relative to the current and output directories.

```
al /out:WalkingThruEvidence.exe /keyfile:MyKeyPair.snk
```

The other technique for signing an assembly is to use code attributes. You can add either the **AssemblyKeyFileAttribute** or the **AssemblyKeyNameAttributeassembly** attribute to your source code. The **AssemblyKeyFileAttribute** specifies the name of the file that contains the desired key pair. The **AssemblyKeyNameAttributeassembly** specifies the name of a key container within the CSP that contains the key pair. The following code uses the **AssemblyKeyFileAttribute** with the key file named **MyKeyPair.snk**. The full path must be specified, but in this example it has been shortened to fit onto a single line in this book. This attribute is typically added to the source file named **AssemblyInfo.cs**, which is automatically generated for you when you create a C# project in Visual Studio .NET.

```
[assembly:AssemblyKeyFileAttribute(@"...\MyKeyPair.snk ")]
```

The **WalkingThruEvidence** example first obtains the current **Evidence** object, and then it loops through all the evidence that it contains. Then, for each piece of evidence, it displays the details found. Here is the source code.

```
//obtain appdomain security evidence
Evidence evidence =
   AppDomain.CurrentDomain.Evidence;

//obtain evidence enumerator
IEnumerator enumerator = evidence.GetEnumerator();

//walk thru evidence
while (enumerator.MoveNext())
{
   object item = enumerator.Current;

   //display the evidence
   Type type = item.GetType();
   Console.WriteLine(type.Name + ": ");
   if (type == typeof(Url))
   {
      Console.WriteLine(
         "   Value: " +
         ((Url)item).Value);
   }
   if (type == typeof(Zone))
   {
```

```
        Console.WriteLine(
            "     SecurityZone: " +
            ((Zone)item).SecurityZone);
    }
    if (type == typeof(Hash))
    {
        Console.WriteLine(
            "     MD5: " +
            BitConverter.ToString(((Hash)item).MD5));
        Console.WriteLine(
            "     " + "SHA1: " +
            BitConverter.ToString(((Hash)item).SHA1));
    }
    if (type == typeof(StrongName))
    {
        Console.WriteLine(
            "     Name: " +
            ((StrongName)item).Name);
        Console.WriteLine(
            "     Version: " +
            ((StrongName)item).Version);
        Console.WriteLine(
            "     PublicKey: " +
            ((StrongName)item).PublicKey);
    }
    if (type == typeof(Site))
    {
        Console.WriteLine(
            "     Name: " +
            ((Site)item).Name);
    }
}
```

Here is the output of the **WalkingThruEvidence** example that results from running it directly from the local file system. Output lines that are too long to fit on the printed page have been shortened where necessary. As you can see, the zone is the local computer, and the URL specifies the file protocol followed by the file path where the assembly is located. Because the assembly was digitally signed, you can see the strong name evidence, including the public key. Finally, the MD5 and SHA-1 hash information is present. If you were to rebuild the assembly without the digital signature, then the strong name evidence would be missing. Since this was run directly from the local file system, and not via Internet Explorer, the Web site evidence is absent.

```
Zone:
    SecurityZone: MyComputer
Url:
    Value: file://C:/.../WalkingThruEvidence.exe
```

```
StrongName:
   Name: WalkingThruEvidence
   Version: 1.0.1010.20177
   PublicKey:
002400000480000094000000060200000002400005253...
     5C5703B8AEEA06C1CFD72327CD0F35FD650345ACA6806F7
Hash:
   MD5: A6-AB-D6-AD-42-41-38-67-BF-57-32-4C-55-A4-6C-A4
   SHA1: F6-E1-17-1A-4B-6C-BE-DB-4B-ED-...-E4-E2-C3-37
```

Accessing the WalkingThruEvidence Example Via IIS

Let's try something slightly different now by publishing the **WalkingThruEvidence** assembly on the local IIS Web site and then executing it from within Internet Explorer via http. To publish a file on an IIS Web site, you simply copy the file to the **\inetpub\wwwroot** directory. Then, to access it in Internet Explorer, you enter the URL in the form of **http://servername/filename**. To do this locally, you can specify localhost as your server name. The URL that you will then enter in Internet Explorer will therefore be **http://localhost/WalkingThruEvidence.exe**.

Assuming that you have deployed the assembly to the IIS root directory, if you try to run this program in this way, Internet Explorer will attempt to load and run the assembly, but this will only result in a **SecurityException** being thrown. This happens because the assembly is no longer being loaded from the My Computer zone, which is fully trusted, but instead is being loaded from the Local Internet zone, which is not granted full trust by default.

To see this program work properly, you must change the trust level granted to the Local Internet zone to full trust. **Warning**: This is an experiment only. You should *never* set the intranet zone to full trust in a production environment! This experiment should only be done temporarily on a non-networked development machine. Once you are done, you should set the trust level back to its original default level to avoid an obvious security risk. To change this trust level, select Start | Settings | Control Panel | Administrative Tools | Microsoft .NET Framework Wizards, and then select Adjust .NET Security, which opens the Security Adjustment Wizard, as shown in Figure 8–19.

In the Security Adjustment Wizard, select the Make changes to this computer radio button and click Next. Click on the Local Intranet icon and adjust the level of trust to Full Trust. This is shown in Figure 8–20.

Click Next, and then, to complete the wizard, click Finish. Once you have done this, you can again try running the program using Internet Explorer, with the result shown in the following output. The zone, which was previously MyComputer, is now changed to Intranet. The URL, which was previously **file://C:/.../WalkingThruEvidence.exe**, is now **http://localhost/WalkingThruEvidence.exe**. From this, you can see clearly that a completely different protocol (http rather than file) was used this time to locate

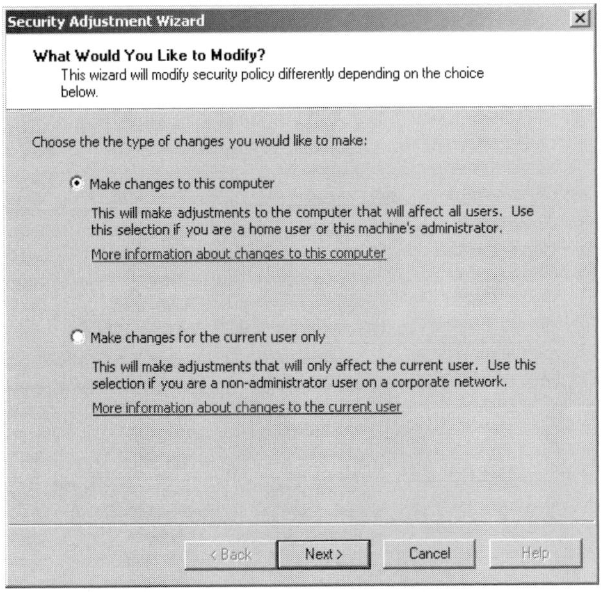

FIGURE 8-19 The Security Adjustment Wizard.

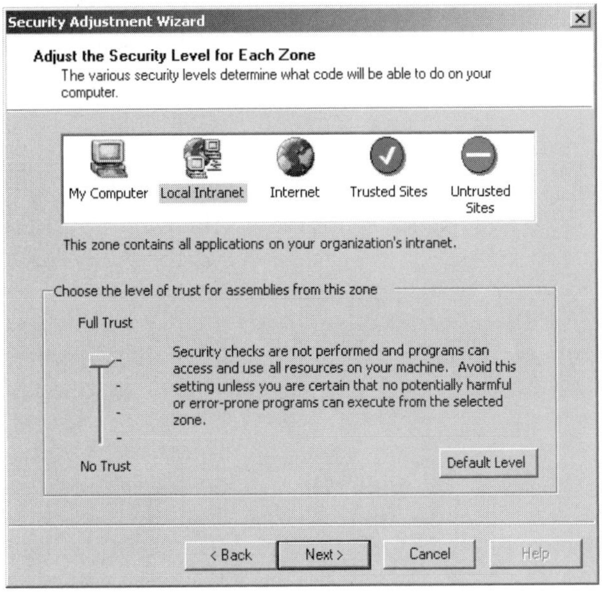

FIGURE 8-20 Local Intranet zone set to full trust.

and load the assembly. The Web site evidence, which was completely missing before, now specifies the localhost machine, and the strong name and hash evidence is no longer available. This all clearly shows that we are now dealing with an entirely different code group.

```
Zone:
    SecurityZone: Intranet
Site:
    Name: localhost
Url:
    Value: http://localhost/WalkingThruEvidence.exe
```

Imperative CAS

Let's turn our attention now to the imperative approach to CAS. We first consider how this is done by browsing through the available evidence, and later we will see how to do the same thing using **CodeAccessPermission** derived classes.

THE IMPERATIVECAS EXAMPLE

The **ImperativeCAS** example program, found together with the associated **TrustedClient** and **EvilClient** programs in the **ImperativeCAS** directory, demonstrates the explicit imperative approach for protecting a component by allowing it to defend itself from being called by certain untrusted client applications. The **EvilClient** and **TrustedClient** programs both attempt to call into the **DoSomethingForClient** method exposed by the **ImperativeCASComponent** assembly, but only the **TrustedClient** is successful.

This example makes explicit use of the **Evidence** class and chooses between two alternative actions (i.e., execute normally or throw a **SecurityException**) based on an **if** statement that tests a particular detail of the available security evidence. Shortly, we will see another imperative security example using permission objects rather than explicitly perusing the contents of an **Evidence** object.

The **EvilClient** program is very simple. It just calls into a static method named **DoSomethingForClient** on an object defined by a class named **ImperativeCASComponent** in a separate assembly named **ImperativeCASComponent.dll**.

```
//EvilClient.cs

using System;
using System.Security;

class EvilClient
```

```
{
   static void Main(string[] args)
   {
      //NOTE: need ref to ImperativeCASComponent.dll

      //try to call on the component
      try
      {
         ImperativeCASComponent.DoSomethingForClient();
      }
      catch (SecurityException se)
      {
         Console.WriteLine(
            "SecurityException: " + se.Message);
      }
   }
}
```

Notice that the following output shows the unsuccessful result of running the **EvilClient** program, indicating that the client is not considered trustworthy. We will see how this happens when we study the code in the **DoSomethingForClient** method.

```
DoSomethingForClient called
SecurityException: Client is not trustworthy
```

Before we study the **DoSomethingForClient** method, let's look at what happens when we run another program that appears to be identical to the **EvilClient** program. As you can see in the following code listing, the **TrustedClient** program looks virtually identical to the **EvilClient** program in every detail. Yet when you run it, you get an entirely different result.

```
//TrustedClient.cs

using System;
using System.Security;

class TrustedClient
{
   static void Main(string[] args)
   {
      //NOTE: need ref to ImperativeCASComponent.dll

      //try to call on the component
      try
      {
         ImperativeCASComponent.DoSomethingForClient();
      }
```

```
      catch (SecurityException se)
      {
         Console.WriteLine(
            "SecurityException: " + se.Message);
      }
   }
}
```

The following output shows the result of running the **TrustedClient** program. Notice that this time, the output shows a successful result, indicating that the client is considered trustworthy. We will see how this happens as well by studying the code in the **DoSomethingForClient** method.

```
DoSomethingForClient called
Permitted: Client is trustworthy
```

Let's now look at the code that implements the **DoSomethingForClient** method. This static method is implemented in the class named **ImperativeCASComponent**. Both the **TrustedClient** and **EvilClient** attempt to call this method in exactly the same way.

The **DoSomethingForClient** method starts by obtaining the current application domain's **Evidence** object. It then obtains an **IEnumerator** interface and enters a while loop where each piece of available evidence is inspected. As we have seen, there are several types of evidence that may be provided by the **Evidence** object, but the type of evidence in which we are interested in this example is represented by the **Url** class, defined in the **System.Security.Policy** namespace. Therefore, we use an **if** statement to determine if the type of the evidence is a **Url**, and, if it is, we test to see if its value ends with the string **TrustedClient.exe**. Only if this match is found do we recognize the client as being trustworthy. All clients with names other than **TrustedClient.exe** are rejected by throwing a **SecurityException**. Of course, this is a simplified example that focuses on concepts rather than realism. In a more realistic scenario, you would probably want to make more elaborate decisions based on a combination of the available evidence.

```
//ImperativeCASComponent.cs

using System;
using System.Security;
using System.Collections;
using System.Security.Policy;

using System.Windows.Forms;

public class ImperativeCASComponent
{
```

```
//this method only works for TrustedClient.exe
public static void DoSomethingForClient()
{
    Console.WriteLine(
        "DoSomethingForClient called");

    //obtain appdomain security evidence
    Evidence evidence =
        AppDomain.CurrentDomain.Evidence;

    //obtain evidence enumerator
    IEnumerator enumerator = evidence.GetEnumerator();

    bool trustworthy = false; //assume the worst
    while (enumerator.MoveNext()) //walk thru evidence
    {
        object item = enumerator.Current;

        //test to see if Url is acceptable
        Type type = item.GetType();
        if (type == typeof(System.Security.Policy.Url))
        {
            String strUrl =
                ((Url)item).Value.ToString();
            if (strUrl.EndsWith("TrustedClient.exe"))
            {
                trustworthy = true; //good news
                break;
            }
        }
    }

    //throw exception if no good evidence found
    if (!trustworthy)
        throw new SecurityException(
            "Client is not trustworthy");

    //if we got this far then all went OK
    Console.WriteLine(
        "Permitted: Client is trustworthy");
}
}
```

Code Access Permissions

We have just seen several examples showing how the **Evidence** class can be used in a direct manner to make CAS decisions within your code according to the discovery of host and assembly evidence. The other way of approaching CAS is to let the code access permission classes automatically detect any mismatch between the current security policy and the permissions required by the running code. Then, if your program attempts something that it is not permitted to perform, a **SecurityException** is automatically thrown.

CodeAccessPermission Derived Classes

CAS programming usually involves using the classes derived from **CodeAccessPermission**, which are shown in the following list. Since these classes are not all contained within the same namespace, their fully qualified names are provided here for clarity. Most of the **CodeAccessPermission**-derived classes have meanings that are made obvious by their names. For example, **DBDataPermission** controls access to a database, **PrintingPermission** controls access to printers, **SocketPermission** represents the permission for making or accepting TCP/IP connections, and so on.

A subset of these code access permission classes are known as identity permissions, since they do not deal with controlling access to resources but rather specialize in dealing with host evidence pertaining to assembly identity. You can easily recognize these classes, since their names contain the word Identity, such as **SiteIdentityPermission** and **ZoneIdentityPermission**.

Note that this list of **CodeAccessPermission**-derived classes does not contain the **PrincipalPermission** class discussed in the previous chapter. This is because **PrincipalPermission** is a peer class derived from **Object**, and it is not a code access permission but a permission that encapsulates user-based security.

- System.Data.Common.**DBDataPermission**
- System.Drawing.Printing.**PrintingPermission**
- System.Messaging.**MessageQueuePermission**
- System.Net.**DnsPermission**
- System.Net.**SocketPermission**
- System.Net.**WebPermission**
- System.Security.Permissions.**EnvironmentPermission**
- System.Security.Permissions.**FileDialogPermission**
- System.Security.Permissions.**FileIOPermission**
- System.Security.Permissions.**IsolatedStoragePermission**
- System.Security.Permissions.**PublisherIdentityPermission**
- System.Security.Permissions.**ReflectionPermission**
- System.Security.Permissions.**RegistryPermission**
- System.Security.Permissions.**ResourcePermissionBase**
- System.Security.Permissions.**SecurityPermission**
- System.Security.Permissions.**SiteIdentityPermission**
- System.Security.Permissions.**StrongNameIdentityPermission**

- System.Security.Permissions.**UIPermission**
- System.Security.Permissions.**UrlIdentityPermission**
- System.Security.Permissions.**ZoneIdentityPermission**

The CodeAccessPermission Class

The **CodeAccessPermission** class has several methods that must be understood, since they are found in all of the derived permission classes that you will be working with. We look at a few of these methods in more detail and see example code demonstrating how they can be used. But first, let's take a look at some brief descriptions of these methods. The methods that are simply inherited from the **Object** class are not shown here.

- **Assert** allows the specified permission in the current method and methods further down the call stack even if code in higher stack-frames[23] have denied the permission. This method works by stopping a stack walk from proceeding further up the call stack, preventing a potential **SecurityException** from being thrown. This method is successful only if the calling code passes the security checks required for granting the specified permission according to security policy and the code is granted assert permission. An assertion is in effect from the time that **Assert** is called until the method that called **Assert** returns or the **RevertAssert** method is called on the current stackframe. Only one assert can be active on a given stackframe, and calling **Assert** more than once on the same stackframe will throw a **SecurityException**. This method should be used judiciously, since it liberalizes permission usage and may introduce luring-attack security risks, but it can be very convenient. For example, you can aggressively deny permissions higher on the stack and then selectively and briefly assert specific permissions in selected methods further down the stack where required.
- **Copy** is an abstract method that each derived class must implement to provide a copy of the permission object.
- **Demand** is used to ensure that calling methods have the specified permission. It does this by performing a stack walk, checking the permissions of each method found higher on the call stack. This method throws a **SecurityException** if any of the calling methods do not have the specified permission. This method is used as an upfront test

---

23. The call stack is conventionally viewed as growing down. Therefore, methods lower in the call stack are called by methods higher in the call stack. Each method being called has its own area on the stack, called a *stackframe*, which contains the parameters and local variables of the current method.

for the specified permission before performing an operation that requires that permission. Many .NET Framework classes make extensive use of the **Demand** method to ensure that they perform only permissible operations according to established security policy. For example, many **FileStream** methods create a **FileIOPermission** object for the appropriate path and operation, and then call its **Demand** method to ensure that it has the necessary permission to carry on with the intended operation. You can also define your own permission classes and call on the **Demand** method for implementing your own security protection mechanisms.

- **Deny** prevents the specified permission in the current method and methods further down the call stack even if code in higher stackframes have been granted the permission. It does this by causing the stack walk to fail on the current stackframe for the specified permission. A denial is in effect from the time that **Deny** is called until the method that called **Deny** returns or the **RevertDeny** method is called on the current stackframe. Only one denial can be active on a given stackframe, and calling **Deny** more than once on the same stackframe will throw a **SecurityException**. This method is used for defensive programming, where you would like to prevent something from happening that you know has no good reason for being permitted within the current and downstream methods.

- **FromXml** is an abstract method that each derived class must implement to reconstruct a permission object from an XML representation.

- **Intersect** is an abstract method that each derived class must implement to create a permission object that is the intersection of two existing permission objects.

- **IsSubsetOf** is an abstract method that each derived class must implement to determine whether one permission object is a logical subset of another permission object.

- **PermitOnly** allows only the specified permission in the current method and methods further down the call stack even if methods in higher stackframes have been granted other permissions. This method is similar to **Deny** except that **Deny** disallows a specific permission and **PermitOnly** disallows all but a specific permission. This method works by causing a stack walk to fail.

- **RevertAll** is a static method that nullifies all calls to **Assert**, **Deny**, and **PermitOnly** on the current stackframe.

- **RevertAssert** is a static method that nullifies any call to **Assert** on the current stackframe.

- **RevertDeny** is a static method that nullifies any call to **Deny** on the current stackframe.

- **RevertPermitOnly** is a static method that nullifies any call to **PermitOnly** on the current stackframe.

- **ToXml** is an abstract method that each derived class must implement to create an XML representation of the specified permission object.
- **Union** is an abstract method that each derived class must implement to create a permission object that is the logical union of two existing permission objects.

Notice that certain methods, such as **Copy** and **IsSubsetOf** are abstract. You do not normally call these abstract methods in application code. Instead, these methods are called by .NET Framework CAS-related code. If you implement your own custom permission class, you will need to implement these abstract methods so that it can work properly with .NET Framework CAS functionality.

To give you an idea of how a couple of these methods work under the covers, the following source code is found in the **codeaccesspermission.cs** file, provided by the Rotor BCL Documentation.[24]

```
[DynamicSecurityMethodAttribute25()]
public void Deny()
{
   CodeAccessSecurityEngine icase =
SecurityManager.GetCodeAccessSecurityEngine();
   if (icase != null)
   {
      StackCrawlMark stackMark =
         StackCrawlMark.LookForMyCaller;
      icase.Deny(this, ref stackMark);
   }
}
...
public static void RevertDeny()
{
   SecurityRuntime isr =
      SecurityManager.GetSecurityRuntime();

   if (isr != null)
   {
      StackCrawlMark stackMark =
         StackCrawlMark.LookForMyCaller;
      isr.RevertDeny(ref stackMark);
   }
```

---

24. Copyright 2002 Microsoft Corporation. The Rotor BCL Documentation is made publicly available by Microsoft and may be used in certain specified ways, but it is not open source in the GNU General Public License sense. Please see the Rotor BCL Documentation for details on this copyright.
25. This attribute indicates that space must be allocated on the caller's stack for a security object to be used for security stack-walking purposes. This gives a small clue how special methods such as **Deny** and **Demand** really are.

```
}
...
[DynamicSecurityMethodAttribute()]
public void Demand()
{
    CodeAccessSecurityEngine icase =
        SecurityManager.GetCodeAccessSecurityEngine();

    if (icase != null && !this.IsSubsetOf( null ))
    {
        StackCrawlMark stackMark =
StackCrawlMark.LookForMyCallersCaller;
        icase.Check(this, ref stackMark);
    }
}
```

A Great Learning Resource: The Rotor BCL Documentation

If you ever wanted to drill down and really understand what's going on in the .NET Framework or you would like to see good examples of C# programming techniques, there is no better place to look than the Rotor Base Class Library Documentation, which contains the source code for the whole .NET library! This is available for viewing at *http://dot-net.di.unipi.it/Content/sscli/docs/doxygen/fx/bcl/index.html.*

In fact, you can download the entire Rotor source tree and build yourself a runtime environment that allows you to step through the .NET Framework code using the **Cordbg.exe** command-line debugger on Windows. You can even get it up and running on FreeBSD! This is all available at *http://msdn.microsoft.com/downloads/default.asp?URL=/downloads/sample.asp?url=/msdn-files/027/001/901/msdncompositedoc.xml.*

Another alternative is from Ximian, sponsor of the Mono project, which is an Open Source effort to implement the .NET Framework, the CLR, and the C# compiler. For details, go *to www.go-mono.com/.*

Happy spelunking!

The UrlIdentityPermission Class

In this section we focus on just one of the **CodeAccessPermission**-derived classes, **UrlIdentityPermission**. This class encapsulates a permission based on the URL from which the assembly originates. We also study the **UrlIdentityPermission** example to see exactly how this class can be used, but we must first understand a bit about the **UrlIdentityPermission** class itself. The **UrlIdentityPermission** class provides implementations for each of the abstract methods of **CodeAccessPermission** described earlier. It also overrides a few nonabstract **CodeAccessPermission** methods. It is sufficient to review the descriptions provided in the previous section to understand the purpose of each method. Beyond that, the **UrlIdentityPermission** does not add much in terms of new functionality. The only new members that have been added are two constructors and one string property named **Url**.

THE URLIDENTITYPERMISSION CONSTRUCTORS

One of the **UrlIdentityPermission** constructors initializes the new permission object with a **PermissionState** parameter. **PermissionState** defines two values: **None** and **Unrestricted**. However, the **UrlIdentityPermission** constructor does not allow the **Unrestricted** value, and you must therefore specify **None** to avoid throwing an **ArgumentException**.

```
public UrlIdentityPermission(
    PermissionState state //None is the only valid
    permission state
);
```

The other constructor initializes a new permission object based on a string parameter that represents a specific URL. The string may contain an optional wild card in the final position. However, the string must not be null and must contain a valid URL syntax, or an **ArgumentNullException**, **FormatException**, or **ArgumentException** will be thrown.

```
public UrlIdentityPermission(
    string site //URL that may contain a wildcard
);
```

THE URLIDENTITYPERMISSION URL PROPERTY

The **Url** read/write property is a string that includes the protocol, such as http or ftp, followed by a colon and two forward slashes, followed by a path and filename separated with single forward slashes. URL matching may be exact or it may make use of a wildcard at the rightmost position. Here are a few examples of valid URL strings.

```
http://www.SomeWebSite.com/SomePath/TrustedClient.exe
http://www.SomeWebSite.com/SomePath/*
file://C:/SomePath/TrustedClient.exe
```

Working with Code Access Permissions

We have already pointed out that, just as was the case with user-based security, there are also two slightly different styles that can be used in the imperative approach. As we saw in the previous **ImperativeCAS** example, you can make security decisions explicitly by choosing the execution path using an **if** statement based on current application domain evidence. The decision was made between two execution branches, where one is successful and the other throws a **SecurityException**. This technique may be quite familiar to many traditional programmers, but the additional code required makes it slightly cumbersome.

In the new-style imperative approach, you create a **CodeAccessPermission**-derived object representing the code access permission that you wish to discriminate on, and then you call on that permission object's **Demand** method. Then, any methods that you call will automatically throw a security exception if the specified permission is not honored. In other words, within the remainder of the current stackframe as well as any called method stackframes, the **SecurityException** will be automatically thrown where appropriate. The advantage of doing it this way is that the code is a little more simple and clean-looking, since there is no visible evidence of inspecting loop, if statement, or exception-throwing code.

Just like the previous **ImperativeCAS** example, this **UrlIdentityPermission** example is an imperative rather than a declarative approach to CAS. The **UrlIdentityPermission** directory contains the **UrlIdentityPermission-Component** project along with the **EvilClient** and **TrustedClient** projects that use the **ImperativeCASComponent** assembly.

THE URLIDENTITYPERMISSION EXAMPLE

The **UrlIdentityPermission** example is similar to the **ImperativeCAS** example in that it discriminates on the basis of URL evidence, but the **UrlIdentityPermission** class is used instead of laboriously enumerating through the evidence information in a loop. The **UrlIdentityPermission** class is used to ensure that the only client code that may successfully call into the component's **DoSomethingForClient** method is the client from a specific URL. Again, this demonstrates a technique for limiting client code to only those clients that are considered trustworthy based on specified evidence. To test this component, we use two programs: **TrustedClient** and **EvilClient**. These two programs are virtually identical in every way in terms of source code. The only significant difference is the URL from which they originate. We now see how a URL is used to represent the protocol, path, and filename of each of these client programs. Here is the code for the **EvilClient** program.

```
//EvilClient.cs

using System;
using System.Security;

class EvilClient
{
```

```
static void Main(string[] args)
{
    //NOTE: need ref to ImperativeCASComponent.dll

    //try to call on the component
    try
    {
        UrlIdentityPermissionComponent.
            DoSomethingForClient();
    }
    catch (SecurityException se)
    {
        Console.WriteLine("Error: " + se.Message);
    }
}
}
```

When you run this **EvilClient** program, you will see the following output. Note that it does in fact throw an exception, indicating that it originates from a URL that differs from the one that is trusted by the server component assembly. As you can see, the specific exception thrown is a **SecurityException**, and its message property states that a request for the **UrlIdentityPermission** failed. When we see the code in the **UrlIdentityPermissionComponent** assembly, we will see why this occurs.

```
Error: Request for the permission of type
System.Security.Permissions.UrlIdentityPermission,
mscorlib, Version=1.0.3300.0, Culture=neutral,
PublicKeyToken=b77a5c561934e089 failed.
```

Here is the source code for the **TrustedClient** program. As you can see, it is indeed virtually identical to the **EvilClient** code. But its output is surprisingly different.

```
//TrustedClient.cs

using System;
using System.Security;

class TrustedClient
{
    static void Main(string[] args)
    {
        //NOTE: need ref to ImperativeCASComponent.dll
```

```
//try to call on the component
try
{
   UrlIdentityPermissionComponent.
      DoSomethingForClient();
}
catch (SecurityException se)
{
   Console.WriteLine("Error: " + se.Message);
}
   }
}
```

Here is the output that results from running the **TrustedClient** program. This time, no exception is thrown, so the error message is not displayed. The only line of output results from a **Console.WriteLine** method in the **UrlIdentityPermissionComponent** assembly, showing that it is quite happy with being called by this particular client program.

```
Client call permitted
```

Why do these apparently identical programs result in such different behavior? To understand this, let's look at the code in the **UrlIdentityPermissionComponent.dll** assembly. As you can see, we create the **UrlIdentityPermission** object, specifying the desired (i.e., trusted) client application, and then call the **Demand** method. Then, it simply goes about its business, and, if the client does not match the URL from which the trusted client should originate, then a security exception is automatically thrown. There is no fussing about with an **Evidence** object or iterating over an enumeration in a loop. You just let CAS do its job.

```
//UrlIdentityPermissionComponent.cs

using System;
using System.Windows.Forms;
using System.Security.Permissions;

public class UrlIdentityPermissionComponent
{
   public static void DoSomethingForClient()
   {
      UrlIdentityPermission urlidperm =
         new UrlIdentityPermission(
            "file://C:/... /TrustedClient.exe");
      urlidperm.Demand();
```

```
    //if we got this far then all is OK
    Console.WriteLine(
        "Client call permitted");
    }
}
```

In the actual source code, the path in the previous listing is fully specified in the **UrlIdentityPermission** object. Since it is too long to display properly in this book, it has been trimmed down in size using three-dot notation. In this code listing the **Demand** method ensures that the CLR will detect any mismatch between the desired permission and the actual current permission in effect at runtime.

Recall that when an assembly is loaded, the CLR reviews all the available host evidence and assigns the assembly all of its identity permissions based on that evidence. The example we have just looked at used the **UrlIdentityPermission** class, which is only one of the available identity permission classes. We could just as easily have used any of the following identity permission classes. Recall that these identity permissions refer to where the assembly came from (site, URL, and zone) or who digitally signed it (strong name and publisher).

- **PublisherIdentityPermission**—X.509 certificate
- **SiteIdentityPermission**—Hostname part of the URL
- **StrongNameIdentityPermission**—Cryptographic signature
- **URLIdentityPermission**—Entire URL in its raw form
- **ZoneIdentityPermission**—MyComputer, LocalIntranet, Internet, Restricted, or Trusted

THE FILEIOPERMISSION EXAMPLE

Let's turn our attention now to an example of a permission class that is not an identity permission. The **FileIOPermission** example shows how the **FileIOPermission** class can be used to control file IO operations in a method. The **FileIOPermission** directory contains three projects: **FileIOPermission**, which is an EXE, as well as **AttemptIO** and **AvoidIO**, which are DLLs. The **FileIOPermission** program creates a **FileIOPermission** object that represents unrestricted file access, but it then calls on its **Deny** method, effectively disallowing all file IO privileges. It then calls into the **DoNoFileIO** and **DoFileIO** methods of the two DLL assemblies.

Although the **Deny** method is called in a different assembly than where the IO will actually be attempted, the call stack will be walked back up to the **Main** method, where the security system will discover that the file IO permission is denied, causing a security exception to be thrown. The source code for all three projects follows.

```
//FileIOPermission.cs

//must add ref to AvoidIO.dll
//must add ref to AttemptIO.dll

using System;
using System.IO;
using System.Security.Permissions;
using System.Security;

class FileIOPermissionExample
{
    public static void Main()
    {
        FileIOPermission fiop = new FileIOPermission(
            PermissionState.Unrestricted);
        fiop.Deny();
        try
        {
            AvoidIO avoidio = new AvoidIO();
            avoidio.DoNoFileIO();

            AttemptIO attemptio = new AttemptIO();
            attemptio.DoFileIO();
        }
        catch(SecurityException se)
        {
            Console.WriteLine(se.Message);
        }

    }
}

//AvoidIO.cs

using System;

public class AvoidIO
{
    public void DoNoFileIO()
    {
        Console.WriteLine("DoNoFileIO called...");
        Console.WriteLine("Nothing written.");
    }
}
```

```
//AttemptIO.cs

using System;
using System.IO;

public class AttemptIO
{
    public void DoFileIO()
    {
        Console.WriteLine("DoFileIO called...");
        String text = "Here is some data to write";
        FileStream fs = new FileStream(
            "outputdata.txt",
            FileMode.Create, FileAccess.Write);
        StreamWriter sw = new StreamWriter(fs);
        sw.Write(text);
        sw.Close();
        fs.Close();
        Console.WriteLine(
            "Written to outputdata.txt: " + text);
    }
}
```

In the previous example, using the **UrlIdentityPermission** class, we explicitly called the **Demand** method to determine whether or not we had that particular permission before proceeding. In contrast, in the above source listings, we never call the **Demand** method explicitly. This is because the **FileStream** class that we are using calls the **Demand** method for us where necessary. In general, the predefined permission classes that do not relate to identity evidence do not require you to call the **Demand** method in your own code. The .NET Framework generally knows when to do that for you. You might want to call the **Demand** method yourself if you would like to test for the permission earlier to improve efficiency or simplicity. If you implement your own custom permission classes, you must take on the responsibility to make the appropriate calls on the **Demand** method where necessary.

The output from running the **FileIOPermission** program follows. As you can see, the method that did not attempt IO worked fine, but the method that attempted file IO threw a **FileIOPermission** exception.

```
DoNoFileIO called...
Nothing written.
DoFileIO called...
Request for the permission of type
   System.Security.Permissions.FileIOPermission,
   mscorlib, Version=1.0.3300.0, Culture=neutral,
   PublicKeyToken=b77a5c561934e089 failed.
```

Declarative Code Access Permissions

Earlier, we saw how to use imperative CAS: We created an instance of a **Code-AccessPermission**-derived class, such as **UrlIdentityPermission**, and then called its **Deny** method to restrict the associated action. It is also possible to accomplish this declaratively using **CodeAccessSecurityAttribute**-derived classes. We will see this shortly, using **UrlIdentityPermissionAttribute**.

The main difference with attributes is that we do not normally instantiate the attribute class in the imperative way using the **new** operator. Instead, we apply the attribute to the target assembly, class, or method, using square bracket declaration syntax. The other difference is that the information declared by a security attribute is stored in the metadata of the assembly and is accessible to the CLR at assembly load time. This also allows the **PermView.exe** tool to display the assembly's permission attributes at the command prompt.

Square Bracket Attribute Declaration Syntax

Attribute-style declarative syntax looks a bit different from traditional imperative-style syntax. The idea is that attributes are applied to a program construct, such as an assembly, a class, or a method, as part of the construct's declaration. Thus, the effect is made at compile time, and the result is stored as part of the assembly's metadata. The special declarative syntax uses square brackets in the following manner.

```
[<attribute_class_name>(
  <default_property_value>
  <property_name>=<property_value>...)]
```

The square brackets contain the name of the attribute class followed by parentheses. The parentheses can contain a number of property values, the first of which may be the default property that does not require a name, followed by property name/value pairs. To make this more concrete, consider the following code snippet taken from the upcoming **DeclarativeCAS** example. The name of the attribute is **UrlIdentityPermission**, and it is being initialized with **SecurityAction.LinkDemand** for its default **Action** property, and "file://C:/.../TrustedClient.exe" for its named **Url** property.

```
[UrlIdentityPermission(
    SecurityAction.LinkDemand,
    Url="file://C:/.../TrustedClient.exe")]
```

You may be wondering how you determine the valid program constructs that the attribute can be applied to and what default property and named properties are provided. The answers can be found in the documentation for the attribute class. First, you locate the documentation for the attribute class, which will have an **AttributeUsage** attribute applied to it that lists the valid program constructs that it can be applied against. Possibilities include assembly, class, and method. Then, take a look at the attribute class's constructor. The constructor parameter indicates which attribute property is the default property.[26] This is the property that does not require an explicit name in the square bracket syntax. To see the named properties supported by the attribute, simply look at the properties defined by the attribute class. The key to all this is the attribute class documentation. Let's look at the **UrlIdentity-PermissionAttribute** class as a concrete example.

The URL Identity Permission Attribute

Before we look at the **DeclarativeCAS** example, we briefly look at the **Url-IdentityPermissionAttribute** class. We are not interested in all of the details of this class. For our needs, it is sufficient to focus on only those aspects that relate to how the attribute works in the context of the square bracket attribute syntax just described.

THE URLIDENTITYPERMISSIONATTRIBUTE CLASS

Here is the **UrlIdentityPermissionAttribute** class declaration. As you can see, its **AttributeUsage** attribute indicates that it can be applied to the following target constructs: assembly, class, struct, constructor, and method.

```
[AttributeUsage(AttributeTargets.Assembly |
  AttributeTargets.Class | AttributeTargets.Struct |
  AttributeTargets.Constructor | AttributeTargets.Method)]
[Serializable]
public sealed class UrlIdentityPermissionAttribute :
  CodeAccessSecurityAttribute
```

THE URLIDENTITYPERMISSIONATTRIBUTE CONSTRUCTOR

Here is the **UrlIdentityPermissionAttribute** constructor. You can see that this constructor takes one parameter of type **SecurityAction**. This means that the attribute has a default property for specifying one of the values defined by

---

26. Actually, every permission attribute exposes a default property named **Action** of type **SecurityAction**. In contrast, the named properties are specialized and vary from one permission attribute to another.

the **SecurityAction** values, such as **LinkDemand**, **InheritanceDemand**, **Demand**, **Deny**, **RequestMinimum**, and so on.

```
[AttributeUsage(AttributeTargets.Assembly |
  AttributeTargets.Class | AttributeTargets.Struct |
  AttributeTargets.Constructor | AttributeTargets.Method)]
[Serializable]
public UrlIdentityPermissionAttribute(
  SecurityAction action
);
```

THE URL PROPERTY

The documentation also shows that the **UrlIdentityPermissionAttribute** class has a string type property named **Url**. This means that this property can be used as a named property in the square bracket attribute syntax described previously. Here is the **Url** property declaration.

```
[AttributeUsage(AttributeTargets.Assembly |
  AttributeTargets.Class | AttributeTargets.Struct |
  AttributeTargets.Constructor | AttributeTargets.Method)]
[Serializable]
public string Url {get; set;}
```

The SecurityAction Class

We have just seen that the **UrlIdentityPermissionAttribute** constructor takes a parameter of type **SecurityAction**. The values defined by the **SecurityAction** enumeration can therefore be used in the square bracket syntax for this attribute. The following list shows the possible values for **SecurityAction** along with a short description of their purposes.

- **Assert**—Requests the specified permission even if callers do not have the permission.
- **Demand**—Ensures that callers have the specified permission.
- **Deny**—Denies the permission even if callers have the permission.
- **InheritanceDemand**—Ensures that derived classes have the permission.
- **LinkDemand**—Ensures that immediate callers have the permission.
- **PermitOnly**—Ensures that the permission is the only permission granted.
- **RequestMinimum**—Requests minimum permissions required by the assembly to load.
- **RequestOptional**—Requests optional permissions useful but not critical to the assembly.
- **RequestRefuse**—Requests refusal of permissions that are not needed by the assembly.

THE DECLARATIVECAS EXAMPLE

The **DeclarativeCAS** example is exactly like the **UrlIdentityPermission** example except that the declarative approach is used rather than the imperative approach. The **EvilClient** and **TrustedClient** source files are identical to the **UrlIdentityPermission** example, and therefore they are not listed again here. Let's now look at how declarative CAS is used in the **DeclarativeCAS-Component.cs** source file. Again, in the actual source code the full path is specified in the **UrlIdentityPermission** attribute, but for display purposes, it has been trimmed down in size using the three-dot notation. As you can see, instead of creating an instance of **UrlIdentityPermission** and calling its **Demand** method, we just declare the **DoSomethingForClient** method using the **UrlIdentityPermission** attribute.

```
//DeclarativeCASComponent.cs

using System;

using System.Security;
using System.Security.Permissions;

public class UrlIdentityPermissionComponent
{
    [UrlIdentityPermission(
        SecurityAction.LinkDemand,
        Url="file://C:/.../TrustedClient.exe")]
    public static void DoSomethingForClient()
    {
        //if we got this far then all is OK
        Console.WriteLine(
            "Client call permitted");
    }
}
```

When you run the **TrustedClient**, it works without throwing any exception. When you run the **EvilClient** program, it throws a **SecurityException**. There is really no difference between this example and the previous one except this one uses the declarative technique involving a permission attribute, and the previous one uses the imperative technique using the **new** operator to instantiate the permission object.

Permission Requests

An assembly can declaratively specify certain permission requests. For example, it can specify a minimal set of permissions that it absolutely requires. If the CLR determines that the required permissions are not to be granted, then the assembly will not even load. The assembly can also specify a nice-to-have set of permissions that, if not granted, will still allow the assembly to load. Assemblies can also specify permissions that are flat-out refused, avoiding the risk of having any dangerous permissions that are simply not needed by the assembly.

The PermissionRequest Example

The **PermissionRequest** example shows how to make permission requests within an assembly. Three attributes are established using the **UIPermission** attribute, which governs the ability to use the clipboard and windowing features of the user interface. The first attribute specifies **RequestMinimum** for all clipboard operations, **RequestOptional** for unrestricted user interface operations, and **RequestRefuse** for all window operations.

The effect of the first permission request is that when the program is run, if the permission to access the clipboard is not granted according to security policy, the assembly load operation aborts with a security exception. There is not much effect in this example from the second permission request, but it essentially specifies that all user interface operations be considered optional. The third permission request states that we would like to proactively prevent any possibility of any type of window usage. When you run the program, the **TryWindowAccess** method attempts to display a message box, which fails with a security exception.

```
//PermissionRequest.cs

using System;
using System.Security;
using System.Security.Permissions;
using System.Windows.Forms;

[assembly:UIPermission(
    SecurityAction.RequestMinimum,
    Clipboard=UIPermissionClipboard.AllClipboard)]
[assembly:UIPermission(
    SecurityAction.RequestOptional,
    Unrestricted=true)]
[assembly:UIPermission(
    SecurityAction.RequestRefuse,
    Window=UIPermissionWindow.AllWindows)]

public class PermissionRequest
{
    public static void Main()
    {
```

```
        Console.WriteLine("Calling TryClipboardAccess");
        TryClipboardAccess();

        Console.WriteLine("Calling TryWindowAccess");
        TryWindowAccess();

        Console.Write("Press any key");
        Console.Read();
    }

    private static void TryClipboardAccess()
    {
        try
        {
            Clipboard.SetDataObject(
                "TryClipboardAccess", true);
        }
        catch (SecurityException se)
        {
            Console.WriteLine(se.Message);
        }
    }
    private static void TryWindowAccess()
    {
        try
        {
            MessageBox.Show("TryWindowAccess");
        }
        catch (SecurityException se)
        {
            Console.WriteLine(se.Message);
        }
    }
}
```

Permission Sets

Permission sets allow you to combine multiple **IPermission** objects together
in a single group that can then be collectively manipulated via familiar methods, such as **Deny**, **Demand**, and **Assert**. You may recall we said earlier that
you cannot call methods such as **Deny** and **PermitOnly** twice in the same
stackframe unless there is an intervening reversion. That effectively means
that you must work with a permission set if you want to work with two or
more permissions at the same time in the same stackframe. We look at the
PermissionSet example now, which uses the **PermissionSet** class to manage multiple permissions simultaneously.

The PermissionSet Class

The **PermissionSet** class has the same basic set of methods as the **IPermission**-derived classes that we have already seen, including **Deny**, **Demand**, and **Assert**. But in addition to those, it has the **AddPermission** method used to combine multiple permission objects into a collection. The **IPermission** interface includes all of the permission classes, such as **FileIOPermission**, **UrlIdentityPermission**, and so on.

```
public virtual IPermission AddPermission(
   IPermission perm
);
```

Let's look now at an example in which we use a permission set to group together several permissions and deal with the collection as a single object.

THE PERMISSIONSET EXAMPLE

The **PermissionSet** example combines the three permissions **Environment-Permission**, **FileIOPermission**, and **UIPermission** into a single permission set. It provides a simple user interface for determining the aspects of these three permissions that are to be put into effect. The user interface also allows you to call on the **Deny** or **PermitOnly** methods of the permission set to demonstrate their effects. Finally, the user interface allows you to call on either of two methods that test the effect of the permission set on file access and environment variable access.

The fact that the program attempts to communicate the resulting effects via a message box also tests the effect of the **UIPermission**. By running this program and experimenting with the effects of the various checkboxes, you gain a sense of how a permission set works. By studying the **EstablishPermissionSet**, **buttonAttemptFileAccess_Click**, and **buttonAttemptEnvVarAccess_Click** methods in this program, you can learn how to achieve these effects within your own programs. Figure 8–21 shows the **PermissionSet** example with file read access denied, and Figure 8–22 shows the result of attempting file read access under that condition.

Here are the three significant method source code listings for this example.

```
//PermissionSetForm.cs
...
namespace PermissionSetForm
{
   ...
   public class PermissionSetForm :
      System.Windows.Forms.Form
```

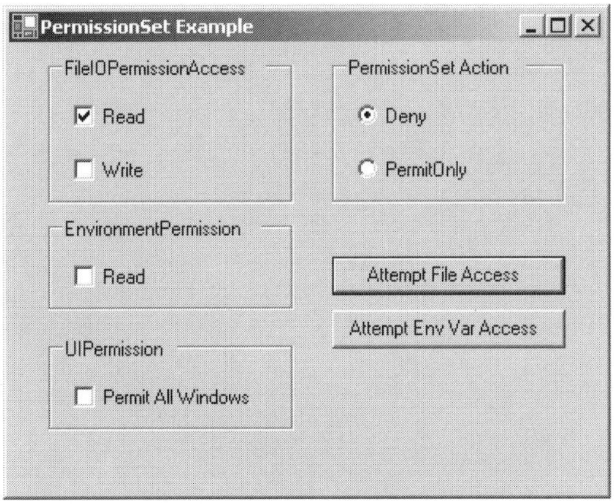

FIGURE 8-21   The PermissionSet example: Denying read access.

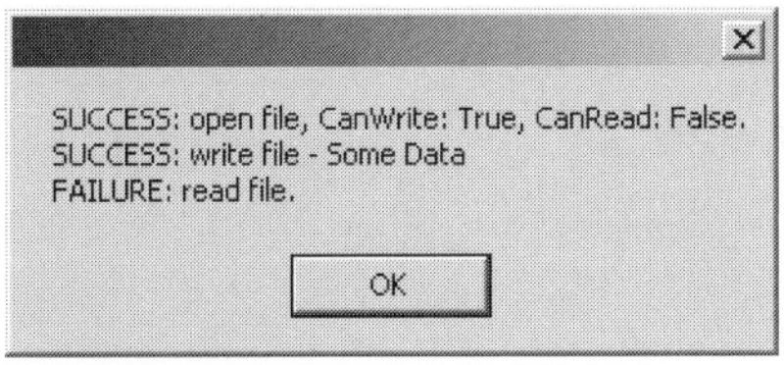

FIGURE 8-22   The PermissionSet example: Attempt File read access.

```
{
  ...
    private void buttonAttemptFileAccess_Click(
       object sender, System.EventArgs e)
    {
       //build perm set according to radio buttons
       EstablishPermissionSet();

       //Deny, or PermitOnly
       if (radioButtonDeny.Checked)
          ps.Deny();
       if (radioButtonPermitOnly.Checked)
          ps.PermitOnly();

       //attempt to open or create file
       FileStream fs = null; //for TestFile.txt file
       try
```

```
    {
        fs = new FileStream(
            "TestFile.txt",
            FileMode.OpenOrCreate,
            FileAccess.ReadWrite);
    }
    catch (Exception)
    {
    }
    if (fs == null)
    {
        try
        {
            fs = new FileStream(
                "TestFile.txt",
                FileMode.OpenOrCreate,
                FileAccess.Read);
        }
        catch (Exception)
        {
        }
    }
    if (fs == null)
    {
        try
        {
            fs = new FileStream(
                "TestFile.txt",
                FileMode.OpenOrCreate,
                FileAccess.Write);
        }
        catch (Exception)
        {
        }
    }
    if (fs == null)
    {
        MessageBox.Show(
            "FAILURE: open file");
        return;
    }

    String strMessageBox =
        "SUCCESS: open file" +
        ", CanWrite: " + fs.CanWrite +
        ", CanRead: " + fs.CanRead +
        ".\n";

    //attempt to write file
    String strDataOut = "Some Data";
```

```
    byte [] bytes=
       Encoding.UTF8.GetBytes(strDataOut);
    try
    {
       fs.Write(bytes, 0, bytes.Length);

       strMessageBox += "SUCCESS: write file - "
          + strDataOut + "\n";
    }
    catch (Exception)
    {
       strMessageBox +=
          "FAILURE: write file.\n";
    }

    //attempt to read file
    bytes = new byte[256];
    try
    {
       fs.Seek(0, SeekOrigin.Begin);
       fs.Read(bytes, 0, bytes.Length);

       String strDataIn = Encoding.UTF8.GetString(
          bytes, 0, bytes.Length);
       strMessageBox +=
          "SUCCESS: read file - " + strDataIn;
    }
    catch (Exception)
    {
       strMessageBox += "FAILURE: read file.\n";
    }

    //show result of attempts
    MessageBox.Show(strMessageBox);

    fs.Close();

    //RevertDeny or RevertPermitOnly
    if (radioButtonDeny.Checked)
       CodeAccessPermission.RevertDeny();
    if (radioButtonPermitOnly.Checked)
       CodeAccessPermission.RevertPermitOnly();

    //clean up permission set
    DestroyPermissionSet();
}

private void buttonAttemptEnvVarAccess_Click(
    object sender, System.EventArgs e)
{
```

```
//build perm set according to radio buttons
EstablishPermissionSet();

//Deny or PermitOnly
if (radioButtonDeny.Checked)
   ps.Deny();
if (radioButtonPermitOnly.Checked)
   ps.PermitOnly();

//attempt to read TEMP environment variable
String ev = null;
try
{
   ev = Environment.GetEnvironmentVariable(
      "TEMP");

   //show result of attempt
   MessageBox.Show(
      "SUCCESS: read environment variable - " +
      ev);
}
catch (Exception)
{
   MessageBox.Show(
      "FAILURE: read environment variable");
}

//RevertDeny or RevertPermitOnly
if (radioButtonDeny.Checked)
   CodeAccessPermission.RevertDeny();
if (radioButtonPermitOnly.Checked)
   CodeAccessPermission.RevertPermitOnly();

//clean up permission set
DestroyPermissionSet();
}

//build permission set according to radio buttons
private void EstablishPermissionSet()
{
   ps = new PermissionSet(PermissionState.None);

   //establish EnvironmentPermission
   EnvironmentPermission ep =
      new EnvironmentPermission(
         EnvironmentPermissionAccess.NoAccess,
         "TEMP");
   if (checkBoxEnvironmentPermissionRead.Checked)
   {
```

```csharp
      ep.AddPathList(
         EnvironmentPermissionAccess.Read,
         "TEMP");
   }
   ps.AddPermission(ep);

   //establish FileIOPermission
   FileIOPermission fp =
      new FileIOPermission(
         FileIOPermissionAccess.NoAccess,
         Path.GetFullPath("TestFile.txt"));
   if (checkBoxFileIOPermissionAccessRead.Checked)
   {
      fp.AddPathList(
         FileIOPermissionAccess.Read,
         Path.GetFullPath("TestFile.txt"));
   }
   if (checkBoxFileIOPermissionAccessWrite.Checked)
   {
      fp.AddPathList(
         FileIOPermissionAccess.Write,
         Path.GetFullPath("TestFile.txt"));
   }
   ps.AddPermission(fp);

   //establish UIPermission
   UIPermission  uip = new UIPermission(
      UIPermissionWindow.NoWindows);
   if (checkBoxAllWindows.Checked)
   {
      uip.Window =
         UIPermissionWindow.AllWindows;
   }
   ps.AddPermission(uip);
}

void DestroyPermissionSet()
{
   ps.RemovePermission(
      typeof(EnvironmentPermission));
   ps.RemovePermission(
      typeof(FileIOPermission));
   ps.RemovePermission(
      typeof(UIPermission));
   ps = null;
}

PermissionSet ps;
   }
}
```

Defining a Permission Set in a Configuration File

Let's see how to configure security for an application by defining a permission set in an application configuration file, which can then be used by the application to grant or deny the permissions defined in the permission set. By configuring the security characteristics in an external XML-based application configuration file, the programmer has less to worry about, and the end user or administrator has greater flexibility in defining security policy for the application. Configuring security after deployment is a very powerful capability, especially considering that an application may be used in many situations that have very different security requirements.

THE CONFIGUREDFILEIOPERMISSION EXAMPLE

The **ConfiguredFileIOPermission** example is very much like the **FileIOPermission** example program we saw earlier in this chapter except that rather than creating a permission object programmatically, the permission[27] is defined in a permission set, which is defined in an XML application configuration file. This example is again composed of three separate projects. Two of them are DLLs, and one is an EXE project. One of the DLLs, **AttemptIO**, attempts to perform IO operations on a particular file, and the other, **AvoidIO**, does not attempt any IO. The EXE project, **ConfiguredFileIOPermission**, calls on the public methods, **DoFileIO** and **DoNoFileIO**, which are exposed by these two DLLs. Here is the source code for the two DLL projects, which is identical to the code we saw earlier in the **FileIOPermission** example.

```
//AttemptIO.cs

using System;
using System.IO;

public class AttemptIO
{
    public void DoFileIO()
    {
```

---

27. Actually, this example is slightly different from the **FileIOPermission** example in a couple of other subtle ways. Rather than working with a single independent permission, we instead work with a permission set containing the single permission. It may be worthwhile to compare this example program with the **PermissionSet** example program as well, since it shows how to work with a permission set directly in a programmatic manner as opposed to defining a permission set in an application configuration file. Also, whereas the **FileIOPermission** example disallowed all file IO privileges, this example is more selective in that it limits only read and write operations on a particular file.

```
        Console.WriteLine("DoFileIO called...");
        String text = "Here is some data to write";
        FileStream fs = new FileStream(
            "outputdata.txt",
            FileMode.Create, FileAccess.Write);
        StreamWriter sw = new StreamWriter(fs);
        sw.Write(text);
        sw.Close();
        fs.Close();
        Console.WriteLine(
            "Written to outputdata.txt: " + text);
    }
}

//AvoidIO.CS

using System;

public class AvoidIO
{
    public void DoNoFileIO()
    {
        Console.WriteLine("DoNoFileIO called...");
        Console.WriteLine("Nothing written.");
    }
}
```

Here is the initial source code for the EXE project. As you can see, the code is almost the same as what we saw in the **FileIOPermission** example; however, there is a small yet significant difference. Unlike the previous example, this example does not create a **FileIOPermission** object directly in the source code. Instead, we have an attribute that denies the permission set defined in an XML file. We shall soon see how this permission set is defined within an application configuration file and brought into play within the program source code.

```
//ConfiguredFileIOPermission.cs

//must add ref to AvoidIO.dll
//must add ref to AttemptIO.dll

using System;
using System.IO;
using System.Security.Permissions;
using System.Security;

class FileIOPermissionExample
{
```

```
public static void Main()
{

    try
    {
        AvoidIO avoidio = new AvoidIO();
        avoidio.DoNoFileIO();

        AttemptIO attemptio = new AttemptIO();
        attemptio.DoFileIO();
    }
    catch(SecurityException se)
    {
        Console.WriteLine(se.Message);
    }

}
}
```

Before we get into configuring the permission set in the configuration file, let's look at the result of running this program without any permission set being defined. The result is shown in the following code, where you can see that the program does in fact perform IO on the file named **outputdata.txt**.

```
DoNoFileIO called...
Nothing written.
DoFileIO called...
Written to outputdata.txt: Here is some data to write
```

Next, we create an XML file named **MyPermissionSet.xml** in the EXE project directory that will serve as an application configuration file for the program. The following XML shows the contents of this file. We use the **PermissionSet** tag to define a permission set, which in turn contains the **IPermission** tag to define a permission object that will be used to control access to the file named **outputdata.txt**. The full path is actually required, but we have shortened the path here so that the XML file can be displayed on this printed page. The permission specifies both read and write permissions on this file.

```
<PermissionSet class="System.Security.NamedPermissionSet"
    version="1"
    Name="MyPermissionSet"
    Description="My Permission set for outputdata.txt IO">
    <IPermission class=
        "System.Security.Permissions.FileIOPermission ...
        Read="C:\OI\...\outputdata.txt"
        Write="C:\OI\...\outputdata.txt"/>
</PermissionSet>
```

Now, for the permission set in this XML file to be used by the application, we use a **PermissionSetAttribute** attribute on the program's **Main** method, which will deny the access permission defined in the permission set. Again, the full path to the file named **MyPermissionSet.xml** is shortened for the printed page. You do not have to deny this permission set via an attribute, as shown here. You could just as easily have done this programmatically. The key difference that we are focusing on here is simply that the permission set is itself defined in a separate XML configuration file rather than in the actual program source code. This can buy us much flexibility, allowing security configuration decisions to be left until deployment time or even later.

```
class FileIOPermissionExample
{
   //PermissionSetAttribute that denies the permissions
   //defined in the MyPermissionSet.xml app config file
   [PermissionSetAttribute(
      SecurityAction.Deny,
      File="C:\\OI\\...\\MyPermissionSet.xml")]
   public static void Main()
   {

      try
      {
         AvoidIO avoidio = new AvoidIO();
         avoidio.DoNoFileIO();

         AttemptIO attemptio = new AttemptIO();
         attemptio.DoFileIO();
      }
      catch(SecurityException se)
      {
         Console.WriteLine(se.Message);
      }
   }
}
```

When you run this program, you will see the following output. As you can see, the program now throws an exception when the attempt is made to perform IO on the specified file. The permission set denial is still made in our program source code, but the permission set itself is defined independently in the **MyPermissionSet.xml** file. Therefore, the permission set can be modified independently after compile time.

```
DoNoFileIO called...
Nothing written.
DoFileIO called...
```

```
Request for the permission of type
   System.Security.Permissions.FileIOPermission,
   mscorlib, Version=1.0.3300.0, Culture=neutral,
   PublicKeyToken=b77a5c561934e089 failed.
```

Summary

In this chapter we explained the major concepts behind CAS and the range of possible security risks that CAS can address. We considered how security is enhanced by way of the execution environment provided by the CLR and the verifiably type-safe nature of .NET managed code. We investigated security policy management and the use of code access permission classes by creating and then denying or demanding those permissions. We also investigated how to implement imperative and declarative CAS and how to manage security using the .NET Framework Configuration Tool and the Caspol.exe utility. Finally, we saw how to define a permission set in an XML application configuration file to enhance the flexibility of application security management.

ASP.NET Security

Security is a significant element in any Web development. Positively ensuring security in Web applications is a major issue. In the present Internet world more real-time Web applications offer their information across Internet and private networks. Even though this widespread connectivity offers better advantages, it also increases the security risks. Web applications that entail sensitive information have to be protected from malicious attacks. That's why Microsoft became aware of these serious security problems in the present environment and engages in Trustworthy Computing.[1] The ASP.NET page framework provides a multilayered, complete set of security features that leverage from the built-in .NET Framework. ASP.NET provides authorization, authentication, impersonation, and delegation techniques that you can employ to enrich Web application and server security.

ASP.NET works in concurrence with IIS[2] to provide authentication and authorization services to Web applications. With Microsoft .NET Framework and IIS, ASP.NET offers better Web application security. The ASP.NET application developer can access all the built-in security features available in the .NET Framework, such as CAS and role-based user-access security, as the ASP.NET is a component of the Microsoft .NET Framework.

---

1. For more information on Trustworthy Computing visit *http://www.microsoft.com/ security/whitepapers/secure_platform.asp* and *http://www.microsoft.com/press-pass/exec/craig/10-02trustworthywp.asp*.
2. IIS (Internet Information Server), Microsoft's Web server, plays a vital role in providing a solution to security issues. IIS security is available even when ASP.NET security is not present.

In this chapter we first look at the ASP.NET security mechanisms, such as ASP.NET Authentication, ASP.NET Authorization,[3] and ASP.NET Impersonation. We explore the security section of the configuration file in detail. ASP.NET authentication is put into practice with the assistance of authentication providers, such as Forms authentication, Passport authentication, and Windows authentication. Then, we drill down on some of the important classes needed for ASP.NET security features. We also look at programming examples that demonstrate how to use these techniques in ASP.NET applications.

Fundamental Security Mechanisms

In developing secure ASP.NET Web applications, you must consider the following three fundamental mechanisms.

- Authentication
- Authorization
- Impersonation[4]

Authentication: Who Are You?

Authentication is the process of verifying the identity of the client application (principal) before permitting the user/application to access a resource. For example, the user or client application has to launch its identity by providing some form of credentials such as a name/password pair to provide the evidence.

Authorization: Are You Allowed to Access This Resource?

Authorization means, what privilege do you have to access this resource? After a user is authenticated, authorization is the process of granting access to the user based on identity. It is the next step to authentication, which validates which resources the authenticated user/application is permitted to access. For example, authorization verifies whether the client application has entire or limited access to the application.

---

3. In ASP.NET, authorization is implemented by two primary ways: *File authorization* and *URL authorization*.
4. Impersonation is useful typically for further authentication or authorization against additional resources.

Impersonation: Application Assumes Client's Identity

Impersonation is the process in which certain actions are performed under a different identity (i.e., assigning a user account to an unknown user). ASP.NET Web applications offer anonymous access to resources on the server by impersonation, where anonymous Web site users are authenticated under a default **IIS_ [ServerName]** account. Impersonation is heavily dependent on what that other resource is. Local resources on the same thread are no problem. Remote resources require delegation, which is an extension of impersonation and requires a delegatable authentication protocol, suitably configured (e.g., Kerberos).

Implementing ASP.NET Authentication

Authentication is one of the primary features in the Web application's security. There are three ways to implement authentication in an ASP.NET Web application with the help of ASP.NET authentication providers:[5] *Forms authentication, Passport authentication,* and *Windows authentication.* To facilitate an authentication provider for an ASP.NET application, you have to configure the **<mode> attribute** of the **<authentication> element** in the application *configuration file* as follows:

```
// Web.config file:
<authentication mode = "[Windows/Forms/Passport/None]">
</authentication>
```

The mode attribute can be set to one of these authentication methods: *Windows, Forms, Passport,* or *None.* The default value is Windows.

- **Forms authentication:** In this mechanism the unauthenticated requests are redirected to a logon Web form, where the user has to provide credentials and submit the form. If the application authenticates the request against a user list or database that the application maintains, then ASP.NET issues a cookie that contains a token or a key to the client. Then, in each subsequent request a cookie is passed in the request headers, which avoid further successive authentications. This method is suitable for commercial Web applications.

---

5. Authentication providers are nothing but the code modules that contain the essential code to authenticate the requester's credentials.

- **Passport authentication:** Centralized single sign-on authentication using Microsoft's Passport service. In this mechanism, the unauthenticated requests (i.e., for new users) are redirected to a site hosted by Microsoft so that the users can register a single username and password that will authenticate their access to multiple Web sites. This method is suitable for multiple commercial Web applications.
- **Windows authentication:** In this mechanism ASP.NET works in concurrence with the IIS authentication scheme. As a first step, the IIS implements authentication by employing any one of these ways: Basic, Digest, Integrated Windows Authentication (formerly known as Windows NT Challenge/Response (NT/CR) or NT LAN Manager (NTLM), or Certificates. When IIS authentication is completed, then in the second step ASP.NET utilizes the authenticated identity to authorize access. This method is best suited in the Intranet and private corporate Web application.
- **None:** Specifies no authentication. Only anonymous users are anticipated. Here ASP.NET does not do any authentication checking, and the authentication services are inactive. You have to be aware that IIS authentication services can still be present. You can employ this when you are not authenticating users at all or are creating your own custom authentication scheme.

ASP.NET Configuration

Let us look at the ASP.NET configuration before moving further, because security is one of the sections in ASP.NET configuration. An ASP.NET configuration file is an XML-based text file that encloses a nested hierarchy of XML tags and subtags with attributes and spells out the configuration settings. Configuration information is stored in XML-based text files, so it is easy to edit and read using any standard text editor or XML parser. In ASP.NET there are two types of XML configuration files: server configuration (**Machine.config**) and application configuration (**Web.config**). ASP.NET configuration files have **.config** as the file extension.

- The root configuration file, **Machine.config**, offers the default configuration settings for the entire Web server. Any system that has the .NET Framework installed will have a **Machine.config** file located in **%windir%\Microsoft.NET\Framework\<version>\CONFIG\Machine.config**. There are separate **Machine.config** files for each version of .NET Framework. This facilitates running different versions of ASP.NET Web applications side by side without any difficulty.

- The **Web.config** file facilitates configuring a specific application or virtual directory. The default **Machine.config** configuration settings are used if the **Web.config** is not available. If the **Web.config** file is present, any settings in **Web.config** supersede the default settings. The **Web.config** file provides configuration settings to the directory in which it is situated and to all child directories.

The tags, subtags, and attributes present in both the **Web.config** and **Machine.config** files are case-sensitive, and the tags must be well-formed XML. The configuration file may be ANSI, UTF-8, or Unicode. The system automatically detects the type of encoding. All the configuration settings are enclosed between **<configuration>** and **</configuration>** tags.

Facts and Benefits of the ASP.NET Configuration System

- Because the configuration files are XML-based,[6] administrators and developers can easily edit or update configuration settings with the assistance of any standard text editor or XML parser. This makes it easy to modify configuration settings both locally and remotely.
- To avoid direct browser access to the configuration files, ASP.NET shields the configuration files by configuring IIS.[7]
- The configuration files are extensible; therefore, custom configuration settings can be added.
- New configuration parameters can be included in the configuration file, and configuration section handlers are added to process those parameters.
- If you apply any new configuration settings to Web resources, the ASP.NET automatically senses the changes to configuration files; it recalculates and acclimatizes the new configuration settings accordingly. Thus there is no need to reboot the server for the alterations to take effect.
- Configuration settings can be locked down by means of the **<location>** tag and the **allowOverride** attribute.

---

6. Like application settings are stored in the Microsoft IIS metabase in Active Server Pages (ASP), configuration settings are stored in Extensible Markup Language (XML) files in ASP.NET.
7. If anyone directly requests or attempts to access a configuration file, then ASP.NET returns HTTP access error 403 (forbidden).

- In an ASP.NET Web application server, configuration information for the ASP.NET resource is contained in multiple configuration files. Those configuration files can be situated in multiple directories, and all are named **Web.config**.
- Configuration settings set in the **Web.config** file apply to its own directory as well as to its associated subdirectories.

Configuration Hierarchy

If a .aspx receives a request, then ASP.NET calculates the configuration settings hierarchically, as follows.

- Configuration setting in a **Web.config** file that is stored in a subdirectory overrides the settings of a **Web.config** file of an application directory.
- Configuration setting in a **Web.config** file that is stored in an application directory overrides the settings of a **Web.config** file of Web site settings (root directory).
- Configuration setting in a **Web.config** file that is stored in a root directory overrides the settings of the **Machine.config** file.

Table 9–1 shows the illustrative configuration file locations for the given URL **http://localhost/Myapplication/Mydir/Page.aspx**.

TABLE 9-1 *Configuration Files Locations*

Level	Path
Configuration settings for the given **<version>** of the .NET Framework	%windir%\Microsoft.NET \Framework\<version>\ CONFIG\Machine.config
Web site settings	Inetpub\wwwroot\Web.config
Application settings	Inetpub\wwwroot\Myapplication\Web.config
Subdirectory settings	Inetpub\wwwroot\Myapplication\Mydir\Web.config

A **Web.config** file at any level is optional; however, a **Machine.config** file is compulsory. The configuration system first explores the machine configuration file. It then explores the application configuration file. ASP.NET utilizes configuration settings to resources in a hierarchical manner. ASP.NET figures out the configuration settings hierarchically by employing all the configuration files situated in the virtual directory. Additional configuration information provided by the child directories is included with the information inherited from parent directories. The very last configuration settings of the child directories overwrite settings for the same section offered by the parent (i.e., configuration is merged across the hierarchy, with the closest configuration being preferred).

Let us consider the URL **http://localhost/Myapplication/Dir1/Dir2/Myresource.aspx**. Myapplication is the application virtual directory. If a client requests the server for the above URL, ASP.NET computes the configuration settings hierarchically by applying **Web.config** file settings in the following order as shown in Figure 9–1.

The ASP.NET configuration[8] system features an extensible and flexible infrastructure that facilitates adjustment of the configuration settings with

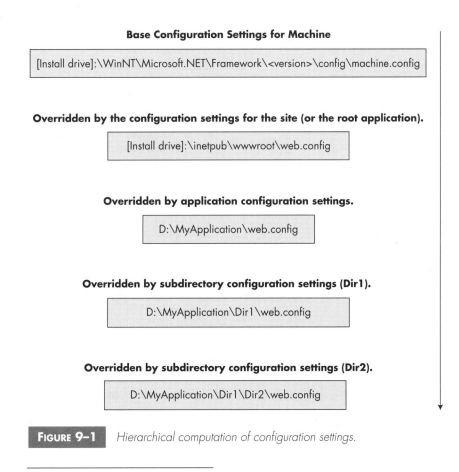

Base Configuration Settings for Machine

[Install drive]:\WinNT\Microsoft.NET\Framework\<version>\config\machine.config

Overridden by the configuration settings for the site (or the root application).

[Install drive]:\inetpub\wwwroot\web.config

Overridden by application configuration settings.

D:\MyApplication\web.config

Overridden by subdirectory configuration settings (Dir1).

D:\MyApplication\Dir1\web.config

Overridden by subdirectory configuration settings (Dir2).

D:\MyApplication\Dir1\Dir2\web.config

FIGURE 9–1   *Hierarchical computation of configuration settings.*

---

8. The ASP.NET configuration system affects only ASP.NET resources, which are registered to be handled by Aspnet_isapi.dll. For example, ASP, HTML, TXT, GIF, and JPEG files are not secured by the Web.config. To secure these files, you must explicitly map them using the IIS administration tool.

minimum impact on Web applications and servers. If you apply any new configuration settings to Web resources, the ASP.NET automatically senses the changes to configuration files, and it recalculates and adapts to the new configuration settings accordingly. That is, ASP.NET listens for file change notifications, restarts the application(s) that are affected, and rereads the changed configuration files in the new application instance. Thus, there is no need to reboot the server for the alterations to take effect. ASP.NET protects certain file types (such as configuration and source code files) from outside access. These file types are located in the Web server's **Machine.config** file in the framework configuration directory and are assigned to the special **HttpForbiddenHandler** as follows.

```
<add verb="*" path="*.asax"
   type="System.Web.HttpForbiddenHandler" />
<add verb="*" path="*.ascx"
   type="System.Web.HttpForbiddenHandler" />
<add verb="*" path="*.config"
   type="System.Web.HttpForbiddenHandler" />
<add verb="*" path="*.cs"
   type="System.Web.HttpForbiddenHandler" />
<add verb="*" path="*.csproj"
   type="System.Web.HttpForbiddenHandler" />
<add verb="*" path="*.vb"
   type="System.Web.HttpForbiddenHandler" />
<add verb="*" path="*.vbproj"
   type="System.Web.HttpForbiddenHandler" />
<add verb="*" path="*.webinfo"
   type="System.Web.HttpForbiddenHandler" />
      . . .
```

The XML format of both **Machine.config** and **Web.config** file is identical. Let's look at the general format of the security section of the **Web.config** file. There are three key subsections: authentication, authorization, and identity.

```
<?xml version="1.0" encoding="utf-8" ?>
<configuration>
<system.web>


   //Authentication section:
   <authentication mode= "[Windows/Forms/Passport/None]">

         //Forms Attributes:
<forms name="[name]" loginUrl="[Url]" protection="[All,
None, Encryption, Validation]" timeout="[time in minutes]"
path="[path]" >
```

```
        //Credentials Attributes:
<credentials passwordFormat="[Clear, SHA1, MD5]">
<user name="[UserName]" password="[password]"/>
</credentials>
</forms>
</authentication>

        //Passport Attributes:
<passport redirectUrl="Internal" />

        //Authorization section:
<authorization>
<allow users="*" /> <!-- Allow all users -->
<!-- <allow    users="[comma separated list of users]"
                roles="[comma separated list of
                roles]"/>
        <deny    users="[comma separated list of users]"
                roles="[comma separated list of
                roles]"/>
-->
</authorization>

        //Identity Attributes section:
<identity impersonate="[true/false]" />
</system.web>
</configuration>
```

Description

All configuration information exists between the **<configuration>** and **</configuration>** root XML tags. The **<system.web>** tag represents all the ASP.NET class settings.

AUTHENTICATION

- This section sets the authentication policies of the application. Possible modes are **"Windows"**, **"Forms"**, **"Passport"**, and **"None"**, enclosed in quotation marks as shown.
- The default setting is **<authentication mode="Windows">**.
- The authentication mode cannot be set at a level below the application root directory.

FORMS ATTRIBUTES

You can employ Forms-based authentication to configure the name of the cookie to use, the protection type, the URL to use for the logon page, the length of the time the cookie is in effect, and the path to use for the issued cookie.

name="[cookie name]": Name of the HTTP cookie used for Forms authentication. The default setting is **<forms name=".ASPXAUTH">**. If many applications want to use Forms authentication on the same machine, it is best to use unique names.

loginUrl="[url]": The custom login page, where the user is redirected if the user has not already been authenticated. The default setting is **<forms loginUrl="default.aspx">**. Redirection may be on the same computer or on a remote one. If it is on a remote computer, both computers should use the same value for the **decryptionkey** attribute.

protection="[All | None | Encryption | Validation]": Protection mode (i.e., the type of encryption and validation used for the cookie) for data in a cookie. The default setting is **<forms protection="All">**, which does validation and encryption. Table 9–2 shows the options for the protection attribute.

TABLE 9-2	*Options for the Protection Attribute*
Item	**Details**
All	Specifies that the cookie can be protected by means of both data validation and encryption. This option uses the configured data validation algorithm (based on the **<machineKey>** element). When Triple DES is accessible and the key is long enough (48 bytes), it can be used for encryption. This is the default and recommended value.
None	This setting offers better performance than any other method of doing personalization with the .NET Framework. This is used in sites where a cookie is used only for personalization. While using this method, you must be careful because both encryption and validation are inactive.
Encryption	The cookie may be encrypted by means of Triple DES or DES, discussed in earlier chapters, but in this method the cookie is not validated. This type of cookie might be subject to chosen plaintext attacks.
Validation	The encryption is not carried out on the cookie. It only validates the cookie data.

timeout="[minutes]": Duration of time in integer minutes for a cookie to be valid (reset on each request). The default setting is **<forms timeout="30">**. The timeout attribute is a sliding value, expiring n minutes from the time the last request was received.

path="/": Sets the path to store the cookie on the user's machine. The default value is "/". The default value is recommended to avoid difficulties with mismatched case in paths, since browsers are strictly case-sensitive and a path-case mismatch could prevent the cookie from being sent with the request.

CREDENTIALS ATTRIBUTES

The **<credentials>** element allows you to store your users list in the **Web.config** file. You can also implement a custom password scheme to use an external source, such as a database, to control validation.

- **passwordFormat="[Clear | SHA1 | MD5]":** Format of user password value stored in **<user>** (Table 9–3).
- The **<credentials>** subtag supports one attribute and one subtag (Table 9–4).
- The **<user>** subtag supports two attributes (Table 9–5).
- The default setting is **<credentials passwordFormat="SHA1">**.

TABLE 9–3	*Options for the Password Format Attribute*	
Attribute	**Option**	**Description**
Password format		Specifies the encryption format for storing passwords.
	Clear	Specifies that passwords are not encrypted.
	MD5	Specifies that passwords are encrypted using the MD5 hash algorithm.
	SHA1	Specifies that passwords are encrypted using the SHA-1 hash algorithm.

TABLE 9–4	*Subtag of the <credentials> Subtag*
Subtag	**Description**
<user>	Allows definition of user name and password credentials within the configuration file.

TABLE 9–5	*Two Attributes of the <user> Subtag*
Attribute	**Description**
Name	The logon user name
Password	The user's password

PASSPORT ATTRIBUTES

The passport attribute **redirectUrl=["url"]** specifies the page to redirect to, whether the page requires authentication, and if the user has not signed on with passport.

AUTHORIZATION

This section sets the authorization policies of the application. You can allow or deny access to the application resources by user or role. Wildcards can be used as follows: "*" means everyone; "?" means anonymous (unauthenticated) users.

IDENTITY ATTRIBUTES

The identity attribute **impersonate="[true | false]"** impersonates a request entity (e.g., Windows user).

Forms Authentication

Forms-based authentication is an ASP.NET authentication service that facilitates Web applications to offer their individual logon user identification and do their own credential verification. It is widely used in Web sites to accomplish customized logic for authenticating the users. When a user logs in by means of forms authentication, a cookie is created, allowing you to track the user all through the site.

In this mechanism unauthenticated users are automatically redirected to a login page where they have to provide suitable credentials (e.g., username/ password). The application code verifies the submitted credentials. Once the user provides proper credentials and is successfully authenticated, the ASP.NET issues the cookie or token to the user and redirects the user to the actual resource that was formerly requested. Otherwise, the user is redirected back to the login page and informed that the username/password is invalid. This sort of authentication is a popular technique used by many Web sites. Forms authentication is often used for personalization, where content is customized for a known user.

Initially, the server issues a cookie,[9] a small piece of data, to the client. In the consecutive HTTP request the client sends back the cookie to the server, illustrating that the client has previously been authenticated. In the following example we show how to create a simple ASP.NET application that implements ASP.NET Forms authentication. There are three files involved:

---

9. ASP.NET provides sophisticated hashing and encryption algorithms, which prevents cookie spoofing.

default.aspx, **login.aspx**, and **Web.config**. Initially, the user requests the secured **default.aspx** page. Since the user is not authenticated, he or she is redirected to the **login.aspx** page, where the user has to submit the suitable username and password. If the user is authenticated, then he or she is redirected to the original default page. Forms authentication uses the classes found in the **System.Web.Security** namespace. Therefore, you should add the **System.Web.Security** namespace to your code.

To implement Forms authentication, follow these steps.

1. Set the authentication mode in the **Web.config** file.
2. Develop a Web form to collect the user's credentials.
3. Store the user's credentials in a file or database.
4. Authenticate the user against the user's file or database.

In Forms authentication mechanism you can store credentials in any of the following.

- Web.config
- XML file
- Database

Method 1: Storing Credentials in the Web.config File

In this method all the user information is stored in the **<credentials>** part of the **Web.config** file that resides in the application root directory. Storing credentials in the **Web.config** file is suitable and convenient only for simple authentication. This method is not suitable if you allow users to create and maintain their own accounts. In those cases you have to store the username and encrypted password in a separate database or XML file. Develop an ASP.NET Web application using Visual Studio .NET, rename the Web page **default.aspx**, and add another Web page named **login.aspx**. Then, configure the **Web.config** file as shown in the next section.

CONFIGURE <AUTHENTICATION> AND <AUTHORIZATION> SECTION IN WEB.CONFIG FILE

You have to configure the **Web.config** configuration file as follows and place it in the application root directory (the directory in which **default.aspx** resides).

```
<configuration>
  <system.web>

//Set the authentication mode to Forms.
    <authentication mode="Forms">
//Set the form's authentication attributes.
        <forms name=".ASPXFormAuth" loginUrl="login.aspx"
          protection="All" timeout="15" path ="/">
```

```
//Storing the UserID and Password in the credential
//section.
            <credentials passwordFormat="Clear">
                <user name="Arun"   password="Spiritual" />
                <user name="Ganesh" password="Divine" />
            </credentials>
          </forms>
      </authentication>
      <authorization>
//Discard the unauthenticated users.
        <deny users="?" />
      </authorization>
    <globalization requestEncoding="UTF-8"
      responseEncoding="UTF-8" />
  </system.web>
</configuration>
```

In the credential section we stored the valid usernames and passwords. Within 15 minutes the authentication cookie will expire because we set the timeout to 15 minutes. The cookie will be regenerated after every 15 minutes so that we can lessen the possibility of another user stealing the cookie.

THE LOGIN.ASPX FILE

If the user is unauthenticated, the request is redirected to this **login.aspx** file. This Web form is identified by name in the **<forms>** element of **Web.config**. Import the namespace **System.Web.Security**. In the design view add two text boxes (**Userid** and **Passid**) and a **Submit** button, as shown in Figure 9–2. The **login.aspx** code is as follows:

```
private void Button1_Click(object sender, System.EventArgs e)
{
/* public static bool Authenticate( string name, string
password );
   Authenticate Userid and Passid against <credentials> */

if (FormsAuthentication.Authenticate( Userid.Text,
   Passid.Text) )
{
FormsAuthentication.RedirectFromLoginPage(Userid.Text,
   false);
}
else
  {
  // Clear the Password text.
Passid.Text = "";
Label3.Text = "Invalid User ID and/or Password!";
}
}
```

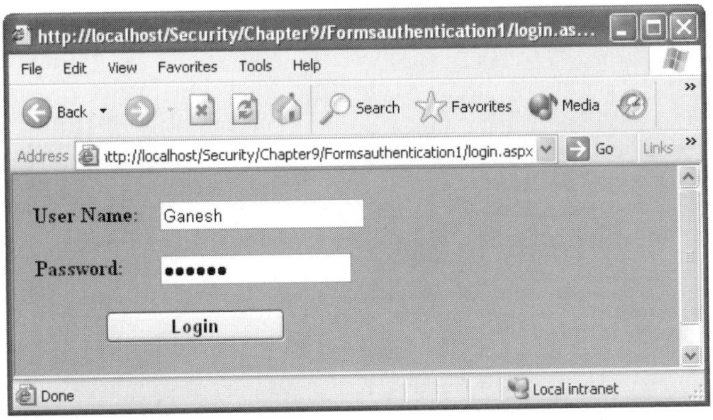

FIGURE 9-2   *Login.aspx page where the user has to submit valid username and password.*

Here, the code **FormsAuthentication.Authenticate(Userid.Text, Passid.Text)** ensures the username and password provided by the user and returns a boolean value of true if the credentials are valid. It returns false if the credentials are not valid. Then, it creates an authentication cookie, appends it to the outgoing response, and redirects the request to the initial requested page using the code **FormsAuthentication.RedirectFromLoginPage(Userid.Text, false)**. In this code the second parameter specifies whether the authentication should be a session cookie (false) or a persistent cookie (true). Here we provide it as a session cookie.

THE DEFAULT.ASPX FILE

The **default.aspx** file is the requested, confined resource. In the **default.aspx** page we simply display the welcome message and a Sign out button, as shown in Figure 9–3. By employing the **FormsAuthentication.SignOut** method, you can easily eliminate or invalidate the authentication cookies. The **default.aspx** code is as follows:

```
private void Page_Load(object sender, System.EventArgs e)
  {

/* Note that in the below code this is chance of a cross site
scripting attack unless the data has been validated before
creating the ticket. So the data entered by the user has to
be validated.*/

Label1.Text= "Welcome, "+ User.Identity.Name+"!"+ "You have
  successfully logged in.";
```

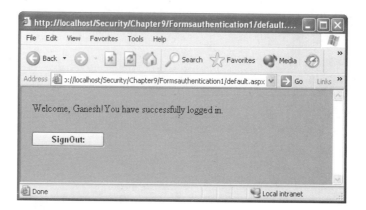

FIGURE 9-3 *Welcome message displayed in the default.aspx page after the user is authenticated.*

```
}
private void SignOut_Click(object sender, System.EventArgs e)
   {
      FormsAuthentication.SignOut();
      Response.Redirect("login.aspx");
   }
```

PROTECTING PASSWORDS WITH ENCRYPTION

It is not recommended to store the password in clear text due to security risks. Even though a user cannot directly access a **Web.config** file, if the server is accessible over a local network, then there is a possibility of accessing a **Web.config** file. Therefore, when storing usernames and passwords in a **Web.config** file or database, you have to encrypt them using the **FormsAuthentication** class's **HashPasswordForStoringInConfigFile** method. This utilizes the SHA-1 or MD5 algorithms to encrypt data, as follows:

```
Passid =
   FormsAuthentication.HashPasswordForStoringInConfigFile
   Passid.Text,"SHA1");
```

For example, the hash value for the password "Divine" using SHA-1 algorithm is C1FF7FB589DDC7CECD412F515709D8DC2B2B2C22.

You can also protect the sensitive information in **Web.config** files by using the Data Protection API (DPAPI). For more information on how to use DPAPI from an ASP.NET Web application or Web service to encrypt sensitive data, visit *http://msdn.microsoft.com/architecture/application/default.aspx?pull=/library/en-us/dnnetsec/html/SecNetHT08.asp.*

Method 2: Storing Credentials in the XML File

In this method all the user information is stored in the XML file. It is impractical to store huge numbers of usernames and passwords in the **Web.config** file. Storing usernames and passwords in the XML or in a database is preferable. In this method there is no credential part in the **Web.config** file. The **Web.config** file is as follows.

```
//Set the authentication mode to Forms.
<authentication mode="Forms">
//Set the form's authentication attributes.
<forms name=".ASPXFormAuthxml" loginUrl="login.aspx"
   protection="All" timeout="60" />
</authentication>
<authorization>
//Discard the unauthenticated users.
<deny users="?"/>
</authorization>
```

As we discussed earlier, ASP.NET verifies whether the request is authenticated. If the request is not authenticated, it redirects the request to the **login.aspx** page. There, the client has to submit the suitable credentials for authentication. The **login.aspx** page evaluates the submitted credentials to a list of credentials in the Users.xml file. The user is redirected to the original requested **default.aspx** page if the submitted credentials are found in the Users.xml file. If not, the request is redirected to another page, where the submitted username and password are added in the XML file.

The Users.xml File

The **Users.xml** file, which encloses the user credentials, is as follows. The **UserPassword** is encrypted using the **FormsAuthentication** class's **HashPasswordForStoringInConfigFile** method (SHA-1 algorithm).

```
<Users>
    <Users>
<UserID>G.A.Gnanavel</UserID>
        <UserPassword>
44DD5C3AA9E4E693A9E394DAA5D3F3A449DC25CA</UserPassword>
    </Users>
    <Users>
<UserID>G.N.Vadivambal</UserID>
        <UserPassword>
FE71C5444F9327DDA2F1D69B7510ABF59B80672F</UserPassword>
    </Users>
    <Users>
        <UserID>G.G.Saratha</UserID>
        <UserPassword>
CF77B1B76919D5D2B8B79D63FCA5E70383A3D7E5</UserPassword>
```

```
      </Users>
</Users>
```

The login.aspx File

```csharp
using System;
using System.Collections;
using System.ComponentModel;
using System.Data;
using System.Data.SqlClient;
using System.Data.OleDb;
using System.Web.Security;
using System.Web;
using System.IO;
using System.Web.SessionState;
using System.Web.UI;
namespace Formsauthenticationxml
{
   public class login : System.Web.UI.Page
   {
   protected System.Web.UI.WebControls.TextBox Passid;
   protected System.Web.UI.WebControls.Button Button1;
   protected System.Web.UI.WebControls.Label Label1;
   protected System.Web.UI.WebControls.Label Label2;
   protected System.Web.UI.WebControls.Label Label3;
   protected System.Web.UI.WebControls.TextBox Userid;

public login()
    {
    Page.Init += new System.EventHandler(Page_Init);
    }
private void Page_Load(object sender, System.EventArgs e)
    {
    }
private void Page_Init(object sender, EventArgs e)
    {
    InitializeComponent();
    }
    #region
    //Web Form Designer generated code
    #endregion
private void Button1_Click(object sender, System.EventArgs e)
    {

/* Encrypt the password entered by the user to verify against
 the encrypted password found in the XML file.*/

string Passidvalue =
FormsAuthentication.HashPasswordForStoringInConfigFile
   (Passid.Text,"SHA1");
       String str = "UserID='" + Userid.Text+ "'";
```

```
        DataSet ds = new DataSet();
        FileStream fs = new
FileStream(Server.MapPath("Users.xml"),
        FileMode.Open,FileAccess.Read);
        StreamReader reader = new StreamReader(fs);
        ds.ReadXml(reader);
        fs.Close();
        DataTable clients = ds.Tables[0];
        DataRow[] items = clients.Select(str);
        if( items != null && items.Length > 0 )
        {
          DataRow row = items[0];
          String pass = (String)row["UserPassword"];
          if (pass == Passidvalue)

FormsAuthentication.RedirectFromLoginPage(Userid.Text,
    false);
          else
            Label3.Text = "Please enter a valid password!";
        }
      else
      {
      Label3.Text = "Invalid User ID and/or Password!";
/* The request is redirected to another page where the
 submitted Username and password will be added to the XML
 file.*/
Response.Redirect("adduser/adduser.aspx?UserID =
    "+Userid.Text);
      }

      }
    }
}
```

We read the XML file, which encloses the authenticated credentials and stores the retrieved data in the **DataSet ds**. Then, we verify the submitted **UserID** with the list of names in Users.aspx. If we find any value in the XML file, we store it in a **DataRow** named *items*. Then we check whether the password value provided by the user matches against the encrypted password found in the XML file. If the password matches, then we redirect the request to the originally requested **default.aspx**. Otherwise, the request is redirected to another page, where the submitted username and password are added to the XML file. But in real-time applications it is recommended to use a relational database for storing the authenticated users.

Method 3: Storing Credentials in a Database

In this method all the user information is stored in the database file instead of in the **Web.config** file. The **default.aspx** and **Web.config** files are similar to the above method. The only difference is in the **login.aspx** page. The code for the **LoginBtn_Click** method in the **login.aspx** code is as follows.

```
// The below code is only for pedagogical purpose.
private void LoginBtn_Click(object sender, System.EventArgs e)
    {

/*SqlConnection conn = new SqlConnection ("Server=(local);" +
"Integrated Security=SSPI;" +
 "database=login");*/
OleDbConnection conn = new
OleDbConnection("Provider=Microsoft.Jet.OLEDB.4.0;Data
Source="+"C:\\NetSecurity\\Chapter9\\Formsauthdatabase\\
   login.mdb");
      try
      {
        conn.Open();

/* Here in the below code there is possibility of
 SQL injection if the user input is not properly
 validated. Therefore validation has to be made before
 processing the user input.*/

String str = "select count (*) from login where UserID=
   '" +Userid.Text+ "' and Password= '" + Passid.Text + "' ";

/* SqlCommand command = new SqlCommand(str, conn);*/

OleDbCommand command = new OleDbCommand(str, conn);

int count = (int)command.ExecuteScalar();
if (count!=0)
FormsAuthentication.RedirectFromLoginPage(Userid.Text, false);
else
Label3.Text = "Please enter a valid password!";
}

  finally
    {
    conn.Close();
    }
}
```

While validating user credentials against a database file, consider the following two things:

- Store one-way password hashes (with a random salt value).
- Avoid SQL injection when validating user credentials.

In real-time applications, it is not recommended to store passwords (cleartext or encrypted) in the database. The problem with storing encrypted passwords is that it is difficult to keep the encryption key safe. Moreover, if an attacker accesses the key, then he or she can decrypt all the passwords that you store in the database. Therefore, the best method is to store a one-way hash of the password (combine the password hash with a salt value).[10]

You can create salt value as follows.

```
public static string GenerateSalt(int size)
{

/* RNGCryptoServiceProvider class in the
  System.Security.Cryptography namespace provides random
  number generation functionality. */

RNGCryptoServiceProvider crypto = new
   RNGCryptoServiceProvider();
byte[] buff = new byte[size];
crypto.GetBytes(buff);
return Convert.ToBase64String(buff);
}
```

You can create a hash value from a given password and salt value as follows.

```
public static string GeneratePasswordHash(string passid,
   string salt)
{
string saltpassid = string.Concat(passid, salt);
string password =
FormsAuthentication.HashPasswordForStoringInConfigFile(
saltpassid, "SHA1");
return password;
}
```

SQL INJECTION

SQL injection means that a user could pass arbitrary, extra (malicious) SQL code, which is typically appended to the valid SQL code. For instance, consider the following code.

```
String str = "select count (*) from login where UserID= '"
+Userid.Text+ "' and Password= '" + Passid.Text + "' ";
```

---

10. Salt value is a cryptographically strong random number.

If the attacker enters the following for the Passid.Text

```
' ;  Any malicious SQL string
```

the above input will execute the malicious SQL string, because the ' (single quotation mark) character indicates that the current string literal in your SQL statement is terminated and the ; (semicolon) character indicates that you are opening a new statement.

To prevent SQL injection, consider the following.

- Employ a strong validator and validate the user input. For instance, you can limit the size and type of input.
- Run SQL code with a least-privileged account.
- Use the **Parameters** collection when building your SQL statements as follows.

```
SqlDataAdapter myCommand = new SqlDataAdapter(
"SELECT * FROM login WHERE UserID= @userid", myConn);
SqlParameter parm =
    myCommand.SelectCommand.Parameters.Add( "@userid
    ",SqlDbType.VarChar, 15);
    parm.Value= Userid.Text;
```

Forms Authentication Classes

The **System.Web.Security** namespace contains all the classes that are used to implement ASP.NET security in Web server applications. Table 9–6 shows the significant .NET Framework classes on Forms authentication.

TABLE 9–6   *.NET Framework Classes on Forms Authentication*

Class	Description
FormsAuthenticationModule	Allows an ASP.NET application to employ Forms authentication.
FormsAuthentication	Provides static methods that deliver helper utilities for manipulating authentication tickets.
FormsAuthenticationTicket	Provides the information represented in an authentication cookie as used by **FormsAuthenticationModule**.
FormsIdentity	Provides an **IIdentity**-derived class to be used by **FormsAuthenticationModule** and allows an application to access the cookie authentication ticket.
FormsAuthenticationEventArgs	Provides data for the **FormsAuthentication_OnAuthenticate** event.

The public static (shared) properties defined in the **FormsAuthentication** class are shown in Table 9–7.

TABLE 9–7	*Public Static (Shared) Properties Defined in the FormsAuthentication Class*
Public Property	**Description**
FormsCookieName	Returns the configured cookie name used for the current application.
FormsCookiePath	Returns the configured cookie path used for the current application.

The public static (shared) methods defined in the **FormsAuthentication** class are shown in Table 9–8.

TABLE 9–8	*Public Static (Shared) Methods Defined in the FormsAuthentication Class*
Public Method	**Description**
Authenticate	Validates the supplied credentials against those contained in the configured credential store and returns true if the credentials are valid or false otherwise.
Decrypt	Returns a **FormsAuthenticationTicket** object, given an encrypted authentication ticket acquired from an HTTP cookie.
Encrypt	Returns a string containing an encrypted authentication ticket suitable for use in an HTTP cookie, given a **FormsAuthenticationTicket**.
GetAuthCookie	Overloaded. Creates an authentication cookie for a given username.
GetRedirectUrl	Returns the redirect URL for the original request that caused the redirect to the logon page. If there is no original URL, **default.aspx** is used.
HashPasswordForStoringInConfigFile	Produces a hash password suitable for storing in a configuration file, given a password and a string specifying the hash type. (The hashed password is not salted. You have to add salt value.) Password algorithms supported are SHA-1 and MD5.

Continued on next page

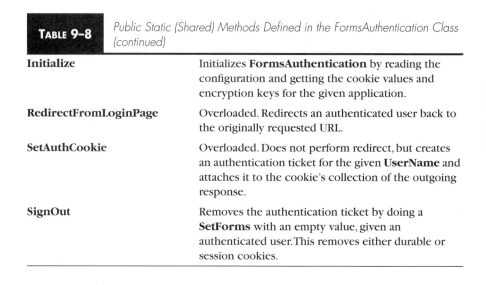

TABLE 9–8	*Public Static (Shared) Methods Defined in the FormsAuthentication Class (continued)*
Initialize	Initializes **FormsAuthentication** by reading the configuration and getting the cookie values and encryption keys for the given application.
RedirectFromLoginPage	Overloaded. Redirects an authenticated user back to the originally requested URL.
SetAuthCookie	Overloaded. Does not perform redirect, but creates an authentication ticket for the given **UserName** and attaches it to the cookie's collection of the outgoing response.
SignOut	Removes the authentication ticket by doing a **SetForms** with an empty value, given an authenticated user. This removes either durable or session cookies.

The public instance properties defined in the **FormsAuthentication-Ticket** class are shown in Table 9–9.

TABLE 9–9	*Public Instance Properties Defined in the FormsAuthenticationTicket Class*

Public Property	**Description**
CookiePath	Returns the path for which the cookie was issued.
Expiration	Returns the date/time at which the cookie expires.
Expired	Returns true if the cookie expired.
IsPersistent	Returns true if a durable cookie was issued. Otherwise, the authentication cookie is scoped to the browser lifetime.
IssueDate	Returns the date/time at which the cookie was originally issued. This can be used for custom expiration schemes.
Name	Returns the username associated with the authentication cookie. A maximum of 32 bytes are stored in the cookie.
UserData	Returns an application-defined string that might have been stored in the cookie.
Version	Returns a byte version number for future use.

The public instance properties defined in the **FormsIdentity** class are shown in Table 9–10.

TABLE 9-10	Public Instance Properties Defined in the FormsIdentity Class

Public Property	**Description**
AuthenticationType	The type of the identity (in this case, "Forms").
IsAuthenticated	Indicates whether authentication took place.
Name	The name of the identity (in this case, the username).
Ticket	Returns the **FormsAuthenticationTicket** associated with the current request.

Passport Authentication

Passport authentication is a centralized, single sign-on authentication service provided by Microsoft. At present a large number of Internet users use Microsoft services such as MSN or Hotmail. They submit their profiles during the registration process in those Microsoft services. The real benefit is that you can utilize the user profile data in your Web sites if you implement passport authentication in your site. That is, information about the user is accessible to your application through a profile that is stored with Microsoft. Many companies, such as McAfee.com and eBay, employ Passport authentication in their Web sites. The benefit of Passport authentication is that the user doesn't have to remember separate usernames and passwords for various Web sites, and the user can keep his or her profile information in a single location. .NET Passport[11] provides users with single sign-in (SSI) and stores the authentication information using encryption technologies such as Secure Sockets Layer (SSL) and the 3DES algorithm for data protection. Figure 9–4 shows the Microsoft .NET Passport home page.

Passport is a Forms-based authentication service. In this mechanism, when a user requests (using an HTTP GET request) a protected resource, the ASP.NET verifies whether the user has a valid Passport ticket (form). If not, the user is redirected to the Passport Logon Service, where the user has to submit the credentials (email address and a password), as shown in Figure 9–5. If the credentials entered are correct, Passport Logon Service redirects the user back to the protected resource. Otherwise, the user must register his or her profile and is then redirected to the protected resource.

---

11. In 1999 Microsoft launched Microsoft .NET Passport, Service-to-Consumer (S2C) Web-based services.

FIGURE 9-4   *Microsoft .NET Passport home page.*

The **PassportAuthenticationModule** provides a wrapper around the Passport software development kit (SDK) for ASP.NET applications. It provides Passport authentication service and profile information from an **IIdentity**-derived class called **PassportIdentity**. You have to register your site with the Passport service, accept the license agreement, and install the passport SDK to employ passport authentication.

The general procedure to implement Passport authentication in an ASP.NET application is as follows:

- Register your site with the passport service.
- Download, install, and configure the Passport SDK from Microsoft Download or in *http://www.passport.com*. To deploy Passport on a real-time Web site, you have to register and get a production key, for which Microsoft charges a licensing fee.[12] For authentication, the user is directed to the page *http://login.passport.com*.

---

12. There are two fees for licensing .NET Passport: a periodic compliance testing fee of $1,500 US and a yearly provisioning fee of $10,000 US. The provisioning fee is charged on a per-company basis.

FIGURE 9-5   *.NET Passport Sign In, where the user has to submit email address and password for credential verification.*

- While testing your site, you cannot employ regular Passport accounts to sign in. Instead, to test the SDK, you have to launch a PREP Passport account or Preproduction key.[13] The Preproduction (PREP) environment allows sites to confirm their development efforts against .NET Passport servers without access to real-world .NET Passport user identifications and profiles. This preproduction registration can be done at *http://current-register.passporttest.com*. For authentication, the user is redirected to the site *http://current-login.passporttest.com* (the address of the PREP Login server).
- Configure the **Web.config** file as

```
<authentication mode="Passport">
<passport redirectURL="login.aspx" />
</authentication>
```

After installing the .NET Passport SDK and configuring the **Web.config** file, you will be able to access the **PassportIdentity** class, which is accessed

---

13. Do not use your Production password for PREP passwords. The PREP system is a separate test environment containing only test data, so it is best for security purposes to keep your Production password unique to the Production system.

by means of the **IIdentity** interface that it implements. The following code
shows how to get an instance of a **PassportIdentity** object.

```
using System.Web.Security;
 ...
 public class WebForm1 : System.Web.UI.Page
 {
   public PassportIdentity pass;

   private void Page_Load(object sender,
     System.EventArgs e)
   {
     pass = (PassportIdentity)User.Identity;
   }
 }
```

With the instance of the **PassportIdentity** object, you can access the
.NET Passport-specific functionality provided by the **PassportIdentity** class.

Let us discuss how to display sign-in and sign-out buttons. Generally,
you can see the **.NET Passport Sign In** or **.NET Passport Sign Out** buttons
in the upper-right corner of the page, and the buttons look like those shown
in Figure 9–6.

The **LogoTag2** method of the **PassportIdentity** object returns an HTML
fragment that includes an **<img>** tag for a Microsoft .NET Passport link. The
link displays either **Sign In** if no valid Ticket cookie is detected or **Sign Out** if
a valid Ticket cookie is detected. The following code illustrates how to use
the **LogoTag2** method in an ASP.NET page.

```
using System.Web.Security;
 ...
 public class WebForm1 : System.Web.UI.Page
 {
   public PassportIdentity pass;

   private void Page_Load(object sender,
     System.EventArgs e)
   {
     pass = (PassportIdentity)User.Identity;
   string returnURL =
       "http://phptr/default.aspx";
```

FIGURE 9–6   *Microsoft .NET Passport Sign In and Sign Out buttons.*

```
string logo = pass.LogoTag2(returnURL,
    10000,true,null,1033,false,Context.Request.
    ServerVariables["SERVER_NAME"],0,false);
Response.Write(logo);
    }
  ...
  }
```

The syntax for the **PassportIdentity.LogoTag2** method is as follows:

```
public string LogoTag2(string strReturnUrl, int
iTimeWindow, bool fForceLogin, string strCoBrandedArgs, int
iLangID, bool fSecure, string strNameSpace, int iKPP, bool
bUseSecureAuth);
```

- The first parameter of the **LogoTag2** method is the **[returnURL]**. It is an optional value. It sets the URL of the location to which the Login server should redirect the user after the .NET Passport sign-in is completed successfully. If **returnURL** is left empty, then it uses the registry default. Usually, the URL is set to the current page so that the user is redirected back to the same page he or she was at before signing in. However, you can set any URL that is favorable.
- The second parameter is **[TimeWindow]** (optional). Time is represented as an integer value in seconds. This indicates the time interval during which the user must have last signed in. This value must be between 100 and 1,000,000.
- The further parameters of the **LogoTag2** method, such as **[ForceLogin]**, **[coBrandArgs]**, **[lang_id]**, **[bSecure]**, **[NameSpace]**, **[KPP]**, and **[SecureLevel]**, specify whether the users should be forced to log on or not, indicate the URL for a co-branding image, stipulate the language for the .NET Passport sign-in page—for example, U.S. English (EN/US, the default) is 1033)—indicate whether it is being accessed over SSL, offer the domain name for the request, indicate Kids Passport consent requirements, and indicate the security level of the sign-in.

The three security-level options for the .NET Passport sign-in are shown in Table 9–11.

As an alternative to the single sign-in mechanism, you can employ an Inline sign-in mechanism, which allows you to embed the sign-in dialog box directly into a page on your site instead of redirecting the user to a .NET Passport-hosted sign-in page. This Inline sign-in mechanism provides more flexibility. The compact and standard inline sign-in modules are shown in

TABLE 9-11	*Three Security-Level Options for the .NET Passport Sign-In*
SecureLevel value	**Description**
0 (or unspecified)	Sign-in UI is served HTTP from the .NET Passport domain authority (default).
10	Sign-in UI is served HTTPS from the .NET Passport domain authority. Requires that return URL be an HTTPS URL; otherwise, the authentication will fail.
100	Sign-in UI is served HTTPS from the .NET Passport domain authority, and sign-in process now requires submission of secure authentication PIN in addition to password.

Figure 9–7. You can also employ a mobile sign-in[14] mechanism in mobile devices.

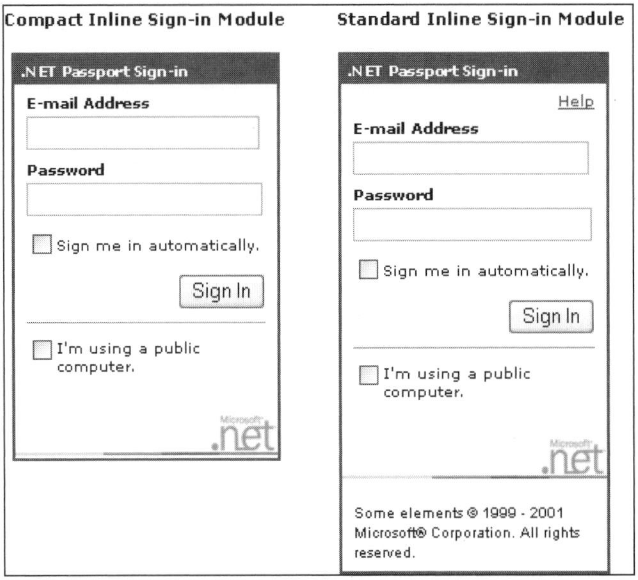

FIGURE 9-7	*Compact and standard inline sign-in modules.*

---

14. Mobile sign-in provides many features and modifications to support general use of .NET Passport on mobile devices. Users can create a Passport using a phone number and personal identification number (PIN) for use on a mobile device (such as a cell phone or PDA).

The considerable benefit of employing Passport authentication is that, as already mentioned, you can access the Passport user's profile data, such as **FirstName** and **Country**, if the user permits his or her profile data to be used, while registering to .NET Passport. But the Passport User ID (PUID) for a .NET Passport-authenticated user is always accessible by means of the **Name** or **HexPUID** properties of the **PassportIdentity** class. You can use the PUID as the index for storing user-specific information at your site. Some other useful attribute names that you can access from the profile data are **FirstName**, **LastName**, **Nickname**, **Gender**, **Birthdate**, **PreferredEmail**, **TimeZone**, **Occupation**, and **Country**. The following code illustrates how to access the user profile data.

```csharp
private void Page_Load(object sender, System.EventArgs e)
  {
  if (pi.IsAuthenticated)
   {
    string name = pi["FirstName"];
      if (name == "")
      {
        Label1.Text = "Warm Welcome!";
      }
      else
      {
        Label1.Text = "Welcome" +name+ "!";
      }
  }
  else
  {
   Label1.Text = "Welcome! Please Sign In!";
   }
}
```

We first verify whether the user has signed in to .NET Passport by using the **IsAuthenticated** method, which returns true if the user is authenticated against a Passport authority. As .NET Passport employs cookies to handle state, you have to create a separate page that takes care of deleting the HTTP cookies that carry the ticket information. Your sign-out page must return an image that can be used to show a successful sign-out to the user. The following code removes the .NET Passport cookies and returns the apposite GIF image to specify a successful sign-out.

```
<%@ Page language="c#" %>
 <%
   Response.ContentType = "image/gif";
   Response.Expires = -1;
   Response.AddHeader("P3P", "CP=TST");
```

```
HttpCookie Cookie1 =
  new HttpCookie("MSPProf","");
Cookie1.Expires = Now();
Response.Cookies.Add(Cookie1);

HttpCookie Cookie2 =
  new HttpCookie("MSPAuth","");
Cookie2.Expires = Now();
Response.Cookies.Add(Cookie2);

HttpCookie Cookie3 =
  new HttpCookie("MSPSecAuth","");
Cookie3.Expires = Now();
Response.Cookies.Add(Cookie3);

HttpCookie Cookie4 =
  new HttpCookie("MSPProfC","");
Cookie4.Expires = Now();
Response.Cookies.Add(Cookie4);

HttpCookie Cookie5 =
  new HttpCookie("MSPConsent","");
Cookie5.Expires = Now();
Response.Cookies.Add(Cookie5);

Response.WriteFile(
  "/images/signout_Clear.gif");
%>
```

We clear the five cookies **MSPProf**, **MSPAuth**, **MSPSecAuth**, **MSP-ProfC**, and **MSPConsent**. You have to incorporate a P3P tag (Platform for Privacy Preferences Project) to clear the cookies in the 6.x generation of Web browsers.

The public instance properties defined in the **PassportIdentity** class are shown in Table 9–12.

TABLE 9–12   *Public Instance Properties Defined in the PassportIdentity Class*

Public Property	Description
Error	Returns an error state associated with the current Passport ticket.
GetFromNetworkServer	Returns true if a connection is coming back from the Passport server (log-on, update, or registration) and if the Passport data contained on the query string is valid. This is actually vitally important, because if it's true, the ticket is on the query string and the application should redirect without the query string to make sure the ticket isn't persisted in browser history (important for things like kiosks).

Table 9-12	*Public Instance Properties Defined in the PassportIdentity Class (continued)*
Public Property	**Description**
HasSavedPassword	Returns true if the Passport member's ticket indicates that the password was saved on the Passport logon page the last time the ticket was refreshed.
HasTicket	Returns true if there is a Passport ticket as a cookie on the query string.
IsAuthenticated	Returns true if the user is authenticated against a Passport authority.
Item	Consists of the default collection. Calling this is the equivalent of calling **GetProfileObject** or **SetProfileObject**.
Name	Consists of the name of the identity. In this case, it is the value of the Passport PUID.
TicketAge	Consists of the time, in seconds, since the last ticket was issued or refreshed.
TimeSinceSignIn	Consists of the time, in seconds, since a member's logon to the Passport logon server.

Windows Authentication

The authentication methods offered by IIS (apart from Anonymous authentication), such as Basic, Digest, Integrated Windows Authentication or its other Forms (NTLM/Kerberos), or Certificates, are employed in the Windows authentication mechanism. This method is very easy to implement because you can implement it with minimal ASP.NET coding, and IIS itself validates the user's credentials. The Windows authentication method is particularly appropriate for intranet applications. Moreover, it works for all content types, not only for ASP.NET resources.

If a user requests the protected resource, the IIS initially authenticates the user and attaches the security token to it. ASP.NET employs the authenticated identities token to decide whether or not the request is granted. You can use impersonation to restrict or permit access to the protected resources. If impersonation is enabled, ASP.NET impersonates the user by means of the security token attached with the request. It then verifies whether the user is authorized to access the resources. If the access is granted, ASP.NET sends the requested resources through IIS; otherwise, it sends an error message to the user.

To enable Windows authentication, configure the **Web.config**[15] file by setting the authentication mode to Windows and denying access to anonymous user, as follows.

```
<configuration>
  <system.web>
    <authentication mode="Windows"/>
```

---

15. Configuring an ASP.NET application has no effect on the IIS Directory Security settings. The systems are completely independent and are applied in sequence.

```
        <authorization>
            <allow
            users="Domainname\GroupName"/>
        <deny users="*"/>
        </authorization>
<identity impersonate="true" />
    </system.web>
</configuration>
```

The public instance properties defined in the **WindowsIdentity** class are shown in Table 9–13.

TABLE 9–13 *Public Instance Properties Defined in the WindowsIdentity Class*

Public Property	Description
IsAnonymous	Gets a value indicating whether the user account is identified as an anonymous account by the system.
IsAuthenticated	Gets a value indicating whether the user has been authenticated by Windows.
IsGuest	Gets a value indicating whether the user account is identified as a Guest account by the system.
IsSystem	Gets a value indicating whether the user account is identified as a System account by the system.
Name	Gets the user's Windows log-on name.
Token	Gets the Windows account token for the user.

The public static (shared) methods defined in the **WindowsIdentity** class are shown in Table 9–14.

TABLE 9–14 *Public Static (Shared) Methods Defined in the WindowsIdentity Class*

Public Method	Description
GetAnonymous	Returns a **WindowsIdentity** object representing an anonymous Windows user.
GetCurrent	Returns a **WindowsIdentity** object representing the current Windows user.
Impersonate	Allows code to impersonate a different Windows user.

To implement Windows authentication, set the authentication mode in the **Web.config** file as shown next, and disable anonymous access. Finally, configure the Windows user accounts on your Web server if they are not already present.

```
<authentication mode="Windows" />
<authorization>
<deny users="?" />
</authorization>
```

In Windows authentication you can retrieve information directly from the **User** object. That is, if a user is authenticated and authorized, then your application can get information about the user by using the **User** object's **Identity** property. For example, for the following code, the output will be as shown in Figure 9–8.

```
private void Page_Load(object sender, System.EventArgs e)
 {
    AuthLabel.Text = "Authentication: " +
User.Identity.IsAuthenticated.ToString();
    UserLabel.Text = "UserName: " + User.Identity.Name;
    AuthtypeLabel.Text = "AuthenticationType: " +
User.Identity.AuthenticationType;

 }
```

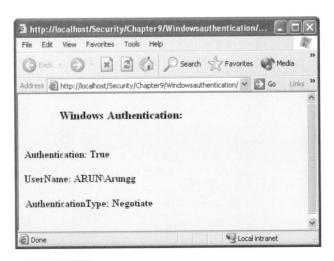

FIGURE 9–8   *Retrieving Windows authentication information (running locally).*

FIGURE 9-9   *Dialog box to connect username and password.*

If you run the project remotely, ASP.NET displays a dialog box in the browser to collect the username and password, as shown in Figure 9–9. If the given username and password match for the network domain, then ASP.NET authenticates you to use the application.

Implementing ASP.NET Authorization

Authorization is a process in which you determine whether an authenticated user is granted access to a certain page or resource. In ASP.NET there are two primary ways to authorize access to a given resource: file authorization and URL authorization. Let us discuss these two types scrupulously.

File Authorization

File authorization is carried out against the authenticated account provided by IIS. It is executed by the **FileAuthorizationModule**. It verifies the Access Control List (ACL)[16] or permissions on a resource to determine whether the authenticated user has privilege to access the protected resource. The **FileAu-**

---

16. The ACL is a list that specifies which users or groups have permission to access or modify a particular file; the Windows discretionary access control list (DACL) and system access control list (SACL) are examples of ACLs.

thorizationModule provides authorization services against the file system ACLs. You can configure the file ACLs for a given file or directory using the Security tab in the Explorer property page. Note that **AccessCheck** is called only if there is a **WindowsIdentity** associated with the request., so it's not strictly useful for Forms authentication or Passport, where there tends to just be one Windows account (the anonymous account).

URL Authorization

URL authorization is executed by the **URLAuthorizationModule**. For URL authorization, the anonymous user is verified against the configuration data. If access is permissible for the requested URL, the request is authorized. By employing the **URLAuthorizationModule**, you can execute both positive and negative authorization assertions. That is, you can allow or deny access to groups of users or roles. To implement the URL authorization, place the list of users and/or roles in the **<allow>** or **<deny>** elements of the **<authorization>** section of a configuration file.

The general syntax for the **<authorization>** section is as follows.

```
<[element] [users] [roles] [verbs] />
```

Here, the elements are **<allow>** and **<deny>**.

The **<allow>** element grants the user access to the resource.

The **<deny>** element revokes the user access to the resource.

The attributes supported by each element are shown in Table 9–15.

TABLE 9–15	*Attributes Supported by the Element (Allow/Deny)*
Attribute	**Description**
Roles	Identifies a targeted role for this element. The associated **IPrincipal** object for the request determines the role membership. You can attach arbitrary **IPrincipal** objects to the context for a given request, and they can determine the role membership in whatever fashion you like. For example, the default **WindowsPrincipal** class uses Windows NT groups to determine the role membership.
Users	Identifies the targeted identities for this element.
Verbs	Defines the HTTP verbs to which the action applies, such as GET, HEAD, and POST.

For example, the following code illustrates access being granted to a user named Arun and a role named Administrator. It will deny all other users.

```
<configuration>
   <system.web>
      <authorization>
         <allow users = "Arun" />
         <allow roles = "Administrator" />
         <deny users= "*" />
      </authorization>
   </system.web>
</configuration>
```

You can specify multiple users or roles by using a comma-separated list:

```
<allow users="Arun,Saru,admin\Gnv" />
```

The domain account (admin\Gnv) has to incorporate both domain and user names.

You can also specify the HTTP method using the **Verb** attribute, as shown in the following code. For example, this code allows Arun and Saru to use POST action and all others to use only GET action.

```
<allow VERB="POST" users="Arun,Saru" />
<deny VERB="POST" users="*" />
<allow VERB="GET" users="*" />
```

There are two special identities

- *—All users
- ?—Unauthenticated (anonymous) users

For example, the following code denies all the unauthenticated users.

```
<authorization>
    <deny users="?" />
</authorization>
```

There is also a **<location>** tag that you can use to specify a particular file or directory.

```
<location path="Required path">
```

The following two authorization sections are different. The first one denies all the users because the first line, <deny users="*" />, discards the upcoming statements. The second one denies all the users except Arun.

```
<authorization>
    <deny users="*" />
    <allow users="Arun" />
</authorization>
<authorization>
    <allow users="Arun" />
    <deny users="*" />
</authorization>
```

Implementing ASP.NET Impersonation

Impersonation, instead of writing ASP.NET code for authentication and authorization, employs IIS to authenticate the user. If the user is authenticated, it passes an authenticated token to the ASP.NET application; otherwise, it passes an unauthenticated token. In an ASP.NET application, if the impersonation is enabled, ASP.NET assumes the client identity and relies on the settings in the NTFS directories and files to permit or deny the request. If impersonation is disabled, it runs with the local machine identity. For ASP compatibility, impersonation is disabled by default.

To enable impersonation, configure the configuration file in the application root directory as follows.

```
<identity impersonate="true" name="Username"
password="Password" />[17]
```

Summary

In this chapter we explained the ASP.NET security in detail. We looked at most of the major .NET classes involved in ASP.NET security programming and at several programming examples that demonstrate how to implement authentication, authorization, and impersonation in ASP.NET applications. In the upcoming chapter we will see the highlights of the Web services security.

---

17. In .NET Framework version 1.1 you can put the password in an encrypted (DPAPI) registry key. There is a hotfix for .NET Framework version 1.0. Read more about it at *http://support.microsoft.com/default.aspx?scid=kb;en-us;329250*.

Web Services Security

*C*urrently, Web service is a buzzword, and it is in the process of revolution-izing the software world. But the security issues prevent the widespread adoption of Web services. According to a Forrester Research study, security concerns are the main barrier in the enterprise Web services world. Certainly, Web service faces critical security challenges, since it exposes sensitive, vital information to the outside world through the Internet. In real-time applications, the triumph depends on secure, reliable communication with business partners. Hence, Microsoft and other software giants give top priority to the security and reliability of Web services. In the heterogeneous environment of Web services that provide security across multitier/multidomain applications, the security issues to be considered are secure communication, authentication, authorization, data protection, privacy (integrity and confidentiality), and nonrepudiation.

In real-time business applications, Web services can establish complex levels of access, and it has to be restricted to authorized clients. For authentication purposes (verification of the identity), the user or the client has to submit some form of credentials, such as username and password. Another area you have to pay attention to is the secure communication between the client and service. To implement secure communication, you can make use of either a transport-level security, such as Secure Sockets Layer (SSL) and Internet Protocol Security (IPSec), or a message-level security, such as WS-Security specification, based on the requirements. Transport-level (point-to-point) security is best suited in a tightly coupled Microsoft Windows operating system environment such as a corporate intranet, and message-level (end-to-end) security is best suited in a heterogeneous Web services environment. You can also employ custom security mechanisms such as SOAP headers. Web services security can be applied in three levels, according to the requirements:

- Transport-level (point-to-point) security, such as SSL/IPSec, ASP.NET authentication and authorization, and IIS authentication.
- Application-level (custom) security, such as SSL/custom SOAP headers.
- Message-level (end-to-end) security, such as the Global XML Architecture (GXA) initiative (WS-Security specification).

In this chapter we first look into the basic security techniques such as firewalls, SSL, virtual private networks (VPNs), and IIS authentication. Then, we learn how to authenticate Web services using SOAP headers and the XML encryption technologies, such as XML Signature, XML Encryption, XKMS (XML Key Management Specification), and Security Assertion Markup Language (SAML). Finally, we talk about the GXA specifications and WS-Security and how to implement that by employing Web Services Enhancements (WSE).

Basic Techniques in Securing Web Services

The basic procedures to be considered to secure Web services are shown in Table 10–1.

TABLE 10–1   *Basic Procedures to Secure Web Services*

Procedures	Description
Secure Connection	Secure Connection means the entire connection between the Web service client and the Web service has to be safe.
Authentication	Authentication is verifying the identity of the sender or receiver. (Who are you?)
Authorization	Authorization determines whether you are allowed to access this service and with what privileges.
Data Protection and Privacy	We have to take care in securing data not only during the transmission but also while storing it in a system. Data protection is the process of providing data confidentiality and privacy. SSL encryption (HTTPS) provides point-to-point data privacy between Web service requesters and Web service providers. XML encryption can be used to provide end-to-end data privacy.

TABLE 10-1	Basic Procedures to Secure Web Services (continued)
Procedures	**Description**
Integrity	Integrity means the assurance that the data is tamper-proof. XML Signature can be used to implement integrity. By means of XML signature, you can sign portions of XML documents so that end-to-end data integrity is provided across multiple systems/entities.
Nonrepudiation	When transactions are carried out, we may later have to prove that a particular action took place. Nonrepudiation confirms the occurrence of an action. It prevents a client or individual from denying an action after accessing it. Digital signatures can be used to implement nonrepudiation.

Secure Connection

The three most widely used and available techniques for the secure connection are

- Firewalls
- SSL
- VPNs

FIREWALLS

A firewall protects a private network from intruders outside the network. A firewall acts as a barrier for information moving into and out of the LAN/WAN. We can provide varied restrictions to different clients based on origin or identity by employing firewalls such as the Microsoft Internet Security and Acceleration (ISA) server. The use of a firewall method is constructive if you can identify which computers should access your Web service. Then, you can implement Internet Protocol Security (IPSec) or firewall rules to restrict access to computers of known IP addresses. But in real time, you may not know the IP address of all the computers. Moreover, any unauthorized user may access the resource by using an IP spoofing technique. IP spoofing is a technique by which an invader simulates the IP of an authorized user and can access the resource. However, a correctly configured firewall is not vulnerable to this.

A Web service is a programmable entity that provides a particular element of functionality, such as application logic, and is accessible to any number of potentially incongruent systems through the use of common data formats and protocols, such as XML and HTTP. In Web services the traffic flows through port 80 and port 443 similar to standard Web site traffic with the help of HTTP. One of the shortcomings in the security of Web services is in the use of HTTP. Of course, HTTP protocol is simple, and, by using it along with XML, we can effortlessly make the application logic accessible to various dissimilar systems and communicate with other applications. But the problem is that HTTP penetrates through the enterprise security firewalls and makes attack and invasion easy to accomplish from outside. Even though firewalls play a vital role in controlling malicious attacks, they cannot examine the SOAP contents to completely prevent the malicious attack from outside. Moreover, firewalls are intended only for network-level security, not for application-level security.

SSL AND HTTPS

SSL has been commonly established on the World Wide Web for authenticated and encrypted communication between clients and servers. At present, SSL along with the Transport Layer Security (TLS)[1] is widely used for securing online transactions. SSL offers confidentiality, data integrity, and authentication (server and client authentication). SSL is already employed by many enterprises to guard data across the Internet. SSL protocol was developed by Netscape, and it is a common technique used to secure the TCP/IP communication between HTTP requesters (Web browsers) and HTTP servers (Web servers). SSL employs public key cryptography[2] for Internet security. HTTPS secures communication by transmitting HTTP request and response over an SSL connection.

SSL provides some degree of protection to Web services. It secures the channel in which the transmission of data between the client and server occurs. In SSL the data is encrypted by the client/sender and then sent to the server. The data received is decrypted by the server/recipient and confirmed as being from a truthful sender. SSL provides a secure, reliable connection between authenticated endpoints. The secure channel is initiated with an exchange of messages through an SSL/TLS handshake. The handshake allows the server to authenticate itself to the client, and optionally the client to authenticate itself to the server. Usually, in business SSL sessions, only the server is authenticated. Then, the successive message is encrypted and digitally signed to assure its confidentiality and integrity. Figure 10–1 shows the transmission of data between the Web service client and a Web service over a secure channel.

The limitation of SSL is its low performance. SSL uses certificates and credentials, which drastically slow the overall performance compared to the performance of HTTP. SSL accelerators sometimes can improve the overall

---

1. TLS is SSL 3.0 with proprietary technology support removed, and it is maintained by the Internet Engineering Task Force (IETF). For more information on TLS visit *http:// www.ietf.org/rfc/rfc2246.txt*.
2. Public key cryptography is a technique that uses a pair of inversely related asymmetric keys for encryption and decryption. Each pair of keys consists of a public key and a private key. The public key is made public by distributing it widely. The private key is never distributed; it is always kept secret. Data that is encrypted with the public key can be decrypted only with the private key. On the other hand, data encrypted with the private key can be decrypted only with the public key. In 1976 researchers at Stanford University developed public key cryptography.

	SSL/TLS handshake	

FIGURE 10-1 *Transmission of data between a Web service client and Web service over a secure channel.*

performance. Another difficulty in using SSL is that it provides only point-to-point (transport-level) security. That means it provides complete security only between two authenticated entities. If there are more than two entities, and each entity is capable of examining and modifying the data, then SSL doesn't provide end-to-end security.

SSL secures communication only at the transport level, not at the message level. Therefore, data is secure only while traveling over the wire. If it reaches the message level, then the data is not secure. But in Web services data normally is passed through various entities before reaching its final destination. For example, suppose entity A wants to communicate with entity B over a secure channel. If there is an intermediate entity C, say, a gateway, then to route the data to entity B, the gateway may need to know the data. In this scenario SSL doesn't provide end-to-end security. Hence, there is a possibility of data corruption or attack in entity C at the message level while the data is transmitted between entity A and entity B. Therefore, for Web services, SSL can be used only in an environment where data does not route through intermediate application nodes and has no multiple hops. That is, we can use SSL in a tightly coupled Microsoft Windows operating system environment.

NEED FOR END-TO-END SECURITY

SSL/TLS provides security features such as data integrity and data confidentiality, and facilitates point-to-point secure sessions. Similar to SSL/TLS, IPSec[3] is also widely employed for the secure sessions.

---

3. IPSec is designed to provide interoperable, high-quality, cryptographically based security for IPv4 and IPv6. It offers security services such as access control, connectionless integrity, data origin authentication, protection against replays (a form of partial sequence integrity), confidentiality (encryption), and limited traffic flow confidentiality. These services are provided at the IP layer, offering protection for IP and/or upper-layer protocols.

Current Web service application topologies comprise a wide range of systems, such as mobile devices, gateways, proxies, load balancers, demilitarized zones (DMZs), and outsourced data centers. Web services have a globally distributed, complex, multidomain and heterogeneous environment, so the SOAP messages must be routed to one or more intermediaries before reaching the final destination, or receiver. The problem is that if the data transmission occurs between the intermediaries beyond the transport layer, then both the data integrity and other security information maybe lost. We need an end-to-end message-level security, and not just point-to-point security, as provided by SSL/TLS. Therefore, for a complete Web service security architecture, we have to incorporate both transport-layer and application-layer end-to-end message-level security mechanisms. Figure 10–2 illustrates the point-to-point and end-to-end configuration.

CONFIGURING SSL IN WINDOWS 2000

To secure XML Web services with SSL in Windows 2000, the following steps have to be done:

- **Configure your Web server for SSL:** To facilitate SSL support, install an SSL server certificate on the server. If you acquire a server certificate from a third-party certificate authority, then skip to next step.
- **Install CA's certificate on the client:** If you use your own certificate services, you have to install your CA's certificate on the client as a trusted root certificate authority.
- **Modify WSDL from HTTP to HTTPS:** The address of your Web service has to start with **https** instead of **http**. Revise the Web Services Description Language (WSDL) files accordingly. Specify an https URL

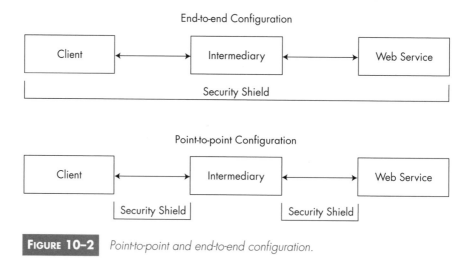

FIGURE 10–2 *Point-to-point and end-to-end configuration.*

as the location of the Web service during the addition of Web reference in Visual Studio .NET. Now we can consume the Web service over SSL.

- **Enforcing SSL-only access:** If the Web service is intended to accept only SSL requests, then configure the virtual directory as follows.

    1. Right-click the virtual directory where the Web service resides, then click Properties.
    2. Click the Directory Security tab, and then click Edit under Secure Communications.
    3. Click Require secure channel (SSL) and then click OK twice.

VIRTUAL PRIVATE NETWORK

1. A VPN connects multiple networks, wireless users, and other remote users. Thus, VPN is an extension of private networks, such as WAN, and is more efficient than WAN, since it uses the already existing Internet infrastructure.
2. A VPN facilitates a secure connection through which data passes between multiple networks over the Internet.

Authentication and Authorization

Authentication is the process of confirming the identity of a client user/application before permitting the user/application to access a resource. For example, users who request the resources have to submit some set of credentials, such as user ID and password. In return, the user receives a security token from the server. In the Web services world, the security token may be in the form of a cookie placed on the user's browser, a session ID stored on the server, and so on. The simplest method to implement an authentication mechanism for a Web service is to use the authentication features of the HTTP.

Authentication Mechanisms for HTTP

Microsoft IIS version 5.0 supports several authentication mechanisms for HTTP, such as Basic, Digest, Windows Integrated, and Client certificate.

BASIC

In Basic authentication, the user is prompted for a login ID and password. If the user provides a valid Windows account, a connection is established. The main drawback in basic authentication is that Web browsers transmit the collected information in an unencrypted plaintext form to the Web server. By observing communications between networks, one can easily interrupt and decipher these passwords by using publicly available tools. We therefore recommend using HTTPS (i.e., Basic over SSL).

DIGEST

Digest authentication is similar to Basic authentication. The only difference is that it entails a different way of transmitting the authentication credentials. In this method hashing is employed to transmit authentication credentials to the server in a secure manner. One cannot decrypt or decipher the original text from the hash or message digest. A message digest is a unique value derived from the message content. However, this method is not supported in many platforms other than Microsoft Windows. Internet Explorer 5.0 and later browsers support Digest authentication, but other browsers, such as Netscape Navigator, do not support Digest authentication natively.

INTEGRATED WINDOWS AUTHENTICATION

This Integrated Windows authentication method is suitable for intranet scenarios. The user's credentials are transmitted to the server using NT LAN Manager (NTLM), NT Challenge/Response (NTCR), or Kerberos.[4] The problem in using Integrated Windows authentication is that it does not work over HTTP proxy connections or other firewalls. IIS authorizes access to the Web service if the credentials submitted by the user match a valid user account. In Integrated Windows authentication it does not initially ask users for a username and password. The current Windows user information on the client computer is utilized for the Integrated Windows authentication. The browser asks the user for a Windows user account if, and only if, there is an occurrence of failure to identify the user during the initial authentication exchange. Figure 10-3 shows the Internet Services Manager settings. To configure this method, check the Integrated Windows authentication box in the Internet Services Manager dialog box, as shown in Figure 10–4.

CLIENT CERTIFICATES

In this method, to access the service, clients have to get a client certificate from a mutually trusted third-party organization. Then, certificates are mapped to user accounts, which are used by IIS for authorizing access to the Web service. Client certificates are electronic documents that contain

---

4. Kerberos is a freely available network-authentication protocol developed at the Massachusetts Institute of Technology (MIT). It is an open-source protocol, which uses shared secret key cryptography to authenticate users and provides a means of verifying the identities of principals (e.g., a workstation user or a network server) on an open (unprotected) network.

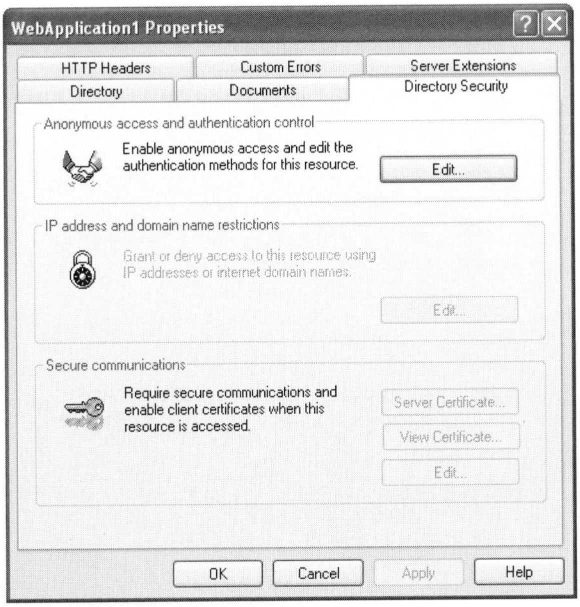

FIGURE 10-3   *Internet Services Manager settings.*

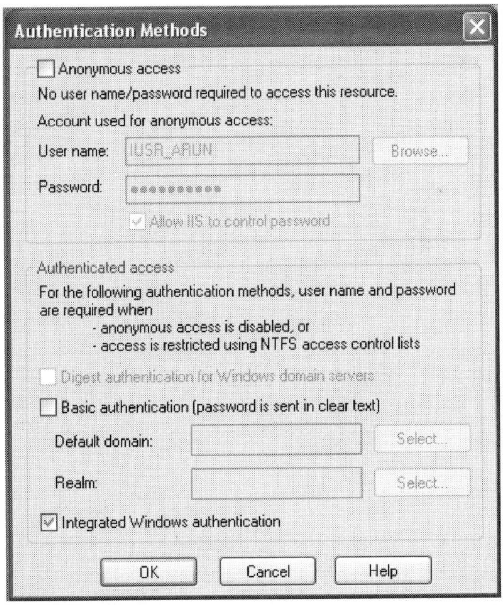

FIGURE 10-4   *Internet Services Manager settings for Integrated Windows authentication.*

identifying information such as the user data and the organization that issued the certificate.

Another alternative to IIS authentication schemes is the use of a custom mechanism, such as transmitting client credentials through a SOAP header.

Authenticate Web Service Using SOAPHEADER

The SOAP Message Architecture

The SOAP message architecture consists of an Envelope which contains an optional Header and a compulsory Body element, as illustrated in Figure 10–5. The Body element includes the data specific to the message. The optional Header element encloses some extra information related to the message. Each child element of the Header element is called a SOAP header. You can employ SOAP headers in ASP.NET Web services to incorporate additional information with SOAP messages. As the SOAP specification doesn't strictly define the contents of a SOAP header, the header usually contains information processed by the infrastructure. **<soap:Header>** may be used to exchange information, such as authentication, session ID, and transaction ID. Thus, SOAP header elements are a means of extending SOAP functionality.

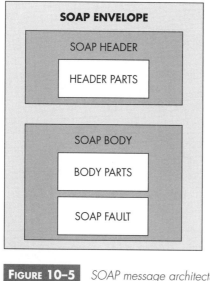

FIGURE 10–5   *SOAP message architecture.*

Let's create an Authenticate Web service that authenticates the user based on username and password using the **SOAPHEADER** base class, and develop a Web client for that Web service using Visual Studio .NET.

```
using System.Web;
using System.Web.Services;
using System.Web.Services.Protocols;
namespace SoapHeader1
{
public class Header : SoapHeader
  {
    public string Username;
    public string Password;
  }
[WebService(Namespace="http://www.phptr.com")]
public class AuthenticateWebService :
System.Web.Services.WebService
  {
    public AuthenticateWebService ()
    { InitializeComponent();
    }
  //Web Service Designer generated code.

[WebMethod(Description = "Using SOAP Headers in ASP.NET Web
Services")][SoapHeader("HeaderMemberVariable")]
    public string Authenticate()
    {
     // Process the SoapHeader.
      if (HeaderMemberVariable.Username == "Adminarun" &&
HeaderMemberVariable.Password == "Anystrongpassword")
      {
      return "Welcome! You have successfully logged in";
      }
      return "Invalid User ID and/or Password!";
    }
  }
}
```

- Create a class named **Header** deriving from **SoapHeader** and representing the data passed in the SOAP header.
- Add two public string members (**Username**; **Password**) to the **WebService** class.
- Add a member variable (**HeaderMemberVariable**) of the type deriving from **SoapHeader**.
- Apply a **SoapHeaderAttribute** to the Web Service method, such as **[SoapHeader("HeaderMemberVariable")]**.
- In the **WebService** method access the **MemberName** property to process the data sent in the SOAP header.

- Check this condition: **HeaderMemberVariable.Username == "** Adminarun " **&& HeaderMemberVariable.Password == "** Anystrongpassword ".
- If it satisfies the condition, return **"Welcome! You have successfully logged in"**.
- If it does not satisfy the condition, return the string **"Invalid User ID and/or Password!"**
- In the test form you will notice the message "No test form is available, as this service or method does not support the HTTP GET protocol."

In the Internet Explorer test page, you can see the sample SOAP request incorporating header elements, as shown in the following code.

```
<?xml version="1.0" encoding="utf-8"?>
<soap:Envelope xmlns:xsi="http://www.w3.org/2001/XMLSchema-
instance" xmlns:xsd="http://www.w3.org/2001/XMLSchema"
xmlns:soap="http://schemas.xmlsoap.org/soap/envelope/">
  <soap:Header>
    <MyHeader xmlns="http://www.phptr.com/">
      <Username>string</Username>
      <Password>string</Password>
    </MyHeader>
  </soap:Header>
  <soap:Body>
    <Authenticate xmlns="http://www.phptr.com/" />
  </soap:Body>
</soap:Envelope>
```

Creating a Proxy with Visual Studio .NET

Create an ASP.NET Web form and rename it **Authenticateclient.aspx**. Add two text boxes for Username and Password, a Label to display the result, and a button. After completing the GUI, add a reference to the project by clicking Project | Add Web Reference. Then click the link Web References on Local Web Server or type the required service name in the address. You can view the test page, shown in Figure 10–6. Click the Add Reference button. You can view the Discovery file (DISCO) and WSDL file in the Web References node in the Solution explorer.

CREATING A WEB FORM CLIENT

To process SOAP headers in a Web service client, the basic procedures are as follows. Create a new instance of the class representing the SOAP header.

```
localhost.Header aa = new localhost.Header();
```

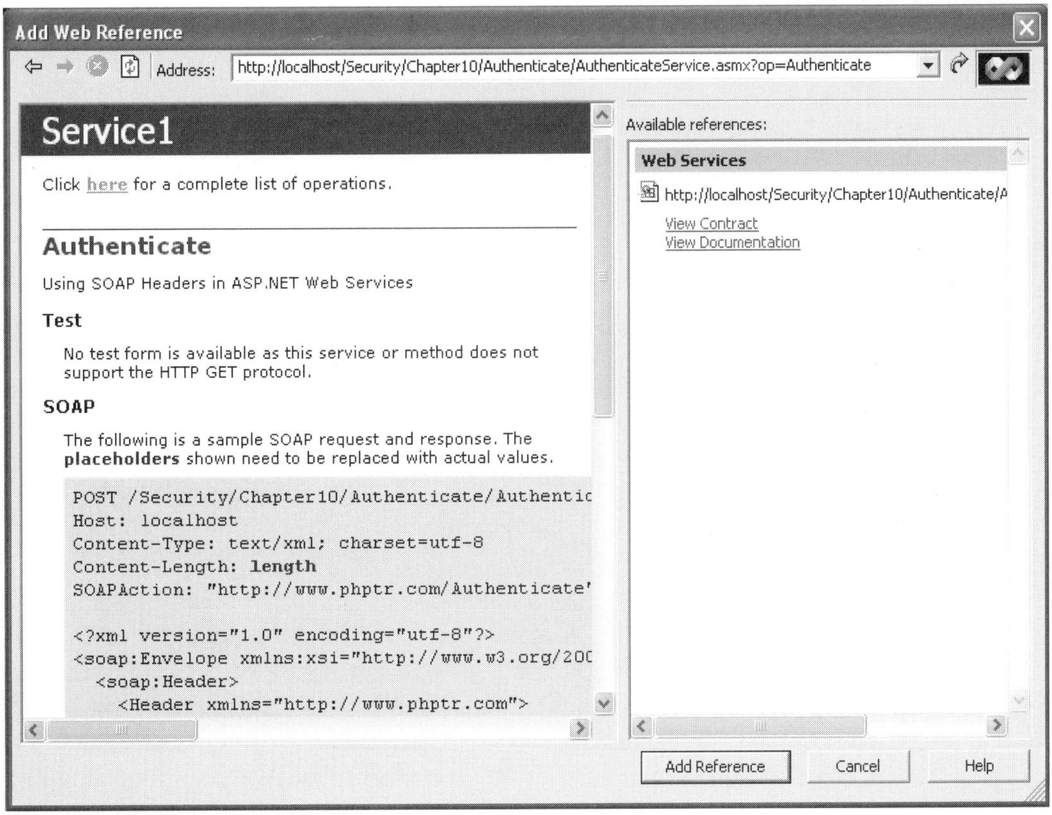

FIGURE 10-6   Add Web Reference dialog box.

Assign the text box values for the SOAP header.

```
aa.Username = TextBox1.Text;
aa.Password = TextBox2.Text;
```

Create a new instance of the proxy class.

```
localhost.AuthenticateWebService proxy = new
localhost.AuthenticateWebService();
```

Assign the SOAP header object to the member variable of the proxy class.

```
proxy.HeaderValue = aa;
```

Invoke the method on the proxy class that communicates with the Web service method, and display the result in the label control.

```
string results = proxy.Authenticate();
Label1.Text =results;
```

The output of the **Authenticateclient.aspx** is shown in Figure 10–7.

Again, if you transmit SOAP messages through HTTP instead of HTTPS, the client credentials will be passed as plaintext.

XML Security Technologies

XML security technologies work at the message layer, so they provide end-to-end security. XML security technologies that address the security issues are

- XML Signature
- XML Encryption
- XKMS
- SAML

Integrity

Integrity means the assurance of whether the data is tamper-proof. Integrity is achieved by employing XML Signature and hash algorithms. In using hash

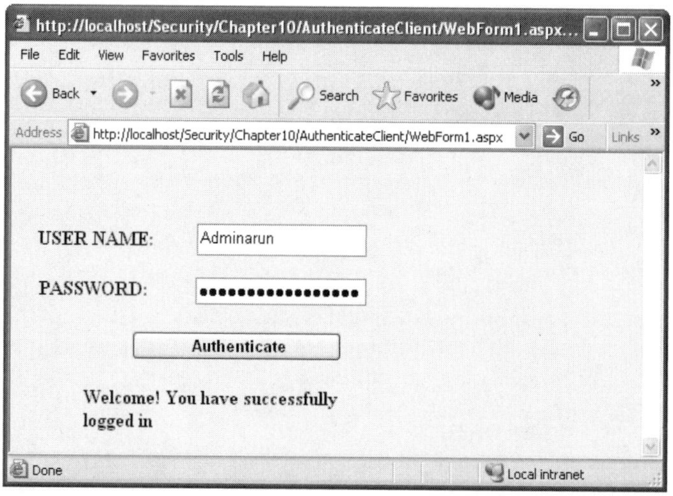

FIGURE 10–7   *Output of Authenticateclient.asmx with correct username and password.*

algorithms while transmitting the data, a hash of that data can be sent along with it. The server can then compare a hash that it computes on the received data with the hash that accompanied the received data. If the two values are equivalent, then the received data must be the same as the data from which the received hash was created. It is computed using a hashing algorithm such as Message Digest 5 (MD5) or Secure Hash Algorithm (SHA-1). One cannot reconstruct the original data from it, since hashing is a one-way process. A digital signature is nothing but an encrypted hash.

XML Signature

XML digital signature technology is a combined effort of the W3C (World Wide Web Consortium) and the IETF (Internet Engineering Task Force). The XML Signature standard facilitates signing parts of XML documents and providing end-to-end data integrity across multiple systems. An XML digital signature confirms the nonrepudiation and message integrity of transmitted XML data across Web services.

XML Signature is the foundation for XKMS, WS-Security, SAML, and other XML-related technologies that authenticate using digital signature. XML digital signatures are signatures available in the XML format that ensure authentication and originality of the parent document. A basic feature of XML signature is the ability to sign a particular portion of the XML document rather than the entire document. An XML Signature can sign more than one type of resource, such as a particular portion of an XML document, character-encoded data (HTML), and binary-encoded data (JPG).

HOW XML DIGITAL SIGNATURE OFFERS NONREPUDIATION AND INTEGRITY

By employing an XML digital signature, you can ensure that the received message is valid and has not been tampered with. With the help of the sender's private key, the service requester signs the document and sends it together with the data of the message. The service provider can then verify the signature with the sender's public key and thereby ensure message integrity.

A digital signature is created by employing the sender's private key. The private key is retained by the sender. No one except the sender can access the private key. Hence, the sender is accountable for keeping the private key private. The recipient verifies the digital signature by employing the associated public key. The public key can be used only when the private key is authentic. Thus, by using an XML digital signature, you can assure message integrity and nonrepudiation. Usually, a small portion of the document (hash or digest) rather than the entire document is transformed by employing a private key. The hashing algorithm is very sensitive to any modifications in the source document. Hence, a recipient can confirm that the document was not altered by comparing the hash that was sent to the recipient with the hash computed from the received document.

TYPES OF XML DIGITAL SIGNATURES

- **Enveloped Signatures:** The generated signature is implanted within the signed XML element itself.
- **Enveloping Signatures:** The generated XML digital signature enfolds the signed XML elements, which it authenticates.
- **Detached Signatures:** The signed XML document and the signature are detached separately.

EXAMPLE OF AN XML DIGITAL SIGNATURE

```
<?xml version='1.0'?>
<!-- Detached XML Signature -->
<Signature Id="MySignature"
xmlns="http://www.w3.org/2000/09/xmldsig#">
<SignedInfo>
<CanonicalizationMethod Algorithm= "http://www.w3.org/TR/
    2001/REC-xml-c14n-20010315"/>
<SignatureMethod Algorithm= "http://www.w3.org/2000/09/
    xmldsig#dsa-sha1"/>
<Reference URI=              "http://www.w3.org/TR/2000/
    REC-xhtml1-20000126/">
<Transforms>
<Transform Algorithm=       "http://www.w3.org/TR/2001/
    REC-xml-c14n-20010315"/>
</Transforms>
<DigestMethod Algorithm=    "http://www.w3.org/2000/09/
    xmldsig#sha1"/>
<DigestValue>ak2r9u45n1045gan3435es503hkk8543fh68...
    </DigestValue>
</Reference>
</SignedInfo>
<SignatureValue>kf84jflk40klfk030klkdf0g55tdghdh6...
    </SignatureValue>
<KeyInfo>
   <KeyValue>
      <DSAKeyValue>
         <p>...</p><X>...</X><A>...</A><Y>...</Y>
      </DSAKeyValue>
   </KeyValue>
</KeyInfo>
</Signature>
```

XML SIGNATURE ELEMENTS

The **Signature** element is the root element of all the standard XML Digital Signatures. It contains the following three main elements.

- SignedInfo (<SignedInfo>...</SignedInfo>)
- SignatureValue (<SignatureValue>...</SignatureValue>)
- KeyInfo (<KeyInfo>...</KeyInfo>)

Let's look at the elements of the XML signature in detail.

- **<Signature ID>** attribute: This attribute identifies the signature.
- **<SignedInfo>** element: This element contains all the necessary information concerning the signed resource.
- **<CanonicalizationMethod Algorithm= "http://www.w3.org/TR/ 2001/REC-xml-c14n-20010315"/>**: It is feasible that two similar XML documents may enclose the same data but diverge only in their textual representations, such as white spaces, line breaks, and element representations. *Canonicalization* is the process of ignoring the small variations in the XML documents so that the logically equivalent documents create the same message digest in spite of structure. Therefore, XML information sets have to be canonized before their bit representation is extracted for signature processing. This helps prevent erroneous confirmation results. The above line indicates the algorithm used for canonicalization.
- **<SignatureMethod Algorithm= "http://www.w3.org/2000/09/ xmldsig#dsa-sha1"/>**: This is the algorithm used for digital signature generation (convert the canonicalized **SignedInfo** into the **SignatureValue**).
- **<Reference URI= "http://www.w3.org/TR/2000/REC-xhtml1-20000126/">**: This attribute contains the location of the signed data (optional).
- **<Transforms>**: This element denotes an ordered list of processing steps that were carried out on the referenced resource's content before it was digested.
- **<DigestMethod Algorithm= "http://www.w3.org/2000/09/ xmldsig#sha1"/>**: This attribute specifies the digest algorithm that was used (compulsory).
- **<DigestValue>ak2r9u45n1045gan3435es503hkk8543fh68... </DigestValue>**: The **Digest** value contains the message digest generated by employing the algorithm specified in the **DigestMethod Algorithm** attribute.

- **<SignatureValue>kf84jflk40klfk030klkdf0g55tdghdh6...</Signa-
tureValue>**: The **Signature** value contains the message digest generated by employing the algorithm specified in the **SignatureMethod
Algorithm** attribute.
- **<KeyInfo>** element: This element provides references to the public
key of the sender, which can then be used by the receiver to validate
the digital signature and resources (optional). Normally, the **KeyInfo**
element encloses public keys, key names, certificates and so on. In
the previous example we employ a DSA type of key.

Data Protection and Privacy

Data protection is the process of offering data confidentiality and privacy.
Confidentiality and privacy mean protecting the sensitive information or data
from unauthorized persons. Confidentiality and privacy can be achieved by
encrypting the data using a crypto-algorithm. In SSL we encrypt the entire
data and send the data to one or more receivers through a secure channel.
But if we want to encrypt the different parts of the same XML document separately, then XML encryption comes into the picture. By means of XML
encryption, you can encrypt the needed sensitive data (portions of the message), such as credit card information, and permit header information and
other data to be used for routing purposes. This facilitates end-to-end data
privacy by keeping the encrypted data up to the final destination.

XML Encryption

The W3C XML Encryption Working Group, the joint effort of the W3C (World
Wide Web Consortium) and the IETF (Internet Engineering Task Force),
launched the XML encryption standards and specifications. In March 2002 the
Working Group released the Candidate Recommendation Specification for
XML encryption. XML encryption stipulates encryption syntax for XML and the
process for encrypting whole or partial XML documents. XML encryption is
the process of encrypting and decrypting digital XML content, using certain
algorithms. The main element in the XML encryption syntax is the **EncryptedData** element, which, with the **EncryptedKey** element, is used to transport encryption keys from the creator to a known receiver.

Data to be encrypted can be arbitrary data, an XML document, an XML
element, or XML element content. When an XML element or element content
is encrypted, the **EncryptedData** element replaces the element or content,
respectively, in the encrypted version of the XML document. When an entire
XML document is encrypted, then the **EncryptedData** element may become

the root of a new document or a child element in an application-chosen XML document.

XML ENCRYPTION SYNTAX

Expressed in shorthand form, the **EncryptedData** element has the following structure, where

- ? denotes zero or one occurrence.
- + denotes one or more occurrences.
- * denotes zero or more occurrences.

The empty element tag means the element must be empty.

```
<EncryptedData Id? Type?>
  <EncryptionMethod/>?
    <ds:KeyInfo>
      <EncryptedKey>?
      <AgreementMethod>?
      <ds:KeyName>?
      <ds:RetrievalMethod>?
      <ds:*>?
    </ds:KeyInfo>?
    <CipherData>
      <CipherValue>?
      <CipherReference URI?>?
    </CipherData>
  <EncryptionProperties>?
</EncryptedData>
```

The **CipherData** element can either envelop or reference the raw encrypted data.

EXAMPLE OF XML ENCRYPTION SYNTAX

```
<?xml version='1.0'?>
  <AuthorInfo xmlns='http://objectinnovations.com/Author'>
    <CompanyName>Object Innovations</CompanyName>
      <Author>
        <Name>G.GNANA ARUN GANESH</Name>
        <Age>23</Age>
        <Salary>50000</Salary>
        <Department>.NET</Department>
      </Author>
  </AuthorInfo>
```

ENCRYPTING XML ELEMENT CONTENT (ELEMENTS)

The following code shows an XML structure with the **<Salary>** element encrypted.

```
<?xml version='1.0'?>
  <AuthorInfo xmlns='http://objectinnovations.com/Author'>
   <CompanyName>Object Innovations</CompanyName>
   <Author>
     <Name>G.GNANA ARUN GANESH</Name>
     <Age>23</Age>
       <EncryptedData Type='http://www.w3.org/2001/04/
          xmlenc#Element' xmlns='http://www.w3.org/2001/
          04/xmlenc#'>
       <CipherData>
          <CipherValue>A23d42U56N</CipherValue>
       </CipherData>
     </EncryptedData>
   </Author>
  </AuthorInfo>
```

ENCRYPTED DOCUMENT WITH THE ENTIRE CONTENTS HIDDEN

```
<?xml version='1.0'?>
  <EncryptedData xmlns='http://www.w3.org/2001/04/xmlenc#'
Type='http://www.isi.edu/in-notes/iana/assignments/media-
types/text/xml'>
    <CipherData>
       <CipherValue> A23d42U56N </CipherValue>
    </CipherData>
  </EncryptedData>
```

SUPER-ENCRYPTION: ENCRYPTING ENCRYPTEDDATA

Super-encryption enables encryption of XML documents containing sections that are already encrypted. During super-encryption of an **EncryptedData** or **EncryptedKey** element, you must encrypt the entire element. Encrypting only the content of these elements or encrypting selected child elements is invalid.

Different elements of an XML document can be encrypted separately using XML encryption. When the data is encrypted, the ciphertext is created. It is represented in base64 encoding, which uses 64 characters to represent binary data. In both enveloped and enveloping signatures, the ciphertext is stored in the **CipherValue** inside the **CipherData** element. The **CipherReference** references a URL of the location of the ciphertext in a detached signature.

XML Key Management Specification (XKMS)

XKMS is a specification that facilitates acquisition of key information (values, certificates, and management or trust data) from a Web service. The XKMS contains two parts:

- XML Key Information Service Specification (X-KISS)
- XML Key Registration Service Specification (X-KRSS)

XKMS provides an XML interface to PKI (Public Key Infrastructure),[5] including distribution, confirmation, and key management. The PKI may be based upon a different specification, such as X.509/PKIX, SPKI, or PGP. XKMS stipulates a method for XML-based clients to obtain cryptographic keys in a secured manner. A key objective of the X-KISS protocol design is to minimize the complexity of applications using XML signature. X-KRSS describes a protocol for registration of public key information.

Security Assertion Markup Language (SAML)

The SAML specification is an XML-based standard and messaging protocol designed to assist the secure exchange of authentication and authorization information between business partners in spite of their security systems. The Organization for the Advancement of Structured Information Standards (OASIS) establishes this emerging standard SAML (single sign-on).

SAML substitutes two previous efforts by OASIS to create an authorization and authentication protocol: S2ML and AuthXML. SAML addresses the authentication and authorization of users. SAML is designed not only for user logon to a system, but also for automated B2B transactions that need a secure transaction between the two parties. Single sign-on is the ability of the system to authenticate a client only once and permit the client to access other resources available with the same credentials.

Global XML Web Services Architecture (GXA)

Web services are built on XML, SOAP, WSDL, and Universal Description, Discovery, and Integration (UDDI) specifications. These baseline specifications offer the foundation for application integration and aggregation. But higher-level functionality, such as security, routing, reliable messaging, and transactions, have to be added to the Web services architecture to facilitate the development of Web services in real-time scenarios at the enterprise level. In April 2001 Microsoft and IBM offered an architectural sketch for the evolution of

---

5. PKI is a network security architecture that offers an improved security with the help of cryptographically derived keys. PKI incorporates public key cryptography with digital signatures for authenticating users in a transaction.

XML Web services at the W3C Workshop on Web Services to provide a solution to the current problems faced by the programmers and for the requirement of additional specifications.[6]

This sketch was the prototype of the Microsoft Global XML Web Services Architecture. The GXA[7] is a protocol framework designed to provide a consistent model for building infrastructure-level protocols for Web services and applications. Microsoft plans to submit the GXA specifications for standardization, which enables GXA as an open architecture. GXA is simply a series of modular, additional specifications that extend SOAP and facilitate the development of better real-time Web services. GXA is intended for a wide range of Web services scenarios, ranging from B2B and EAI solutions to peer-to-peer applications and B2C services.

GLOBAL XML WEB SERVICES SPECIFICATIONS

The GXA specifications and the definitions provided by Microsoft are as follows:

- **WS-Security:** WS-Security is flexible and is designed to be used as the basis for the construction of a wide variety of security models, including PKI, Kerberos, and SSL. Particularly WS-Security provides support for multiple security tokens, multiple trust domains, multiple signature formats, and multiple encryption technologies.
- **WS-Routing:** WS-Routing is a simple, stateless, SOAP-based protocol for routing SOAP messages in an asynchronous manner over a variety of transports like TCP, UDP, and HTTP.
- **WS-Inspection:** The WS-Inspection specification provides an XML format for assisting in the inspection of a site for available services and a collection of rules for how inspection-related information should be made available for consumption. A WS-Inspection document provides a means for aggregating references to preexisting service description documents that have been authored in any number of formats.
- **WS-Referral:** WS-Referral is a protocol that enables the routing strategies used by SOAP nodes in a message path to be dynamically configured.
- **WS-Coordination:** This specification is an extensible framework for providing protocols that coordinate the actions of distributed applications. Such coordination protocols are used to support a number of applications, including those that need to reach consistent agreement on the outcome of distributed transactions.

---

6. For more information on the sketch "Security in a Web Service World: A Proposed Architecture and Roadmap," visit *http://msdn.microsoft.com/webservices/ default.aspx?pull=/library/en-us/dnwssecur/html/securitywhitepaper.asp*.
7. For more information on Microsoft GXA and its specifications, visit *http:// msdn.microsoft.com/webservices/understanding/gxa/*.

- **WS-Transaction:** This specification explains coordination types that are used with the extensible coordination framework described in the WS-Coordination specification.
- **WS-ReliableMessaging:** WS-ReliableMessaging describes a protocol that allows messages to be delivered reliably between distributed applications in the presence of software component, system, or network failures.
- **WS-Addressing:** WS-Addressing offers transport-neutral mechanisms to address Web services and messages.
- **WS-Attachment:** This specification defines an abstract model for SOAP attachments and, based on this model, defines a mechanism for encapsulating a SOAP message and zero or more attachments in a Direct Internet Message Encapsulation (DIME) message.

Figure 10–8 shows Microsoft's Web Services Architecture (Extended Foundation).

WS-Security

WS-Security[8] is a specification that facilitates development of secure Web services. On April 11, 2002, IBM, Microsoft, and VeriSign jointly developed a

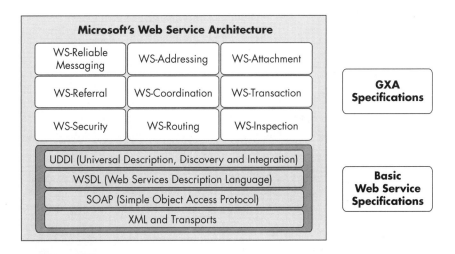

FIGURE 10-8   *Microsoft's Web Services Architecture (Extended Foundation).*

---

8. For more information on the WS-Security specification and for the latest specifications, visit *http://msdn.microsoft.com/webservices/understanding/ default.aspx?pull=/library/en-us/dnglobspec/html/wssecurspecindex.asp.*

specification for Web Services Security (WS-Security). The specification aims to help enterprises build secure and broadly interoperable Web services and applications. Even though WS-Security doesn't offer an absolute solution to the security problems, it provides a way to build other specifications, keeping WS-Security as groundwork. Figure 10–9 illustrates the evolving WS-Security Roadmap.

WS-Security is a baseline specification and assists in sending secure messages. It explains how to attach security tokens, including binary security tokens such as X.509 certificates and Kerberos tickets, to SOAP messages.

WS Initial Specifications

WS-SECURITY

WS-Security is a specification that provides different ways of authentication by attaching signature and encryption header elements to SOAP messages that facilitate protection of the integrity and confidentiality of messages exchanged between business applications.

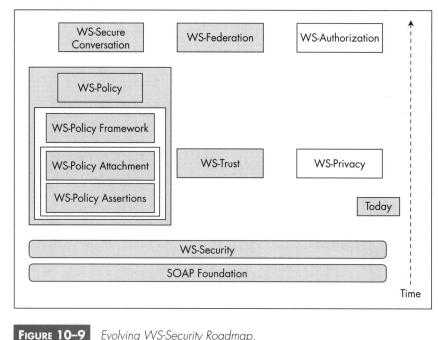

FIGURE 10–9 *Evolving WS-Security Roadmap.*

WS-POLICY

WS-Policy is a specification that describes the capabilities of the security policies on intermediaries and endpoints (e.g., required security tokens, supported encryption algorithms, privacy rules). It describes the business, security, trust, and privacy policies that manage how business applications integrate with one another. The WS-Policy has been further refined to include four documents: Web Services Policy Framework (WS-Policy), Web Services Policy Attachment (WS-PolicyAttachment), Web Services Policy Assertions Language (WS-PolicyAssertions), and Web Services Security Policy (WS-Security Policy). WS-Security-Policy was published as a public specification on December 18, 2002.

WS-TRUST

WS-Trust defines extensions that build on WS-Security to request and issue security tokens, and it defines how to manage trust relationships between businesses. It is a specification that defines a framework for trust models that enable Web services to interoperate securely. WS-Trust was published as a public specification on December 18, 2002.

WS-SECURE CONVERSATION

WS-SecureConversation is a specification that describes how to control and authenticate message exchanges between Web services and clients, including security context exchange in a complex business transaction. WS-SecureConversation was published as a public specification on December 18, 2002.

WS-FEDERATION

WS-Federation is a specification that defines mechanisms that are used to enable identity, account, attribute, authentication, and authorization federation across different trust realms. WS-Federation explains a model for integrating mismatched security mechanisms (e.g., one party using PKI system and another one using Kerberos system) or similar mechanisms (e.g., both parties using Kerberos system) that are deployed within different domains. WS-Federation and the Federation profiles (WS-Federation Active Requestor Profile and WS-Federation Passive Requestor Profile) were published as public specifications on July 8, 2003.

Next Steps of Specifications

These Web services specifications are in the works under OASIS.

WS-PRIVACY

WS-Privacy is a specification that describes how Web services and requesters specify privacy policies and preferences.

WS-AUTHORIZATION

WS-Authorization facilitates the management of authorization data and authorization policies.

Why WS-Security?

As we discussed, present HTTP-based and HTTPS-based security offers point-to-point security only. But real-time Web services need end-to-end security. The data security and integrity have to be protected over multiple hops. WS-Security addresses how to maintain a secure context over a multipoint message path and provide an end-to-end security. Moreover, WS-Security is flexible and extensible. It incorporates a wide variety of existing security models and encryption technologies.

WS-SECURITY IN DETAIL

WS-Security makes use of various familiar and existing security standards and specifications. WS-Security facilitates the combination of current, existing security standards, such as Kerberos, PKI, XML Encryption, XML Signature, and SSL, for securing Web services. WS-Security offers a framework to implant the existing technologies into a SOAP message in a transport-neutral fashion. WS-Security also supports propagating security tokens, such as X.509 certificates and Kerberos tickets, along with multiple security tokens across multiple trust domains by employing multiple signature formats and multiple encryption technologies.

In WS-Security the SOAP header element is employed to transmit security-related data. For example, when an XML signature is used, the header can enclose information such as the key type used, and signature value. Likewise, the header contains encryption information when we employ XML encryption. Thus, the WS-Security indicates how to implant the security information provided by other specifications within a SOAP message instead of specifying the format.

Apart from implementing the existing security specifications in the SOAP header, WS-Security spells out a method by which we can transmit simple user credentials through the **UsernameToken** element. It also defines how to send binary tokens. As all the security information is enclosed in the SOAP part of the message, WS-Security provides end-to-end security for Web services. WS-Security provides enrichments to the existing SOAP messaging to offer quality of protection. Figure 10–10 illustrates the SOAP message format. For securing Web services, WS-Security offers three key mechanisms:

- Security token propagation
- Message integrity
- Message confidentiality

Security Token Propagation

In this standard mechanism the security token is incorporated into the SOAP message. Security token propagation means the security credentials are transmitted from a sender to a receiver. The sender and receiver may be the client, the XML Web service, or an intermediary. Since the token is included with the SOAP message, it is transparent to the outside world. The possibility of tampering with the security tokens by intermediaries is high, as the security token is in cleartext. Proper safety measures have to be taken by employing message integrity and message confidentiality. WS-Security offers only a general-purpose mechanism for associating the token with the SOAP message. It doesn't demand a particular type of security token. It is flexible and supports a variety of security tokens.

The necessary security-related information, including security tokens, are added to a **<Security>** SOAP header for the targeted receiver (SOAP actor) by the client or intermediaries. If the security-related information present in the SOAP message is valid, then the request is accepted; otherwise, it is rejected. A SOAP message, before reaching the receiver, can contain zero or more **<Security>** SOAP headers, since the SOAP message is routed via multiple intermediaries.

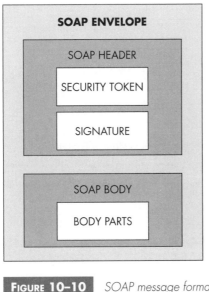

FIGURE 10–10   *SOAP message format in WS-Security.*

WS-SECURITY EXAMPLE

The following sample SOAP message with a **<Security>** SOAP header illustrates a message sender's credentials (X.509 certificate) for the recipient **http://www.arunmicrosystems.netfirms.com/Gnv.asmx.**

```
<S:Envelope xmlns:S="http://www.w3.org/2001/12/soap-envelope"
xmlns:wsse="http://schemas.xmlsoap.org/ws/2002/04/secext">
    <S:Header>
        ...
        <wsse:Security S:actor=" http://
www.arunmicrosystems.netfirms.com/Gnv.asmx " >
            <wsse:BinarySecurityToken
xmlns:wsse="http://schemas.xmlsoap.org/ws/2002/04/secext"
            ValueType="wsse:X509v3"
            wsu:Id="X509Token"
            EncodingType="wsse:Base64Binary">
            AwSaRgguTQmVkopX...
        </wsse:BinarySecurityToken>
    </wsse:Security>
        ...
    </S:Header>
    ...
</S:Envelope>
```

The namespaces used in the WS-Security document are shown in Table 10–2.

TABLE 10–2	*Namespaces Used in WS-Security*
Prefix	**Namespace**
S	http://www.w3.org/2001/12/soap-envelope
Ds	http://www.w3.org/2000/09/xmldsig#
Xenc	http://www.w3.org/2001/04/xmlenc#
M	http://schemas.xmlsoap.org/rp
Wsse	http://schemas.xmlsoap.org/ws/2002/07/secext
Wsu	http://schemas.xmlsoap.org/ws/2002/07/utility

Any recipient can use the security-related information within the **<Security>** header if the actor attribute is absent. The **<Security>** header block contains the security-related information for the message.

```
<wsse:BinarySecurityToken
...
</wsse:BinarySecurityToken>
```

The previous code denotes a security token that is associated with the message. In this case we specify an X.509 certificate that is encoded as base64.

Message Integrity

WS-Security defines a mechanism by which the recipients can confirm whether the message originated from the appropriate sender and the message was not tampered with during the transit. For this purpose WS-Security employs the XML Signature specification. The integrity mechanisms are designed to support multiple signatures, potentially by multiple actors, and to be extensible to support additional signature formats. As we discussed, the XML Signature specification defines a **<Signature>** element along with subelements for specifying the details of a signature.

WS-Security builds upon this XML Signature, incorporating a **<SecurityTokenReference>** element and a **<Signature>** element to reference the security token specified in the **<Security>** SOAP header. With the contents of the SOAP message and the security token, the XML Signature is cryptographically computed. The message recipient verifies the validity of the signature by employing a cryptographic decoding algorithm.

The following SOAP message with a **<SecurityTokenReference>** element illustrates the addition of an XML Signature to a SOAP message.

```
<S:Envelope xmlns:S="http://www.w3.org/2001/12/soap-envelope"
xmlns:ds="http://www.w3.org/2000/09/xmldsig#"
mlns:wsse="http://schemas.xmlsoap.org/ws/2002/04/secext" >
    <S:Header>
        <wsse:Security>
            <wsse:BinarySecurityToken
                    ValueType="wsse:X509v3"
                    EncodingType="wsse:Base64Binary"
                    wsu:Id="X509Token">
                AwSaRgguTQmVkopX...
            </wsse:BinarySecurityToken>
            <ds:Signature>
                . . .
                <ds:KeyInfo>
                    <wsse:SecurityTokenReference>
                        <wsse:Reference URI="#X509Token"/>
                    </wsse:SecurityTokenReference>
                </ds:KeyInfo>
            </ds:Signature>
        </wsse:Security>
    </S:Header>
    . . .
</S:Envelope>
```

The signature is computed based on the X.509 certificate, which is specified in the **<Security>** header.

Message Confidentiality

We discussed how to implement message integrity and how to propagate security tokens by employing WS-Security. But integrity and authentication alone are not sufficient. Imagine a scenario in which the sent message containing sensitive information is both authenticated and signed but not encrypted. What might happen? The attacker could easily access the sensitive information and verify whether it is tamper-proof (confirms no other attacker has modified the message) and from the appropriate sender! So, it is necessary to encrypt the message. During encryption, you can employ either symmetric or asymmetric encryption according to the situation. WS-Security defines a mechanism to make sure the SOAP message is confidential between the sender and receiver. WS-Security employs this by using the XML encryption standard to encrypt portions of the SOAP message. It describes how the **<ReferenceList>**, **<EncryptedData>**, **<EncryptedKey>**, and **<DataReference>** elements defined by XML encryption can be used in the **<Security>** header.

The following code encrypts the body of a SOAP message using a secret key shared by the sender and receiver.

```
<S:Envelope
    xmlns:S="http://www.w3.org/2001/12/soap-envelope"
    xmlns:ds="http://www.w3.org/2000/09/xmldsig#"
xmlns:wsse="http://schemas.xmlsoap.org/ws/2002/04/secext"
    xmlns:xenc="http://www.w3.org/2001/04/xmlenc#">
  <S:Header>
      <wsse:Security>
          <xenc:ReferenceList>
              <xenc:DataReference URI="#enc1"/>
          </xenc:ReferenceList>
      </wsse:Security>
  </S:Header>
<S:Body>
<xenc:EncryptedData
xmlns:xenc="http://www.w3.org/2001/04/xmlenc#"
xmlns:wsu="http://schemas.xmlsoap.org/ws/2002/07/utility"
Type="http://www.w3.org/2001/04/xmlenc#Element"
wsu:Id="enc1">
    <xenc:EncryptionMethod
    Algorithm="http://www.w3.org/2001/04/xmlenc#3des-cbc"/>
        <xenc:CipherData>
            <xenc:CipherValue>dwSaRgguTQmVkopX...
            </xenc:CipherValue>
        </xenc:CipherData>
```

```
</xenc:EncryptedData>
</S:Body>
</S:Envelope>
```

An overview of the Web services security standards is shown in Table 10–3.

TABLE 10-3   *Web Services Security Standards*

Technology	Security Function	Description
Basic HTTP	Authentication	HTTP and its security mechanisms address only point-to-point security.
HTTPS (SSL 3.0/TLS 1.0)	Confidentiality, data integrity, and authentication (encryption)	Point-to-point security sessions between client and server.
XML Signature	Authentication, integrity, and nonrepudiation (authentication)	Prerequisite for WS-Security. It ensures the received message is tamper-proof.
XML Encryption	Integrity and privacy (encryption)	Prerequisite for WS-Security. It prevents the attacker from reading the content of the XML message.
XML Key Management Specification (XKMS)	Authentication, privacy, and integrity (key exchange)	XKMS provides an XML interface to PKI, including distribution, confirmation, and key management.
Security Assertion Markup Language (SAML)	Authentication and authorization	Provides interoperable authentication and authorization (single sign-on).
WS-Security	Authentication, encryption, and integrity	WS-Security is a baseline specification and assists in sending secure messages. It illustrates the use of XML Encryption and XML Signature to SOAP headers.

WEB SERVICES ENHANCEMENTS 1.0 FOR MICROSOFT .NET

Microsoft released WSE 1.0 for Microsoft .NET on December 5, 2002. It replaces the WSDK Technical Preview. WSE 1.0 for Microsoft .NET is a new .NET class library by which you can implement the latest Web services protocols, including WS-Security, WS-Routing, DIME, and WS-Attachments.

With the help of WSE, .NET Framework developers can incorporate features such as security, routing, and attachments to their Web services applications. WSE sits on top of the .NET Framework and allows developers to implement the latest Web services protocols in XML Web services. The key part of the WSE is the **Microsoft.Web.Services.SoapContext** class that provides an interface for examining the WS-Security header and other headers for incoming SOAP messages, and adding WS-Security and other headers for outgoing SOAP messages.

If you install the WSE 1.0 setup, the following items will be installed.

- The Microsoft.Web.Services assembly (Microsoft.Web.Services.dll) in the application folder.
- The following elements are added into the **Machine.config** file by WSE 1.0.

```
<mscorlib>
   <cryptographySettings>
     <cryptoNameMapping>
       <cryptoClasses>
          <cryptoClass
Sha1="System.Security.Cryptography.SHA1Managed" />
       </cryptoClasses>
       <nameEntry name="SHA1" class="Sha1" />
       <nameEntry
name="System.Security.Cryptography.SHA1"
class="Sha1" />
     </cryptoNameMapping>
   </cryptographySettings>
</mscorlib>
```

- WSE documentation
- WSE QuickStart Samples Release Notes and Release Notes

The WSE provides the following features for the secure transmission of SOAP messages:

- **Adding Security Credentials to a SOAP Message:** By means of WSE, you can add one or more security credentials to a SOAP message. The purpose of adding security credentials to a SOAP message is that it secures the XML Web services over the entire route even though the SOAP message is routed through intermediaries before reaching the final entity. That is, instead of adding security credentials at the transport level, you add the security credentials to the SOAP message (message level).
- **Digitally Signing a SOAP Message:** By means of WSE, you can digitally sign a SOAP message so that it facilitates cryptographic verification that a SOAP message has not been altered since it was signed.

- **Encrypting a SOAP Message:** By means of WSE, you can encrypt a SOAP message and confirm that only the intended recipient can read the contents of a message.

PROCESS SOAP MESSAGES SIGNED USING A USERNAMETOKEN

Let's see how an XML Web service processes a SOAP message signed using a **UsernameToken**. The steps are as follows:

1. In the ASP.NET Web service project add a reference to the Microsoft.Web.Services assembly.
2. Add the **microsoft.web.services** configuration section handler to the configuration file. Add a **<section>** element to the **<configuration>** section of the needed **Web.config** file. The following code shows how to add the **microsoft.web.services** configuration section handler. The type attribute of the **<section>** element must be on one line, although the following code is broken up for readability.

```
<configuration>
    <configSections>
        <section name="microsoft.web.services"
type="Microsoft.Web.Services.Configuration.
WebServicesConfiguration, Microsoft.Web.Services,
Version=1.0.0.0, Culture=neutral,
PublicKeyToken=31bf3856ad364e35" />
    </configSections>
</configuration>
```

3. In the **Web.config** file for the XML Web service, add an **<add>** element to the **<soapExtensionTypes>** section. The following code is the configuration entry that must be placed in the **Web.config** file for the WSE to run with an XML Web service. The type attribute of the **<add>** element for **<soapExtensionTypes>** must be on one line, although the following code is broken up for readability.

```
<configuration>
    <system.web>
        <webServices>
            <soapExtensionTypes>
                <add
type="Microsoft.Web.Services.WebServicesExtension,
Microsoft.Web.Services,Version=1.0.0.0,
Culture=neutral, PublicKeyToken=31bf3856ad364e35"
                    priority="1"
                    group="0"/>
            </soapExtensionTypes>
        </webServices>
    </system.web>
</configuration>
```

The Microsoft.Web.Services assembly has to be accessible from within this ASP.NET application; otherwise, the above configuration setting doesn't work. So, the Microsoft.Web.Services assembly has to be either in the bin folder of the ASP.NET application or in the Global Assembly Cache (GAC). In Visual Studio .NET after a reference is made to the Microsoft.Web.Services assembly; set the Copy Local property for the reference to true. This copies the assembly to the bin folder.

Now, let's see how to develop a Web service that processes a SOAP message signed using **UsernameToken**.

```
using System;
using System.Collections;
using System.ComponentModel;
using System.Data;
using System.Diagnostics;
using Microsoft.Web.Services.Security;
using Microsoft.Web.Services;
using System.Security.Cryptography;
namespace WSEUsernameToken
{
 public class Service1 : System.Web.Services.WebService
 {
[WebMethod]
public string Hello ()
 {
    SoapContext requestContext =
HttpSoapContext.RequestContext;
   // Verifies whether a SOAP request was received.
   if (requestContext == null)
   {
       throw new
         ApplicationException("Non-SOAP request or the
WSE is not properly installed.");
   }
    UsernameToken Token1 =
       GetToken( requestContext.Security );
    if ( Token1 != null )
    {
       value = "Hello";
    }
    return value;
 }
private UsernameToken GetToken(Security sec )
 {
    UsernameToken value = null;
            if ( sec.Tokens.Count > 0 )
            {
```

```
            foreach ( SecurityToken tok in sec.Tokens )
              {
                  value = tok as UsernameToken;
                  if ( value != null )
                  {
                   return value;
                  }
              }
          }
    return value;
  }
 }
}
```

Since each WS-Security SOAP header may contain zero or more security tokens, we iterate through a for-each loop and return the **UsernameToken**.

Two major steps are required for the Web services to process SOAP messages signed using a **UsernameToken**. First, add a class that implements the **IPasswordProvider** interface. The code is as follows.

```
/* It is recommended to insist that an assembly accessing
this class already have permission to call unmanaged code,
since Microsoft.Web.Services is the only assembly that
should call this class. Therefore apply the
SecurityPermissionAttribute attribute to the
class implementing IPasswordProvider, demanding the
UnmanagedCode permission. */

[SecurityPermission(SecurityAction.Demand,
  Flags= SecurityPermissionFlag.UnmanagedCode)]
public class PasswordProvider: IPasswordProvider
// Implement the GetPassword method of the IPassword
// Provider interface.
public string GetPassword(UsernameToken userName)
{
  // This below code is only for pedagogical purpose.
  // In real time applications the code
  // typically consults an external database of
  // (userName,hash) pairs.
  // Here for simplicity we employ the UTF-8
  // encoding of the user name.
  byte[] encodedUsername =
        System.Text.Encoding.UTF8.GetBytes
            (userName.Username);
  return System.Text.Encoding.GetString(encodedUsername)
}
```

When this class is registered in the Web.config file, the WSE calls the **GetPassword** method of this class whenever a message is signed using a **UsernameToken** to get the password for the input user name.

Now, configure the class implementing **IPasswordProvider** in the **Web.config** file for the XML Web service, as shown below. The value of the type attribute must be on one line, although this code is broken up for readability.

```
<microsoft.web.services>
 <security>
   <passwordProvider type=
     "MyNamespace.PasswordProvider, MyAssemblyName,
     Version=1.0.0.0,
     Culture=neutral,
     PublicKeyToken=81f0828a1c0bb867" />
 </security>
</microsoft.web.services>
```

We configure the **MyNamespace.PasswordProvider** type to be called whenever a SOAP message signed with a **UsernameToken** is received for XML Web services affected by this **Web.config**.

SIGNING A SOAP MESSAGE USING A USERNAME TOKEN

Let's see how an XML Web service client signs a SOAP request using a **UsernameToken**.

1. Add a Web reference to **Microsoft.Web.Services.dll** and **System.Web.Services.dll**.
2. Add a Web reference to the Web service that is to receive the SOAP message.
3. Edit the proxy class to derive from **WebServicesClientProtocol**. To edit the class, right-click the **Reference.cs** file in the Solution Explorer, and then click View Code. In the code edit the class from

```
public class Service1 :
System.Web.Services.Protocols.SoapHttpClientProtocol
to public class Service1 :
Microsoft.Web.Services.WebServicesClientProtocol.

/* In Visual Studio .NET, if you click Update Web
Reference, the proxy class is regenerated, the base
class is reset to SoapHttpClientProtocol, therefore you
have to edit the proxy class again. */
```

4. Add the following using directives to the Web service client code:

```
using Microsoft.Web.Services;
using Microsoft.Web.Services.Security;
```

The client code looks like this:

```
localhost.Service1 proxy = new localhost.Service1();
/* Create a new instance of UsernameToken, specifying the
user name, password, and how the password is sent in the
SOAP message.*/
UsernameToken userToken = new UsernameToken(userName,
password,PasswordOption.SendHashed);
proxy.RequestSoapContext.Security.Tokens.Add(userToken);
// Signs the SOAP message using the UsernameToken.
Proxy.RequestSoapContext.Security.Elements.Add(new
Signature(userToken));
//Call the Web service.
label1.Text = proxy.Hello();
```

WEB SERVICES ENHANCEMENTS 2.0 FOR MICROSOFT .NET

Microsoft released WSE 2.0 for Microsoft .NET on July 15, 2003.[9] It replaces the WSE1.0 Technical Preview which was released on December 5, 2002. With WSE 2.0 for Microsoft .NET, you can implement the latest Web services protocols, including WS-Addressing, WS-Policy, WS-SecurityPolicy, WS-Trust, and WS-SecureConversation.

The new features added to the WSE 2.0 Technology Preview are as follows.

1. The WSE version 2.0 provides support for new Web Services specifications including WS-Addressing, WS-Policy, WS-SecurityPolicy, WS-Trust, and WS-SecureConversation.
2. In WSE version 2.0, you can express the receiving and sending message requirements using configuration files (configuration-based declaration of security or other policies).
3. The WSE version 2.0 provides the capability to programmatically request a security token using a SOAP message, and that token can be used for a series of SOAP messages between a SOAP message sender and a target Web service.
4. The WSE version 2.0 supports role-based authorization for SOAP messages by constructing a principal from a security token within the SOAP message.
5. The WSE version 2.0 provides support for Kerberos tokens. This support is operating system platform dependent.
6. With SOAP messaging, the WSE version 2.0 supports a flexible mechanism for sending and receiving SOAP messages. This lightweight, message-oriented SOAP programming model facilitates applications to switch between the TCP and HTTP transport protocols easily.

---

9. For more information on WSE 2.0, visit *http://msdn.microsoft.com/webservices/ building/wse/default.aspx*.

7. The WSE version 2.0 provides support for XML security tokens, such as XrML and SAML security tokens.

8. QuickStart samples are provided in C# and Visual Basic languages.

Note that this Technology Preview release is for testing purposes only; the software must not be used in a production environment, must not be redistributed, and is not supported by Microsoft. Get in touch with WSE 2.0 Technology Preview for testing purpose, until the final version of WSE 2.0.

Organizations Involved

Various organizations are involved in the process of finding solutions to the shortcomings of Web services:

- Worldwide Web Consortium (W3C)
- Organization for the Advancement of Structured Information Standards (OASIS)
- Internet Engineering Task Force (IETF)
- Web services Interoperability Organization (WS-I)
- Vendors like Microsoft, IBM, Sun, BEA, e-Speak, IONA and Hewlett-Packard

W3C working groups are refining both SOAP 1.1 and WSDL 1.1 specifications. The XML Protocol Working Group and Web Services Description Working Group are working in parallel to standardize SOAP 1.2 and WSDL 1.2, respectively. In addition to XML digital signature and XML encryption, W3C is developing the XML Key Management Specification and a Web service architecture that includes a security framework.

The following are the mission statements of the important organizations involved in developing the foundation for the Web services security standards.

- **OASIS Web Services Security Technical Committee (WSS TC):** On April 11, 2002, IBM, Microsoft, and VeriSign announced a set of specifications called WS-Security that extend SOAP security and build on other existing Web services security standards. WSS TC continues to work on the Web Services security foundations as described in the WS-Security specification. The work of the WSS TC will form the necessary technical foundation for higher-level security services, which are to be defined in other specifications.
- **XML Signature WG:** The mission of this working group is to develop an XML-compliant syntax used for representing the signature of Web resources and portions of protocol messages (anything referenceable

by a URI) and procedures for computing and verifying such signatures. This is a joint working group of the IETF and W3C.

- **XML Encryption Working Group:** The mission of this working group is to develop a process for encrypting/decrypting digital content (including XML documents and portions thereof) and XML syntax used to represent both encrypted content and information that enables an intended recipient to decrypt it.
- **XML-Based Security Services Technical Committee (SSTC):** This technical committee works on SAML, an XML-based security standard for exchanging authentication and authorization information.
- **Web Services Interoperability Organization (WS-I):** WS-I is an open industry organization chartered to promote Web services interoperability across platforms, operating systems, and programming languages. The organization works across the industry and standards organizations to respond to customer needs by providing guidance, best practices, and resources for developing Web services solutions.

OASIS and the W3C focus on the key areas listed in Table 10–4 to form the groundwork of a Web services security framework.

TABLE 10–4 *Web Services Security Standards and Status*

Standard (proposed or final)	Standards body and status
WS-Security	OASIS: Forming technical committee, WSS TC
XML Digital Signature	W3C: Completed
XML Encryption	W3C: Final vote in committee
XKMS	W3C: Working draft
SAML	OASIS: Final vote
XACML	OASIS: Committee review
SSL/TLS	IETF: RFC 2246
Kerberos	IETF: RFC 1510

SUMMARY

In this chapter we studied the Web services security. First, we looked at some of the present Web services security methods, such as SSL/TLS and firewall. Then, we explored the XML encryption technologies: XML signature, XML encryption,

XKMS, and SAML. Finally, we discussed WS-Security and how to implement it by employing WSE. SSL/TLS and other existing technologies are temporary solutions that work reasonably well within a constrained environment. If you are using Web services right now, we suggest you employ these solutions. We suggest also that you stay informed about the development of the WSE, which implements WS security, and make use of it after its final release.

A Security Attack Example: The Stack Overrun

Stack overruns are a good example of the kind of vulnerability that attackers often enthusiastically exploit. A famous example from the history of the Internet of such an attack was the Morris Internet Worm. This is just one of many interesting types of attacks that must be considered in secure programming. This particular type of attack is much more difficult to mount in a managed runtime environment, such as .NET or Java, but has been exploited in many large C or C++ programs, including SQL Server and IIS. Studying this simple example may help you get a feel for the resourcefulness and state of mind of your potential adversaries.

The **Win32ProjectBufferOverflow** example described in this appendix demonstrates the concept behind the stack-overrun attack.[1] This technique is a simple exploit that is designed to write code onto the parameter area of the stack in a way that overlaps the function return address, causing execution to jump into the attacker's code rather than return normally. In the following code listing, you can see that the attacker's code is represented by the **AttackerInsertedCode** function. If you run this program, you will see that the **AttackerInsertedCode** function does get executed, even though there is no code in the source listing that actually calls this function.

To keep things simple and compact, this example has both the code being attacked and the code that performs the attack all in one small program. In fact, they are both in the same source file, which is convenient for our purposes of demonstration, but not all that realistic. In a real-world example, the target code and the attack code would be in separate programs, typically communicating via a socket rather than a direct function call. However,

---

1. Note that the **/GS** option can be used in Visual C/C++ programs to detect buffer overruns, effectively preventing most vulnerabilities to the stack-overrun attack.

precisely the same concept would still be in effect in both the realistic scenario and the example given here. Another point to remember when trying out this example program is that if you recompile it with a different version of the compiler, or if you change any of the source code and then recompile, you will probably have to modify the data that is used to overwrite the stack, since both code and stack layout may have changed. This project has not turned on stack runtime checks, and if you turn this compiler option on, it will not work properly.

```cpp
// Win32ProjectBufferOverflow.cpp
...

#define BUFLENGTH 16

//the following code was written by a sloppy programmer
void VulnerableFunction(char * str)
{
   char buf[BUFLENGTH];
   strcpy(buf, str); //danger here!

   printf("VulnerableFunction called.\n\n");
}

//the following code was written by a nasty programmer
void AttackerInsertedCode()
{
   printf("Nyahahaha... AttackerInsertedCode called.\n");
   while (true); //never return
}
void main()
{
   //call the vulnerable function in a safe way
   printf("Call VulnerableFunction in a safe way.\n");
   VulnerableFunction("hello");

   //call the vulnerable function in a nasty way
   printf("Call VulnerableFunction in nasty way.\n");
   char bufNasty[25];
   //make sure there are no intervening nulls
   for (int i=0; i<20; i++)
      bufNasty[i] = 0x01;
   //overwrite return address with AttackerInsertedCode
   int * pRetAddres = (int *)&(bufNasty[20]);
   *pRetAddres = 0x004119A0;
   //final null terminator
   bufNasty[24] = (char)0x00; //actually redundant
   //do the dirty deed
   VulnerableFunction(bufNasty);
}
```

The key weakness that is exploited in this example is the sloppy workmanship in the function named **VulnerableFunction**. In particular, the call to **strcpy** is not done in a safe manner. The **strcpy** function copies the buffer pointed to by the second parameter, including its terminating null, to the buffer pointed at by the first parameter. But this copying is done without any buffer-length checking. Within **VulnerableFunction**, the local buffer **buf** is allocated on the current stack frame with a capacity of 16 bytes. If you call **VulnerableFunction** with a parameter that points to a zero-terminated buffer that is no more than 16 bytes, it will work normally. If you pass in a pointer to a buffer that has more than 16 bytes, the additional bytes are written into the next available bytes on the stack, which contain, among other things, the return address used upon returning from the function to resume at the next instruction within the calling function.

If you run the program, you will see the following output. Note that the first time that **VulnerableFunction** is called, it works normally. This is because it is called safely, passing a buffer containing fewer than 16 bytes. But the second call to **VulnerableFunction** is a different story. The buffer passed in contains 25 bytes. Normally, this would just be a bug that causes a random amount of arbitrary data to overwrite the stack, which would cause an access violation (or perhaps have no deleterious effect). But in this example, the data being written over the stack is not a random length, and the data being written is specially crafted to have a very specific effect. Rather than producing an access violation, the **AttackerInsertedCode** is executed, as evidenced by the appearance of the output Nyahahaha... being displayed on the console.

```
Call VulnerableFunction in a safe way.
VulnerableFunction called.

Call VulnerableFunction in nasty way.
VulnerableFunction called.

Nyahahaha... AttackerInsertedCode called.
```

So, how do you figure out exactly how long your stack overwriting buffer should be, and how do you figure out exactly what data should be placed into this buffer to ensure that your own nasty code gets executed in place of a normal, orderly function return? To sort this out, you have to get into the debugger and set breakpoints, view the disassembly of the code, study a few of the CPU registers, and view the contents of memory containing the stack. Then, you can locate the address that contains the four bytes containing the return address for **VulnerableFunction**. You can also determine the address of your own **AttackerInsertedCode** function.

Let's see how to determine the address of the **AttackerInsertedCode** function. Set a breakpoint on the **AttackerInsertedCode** function, and run the program under the debugger. Then, click on the Disassembly tab and note the address of this function. This is shown in Figure A–1, where you can see that this address is 004119A0 in this example.

Next, let's see how to determine where the return address is stored for returning from the call to the **VulnerableFunction** function. This is a bit tricky, but here is the basic approach to use. First, set a breakpoint on the function to be called (Figure A–2), and then run the program under the debugger. When you hit the breakpoint, switch the source code view to show the disassembly of the function call.

From this information, you can determine the return address that you would like to switch to (pRetAddress = 0x004119A0) and also exactly where in the parameter stack you need to place this new return address (buf-Nasty[20]).

```
Disassembly                                                    ×
Address  AttackerInsertedCode(void)           ▾

    //the following code was written by a nasty programmer
    void AttackerInsertedCode()
    {
⇨  004119A0   push        ebp
    004119A1   mov         ebp,esp
    004119A3   sub         esp,40h
    004119A6   push        ebx
    004119A7   push        esi
    004119A8   push        edi
       printf("Nyahahaha... AttackerInsertedCode called.\n");
    004119A9   push        offset string "Nyahahaha... Attacker
    004119AE   call        @ILT+1080(_printf) (41143Dh)
    004119B3   add         esp,4
       while (true); //never return
    004119B6   mov         eax,1
    004119BB   test        eax,eax
    004119BD   je          AttackerInsertedCode+21h (4119C1h)
    004119BF   jmp         AttackerInsertedCode+16h (4119B6h)
    }
    004119C1   pop         edi
    004119C2   pop         esi
```

FIGURE A–1   *Determining the address of the AttackerInsertedCode function.*

```
//the following code was written by a nasty programmer
void AttackerInsertedCode()
{
    printf("Nyahahaha... AttackerInsertedCode called.\n").
    while (true); //never return
}
void main()
{
    //call the vulnerable function in a safe way
    printf("Call VulnerableFunction in a safe way.\n");
    VulnerableFunction("hello");

    //call the vulnerable function in a nasty way
    printf("Call VulnerableFunction in nasty way.\n");
    char bufNasty[25];
    //make sure there are no intervening nulls
    for (int i=0; i<20; i++)
        bufNasty[i] = 0x01;
    //overwrite return address with AttackerInsertedCode
    int * pRetAddres = (int *)&(bufNasty[20]);
    *pRetAddres = 0x004119A0;
    //final null terminator
    bufNasty[24] = (char)0x00; //actually redundant
```

FIGURE A-2   *Setting the breakpoint on the VulnerableFunction.*

How the RSA Cipher Works

*I*n order to appreciate the inner workings of a cryptographic system, such as RSA, it is helpful to see a simple implementation in code. This appendix provides some insight into the workings of the RSA algorithm, but it is not entirely necessary for those with a purely pragmatic interest in applying existing cryptographic solutions, such as the security and cryptographic classes in the .NET Framework. However, even pragmatists may benefit from a background understanding of the algorithms that they use.

This appendix provides an example program that explores the inner workings of the RSA algorithm named **BigRSA**, which is a multiprecision implementation. You will probably never implement your own RSA algorithm like this from scratch, since most cryptographic libraries, including the .NET Security Framework, provide excellent implementations. This example is provided purely for deeper understanding.

Modular Arithmetic

Before we look at the code in the RSA program example, let's first understand a bit more about modular arithmetic. Modular arithmetic is used in many cryptographic systems, including RSA, DSA, and SSL. The algebraic structure that is used is referred to as Z_n, which is the set of nonnegative integers modulo n. Z_n consists of the set $\{0, 1, 2, \ldots, n-1\}$ along with operators defined for addition and multiplication. Note that Z_n is integer arithmetic on a finite circle, not an infinite number line. Z_n is sometimes referred to as clock arithmetic, since a twelve hour clock implies Z_{12} arithmetic.

For example, Z_{12} would be the set of numbers from 0 to 11, with addition defined much like regular addition, but any result over 11 (the modulus minus one) is wrapped around starting back at zero. So, in Z_{12}, $1 + 0 = 1$, $1 + 1 = 2$, and $3 + 5 = 8$. However, when an addition would normally go beyond 11, then the modular wraparound takes effect. For example, $10 + 5 = 3$, not 15. Regular arithmetic would have $10 + 5 = 15$, but 15 is greater than 11, so in modular arithmetic, with a modulus of 12, $10 + 5$ is actually $15 - 12$, which is 3. As another example, $5 + 7$ would produce 0 rather than 12, since $12 - 12 = 0$. The idea behind modular arithmetic is that given a value for a modulus, you will never have to deal with any quantities equal to or greater than the modulus. In powerful and peculiar ways, this trick provides extraordinary advantages when dealing with the implementation of asymmetric cryptographic algorithms. Of course, in algorithms such as RSA, you never work with a tiny modulus like 12, but, rather, you work with a much more computationally significant modulus.

The BigRSA Example Program

If you have read Chapter 4, you may recall the basic algorithmic steps involved in RSA. In the example program **BigRSA**, you will see similarities to the implementation shown in the **TinyRSA** example program provided in Chapter 4. The main difference you will see in the **BigRSA** example program is that we are using the GnuMP multiprecision math library. For details on installing and using this library, see Appendix C.

Note that in the **BigRSA** example program, the value of *e* is selected randomly. This was done just to prove that any value of *e*, such that *e* < phi and GCD(*e*, phi) = 1 are true, will work. However, the values of *e* that are most frequently used in practice are 3, 17, and 65535 (or 0xFFFF).

```
unsafe static void Main(string[] args)
{
  //initialize random state with default algorithm
  gmp_randstate_struct state =
    new gmp_randstate_struct();
  GmpWrapper.__gmp_randinit_default(&state);

  //set seed to current time
  DateTime dt = DateTime.Now; //current date and time
  GmpWrapper.__gmp_randseed_ui(
    &state, (ulong)dt.Ticks);

  //get 256 bit uniformly distributed random prime p
  mpz_struct p;
  GmpWrapper.__gmpz_init(&p);
```

```
GmpWrapper.__gmpz_urandomb(&p, &state, 256);
GmpWrapper.__gmpz_nextprime(&p, &p);

//display random prime p
Console.WriteLine(
  "p: " +
  GmpWrapper.__gmpz_get_str(null, 10, &p));

//get 256 bit uniformly distributed random prime q
//in theory, we should ensure that p != q
//but we don't bother here ...
//i.e. have you won the lottery lately?
mpz_struct q;
GmpWrapper.__gmpz_init(&q);
GmpWrapper.__gmpz_urandomb(&q, &state, 256);
GmpWrapper.__gmpz_nextprime(&q, &q);

//display random prime q
Console.WriteLine(
  "q: " +
  GmpWrapper.__gmpz_get_str(null, 10, &q));

//pq = p*q
mpz_struct pq;
GmpWrapper.__gmpz_init(&pq);
GmpWrapper.__gmpz_mul(&pq, &p, &q);

//display product pq
Console.WriteLine(
  "\npq:   " +
  GmpWrapper.__gmpz_get_str(null, 10, &pq));

//initialize euler totient phi = (p-1)*(q-1)
mpz_struct phi;
GmpWrapper.__gmpz_init(&phi);
mpz_struct one;
GmpWrapper.__gmpz_init(&one);
GmpWrapper.__gmpz_set_str(&one, "1", 10);
mpz_struct pminusone;
GmpWrapper.__gmpz_init(&pminusone);
GmpWrapper.__gmpz_sub(&pminusone, &p, &one);
mpz_struct qminusone;
GmpWrapper.__gmpz_init(&qminusone);
GmpWrapper.__gmpz_sub(&qminusone, &q, &one);
GmpWrapper.__gmpz_mul(&phi, &pminusone, &qminusone);

//display phi
Console.WriteLine(
  "phi: " +
  GmpWrapper.__gmpz_get_str(null, 10, &phi));
```

```
//get value for e rel prime to phi and < phi
mpz_struct e;
GmpWrapper.__gmpz_init(&e);
while(true)
{
  //get random number as candidate for e
  GmpWrapper.__gmpz_urandomb(&e, &state, 256);

  //is e < phi?
  bool goodsize =
    GmpWrapper.__gmpz_cmp(&e, &phi) < 0;

  //is gcd of e and phi = 1?
  mpz_struct gcd;
  GmpWrapper.__gmpz_init(&gcd);
  GmpWrapper.__gmpz_gcd(&gcd, &e, &phi);
  bool relprime =
    GmpWrapper.__gmpz_cmp(&gcd, &one) == 0;

  //bail out if we have what we want
  if (goodsize && relprime)
    break;
}

//display random rel prime e
Console.WriteLine(
  "\ne: " +
  GmpWrapper.__gmpz_get_str(null, 10, &e));

//calculate d = e^-1 mod phi
mpz_struct d;
GmpWrapper.__gmpz_init(&d);
GmpWrapper.__gmpz_invert(&d, &e, &phi);

//display d
Console.WriteLine(
  "d: " +
  GmpWrapper.__gmpz_get_str(null, 10, &d));

//initialize plaintext message m
mpz_struct m;
GmpWrapper.__gmpz_init(&m);

while (true)
{
  //get 256 bit uniformly dist random message m
  GmpWrapper.__gmpz_urandomb(&m, &state, 256);

  //must ensure that m < pq, or algebra fails
  if (GmpWrapper.__gmpz_cmp(&m, &pq) < 0)
```

```
        break;
    }

    //display plaintext message m
    Console.WriteLine(
      "\nm: " +
      GmpWrapper.__gmpz_get_str(null, 10, &m));

    //calculate ciphertext c = m^e mod pq
    mpz_struct c;
    GmpWrapper.__gmpz_init(&c);
    GmpWrapper.__gmpz_powm(&c, &m, &e, &pq);

    //display ciphertext message c
    Console.WriteLine(
      "c: " +
      GmpWrapper.__gmpz_get_str(null, 10, &c));

    //calculate deciphered  x = c^d mod pq
    mpz_struct x;
    GmpWrapper.__gmpz_init(&x);
    GmpWrapper.__gmpz_powm(&x, &c, &d, &pq);

    //display deciphered message x
    Console.WriteLine(
      "x: " +
      GmpWrapper.__gmpz_get_str(null, 10, &x));
}
```

The CrackRSAWorkFactorDemo Example Program

The **CrackRSAWorkFactorDemo** example shows the exponential growth in time required to crack RSA. Figure B–1 shows the output from this program. These results are from a 900 MHz PC.

If you want to compare these results on your own machine, and you want to know your machine's clock speed, see the following using **Regedt32.exe**.

```
HKEY_LOCAL_MACHINE/HARDWARE/DESCRIPTION/System/
CentralProcessor/0
```

For numbers up to 13 bits, less than one millisecond is required. When 22 bits are used, it takes almost one second; 28 bits takes an hour; and if you had the patience, you would see that 38 bits takes more than a day. How many bits would take a human lifetime? Assume that you would live 2^{15} = 32768 days, which is 89 years and about 9 months, just a few years higher than average life expectancy in most of the developed world. If 38 bits takes

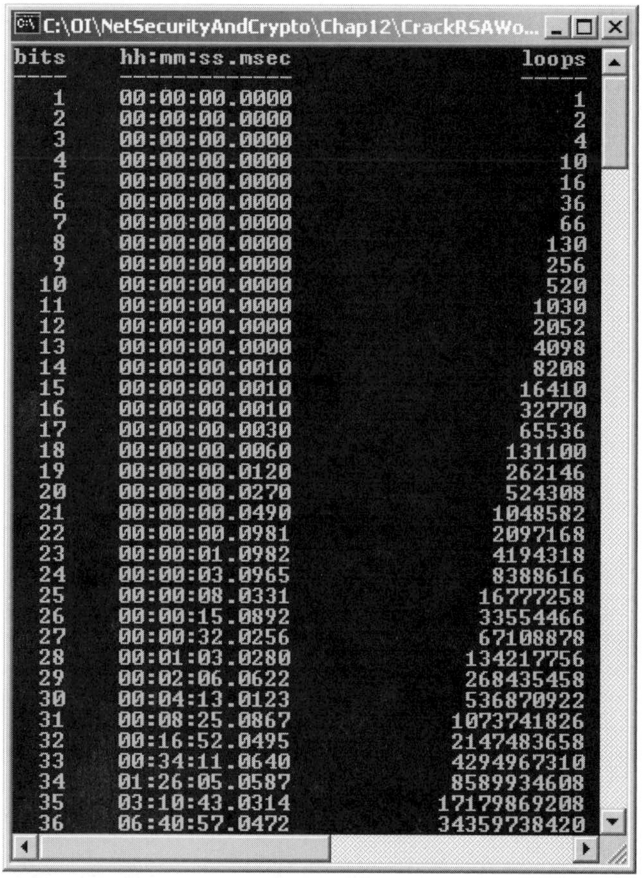

bits	hh:mm:ss.msec	loops
1	00:00:00.0000	1
2	00:00:00.0000	2
3	00:00:00.0000	4
4	00:00:00.0000	10
5	00:00:00.0000	16
6	00:00:00.0000	36
7	00:00:00.0000	66
8	00:00:00.0000	130
9	00:00:00.0000	256
10	00:00:00.0000	520
11	00:00:00.0000	1030
12	00:00:00.0000	2052
13	00:00:00.0000	4098
14	00:00:00.0010	8208
15	00:00:00.0010	16410
16	00:00:00.0010	32770
17	00:00:00.0030	65536
18	00:00:00.0060	131100
19	00:00:00.0120	262146
20	00:00:00.0270	524308
21	00:00:00.0490	1048582
22	00:00:00.0981	2097168
23	00:00:01.0982	4194318
24	00:00:03.0965	8388616
25	00:00:08.0331	16777258
26	00:00:15.0892	33554466
27	00:00:32.0256	67108878
28	00:01:03.0280	134217756
29	00:02:06.0622	268435458
30	00:04:13.0123	536870922
31	00:08:25.0867	1073741826
32	00:16:52.0495	2147483658
33	00:34:11.0640	4294967310
34	01:26:05.0587	8589934608
35	03:10:43.0314	17179869208
36	06:40:57.0472	34359738420

FIGURE B–1 *Cracking RSA work factor demo.*

more than one day, then 53 = 38 + 15 (multiplying is done by adding exponents) will take considerably more than a human lifetime.

Here is the source code for this example program.

```
unsafe static void Main(string[] args)
{
  //initialize prime p
  mpz_struct p;
  GmpWrapper.__gmpz_init(&p);

  //initialize prime q
  mpz_struct q;
  GmpWrapper.__gmpz_init(&q);
```

```
//initialize pq
mpz_struct pq;
GmpWrapper.__gmpz_init(&pq);

//string representation of n-bit binary number
String strBits = "1";

Console.WriteLine(
  "bits     hh:mm:ss.msec                loops");
Console.WriteLine(
  "----     -------------                -----");

//iterate over n-bit binary numbers 2^1 to 2^256
for (ulong n= 1; n<=256; n++)
{
  //get p = next prime after 2^n
  GmpWrapper.__gmpz_set_str(&p, strBits, 2);
  GmpWrapper.__gmpz_nextprime(&p, &p);

  //get q = next prime after p
  GmpWrapper.__gmpz_nextprime(&q, &p);

  //get product of primes pq = p*q
  GmpWrapper.__gmpz_mul(&pq, &p, &q);

  //display number of bits n
  Console.Write("{0,4}    ", n);

  //do the factoring work and show loop count
  WorkFactor(&pq);

  //one more bit next time around
  strBits = strBits + "0";
}
}
unsafe static void WorkFactor(mpz_struct* pq)
{
  //initialize candidate
  mpz_struct candidate;
  GmpWrapper.__gmpz_init(&candidate);
  GmpWrapper.__gmpz_set_ui(&candidate, 2);

  DateTime dtStart = DateTime.Now;

  //brute force search
  while (true)
  {
    if (GmpWrapper.__gmpz_divisible_p(
      pq, &candidate) != 0)
      break; //factor found
```

```
        GmpWrapper.__gmpz_add_ui (
           &candidate, &candidate, 1L);
    }

    DateTime dtEnd = DateTime.Now;
    TimeSpan ts = dtEnd-dtStart;
    Console.Write(
       "{0,2:d2}:{1,2:d2}:{2,2:d2}.{3,2:d4}     ",
       ts.Hours,
       ts.Minutes,
       ts.Seconds,
       ts.Milliseconds);

        GmpWrapper.__gmpz_sub_ui(
       &candidate, &candidate, 1);
    String str = GmpWrapper.__gmpz_get_str(
       null, 10, &candidate);

    Console.WriteLine("{0,18}", str);
}
```

Using the GNU GMP Library

As explained in Chapter 4, public key cryptography involves a mathematical function that is relatively easy to calculate in the forward direction, but the inverse function is extremely costly to calculate in the reverse direction unless a secret backdoor (i.e., key) is provided. All such mathematical functions suitable for use in public key cryptography require the use of arbitrary precision arithmetic.

Since the .NET Framework currently has no explicit support for such arithmetic, we must look elsewhere if we want to experiment with asymmetric algorithm implementations. There are numerous multiprecision libraries available; however, the most obvious choice is probably the GNU MP library, also known as GMP, from the open-source world. You can learn more about this library at *http://www.gnu.org/directory/gnump.html*.

The GNU GPL (General Public License) covers the GMP library. This means that you can freely copy the library source code and distribute your programs that use it, but you are required to make your own source code available under the GPL. For more information on GPL, see *http://www.gnu.org/*.

Installing Cygwin

Before you can use the GMP library, you need to have a platform that you can use it on. As is usually the case with GNU software, the assumed platform is Linux, or some form of UNIX. This book is intended for .NET programmers, which makes the implicit assumption that you are programming on some flavor of Microsoft Windows. The resulting problem is that the GMP library will not run directly on Windows without some help.

To solve this problem, we use an open-source product from Red Hat, named Cygwin. Cygwin provides Microsoft Windows with a UNIX programming environment. This is comprised of an emulation layer for POSIX API support and a set of UNIX command-line utilities, including gcc, make, and so on. The Cygwin.dll library provides a very useful subset of the standard UNIX programming environment. You can learn more about it at the Cygwin home page: *http://cygwin.com/*.

The GNU GPL also covers Cygwin. This means that the source code of any application that you build using Cygwin must also be distributed freely along with those applications unless the Cygwin buy-out license is purchased from Red Hat.

The Cygwin installation program, named **setup.exe**, can be downloaded from *http://www.cygwin.com/setup.exe*. You can then install Cygwin by running this **setup.exe** program. However, the default installation provides only a basic set of packages. In particular, the default installation package does not include the utilities you will need to build programs, such as gcc, binutils, and make. These utilities are provided under the Devel category of Cygwin packages. Therefore, when you run **setup.exe**, make sure that you select the install option for the Devel category, as described in the next paragraph.

When you run **setup.exe**, you will see the resulting wizard dialogs, as shown in Figures C–1 to C–9. Notice that in Figure C–7, you must click on the Devel node to change it from Default to Install. This causes the program development utilities to be included in your Cygwin installation.

FIGURE C-1   *Cygwin Setup Dialog 1.*

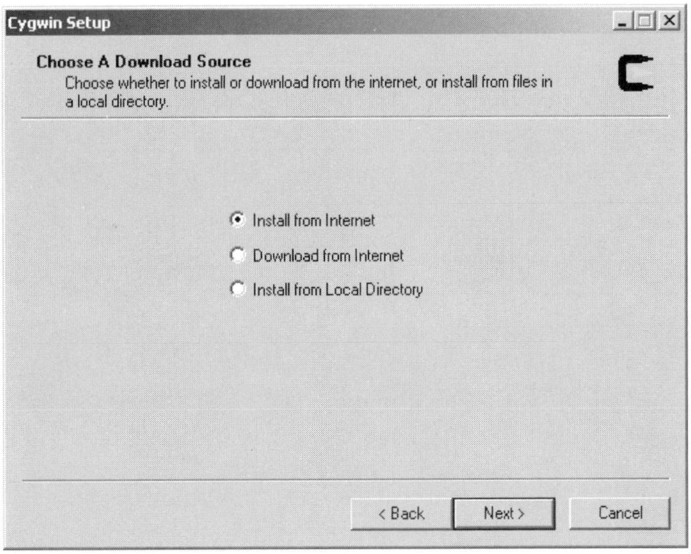

FIGURE C-2   Cygwin Setup Dialog 2.

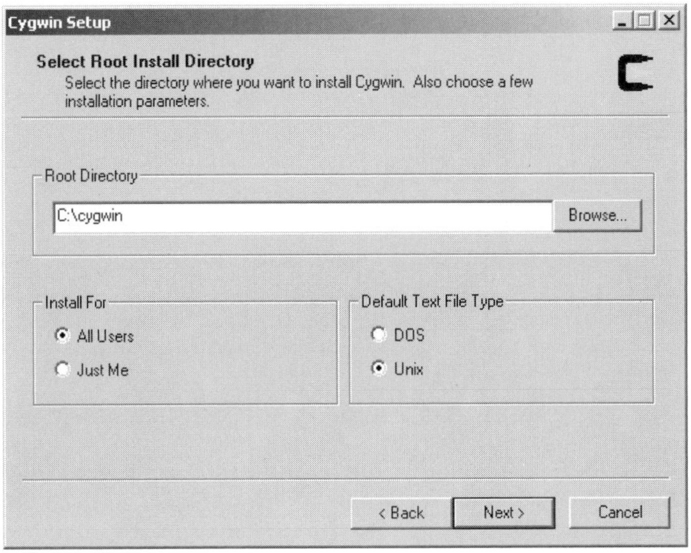

FIGURE C-3   Cygwin Setup Dialog 3.

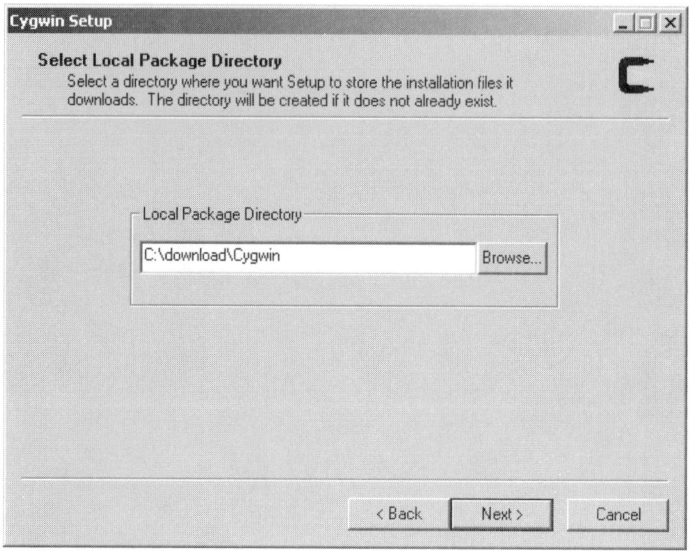

FIGURE C-4   Cygwin Setup Dialog 4.

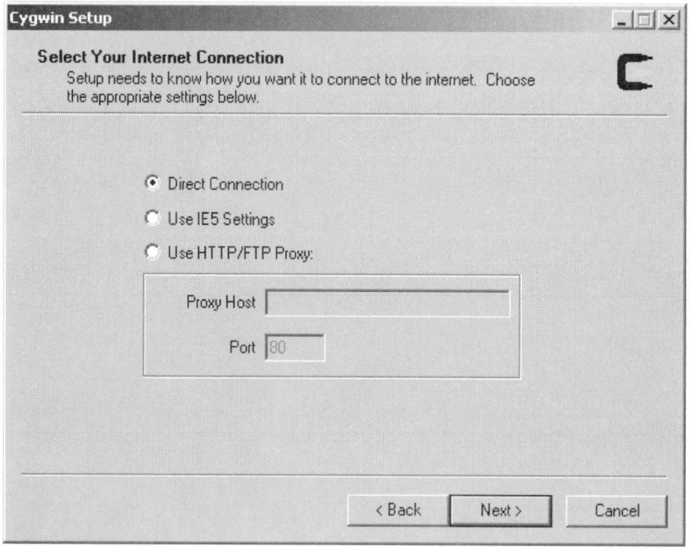

FIGURE C-5   Cygwin Setup Dialog 5.

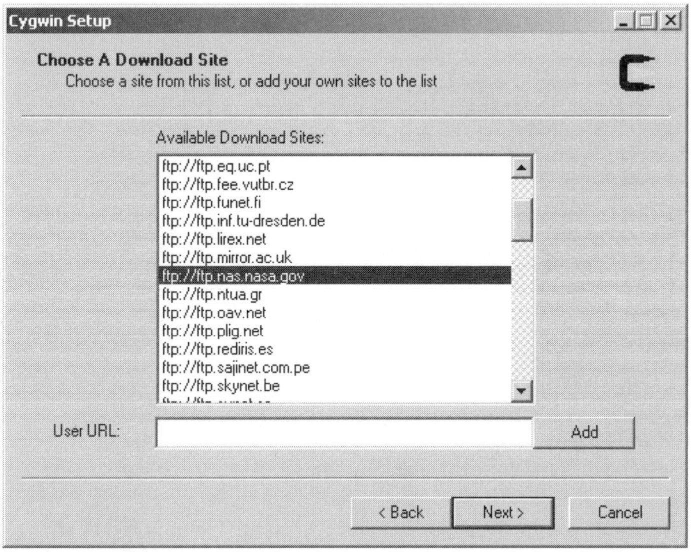

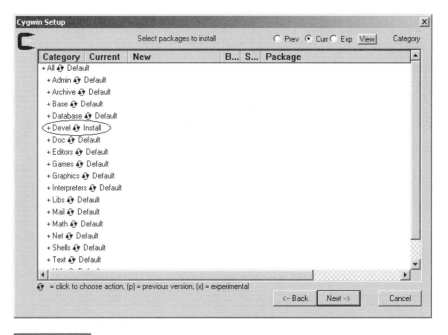

FIGURE C-6   Cygwin Setup Dialog 6.

FIGURE C-7   Cygwin Setup Dialog 7.

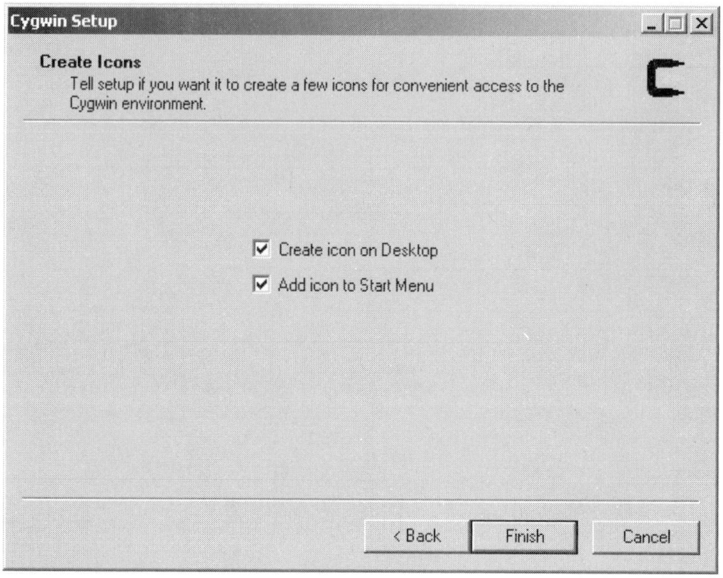

FIGURE C-8 *Cygwin Setup Dialog 8.*

FIGURE C-9 *Cygwin Setup Dialog 9.*

Cygwin provides a UNIX-style command-prompt window. All of the GNU tools can be used at the Cygwin command prompt, using normal Windows path names. To make this available from any directory, you should add the appropriate path (c:\cygwin\bin by default) to your PATH environment variable, as shown in Figure C–10, so that you can use the bin utilities in any directory.

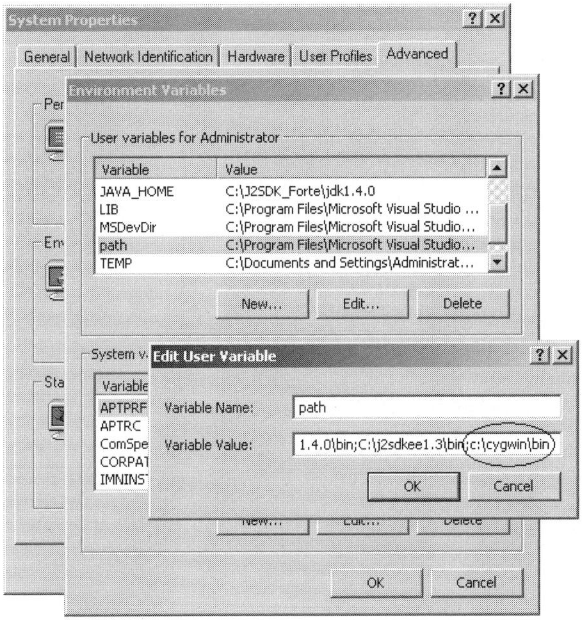

FIGURE C-10   *Adding Cygwin to the PATH environment variable.*

Testing Your Cygwin Installation

You can now test your Cygwin installation by compiling a simple DLL with the gcc utility and calling it from a C# .NET program. Here is an example of how to do this.

Create the following C source code file named **MyDll.c**. This will be compiled with the gcc utility to create a Windows DLL.

```
//MyDll.c

#include <windows.h>

int WINAPI DllMain(
    HANDLE hInst,
    ULONG reason,
    LPVOID lpReserved)
{
    return 1;
}
```

```c
__declspec(dllexport) char* SomeDllFunction()
{
   return "SomeDllFunction called!";
}
```

Here is the command line for compiling and generating **MyDll.dll**. This can be executed at an ordinary Windows command prompt or at the Cygwin Bash Shell prompt.

```
gcc -shared MyDll.c -o MyDll.dll -e DllMain@12
```

Here is the C# client program that will be used to test **MyDll.dll**.

```csharp
//MyDllClient.cs
using System;
using System.Runtime.InteropServices;

class MyDllClient
{
   //NOTE: MyDll.dll must be in dll search path

   [DllImport("MyDll.dll")]
   public static extern String SomeDllFunction();

   static void Main(string[] args)
   {
      String str = SomeDllFunction();
      Console.WriteLine(
         "SomeDllFunction in MyDll.dll returned: " +
         str);
   }
}
```

The result of running this C# client program is shown in Figure C–11. If you achieve this result, then you have set up your Cygwin installation properly.

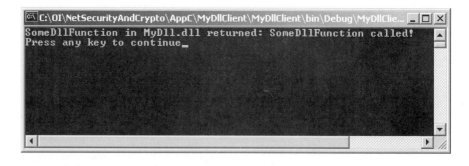

FIGURE C–11   *The result of running the C# client program.*

If this simple example worked, you should now install and test the GMP library.

Installing GMP

Now, you will want to download and build the GMP library. You can obtain the most recent version of GMP in source code format from *http://www.gnu.org/directory/gnump.html*. At the time of writing, the most recent version was **gmp-4.0.1.tar.gz**, as shown in Figure C–12.

After you download the GMP tarball (i.e., gmp-4.0.1.tar.gz), you will have to decompress it, using WinZip or an equivalent utility. This creates a directory named **gmp-4.0.1** (depending on the specific version you have downloaded), which you can put in some convenient place, such as at the root c:\ directory. At this point, the **c:\gmp-4.0.1** directory contains the GMP source tree, but it is not compiled and linked yet. To do this, you must start up a Cygwin command window by selecting Start | Programs | Cygwin | Cygwin Bash Shell.

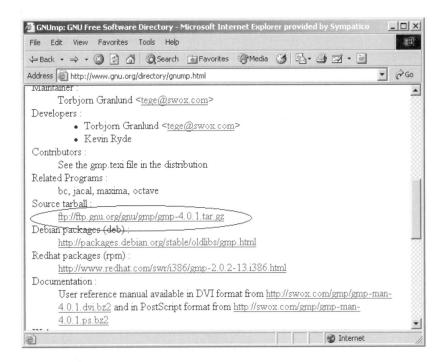

FIGURE C–12   *Getting GnuMP.*

To build the GMP library, enter the following commands at the Cygwin Bash Shell prompt.

```
cd c:/gmp-4.0.1
./configure --disable-static --enable-shared
make
make install
```

Your working directory may be different, according to where you unzipped the GMP tarball. We do not want a static library for linking with C/C++ programs. For .NET programs, we need a DLL that provides PInvoke services to access the functionality of the GMP library. This means that we must generate a DLL rather than a statically linkable LIB file. This is why we are using the **--disable-static --enable-shared** parameters in the configure command. The first **make** command is used to perform a build on the GMP project, and the second **make** command installs it on your Cygwin system. The result of this installation is that a header file named **gmp.h** is placed in the **c:\gmp-4.0.1** directory, and a DLL named **cyggmp-3.dll** is placed in the **c:\gmp-4.0.1\.libs** directory. You should make this DLL available to the DLL search path by adding **c:\gmp-4.0.1\.libs** to the PATH environment variable.

The details on how to use the entire functionality of the GMP library are beyond the scope of this book. To learn more about all the functions supported by the GMP library, see the documentation at *http://www.swox.com/gmp/manual/*. However, to get you started and to test the newly built GMP library with a C# .NET program, try creating the following C# client program. If you want to access any of the other GMP functions exposed by **cyggmp-3.dll**, just add the appropriate **DllImport** attributed external methods to the **CygGmpWrapper** class, according to the signature you find in **gmp.h**.

```
//MyCSharpGMPClient.cs

using System;
using System.Runtime.InteropServices;

//GMP's structure for multiprecision integer
[StructLayout(LayoutKind.Sequential)]
unsafe public struct mpz_struct
{
    public int _mp_alloc;
    public int _mp_size;
    public uint *_mp_d;
};

//NOTE: cyggmp-3.dll must be in dll search path
class CygGmpWrapper //wrapper for calling GMP library
{
```

```csharp
    [DllImport("cyggmp-3.dll")]
unsafe public static extern
    void __gmpz_init(
    mpz_struct* val);
    [DllImport("cyggmp-3.dll")]
unsafe public static extern
    int __gmpz_set_str(
    mpz_struct* val,
    String strval,
    int baseval);
    [DllImport("cyggmp-3.dll")]
unsafe public static extern
    int __gmpz_mul(
    mpz_struct* valprod,
    mpz_struct* val1,
    mpz_struct* val2);
    [DllImport("cyggmp-3.dll")]
unsafe public static extern
    String __gmpz_get_str(
    String str,
    int baseval,
    mpz_struct* val);
};

class MyCSharpGMPClient
{
    unsafe static void Main(string[] args)
    {
        //initialize gmp integer variables a, b, and p
        mpz_struct mpzs_a;
        mpz_struct* a = &mpzs_a;
        CygGmpWrapper.__gmpz_init(a);
        mpz_struct mpzs_b;
        mpz_struct* b = &mpzs_b;
        CygGmpWrapper.__gmpz_init(b);
        mpz_struct mpzs_prod;
        mpz_struct* prod = &mpzs_prod;
        CygGmpWrapper.__gmpz_init(prod);

        //assign a and b using base 10 strings
        CygGmpWrapper.__gmpz_set_str (
            a, "123456789123456789", 10);
        CygGmpWrapper.__gmpz_set_str (
            b, "123456789123456789", 10);

        //multiply a and b and put the result in prod
        //result is 15241578780673678515622620750190521
        CygGmpWrapper.__gmpz_mul(prod, a, b);
```

```
    //print prod in base 10
    String strProd =
        CygGmpWrapper.__gmpz_get_str(null, 10, prod);
    Console.WriteLine(
        "123456789123456789 * 123456789123456789 = \n" +
        strProd);
    }
}
```

When you run this program, you should see the following output.

```
123456789123456789 * 123456789123456789 =
15241578780673678515622620750190521
```

Uninstalling Cygwin

Cygwin does not have an automatic uninstall capability. To uninstall Cygwin, perform the following manual steps.

1. Delete the Cygwin shortcuts on the Desktop and Start Menu.
2. Delete the registry node **Software\Cygnus Solutions** under **HKEY_LOCAL_MACHINE** and **HKEY_CURRENT_USER**.
3. Delete the Cygwin directory (typically **C:\cygwin**).
4. Delete any files created in the setup temporary directory.
5. Delete **C:\cygwin\bin** from the **PATH** environment variable if you have it.

Cryptography and Security Resources

*T*his appendix provides a handy list of resources that you may find useful in gaining a deeper and broader understanding of cryptography and security. Some of the more notable books that you may find useful are listed here under each of several categories. Following that, you will find a list of useful Web sites that provide reference and product information related to several important aspects of cryptography and security.

Background Knowledge and Conceptual Books

The following books provide useful general-purpose background knowledge and conceptual information related to modern cryptography.

- *The Handbook of Applied Cryptography* by Alfred J. Menezes, Paul C. van Oorschot, and Scott A. Vanstone. This is also freely available online at *www.cacr.math.uwaterloo.ca/hac/*. This is one of the best and most comprehensive general technical references available. It introduces symmetric and asymmetric algorithms and provides excellent mathematical descriptions. Areas covered include pseudorandom number generator, symmetric and asymmetric algorithms, stream and block ciphers, hash functions, and digital signatures, along with descriptions of several important protocols and standards.
- *Introduction to Cryptography* by Johannes A. Buchmann. This is another great book that shows how several important cryptographic techniques work and how to estimate algorithmic efficiency and security strength. This book explains the important mathematical

methods of modern cryptography, but it assumes only basic mathematical knowledge on the part of the reader.

● *Applied Cryptography* by Bruce Schneier. This book has become enormously popular, especially as a reader's first background book. It provides a nice light overview of most of the significant aspects of modern cryptography, and it comes with a set of C source files for all of the most notable algorithms, which is great for learning about cryptography from the inside out.

● *Cryptography: Theory and Practice,* Second Edition, by Douglas Stinson. This book provides a highly readable and thorough coverage of cryptographic mathematics, including DES, RSA, one-way hash functions, pseudorandom number generator, and digital signatures.

Cryptographic Mathematics Books

Once you have a good understanding of the background basics, you may want to further your studies with deeper insights into the mathematical and theoretical aspects of cryptography and security. The following books provide a more mathematically focused treatment of cryptographic algorithms.

● *A Course in Number Theory and Cryptography* by Neal I. Koblitz. This mathematically intensive book introduces number theoretic concepts relevant to cryptography. No background in algebra or number theory is assumed, and the reader is methodically introduced to each important concept in a highly descriptive manner. Important algorithms are described along with an introduction to the analysis of complexity. This book also provides an introduction to the use of elliptic curves in cryptography, which is a rather advanced cutting-edge topic. Exercises and solutions are provided in each chapter.

● *The Mathematics of Ciphers: Number Theory and RSA Cryptography* by S. C. Coutinho. This compact book (less than 200 pages) provides an easygoing introduction to relevant number theory and algorithms that pertain to RSA cryptography. It describes their relation to asymmetric encryption and works toward a good understanding of the RSA algorithm itself. The book takes you through many basic concepts, developing thorough understanding of how RSA works, which is described in its final chapter.

Learning about cryptographic mathematics is only the first step in gaining a thorough understanding of cryptographic theory. The second step is to learn about cryptanalysis, which is the task of analyzing and breaking existing ciphers. Generally, an understanding of cryptanalysis is not necessary for regular programmers who simply need to implement existing cryptographic algorithms into their applications. However, to design new algorithms, you must have a good grounding in modern cryptanalysis theory. Cryptanalysis is rather difficult, and it is virtually always simpler and safer to use existing, well-tested algorithms than to design your own. Thus, in almost all cases, algorithm design should be left to professional cryptographers. However, if you are interested in eventually becoming a professional cryptographer, or if you simply have a personal desire to learn as much as you can about cryptanalysis, then you should study the following books.

- *Differential Cryptanalysis of the Data Encryption Standard* by Eli Biham and Adi Shamir. This is a mathematically advanced (you might even say scary) book that describes differential cryptanalysis as applied to the DES algorithm. It shows how to analyze the evolution of differences that result from related plaintexts that are encrypted using the same key. This technique is able to break the 16-round DES algorithm faster than any previously published attack. The same approach can be applied to some other symmetric algorithms as well.
- *Elementary Cryptanalysis: A Mathematical Approach* by Abraham Sinkov. This explains, in an easy-to-understand manner, some fundamental approaches used in cryptanalysis. Topics covered include some statistics, modular arithmetic, simple number theory, and a smattering of linear matrix algebra.
- *Cryptanalysis: A Study of Ciphers and Their Solutions* by Helen F Gaines. This book, which was published in 1939, is the bible of classical cipher analysis. Although classic ciphers are no longer seriously used today, making this book rather dated, it is still a very interesting read. It also provides many insights into the cryptanalysis mindset and gives you a feel for how cryptanalysis is planned and applied, without the bewildering mathematical complexity of modern cryptanalysis. It is also very interesting from a historical point of view.

Implementing Security Guide Books

In this book, we focused on security and cryptography from the programmer's point of view. Ultimately, however, security technologies that have been implemented by programmers must be put to use by administrators and end users. The programmer should therefore gain some familiarity with important security protocols and should also be aware of some of the administrative aspects of operating-system security features. The following provide hands-on, practical guides to implementing security on real systems, using actual protocols and products:

- *Cryptography and Network Security: Principles and Practice* by William Stallings. This is an introductory reference book on real-world security protocols and systems. It covers symmetric and asymmetric techniques for encryption and authentication. It also covers important security protocols, such as PGP, S/MIME, SSL, and Kerberos.
- *Windows 2000 Security* by Roberta Bragg. This provides network administrators with practical information on how to secure the Windows 2000 operating system, including security-related aspects of configuring Active Directory.

Human Interest Books on Cryptography

The following books provide a technically lighter and somewhat more historical approach to the topics of cryptography. These books are all great for times when you want to forget about programming and mathematics, and you simply want a relaxing read by the fireplace.

- *The Codebreakers* by David Kahn. This book provides a very interesting historical account of cryptography, but it does not have much to say about truly modern cryptography (after all, it was published in 1967). However, it provides a fascinating light read and is written in a captivating and nontechnical style.
- *The Code Book: The Science of Secrecy from Ancient Egypt to Quantum Cryptography* by Simon Singh. This book also offers a rather nontechnical look into the world of cryptography and codes through history, including some of the more recent developments not covered in *The Codebreakers*. This is also a very interesting read.
- *Decrypted Secrets* by Friedrich Bauer. This book continues in the style of *The Codebreakers* but is somewhat more technical, especially as it pertains to cryptanalysis of historically important WWII ciphers. Again, this is an interesting book for the casual reader.

Cryptography News Groups

- The news:sci.crypt newsgroup is a great place to post questions about cryptography. However, to avoid getting flamed, you should first read the FAQ at *www.faqs.org/faqs/cryptography-faq/*. Several very knowledgeable people frequent this newsgroup and can give you very high-quality answers to your questions. However, a few of them have zero tolerance for those who do not follow the guidelines outlined in the FAQ. In particular, if you do not have a considerable theoretical understanding of modern cryptography and cryptanalysis theory, then do not post any of your own algorithm designs to the group for comment and do not provide incorrect answers to other posted messages. If you do, then you will suffer the wrath of countless insults and flames, and you will receive no helpful feedback whatsoever. However, even the simplest novice questions are usually tolerated and politely answered if they comply with the FAQ guidelines.

- The news:sci.crypt.research newsgroup is a moderated newsgroup (and therefore it is more civilized and focused than news:sci.crypt) that is intended for serious discussion among experts. It is recommended that newbies lurk much more frequently than post to this newsgroup. In spite of the high intimidation level found within this newsgroup, it can still be a very good learning resource for the newcomer.

Useful Cryptographic and Security Web Sites

- Counterpane Internet Security is located at *www.counterpane.com*. The founder and CTO of Counterpane is Bruce Schneier, the author of the popular book *Applied Cryptography* and inventor of the Blowfish and Twofish algorithms. This Web site has some interesting literature, and it also provides access to *Crypto-Gram*, which is a free monthly email newsletter on computer security and cryptography.
- RSA Security is located at *www.rsasecurity.com*. This Web site provides a great deal of useful information, including the *CryptoBytes* newsletter, white papers, technical notes, and bulletins on RSA-based cryptography.
- The CERT Coordination Center is located at *www.cert.org*. CERT is a federally funded security issue clearing center operated by Carnegie Mellon University. It provides a large resource of important up-to-date information on known security issues. This Web site provides the latest information on significant security incidents, vulnerabilities, and security alerts.
- *The Handbook of Applied Cryptography* (also known as HAC) is freely available online at *www.cacr.math.uwaterloo.ca/hac/*. We mentioned this book earlier in this appendix, but we mention it here again simply because it is such an incredibly useful Web site resource for learning about cryptographic theory.

- The Bureau of Industry and Security is located at *www.bxa.doc.gov/ Encryption/Default.htm*. It provides information on U.S. government regulations governing exports of encryption technologies. Note that each country has its own set of laws regulating encryption and security technologies, so please consult any relevant country-specific information that you may need accordingly.

Exploring Web Services

I think there is a world market for maybe five computers.
—Thomas Watson, chairman of IBM, 1943

*It is not the strongest of the species that survives,
nor the most intelligent, but the one responsive to change.*
—Charles Darwin

*T*he Internet and World Wide Web are the most important and significant creations of the 20th century. These technologies have significantly changed the software world, making one wonder whether Darwin's comment refers to the human race or the Internet race. Such is the impact of the Internet that there has been a total paradigmatic shift in technology. A similar shift in perception is presently happening, this time with application programs using Web services. As the next revolutionary advancement of the Internet, Web services will become the elemental structure that links together all computing devices.

Microsoft explains Web services in the ASP.NET Quick Starts: "The Internet is quickly evolving from today's Web sites that just deliver user interface pages to browsers to a next generation of programmable Web sites that directly link organizations, applications, services, and devices with one another."

Motivation for Web Services

You may wonder, what is special in Web services compared to traditional distributed programming models like Microsoft's Distributed Component Object Model (DCOM), the Object Management Group's Common Object Request Broker Architecture (CORBA), or Sun's Remote Method Invocation (RMI).

The main drawbacks in the present distributed programming models include the following:

- Interoperability (ability to communicate and share data with applications from different vendors and platforms).
- Many businesses can't afford the cost of CORBA or even Enterprise Java Beans (EJBs) development and administration.
- These technologies face issues with firewalls. Since most firewalls block all but a few ports, such as the standard HTTP port 80, all of today's distributed object protocols, such as DCOM, suffer because they depend on dynamically assigned ports for remote procedure calls.

DCOM is proprietary, thus negating the goal of standards-based interoperability. DCOM systems cannot interoperate with CORBA or EJB systems without significant extra effort. RMI is Java-based and thus does not easily play well with other languages. CORBA comes closer. It is standards-based, vendor-neutral, and language-agnostic. It is limited, however, by its inability to utilize the power and flexibility of the Internet. DCOM and CORBA components often communicate via a COM/CORBA bridge. Even if a small change occurs in any part of the component model, we have to modify the entire model along with the bridge to reflect the changes. DCOM, IIOP, and Java/RMI require tight integration between the client and the server, and the platform used. These technologies also require specific binary data formats and a particular component technology or object-calling convention. Thus, the failure of the industry to find a single standard motivates the Web services.

Web services perk up distributed computing capabilities and solve these problems. In a Web services-based computing model the client need not worry about the language or operating system in which Web services are implemented (because Web services are loosely coupled Web programming models based on standard data formats and protocols such as XML, SOAP, and HTTP). The Web service client has to identify only the location of a Web service and the methods that the client can call on the service. The only assumption between the Web service client and the Web service is that recipients will understand the SOAP messages they receive. As a result, applications written in different programming languages, using different component models, running on different operating systems, and devices can access Web services.

Web Services Definition

Web services are defined in many different ways. The following definitions are from leading companies who are involved in Web services.

1. **W3C:** A Web service is a software application identified by a URI, whose interfaces and binding are capable of being defined, described, and discovered by XML artifacts and supports direct interactions with other software applications using XML-based messages via Internet-based protocols.
2. **Microsoft:** Web services provide the ability to exchange messages in a loosely coupled environment using standard protocols such as HTTP, XML, XSD, SOAP, and WSDL.
3. **IBM:** Web services are a new breed of Web application. They are self-contained, self-describing, modular applications that can be published, located, and invoked across the Web.
4. **Rogue Wave:** Applications that interoperate in a loosely coupled system using Internet protocols.
5. **The Stencil Group:** Loosely coupled software components that encapsulate discrete functionality and that are accessible over standard Internet protocols.
6. **Sun Microsystems:** A Web service is an application that exists in a distributed environment, such as the Internet. A Web service accepts a request, performs its function based on the request, and returns a response.

Backbones of Web Services

Let us explore the baseline XML Web services specifications, such as XML, SOAP, WSDL and UDDI.

XML (Extensible Markup Language): XML is the foundation on which Web services are built. XML provides the description, storage, and transmission format for data exchanged via Web services. XML is a simple, platform-independent, and broadly adopted standard.

SOAP (Simple Object Access Protocol): SOAP is a lightweight and simple XML-based protocol that is designed to exchange structured and typed information on the Web. SOAP is a protocol that defines how to access services, objects, and servers in a platform-independent manner using HTTP and XML. SOAP uses XML as a wire protocol to describe how the data and its associated type definitions are transmitted. SOAP was developed by Microsoft, IBM, and others, and then handed over to the W3C for further development. At present, SOAP 1.2 is emerging as a W3C-defined specification and has been sent to the W3C membership for final review.

The WSDL (Web Service Description Language): The WSDL is an XML-based grammar for describing Web services and their functions, parameters, and return values. WSDL defines the methods and the data associated with a Web service. Since WSDL is XML-based, it is both human- and machine-readable.

The UDDI (Universal Description, Discovery, and Integration): UDDI is a comprehensive industry initiative enabling businesses to share information about Web services in a global registry. UDDI enables businesses to find and transact with one another dynamically. UDDI facilitates locating the WSDL-formatted protocol description of a given SOAP-based Web service (standard way to publish and discover information about Web services). UDDI is a business registry that allows businesses and developers to programmatically locate information about Web services exposed by other organizations. At present, UDDI is not a standard, but a joint initiative of businesses and vendors. The latest UDDI version 3 has some unique features such as multiregistry topologies, increased security features, improved WSDL support, a new subscription API, and core information model advances.

Next Generation of Distributed Computing: Web Services

An XML Web service is a programmable application component that provides some serviceable, useful functionality, such as application logic, and is available to any number of potentially incongruent systems through the use of standard protocols, such as XML and HTTP. Web services provide the ability to exchange messages in a loosely coupled environment (whereas DCOM, IIOP, and Java/RMI require tight integration between the client and the server) through the use of common data formats and standard protocols, such as XML, SOAP, and HTTP.

Since Web services are based on standard data formats and protocols, Web service applications can communicate with a wide range of implementations, platforms, and devices. As XML messaging is the fundamental means of data communication in Web services, it bridges the differences that exist between systems that use dissimilar component models, programming languages, and operating systems.

Since Web services use the underlying infrastructure provided by HTTP, Web services can move data through firewalls and between diverse systems.

Therefore, we see Web services as the next generation of distributed computing. Web services are enabling a new era of distributed application development.

Benefits of Web Services

Let us see some momentous advantages of Web services.

1. Web services offer new business opportunities by making it easy to connect with partners (business-to-business integration).
2. Web services reduce application development and maintenance costs (save time and money).
3. You can create new sources of revenue by modifying the present functionality as the Web services.
4. Web services provide a solution to systems interoperability problems.
5. Web services enable crossplatform, program-to-program communications (application integration).
6. Software reuse is a time- and cost-saving benefit of Web services.
7. Web services connect information, applications, people, systems, and devices.

ASP.NET Web Services

Since ASP.NET Web services are built on top of ASP.NET, you can use the features of ASP.NET to build Web services. Distinctively, ASP.NET takes advantage of performance and security enhancements found in the .NET Framework and the CLR. Because ASP.NET is built upon the .NET Framework, ASP.NET Web services can utilize many .NET Framework features, such as authentication, caching, memory management, interoperability, and state management. Visual Studio .NET is a powerful tool for building Web applications, Web services, desktop applications, and mobile applications. The Visual Studio .NET IDE (integrated development environment) facilitates rapid application development (RAD), which enables developers to quickly create, consume, and deploy Web services. The ASP.NET and Visual Studio .NET provides an easy and simple programming model to develop and deploy Web services. For example, developers do not need to generate WSDL documents, since ASP.NET itself takes care of generating the required WSDL documents.

Web Services Architecture

The Web service infrastructure consists of the following four sections.

1. Wire Format (HTTP and SOAP)
2. Description and Discovery Stack (WSDL and Disco)
3. Directory Stack (UDDI)
4. Request/Response Service (Soap Message)

Figure E–1 shows the basic Web services architecture. Figure E–2 illustrates the four sections of the Web service infrastructure and their relationships in detail.

Figure E–3 and Figure E–4 show the Web services interaction. The various steps involved in Web services interaction are as follows.

- The service provider, in order to publish a Web service as a one-time activity, registers the Web service definition (the WSDL) in a UDDI registry.
- The client application queries the UDDI using a description of the service it needs.

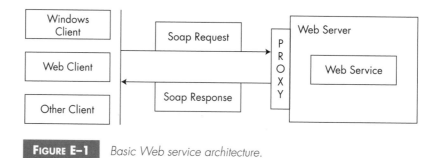

FIGURE E–1   *Basic Web service architecture.*

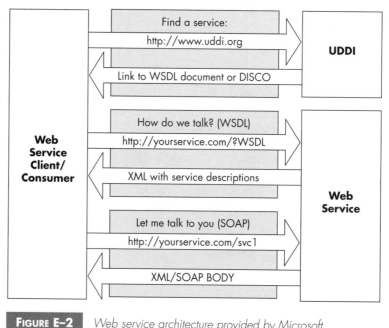

FIGURE E–2   *Web service architecture provided by Microsoft.*

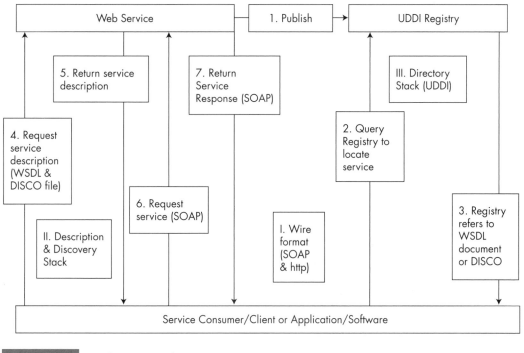

FIGURE E-3   *Web service architecture.*

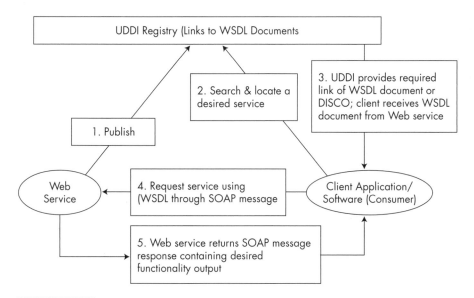

FIGURE E-4   *Web service interaction.*

- If a proper Web service is found, UDDI provides a link to the WSDL document describing that Web service.
- The client uses the link to request the WSDL document for that Web service.
- The Web service returns WSDL, which describes the interface(s) for calling the Web service.
- The client makes a SOAP request, formatted according to the WSDL.
- The Web service returns a SOAP body based on the request.

Code Model for Web Services

A Web service created using Visual Studio .NET has two parts:

1. The first part is a file with extension **.asmx**, which serves as the address-able entry point for the Web service.
2. The second part is the code behind file with extension **.asmx.cs** (**.asmx.vb** for VB.NET), which provides the implementations for the methods that the Web service provides.

The **WebService** directive present in the **.asmx** file specifies the public class that implements the Web service logic. In ASP.NET, the **.asmx** file references code in pre-compiled assemblies, a code-behind file, or the code contained in the **.asmx** file itself. The Web service class contains one or more public methods for exposure in a Web service. These Web service methods are prefaced with the **WebMethod** attribute. By default, Visual Studio .NET uses code-behind files—for instance, **Service1.asmx.cs** or **Service1.asmx.vb**—when you develop a Web service with the ASP.NET Web service project template.

Developing a Simple Concatenate Web Service

From the File menu select New | Project…. The dialog box with different types of projects will be displayed, as shown in Figure E–5. Select ASP.NET Web service from the Visual C# Projects and type the location of the localhost Web server (or the name of the IIS Web server on which to host the XML Web service). After typing the location, press the OK button. Visual Studio automatically creates the necessary files and references to support a Web service. After you press OK, the IDE displays the **.asmx** file in Design View (since

FIGURE E–5   *Creating a Concatenate ASP.NET Web application project.*

XML Web services are inherently nonvisual, you cannot drag and drop controls or other visual elements in Design View). Click the link Click here to switch to code view in the Design View to add the code to the Web service.[1]

When the project is created, the Web service has the name **Service1.asmx**. Rename the **Service1.asmx** file in the Solution Explorer **Concatenate.asmx**. The addressable entry point for the Web service is specified by the **.asmx** file **Concatenate.asmx**. The implementation for the methods that the Web service provides is in the file **Concatenate.asmx.cs**. To view the **.asmx** file, right-click the **.asmx** file in the Solution Explorer and select Source Code (Text) Editor in the Open With dialog box, and then click Open, as shown in Figure E–6.

Use the following URL to access the program: *http://localhost/Security/ AppendixE/Concatenate/Concatenate.asmx.*

---

1. The project created by Visual Studio has commented-out code already provided for a simple "Hello World" Web service. To implement that Web service, just uncomment the code, then build and run.

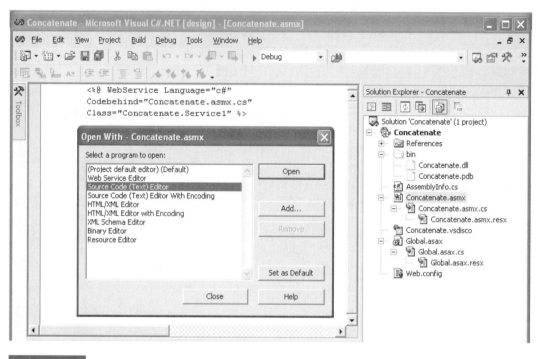

FIGURE E-6 *Open With dialog box.*

Concatenate.asmx and Concatenate.asmx.cs

The code of the **Concatenate.asmx** file has just the following **WebService** directive:

```
<%@ WebService Language="c#"
Codebehind="Concatenate.asmx.cs"
Class="Concatenate.Service1" %>
```

The code of **Concatenate.asmx.cs** file is as follows.

```
using System;
using System.Collections;
using System.ComponentModel;
using System.Data;
using System.Diagnostics;
using System.Web;
using System.Web.Services;
```

```
namespace Concatenate
{

[WebService(Namespace="http://www.phptr.com",
Description="A Simple Web Service.", Name="Concatenation")]

public class Service1 : System.Web.Services.WebService
{
  public Service1()
    {
     InitializeComponent();
    }
//Component Designer generated code

   protected override void Dispose( bool disposing )
   {
   }

//If you add "WebMethodAttribute" to a method in a Web
//service then it makes the method callable from a remote
//client.

[WebMethod (Description="Web Service which provides
Concatenation functionality.")]
public string Concatenate(string s1, string s2)
    {
        string s3="Concatenated String =";
        return s3+s1+s2;
    }
   }
}
```

TESTING CONCATENATE WEB SERVICE

Even without creating a client for your Web service, you can view and test it by employing ASP.NET. After creating the Concatenate Web service in Visual Studio .NET, just click the Run button to view the IE (Internet Explorer) test page.[2] Figure E–7 shows the IE test page, which lists all the available Web service methods. (In our example, only one, **Concatenate**, is available.)

Now, let us test our Web service by clicking the link Concatenate in the IE test page. Figure E–8 shows the test page that is displayed when you click the link. This test page has two sections. The first part consists of two textboxes and an Invoke button that allows you to run the Concatenate Web service method without needing to create a client. The second part consists of a

---

2. The Internet Explorer test page is an automatically created HTML page with which you can execute and test a Web service's methods and review its WSDL document.

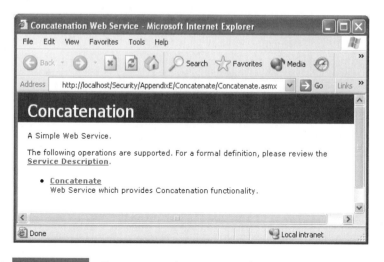

FIGURE E-7   *The Internet Explorer test page for the Concatenate Web service.*

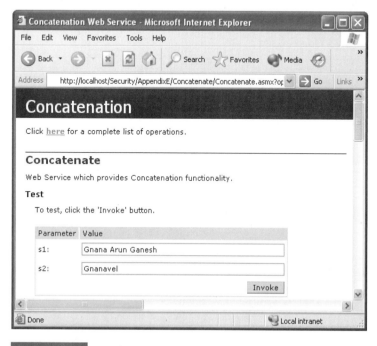

FIGURE E-8   *Invoking Concatenate Web service method.*

list of different protocols (HTTP POST, HTTP GET, and SOAP) you can employ to connect with the Web service and a description for each message format. If you press the Invoke button, the result is displayed inside a new browser window in the XML format, as shown in Figure E–9.

SERVICE DESCRIPTION

If you click the Service Description link, WSDL is displayed that defines the service description of that Web service, as shown in Figure E–10. A WSDL document can be logically divided into two sections:

- **Abstract definitions:** Types, messages, and port types
- **Concrete definitions:** Bindings and services

WSDL Element: type • This element provides the definition for the datatypes in a SOAP message. The **<types>** element contains an XSD schema. For example, the **<types>** section in the WSDL file of the concatenate Web service defines the following types:

- **Concatenate** is used when SOAP invokes the Web service.
- **ConcatenateResponse** is used when the SOAP Web service invocation returns. **Concatenate** has two elements, **s1** and **s2,** which are defined with the XSD type's string.

WSDL Element: message • The **<message>** section offers a description of the message.

WSDL Element: portType • The **<portType>** section describes the service interfaces of the operations that the Web service supports. If there had been

FIGURE E–9   *The result from Concatenate Web service method in XML format.*

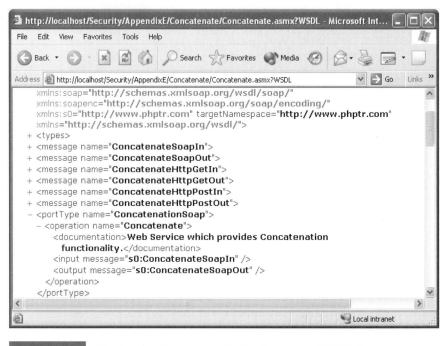

FIGURE E-10   *Viewing the Concatenate Service Description (WSDL document).*

more Web methods in the Web service, there would have been more operation elements allied with the **portType**.

WSDL ELEMENT: SERVICE • The **<service>** section describes the URL of the Web service on the server.

WSDL ELEMENT: BINDING • The **<binding>** section defines the data encodings and protocols to be used for each operation.

Later, we discuss how to consume the developed Web service. Now, let us study in detail the **WebService** directive and the **System.Web.Services** namespace.

@ WebService Directive

To declare a Web service, place the **WebService** directive at the top of a file with an **.asmx** extension.

```
<%@ WebService class="Service1" Language="cs" %>
```

The **WebService** directive indicates the class implementing the Web service and the programming language used in the implementation. The essential attributes of the **WebService** directive include the following:

Class attribute: This attribute indicates the class with Web service implementation. It can be set to a class that exists in the same file as in our previous example or within a separate file placed in the Bin folder under the directory where **.asmx** is situated.

Language attribute: This attribute indicates the programming language used to create the Web service. You can develop Web services in any .NET-compatible language, such as C#, Visual Basic.NET, and JScript.NET.

Codebehind attribute: If the implementation of the Web service resides in a code-behind file, then this **Codebehind** attribute specifies the file.

If the implementation of the Web service resides in an assembly, then declare as follows:

```
<%@ WebService Language="cs" Class="Class Name, Assembly
Name" %>
```

System.Web.Services Namespace

The **System.Web.Services** namespace consists of the classes that facilitate development and use of Web services. Let us investigate the classes in **System.Web.Services** namespace in detail. Table E–1 shows the classes in the **System.Web.Services** namespace.

TABLE E–1   *Classes in System.Web.Services Namespace*

Item	Details
WebServiceAttribute (Optional)	May be used to add more information to Web services, such as a string describing its functionality.
WebService (Optional)	Delineates the base class for Web services if you want to use common ASP.NET objects such as **Server**, **Session**, **User**, **Context**, and **Application**.
WebMethodAttribute	If you add this attribute to a method in a Web service, it makes the method callable from a remote client.

WebServiceAttribute

You can use the **WebServiceAttribute** to add information to a Web service. It is optional. This is used in the service description and the service help page of the Web service. The attribute is not required for a Web service to be published and executed. Table E–2 shows the instance properties of the **WebServiceAttribute class**.

TABLE E–2	Instance Properties of the WebServiceAttribute Class
Properties	**Description**
Description	Provides descriptive comments about the Web services.
Name	Provides the name for the ASP.NET Web service.
Namespace	Provides the default XML namespace for the Web service.

In our first example, **Concatenate.asmx**, you may notice these properties in the code and in the program output as follows.

- Description: "A Simple Web Service."
- Name: "Concatenation"
- Namespace: http://www.phptr.com

The default value of the namespace is **http://tempuri.org/** for Web services that are under development, but published Web services should use a more permanent namespace. It is highly suggested that this default namespace should be personalized before the Web service is made publicly consumable. This is important because the Web service needs to be distinguished from other Web services. To apply the **WebService** attribute, insert the **WebService** attribute before the class declaration and set the **Namespace** and **Description** properties. Separate multiple properties with a comma.

```
[WebService(Namespace="http://www.phptr.com",
Description="A Simple Web Service.", Name="Concatenation")]
public class Service1 : System.Web.Services.WebService
    {
     //Implementation
    }
```

When you run the **Concatenate** program without the **WebService** attribute, you can see more details concerning the need for the **WebService** attribute in the test page.

WebService Class

System.Web.Services.WebService class is an optional base class for Web services, which provides access to common ASP.NET objects such as **Session**, **Server**, **Application**, **Context**, and **User**. You can derive Web services directly from **System.Object**, but, by default, Web services created using Visual Studio .NET automatically derive from the **WebService** base class. If you create a Web service without deriving from the **WebService** class, then you cannot access the ASP.NET objects. If the Web service does not inherit from the **WebService** base class, it can access the ASP.NET intrinsic objects from **System.Web.HttpContext.Current**. Let's scrutinize the properties of the **WebService** class. Table E–3 shows the properties of the **WebService** Class.

TABLE E-3   *Properties of the WebService Class*

Properties	Description
Application	Gets the **Application** object for the current HTTP request.
Context	Gets the ASP.NET **HttpContext** for the current request, which encapsulates all HTTP-specific contexts used by the HTTP server to process Web requests.
Server	Gets the **HttpServerUtility** for the current request.
Session	Gets the **HttpSessionState** instance for the current request.
User	Gets the ASP.NET server **User** object, which can be used to authenticate a given user.

WebMethod Attribute

If you want to expose your public method as part of the Web service, add the **WebMethod** attribute to that public method. The **WebMethod** attribute provides the following properties:

- **BufferResponse**
- **Description**
- **MessageName**
- **CacheDuration**
- **EnableSession**
- **TransactionOption**

WEBMETHOD ATTRIBUTE: BUFFERRESPONSE

The **BufferResponse** property of the **WebMethod** attribute facilitates buffering of responses before they are sent to the client for a Web service method. If this property value is true, then it serializes the response of the Web service method into a memory buffer until either the response is completely serialized or the buffer is full. After the response is buffered, it is returned to the Web service client over the network. The default value is true. The buffering technique improves performance by reducing the communication between the worker process and the IIS process. If you set this property to false, ASP.NET buffers the response in 16-KB chunks. If you don't need to place the whole contents of the response in the memory, or if the Web service method returns large amounts of data to the client, then you might set this property to false. SOAP extensions are disabled for the Web service method if this property value is false.

```
[WebMethod(BufferResponse=false)]
Public string GetData()
{
// Implementation code
}
```

WEBMETHOD ATTRIBUTE: DESCRIPTION

You can make use of the **Description** property of the **WebMethod** attribute to provide a name for the Web method which is to be published. It is optional. This is used in the service description and the service help page of the Web service.

The default value is **String.Empty**. In the following example the string **"Web Service which provides Concatenation functionality"** is used to describe the Web service method, and the same can be used in the WSDL file, as shown in Figure E–10.

```
[WebMethod (Description="Web Service which provides
Concatenation functionality.")]
public string Concatenate(string s1, string s2)
    {
        string s3="Concatenated String =";
        return s3+s1+s2;
    }
```

WEBMETHOD ATTRIBUTE: MESSAGENAME

The **MessageName** property of the **WebMethod** attribute facilitates a unique name to the overloaded or polymorphic methods. The **MessageName** property can be used to alias method or property names. To exemplify this property, let's look at a simple add Web service that has three methods.

```
[WebMethod (Description="Add two floats.")]
 public float Add(float s1, float s2)
 {
   return s1+s2;
 }

[WebMethod (Description="Add two integers.")]
 public int Add(int s1, int s2)
 {
   return s1+s2;
 }

[WebMethod (Description="Add three integers.")]
 public int Add (int s1, int s2, int s3)
 {
   return s1+s2+s3;
 }
```

The program compiles nicely without a problem. But if you request the Web service, you come across the following errors for overload and polymorphic methods, respectively.

> **System.Exception: Both Int32 Add(Int32, Int32) and Single Add(Single, Single) use the message name 'Add'. Use the MessageName property of the WebMethod custom attribute to specify unique message names for the methods.**

> **System.Exception: Both Int32 Add(Int32, Int32, Int32) and Int32 Add(Int32, Int32) use the message name 'Add'. Use the MessageName property of the WebMethod custom attribute to specify unique message names for the methods.**

If you alter the program as follows, using the **MessageName** property, the program runs smoothly.

```
[WebMethod(Description="Add two
Floats.",MessageName="Add2Floats")]
public float Add (float s1, float s2)
{ return s1+s2;}

[WebMethod (Description="Add two
integers.",MessageName="Add2Integers")]
public int Add (int s1, int s2)
{ return s1+s2;}

[WebMethod (Description="Add three
integers.",MessageName="Add3Integers")]
public int Add (int s1, int s2, int s3)
{ return s1+s2+s3;}
```

You can see that the WSDL description names are unique now.

CACHING IN ASP.NET WEB SERVICE

You can incorporate the caching behavior to an ASP.NET Web service by setting the **CacheDuration** property of the **WebMethod** attribute as follows.

```
[WebMethod(CacheDuration=30)]
```

The value of the **CacheDuration** property indicates how many seconds ASP.NET should cache the results. You should set the **CacheDuration** property of the **WebMethod** attribute to any value greater than zero. The default value of **CacheDuration** property is zero.

TRANSACTION IN ASP.NET WEB SERVICE

You can incorporate the transaction behavior (new transaction) of an ASP.NET Web service by setting the transaction property of the **WebMethod** attribute as follows.

1. Add a reference to **System.EnterpriseServices.dll**.
2. Use the **TransactionOption** property of the **WebMethod** attribute

```
[WebMethod(TransactionOption=TransactionOption.RequiresNew)]
```

System.EnterpriseServices.dll namespace contains methods and properties that expose the distributed transaction model found in COM+ services. If an exception is thrown during the execution of the transaction process in a Web service method, the transaction is automatically aborted (using the **SetAbort** method of the **System.EnterpriseServices.ContextUtil** class). If no exception happens, then the transaction is automatically committed (using the **SetComplete** method of the **System.EnterpriseServices.ContextUtil** class). The **TransactionOption** property of the **WebMethod** attribute specifies how a Web service method participates in a transaction. Table E–4 shows **TransactionOption** enumeration members.

TABLE E–4	*TransactionOption Enumeration Members*
Item	**Description**
Disabled	Ignore any transaction in the current context.
NotSupported	Create the component in a context with no governing transaction.
Required	Share a transaction if one exists; create a new transaction if necessary.
RequiresNew	Create the component with a new transaction regardless of the state of the current context.
Supported	Share a transaction if one exists.

The **TransactionOption** property can be set to any of the **Transaction-Option** enumeration values. But the **TransactionOption** enumeration of a Web service method has only two possible behaviors.

- Doesn't participate in a transaction (**Disabled**, **NotSupported**, **Supported**).
- Creates a new transaction (**Required**, **RequiresNew**).

The default value is **TransactionOption.Disabled**.

Session Management

The **EnableSession** property of the **WebMethod** attribute facilitates session state for a Web service method. The basic steps are as follows:

- Add a reference to the **System.Web.Services** namespace.
- Set the **EnableSession** property of the **WebMethod** attribute to true as below.

You can access the stored information in the **Session** object if you set this property to true.

```
[WebMethod(EnableSession=true)]
public String SessionCount()
{
// Code
}
```

Protocols

When you create an ASP.NET Web service, it automatically supports clients using the SOAP, HTTP GET, and HTTP POST protocols to invoke Web service methods. In HTTP GET the data is sent in a query string (name/value pairs) that is appended to the URL. In HTTP POST the data is not appended to the query string as in HTTP GET, but instead name/value pairs are written to a separate line sent with the HTTP header, and the data is not directly visible to the outside world.

The datatypes supported by HTTP GET and HTTP POST are string (Int16, Int32, Int64, Boolean, Single, Double, Decimal, DateTime, etc.), enumerations, and simple arrays. You cannot use HTTP GET and HTTP POST to represent some complex datatypes. However, SOAP supports a richer set of datatypes, such as object instances, ADO.NET datasets, XML nodes, and complex arrays.

Accessing a Web Service

There are two primary steps when working with Web services: creating a Web service and accessing a Web service. We discussed how to create a Web service and test it in the IE test page. Let us now explore how to develop a Windows Form client. In consuming a Web service, the client application has to locate, reference, and invoke the functionality in a Web service. A Web service client can be any type of .NET application, such as a Web or Windows application. Let's create a simple Windows Form client for the Concatenate Web service. The fundamental steps in consuming Web services are as follows:

- Locate the Web service by using the Add Web Reference dialog box (if you are using Visual Studio .NET).
- Generate a proxy class for the Web service either by using the WSDL.exe tool or by adding a Web reference to your project.
- Reference the proxy class in the client code by including its namespace.
- Create an instance of the Web service proxy class and invoke the Web service methods using that proxy.

Generating a Proxy

A proxy class acts as an intermediary between the Web service and the client. It transmits the required arguments from the client to the Web service and also returns of the result back to the client. By default, the proxy class uses SOAP to access the Web service method. Generating a proxy class is very easy. You can create it in two ways.

- Using the Wsdl.exe command-line tool.[3]
- Using Visual Studio .NET.

Creating a Proxy Using Wsdl.exe

Now let us create a proxy for **Concatenate.asmx** and explore the proxy class in detail. You have to specify the name of the proxy file to be created and the URL where the service description is available, as follows:

```
Wsdl /out:Concatenate.cs http://localhost/Security
/AppendixE/Concatenate/Concatenate.asmx?wsdl
```

---

3. The Wsdl.exe tool is in the .NET Framework directory, such as **C:/Program Files/Microsoft.NET/ FrameworkSDK/Bin**.

The Wsdl.exe tool creates a C# proxy class by default. For other languages, such as VB.NET or JScript.NET, you have to use the optional **/l:** language flag.

CONSTRUCTING THE ASSEMBLY

To make use of the generated proxy class, you have to build an assembly to contain the proxy code. Construct the assembly in the command prompt as follows:

```
csc /r:system.xml.dll /r:system.web.services.dll
/out:c:\Concatenate.dll /t:library Concatenate.cs
```

The syntax for the Wsdl tool is as follows:

```
Wsdl /language:language  /protocol:protocol
/namespace:myNameSpace /out:filename /username:username
/password:password /domain:domain <url or path>
```

Figure E–11 shows the **Concatenate.dll** assembly in IL DASM.[4]

Creating a Windows Form Client

Now we create a simple Windows Form client using Visual Studio .NET, which consumes the Concatenate Web service. Create a Windows application

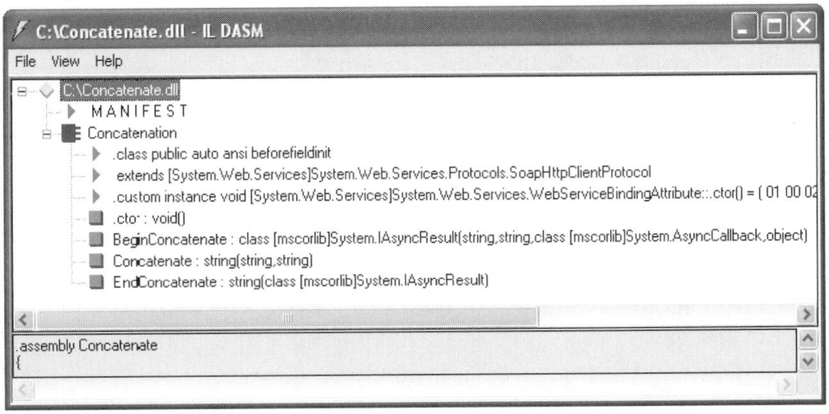

FIGURE E-11   *Viewing the Concatenate.dll assembly in IL DASM.*

---

4. The Microsoft .NET Framework SDK offers a tool called MSIL Disassembler (ILDasm.exe) that allows you to load any Microsoft .NET assembly (EXE or DLL) and investigate its contents, including the associated manifest, type metadata, and IL instruction set.

project and add a reference to the **Concatenate.dll** assembly and **System.Web.Services**. Then, you can easily access the Web service by creating an instance of the proxy object in the client code, as follows:

```
private void button1_Click(object sender, System.EventArgs e)
  {
    string s1,s2;
    Concatenation proxy = new Concatenation();
          s1=textBox1.Text.ToString();
          s2=textBox2.Text.ToString();
    textBox3.Text=proxy.Concatenate(s1,s2);
  }
```

Figure E–12 shows the output of the Windows Form client program.

CREATING A WEB REFERENCE IN VISUAL STUDIO .NET

In Visual Studio .NET creating a Web reference is straightforward. The only limitation when you use Visual Studio .NET is that you can specify the protocol as SOAP only. But you can specify the protocol as HTTP GET, HTTP POST, or SOAP in the Wsdl.exe utility using the **/protocol** flag. To add a reference to the Web service, click Project | Add Web Reference. Then click the link Web References on Local Web Server or type the required Web service path name in the address. You can view the test page and WSDL file, and then click the Add Reference button. You can view the **disco**[5] and WSDL files in the Web Refer-

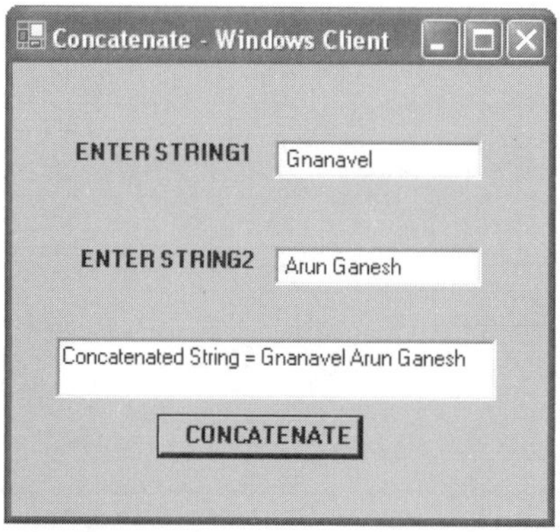

FIGURE E-12   *Output of the Concatenationwinclient program.*

---

5. The DISCO specification defines an algorithm for locating service descriptions. The **disco** file is an XML document that contains links to Web services, or it can offer a dynamic list of Web services in a specified path.

ences node in the Solution Explorer[6]. Then, you can easily access the Web service by creating an instance of the proxy object in the client code, as follows:

```
private void button1_Click(object sender, System.EventArgs e)
    {
        string s1,s2;
        localhost.Concatenation proxy = new
localhost.Concatenation();
        s1=textBox1.Text.ToString();
        s2=textBox2.Text.ToString();
        textBox3.Text=proxy.Concatenate(s1,s2);
    }
```

Asynchronous Programming in Web Services

You can also employ an asynchronous call for a method on a Web service along with a synchronous call. What's special about asynchronous programming? The unique thing in asynchronous programming is that after sending the request to the Web service, the client need not wait for the request to be completed.

If a large amount of data is to be returned from a Web service, you can use the asynchronous method. This will greatly improve the application performance. The client can do any further useful execution until the result is returned from the Web service. It is imperative to note that a Web service does not have to be exclusively written to handle asynchronous requests to be called asynchronously.

When the proxy class is created using either Wsdl.exe or Visual Studio .NET for synchronous call, the methods needed for calling the Web service method asynchronously are also created automatically.

Two Asynchronous Methods (Begin and End)

For each synchronous method, there is a **Begin** and an **End** asynchronous method. For example, in the proxy **Concatenate.cs** file, for the synchronous **Concatenate()** method, there are two asynchronous methods: **BeginConcatenate()** and **EndConcatenate()**, as shown next.

```
public string Concatenate(string s1, string s2)
{
object[] results = this.Invoke("Concatenate", new object[]
{ s1,   s2});
```

---

6. If the Web service is changed, then you have to update the proxy class by right-clicking on the server name (in our case, localhost) and click Update Web Reference.

```
return ((string)(results[0]));
}

public System.IAsyncResult BeginConcatenate(string s1,
string s2, System.AsyncCallback callback, object
asyncState)
{
return this.BeginInvoke("Concatenate", new object[]
{s1,s2}, callback, asyncState);
}

public string EndConcatenate(System.IAsyncResult
asyncResult)
{    object[] results = this.EndInvoke(asyncResult);
     return ((string)(results[0]));
}
```

The **Begin** method is called by a client to start the process of the Web service method (request). The **End** method is called by the client to get the results of the processing done by the Web service method call (response). After calling the **Begin** method to start the process, when do we have to call the **End** method? How will we know the asynchronous Web service call has completed?

There are four ways to determine when the asynchronous Web service call has completed.

1. A callback delegate is passed along with the **Begin** method, and that callback function is called by the proxy when the Web method has completed processing.
2. A client waits for the method to complete using one of the methods of the **WaitHandle** class.
3. The value of **IAsyncResult.IsCompleted** is polled to check the completion of the process. When this property returns true, the Web service response is available.
4. The **End** method is called directly.

Let us discuss the first two methods in detail.

Creating an ASP.NET Calculator Web Service

Create a Web service with C# as project type, and enter **http://localhost/Security/AppendixE/Calculator** as the location of your project. Write a Web method named **Calculator** that accepts three arguments: first operand operation (+, - , *, /, Pow), second operand, and gives the result as double, as shown in the following code.

```
[WebMethod(Description="Simple Calculator Web Service.")]
public double Calculator(System.Double a,string c,
System.Double  b)
{
switch (c)
  {
  case "+":
    return a + b;
    case "-":
    return a - b;
    case "/":
    if (b == 0)
    {
    return 0;
    }
    return a /b;
    case "*":
    return a * b;
    case "Pow":
    return Math.Pow(a, b);
    default:
    return 0;
  }
 }
```

Test the Web service in the test form and check the results.

EXAMPLE: ASYNCHRONOUS PROGRAMMING (METHOD 1)

To illustrate the asynchronous programming of method 1, we look at a simple Windows example. Open a new Windows application and add a Web reference to the Web service **http://localhost/Security/AppendixE/Calculator/Service1.asmx**. In this method, the **Callback** function is passed with the **Begin** method, and it will be called by the proxy when the Web method has completed processing and returns the result to the proxy.

In the following example we show the asynchronous programming of method 1.

```
private void button1_Click(object sender, System.EventArgs e)
{
  localhost.Service1 proxy = new localhost.Service1();
  AsyncCallback cb = new AsyncCallback(AddCallback);
  double s1,s3;
  string s2;
  s1=Convert.ToDouble(textBox1.Text);
  s3=Convert.ToDouble(textBox3.Text);
  s2 = textBox2.Text;
  IAsyncResult ar =
proxy.BeginCalculator(s1,s2,s3,cb,proxy);
```

```
/* Do any useful work! Callback function is called by the
proxy when the method has completed processing and returning
the result to the proxy.*/
}

public static void AddCallback(IAsyncResult ar)
{
localhost.Service1 proxy = (localhost.Service1)
ar.AsyncState;
double a;
// End the Method Call.
// EndCalculator (System.IAsyncResult asyncResult).
a=proxy.EndCalculator(ar);
MessageBox.Show(a.ToString(),"Output:");

}
```

Figure E–13 shows the output of **Calculate.cs**.

EXAMPLE: ASYNCHRONOUS PROGRAMMING (METHOD 2)

To illustrate the second method of calling the **End** method, let us look at a simple Web example. Open a new ASP.NET Web application and add a Web reference to the Web service **http://localhost/Security/AppendixE/Calculator/ Service1.asmx**. Include the namespace **System.Threading**. You will require this namespace to access the **WaitHandle** class. In this method the client waits for the method to complete, using one of the methods of the **WaitHandle** class.

After asynchronously calling the desired Web service or Web services, the **WaitHandle** class waits for

- A single Web service (**WaitHandle.WaitOne**).
- The first of many Web services (**WaitHandle.WaitAny**). This method is favored if you wish to process the results as they are available one by one.

FIGURE E–13   Output of Calculate.cs (asynchronous method 1).

- All of many Web services (**WaitHandle.WaitAll**). This method is preferred if you desire to process the results after the completion of all asynchronous calls.

In the following example we show the asynchronous programming of method 2.

```
private void Button1_Click(object sender, System.EventArgs e)
{
localhost.Service1 proxy = new localhost.Service1();
double  s1,s3,a;
string s2;
s1=Convert.ToDouble(TextBox1.Text);
s2 = TextBox2.Text;
s3=Convert.ToDouble(TextBox3.Text);
IAsyncResult ar = proxy.BeginCalculator(s1,s2,s3,null,null);
/*Do any Useful further works and then wait for the output
from Web Service.*/
ar.AsyncWaitHandle.WaitOne();
a=proxy.EndCalculator(ar);
TextBox4.Text=a.ToString();
}
```

Figure E–14 shows the output of **Calculate.aspx**.

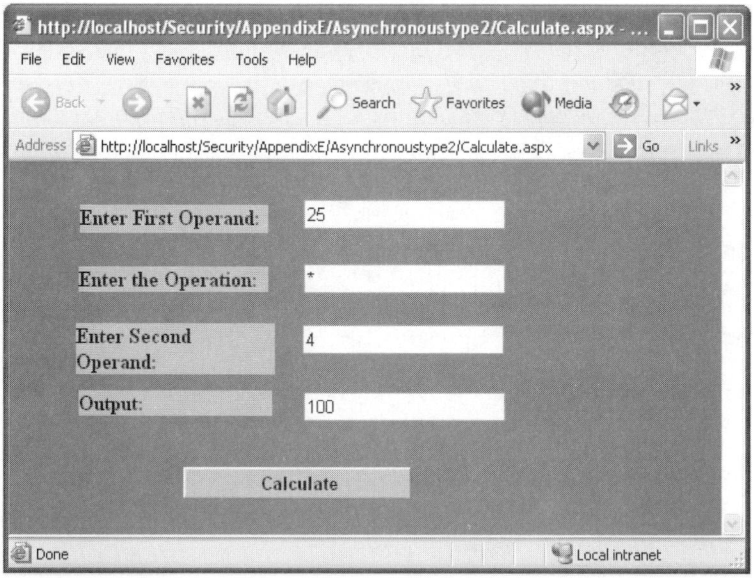

FIGURE E-14   *Output of Calculate.aspx (asynchronous method 2).*

Web Services Are Still Evolving

We have explored Web services in detail, including various programming techniques and how to build the distributed applications. But you have to be aware of one significant point: Web services are still in an evolving stage. With today's Web service tools and frameworks, you can build distributed applications that communicate by sending SOAP messages.

But you cannot employ Web services simply in mission-critical business, financial, or realistic applications. Why? The baseline specifications, such as WSDL, UDDI, and SOAP, are in a budding process. Moreover, there are some limitations in the present Web services, such as security, reliability, transaction processing, messaging and routing, quality of service, interoperability, and operational management. These limitations must be resolved to make use of Web services in real-time applications. To address these problems, Microsoft, IBM, and others have been working on the Global XML Web Services Architecture platform. The Global XML Architecture (GXA) is a series of specifications such as WS-Security, WS-Routing, WS-Inspection, WS-Addressing, WS-Policy, WS-Referral, WS-Coordination, WS-ReliableMessaging, and WS-Transaction, that extend SOAP and facilitate development of better real-time Web services.

Summary

Web services, an evolving distributed-computing architecture, use standard protocols such as HTTP, XML, XSD, SOAP, and WSDL. Web services trim down development and maintenance costs, provide solutions to interoperability issues, and allow business partners to share information or integrate with legacy systems without having to develop specialized interconnection applications. Microsoft .NET provides powerful tools that make the Web service creation and consumption straightforward. This appendix explored ASP.NET Web services in brief. We learned about the **WebService** directive, **WebMethod** attribute, **WebService** attribute, and **System.Web.Services.WebService** base class. We illustrated asynchronous programming in ASP.NET Web services. Finally, we discussed the demand for higher level functionalities, such as security and reliability for real-time Web services.

INDEX

Note: Letters following numbers:
t = table; f = figure

Developer Training

Object Innovations offers training course materials in fundamental software technologies used in developing applications in modern computing environments. We emphasize object-oriented techniques, with a focus on Microsoft® technologies, XML, Java™, and Linux®. Our courses have been used by businesses, training companies, and universities throughout North America. End clients include Microsoft, IBM®, HP®, Dell®, FedEx®, UPS®, AOL®, U.S. Bank®, Mellon Bank®, and NASA. Our courses are frequently updated to reflect feedback from classroom use. We aggressively track new technologies and endeavor to keep our courseware up-to-date.

Founded in 1993, Object Innovations has a long record of firsts in courseware. Our Visual C++ course was released before Microsoft's, we introduced one of the first courses in JavaServer Pages, and our Linux Internals 2.4 kernel course came out several months before Red Hat's course. Now we are leading the development of comprehensive developer training in Microsoft's .NET technology.

.NET Developer Training

Object Innovations is writing the premier book series on .NET for Prentice Hall PTR. These authoritative books are the foundation of our curriculum and are an ideal supplement to .NET training courses. We provide both comprehensive 5-day courses and also shorter courses focused on specific aspects of .NET technology. Our curriculum is evolving, so please check our Web site www.objectinnovations.com for current information. The following is a representative list of our courses.

402	.NET Overview (2 day)
410	Object-Oriented Programming in C# (5 days)
411	C# Essentials (2 days)
412	.NET Framework Using C# (3 days)
416	ASP.NET Using C# (3 days)
418	Web Service Fundamentals Using C# and ASP.NET (3 days)
420	Object-Oriented Programming in VB.NET (5 days)
421	VB.NET Essentials (2 days)
422	.NET Framework Using VB.NET (3 days)
426	ASP.NET Using VB.NET (3 days)
428	Web Service Fundamentals Using VB.NET and ASP.NET (3 days)
434	.NET Architecture and Programming Using Visual C++ (5 days)
441	XML Parsing Using C# and .NET
451	XML Parsing Using Visual Basic and .NET
482	Application Development Using C# and .NET (5 days)
484	Application Development Using Visual Basic and .NET (5 days)

See our .NET Web site for complete course listings: **www.objectinnovations.com/dotnet.htm**

Microsoft Developer Training

Our Microsoft curriculum is very extensive, with introductory and advanced courses on MFC, COM/DCOM, COM+, Windows Device Drivers, and advanced topics in Visual Basic™. Selected courses include:

123   Programming COM and DCOM Using ATL (5 days)
149   Distributed COM+ Programming (5 days)
133   Distributed COM+ Programming Using Visual Basic (5 days)
145   MFC Windows Programming for C++ Programmers (5 days)
671   Writing Windows Device Drivers (5 days)

XML and Web Services Developer Training

Our XML curriculum covers the broad range of XML technology. We offer courses in "pure" XML—all discussions and exercises based entirely on W3C recommended standards—as well as training in the use of XML through today's dominant enterprise platforms, .NET and Java. We offer Web services training using both .NET and Java. Selected courses include:

418   Web Service Fundamentals Using C# and ASP.NET (3 days)
428   Web Service Fundamentals Using VB.NET and ASP.NET (3 days)
441   XML Parsing Using C# and .NET (2 days)
451   XML Parsing Using Visual Basic and .NET (2 days)
501   Introduction to XML (1 day)
516   XML Transformations (2 days)
517   XML Schema (2 days)
542   XML Programming Using Java (3 days)
551   Overview of Java Web Services (1 day)
552   The Java APIs for SOAP Messaging (2 days)
554   The Java API for XML-Based RPC (2 days)
556   Publishing and Discovery Using UDDI and Java (2 days)
570   Developing Web Services with WebLogic™ (5 days)

Java Developer Training

Java training courses span the spectrum from beginning to advanced and provide extensive coverage of both client-side and server-side technologies. We emphasize distributed application development using Java. Selected courses include:

103   Java Programming (5 days)
105   Using and Developing JavaBeans (4 days)
106   CORBA Architecture and Programming Using Java (4 days)
109   JavaServer Pages (4 days)
110   Java Servlets (2 days)
111   Introduction to Java RMI (1 day)
163   Enterprise JavaBeans (5 days)
172   Java Foundation Classes (5 days)
180   Wireless Programming Using J2ME and MIDP (4 days)

See our Web site for complete course listings: **www.objectinnovations.com**

Object Innovations .NET Training and Consulting Partners

For information about .NET consulting and training using Object Innovations courseware, please check with our .NET Training and Consulting Partners.

Anew Technology Corporation   **www.Anew.net**

Specialized in IT consulting, training, mentoring, and development, Anew Technology has been serving many satisfied clients. Our business mission is threefold: to stay at the forefront of IT technologies, to satisfy client needs by applying these technologies, and to provide the best service in our industry. Anew Technology is a business partner with Object Innovations in operations and courseware development.

Batky-Howell   **www.batky-howell.com**

We specialize in custom, on-site training in Java, Oracle, UNIX, C, C++, XML, Perl and Object-Oriented Design training. Batky-Howell has trained 30,000 programmers, system administrators, database managers and IT leaders in 3,200 classes that range from the fundamentals to advanced topics. We have developed over 40 titles, covering 143 days of training with 14,000+ pages of instruction. With our new VClass capabilities and highly-qualified instructors, we can take a course, tailor it to your specifications, and then deliver it to students in Los Angeles, New York, and Chicago simultaneously.

Computer Horizons   **www.ComputerHorizons.com/Training**

For over sixteen years Computer Horizons Education Division (CHED) has been providing on-site, instructor-led IT training and customized workshops for organizations nationwide. We have developed extensive curriculum offerings in Web Technologies, Relational Databases, Reporting Tools, Process Improvement, UNIX® and LINUX®, Client/Server, Mainframe & Legacy Systems, Windows® 2000, and much more. CHED will design, develop and deliver a training solution tailored to each client's training requirements.

CompuWorks Systems, Inc.   **www.CompuWorks.com**

CompuWorks Systems, Inc. is an IT solutions company whose aim is to provide our clients with customized training, support and development services. We are committed to building long term partnerships with our clients in an effort to meet their individual needs. Cutting-edge solutions are our specialty.

Custom Training Institute   **www.CustomTraining.com**

Custom Training Institute is a provider of high quality High-End training since 1989. Along with our full line of "off-the-shelf" classes, we excel at providing customized Solutions—from technical needs assessment through course development and delivery. We specialize in Legacy Skill Transformation, Oracle, UNIX, C++, Java™ and other subjects for computer professionals.

Devcom   **www.dev-cominc.com**

Devcom Corporation offers a full line of courses and seminars for software developers and engineers. Currently Devcom provides technical courses and seminars around the country for Hewlett-Packard®, Compaq® Computer, Informix® Software, Silicon Graphics®, Quantum/Maxtor® and Gateway® Inc. Our senior .NET/C# instructor is currently working in conjunction with Microsoft to provide .NET training to their internal technical staff.

Focal Point   www.FocalPoint-Inc.com

Focal Point specializes in providing optimum instructor-led Information Technology training for our corporate clients on either an onsite basis, or in regional public courses. All of our course curricula is either developed by our staff of "World Class Instructors" or upon careful evaluation and scrutiny is adopted and acquired from our training partners who are similarly focused. Our course offerings pay special attention to Real World issues. Our classes are targeted toward topical areas that will ensure immediate productivity upon course completion.

I/SRG   www.isrg.com

The I/S RESOURCE GROUP helps organizations to understand, plan for and implement emerging I/S technologies and methodologies. By combining education, training, briefings and consulting, we assist our clients to effectively apply I/S technologies to achieve business benefits. Our eBusiness Application Bootcamp is an integrated set of courses that prepares learners to utilize XML, OOAD, Java™, JSP, EJB, ASP, CORBA and .NET to build eBusiness applications. Our eBusiness Briefings pinpoint emerging technologies and methodologies.

Patni Computer Systems Ltd   www.patni.com

Patni Computer Systems Limited is India's sixth largest software company with offices spanning North and South America, Europe, Asia, and Australia. Patni has over 2 decades of experience in system and application development projects, across all major software platforms. Committed to quality, Patni adds value to client businesses through well-established and structured methodologies, tools and techniques backed by 6 Sigma processes. All Patni centres have been awarded the ISO 9001:2001Certification. Patni is the largest company in the world which has all its development centres SEI CMM Level 5 assessed.

Reliable Software   www.ReliableSoftware.com

Reliable Software, Inc. uses Microsoft technology to quickly develop cost-effective software solutions for the small to mid-size business or business unit. We use state-of-the-art techniques to allow business rules, database models and the user interface to evolve as your business needs evolve. We can provide design and implementation consulting, or training.

SkillBridge Training   www.SkillBridgeTraining.com

SkillBridge is a leading provider of blended training solutions. The company's service offerings are designed to meet a wide variety of client requirements. Offering an integration of instructor-led training, e-learning and mentoring programs, SkillBridge delivers high value solutions in a cost-effective manner. SkillBridge's technology focus includes, among others, programming languages, operating systems, databases, and internet and web technologies.

/training/etc Inc.   www.trainingetc.com

A training company dedicated to delivering quality technical training, courseware development, and consulting in a variety of subject matter areas, including Programming Languages and Design (including C, C++, OOAD/UML, Perl, and Java), a complete UNIX curriculum (from UNIX Fundamentals to System Administration), the Internet (including HTML/CGI, XML and JavaScript Programming) and RDBMS (including Oracle and Sybase).

Watermark Learning   www.WatermarkLearning.com

Watermark Learning provides a wide range of IT skill development training and mentoring services to a variety of industries, software/consulting firms and government. We provide flexible options for delivery: onsite, consortium and public classes in three major areas: project management, requirements analysis and software development, including e-Commerce. Our instructors are seasoned, knowledgeable practitioners, who use their industry experience along with our highly-rated courseware to effectively build technical skills relevant to your business need.

informIT